V&R

Esther P. Wipfler

Martin Luther in Motion Pictures

History of a Metamorphosis

Vandenhoeck & Ruprecht

For Erika Pohl, née Israel

Mit 54 Abbildungen

Bibliografische Information der Deutschen Nationalbibliothek
Die Deutsche Nationalbibliothek verzeichnet diese Publikation in der
Deutschen Nationalbibliografie; detaillierte bibliografische Daten sind
im Internet über http://dnb.d-nb.de abrufbar.

ISBN 978-3-525-55019-9
ISBN 978-3-647-55019-0 (E-Book)

Umschlagabbildung: Filmplakat des Films »Martin Luther«, 1953
© Stiftung Luthergedenkstätten in Sachsen-Anhalt

Satz und Lithographie: SchwabScantechnik, Göttingen
Druck und Bindung: ⊕ Hubert & Co. Göttingen

Content

"It's one of those stories that …
however many times they're told can always be told again."
(Alfred Molina on Martin Luther's life in an interview he gave
on his role as Johann Tetzel in Luther [2003])

I. Introduction

Visual media have always been used for the transmission of religious thought. In the 20th century, the moving image has become its most important form. Therefore, the feature film has done more than any other medium to shape the image of Martin Luther held by the common public in the 20th century. Nonetheless, the Luther film has been largely bypassed by traditional Luther scholarship. The first studies dealing with individual Luther films have come from the fields of theological film criticism and history.[1] They have not, however, covered the temporal dimension of the 'Luther film phenomenon' in the years between 1911 and 2003 and have ignored both the production background and the transatlantic aspect. The present study, supported by the author's previously published contributions to this topic, is intended to explore these areas.[2]

Luther films have always been—apart from the very earliest examples—ambitious undertakings, staffed by a personnel that includes leading representatives of theology and expert consultants in ecclesiastical history. None of the Luther films made for the cinema can be classified as belonging to the 'B picture' category. The status of the historic figure as a national myth in Germany[3] and a Church founder in America was too high and the intentions of those who commissioned the films have been too closely linked to theological issues as well as the self-image of the Lutheran Church. The present study is chiefly concerned with working out the interests brought to bear on each film project by their initiators and the impact each has made on the image of Luther in film in its historical context.

Filmic representation stands at the end of a tradition of text and image, the fundamentals of which were already laid down in Luther's lifetime. Reference to topoi formulated in the reformer's own time continued even into film to lend it an aura of authenticity. Even in the Reformation period, the image of Luther was multifaceted: the spectrum ranges on the one hand from "Luder" ("rascal", "scoundrel": a pun on the name "Luther"), "Septiceps" (the seven-headed dragon of the Apocalypse), "mad dog", "grim bear" to "Devil's apprentice". On the other hand, Luther's followers characterized him as a "man of God", "herald of peace", a "great prophet", "the third Elijah" or "another Plato" as well as "a true Cicero", "father of the Church", "bringer of Enlightenment", "German hero" and "father of his house".[4] The filmic image of Luther is also part of a specific Lutheran approach to the visual arts.[5] By contrast, it is well known that the Swiss Reformed Church tradition has failed to produce any feature films on Jean Calvin or Huldrych Zwingli, apart from documentaries[6], even though it has also studied the religious film.[7] Nor was anything of the kind planned for the Calvin Year 2009.

The representation of Luther in feature films is—apart from the protagonist's physical similarity with the portraits by Lucas Cranach the Elder[8]—anything but uniform, not even when the positive sides played a role in characterization. Problematic stances such as Luther's late tirades against the Jews or his condoning the Landgrave of Hesse's living in bigamy were banished to other filmic formats such as documentaries[9], but this genre is not subject of my study apart from re-enacted scenes.

The person of Luther as a whole was supposed to remain a likeable and admirable character, providing a model for Christian life, depending on the screenplay writer, theological advisers and the Zeitgeist. Therefore Luther appeared on the cinema screen and later on the television screen as a romantic lover, a titan of German nationalism, talented in the arts and fond of children, racked by doubt, a groundbreaking theologian or the passionate antagonist to spiritual and temporal potentates as well as to Thomas Müntzer and the peasantry. The character of Luther was also shaped by those who played him. Invariably one chose actors who were famous, looked back on long years of stage experience and in some cases had even attained 'star' status. Today many of the names (Hermann Litt, Rudolf Essek, Karl Wüstenhagen, Eugen Klöpfer, Niall McGinnis, Hans Dieter Zeidler, Christian Rode, Bernard Lincot, Stacy Keach, Lambert Hamel, Ulrich Thein and Joseph Fiennes) have been forgotten. Through them, the filmic Luther speaks not only German but more recently also French and English, which has considerably expanded an awareness of the historical person. This always matched the—albeit only latent—proselytising character of the films, which, to all appearances, made no impact at all. Rather, film has mainly served to confirm the faith of those who were already members of the Lutheran Church.

Considering the conditions under which the genre originated, the Luther film is recognizably associated with the context of the German middle-class Protestant culture of commemoration.[10] Luther anniversaries always gave the impetus for a new treatment of the Reformer and this equally applied to cinematic history. However, the officially commemorated Luther Years such as 1983 and 1996 have been too rare to serve as an occasion for more regular celebration. Hence, 1913, 1923, 1953, 1973 und 2003 were chosen as years to be commemorated because they give some semblance of regular occurrence. Orientation towards the year of Luther's birth rather than the pivotal dates of Reformation history such as the Nailing of the Theses or the Confessio Augustana reveals how strongly the commemorative culture of the Lutheran Church is centered on the reformer's life. By the 16th century, this cult was stylized, most notably in pictures: a frequently cited example is the 1521 Hans Baldung (known as Baldung Grien) woodcut, in which Luther is hagiographically depicted as a monk with a nimbus and the dove of the Holy Spirit.[11] Luther himself, however, contributed to the stylization of his own person: although enrolled in 1501 at Erfurt University as "Martinus Ludher ex Mansfeldt", in signing the letter he wrote to the Archbishop of Mainz on October 31, 1517, he styled himself 'Luther' for the first time. That was because he saw himself as "Eleutherius", meaning "the One Who Has Been Made Free (by God)".[12] In the films, he is consistently addressed as "Luther".

Viewed against this background and the regularity with which it continued to be revived, the Luther film seems to refute the much cited thesis that views historical biography as a crisis phenomenon.[13] It only seems to apply to the 1927 Luther film: The extremely nationalistic view of the protagonist in this film reflected the situation of Lutheranism as a former state church that was forced into a defensive position during the Weimar Republic. Lutheranism at that juncture wanted to express its claim to spiritual leadership in political terms as well as spiritual and used the nationalist lexis to do so. This aim is easily recognizable in the person of the Cathedral Preacher Bruno Döhring, the advisor for the screenplay. Döhring's role in the creation of that film has hitherto been completely underestimated or even overlooked since focus has always been on the director. In the 1927 film, it becomes clear how the medium of cinema contributed to ensuring the continuity of the culture struggle by means of a visual vehicle.

Even though the anniversary of Luther's birth provided an occasion for representing his life story, most Luther films do not begin with his birth but rather at a biographical turning point such as his entering the monastery or taking monastic vows, that is, with the official beginning of his religious life. This treatment corresponds to the traditional structure of filmic biography, which often only begins at the moment that the idea embodied by the protagonist takes hold.[14]

In German Luther films, this mainly concerns the idea of creating a national church and supporting the 'religion of conscience' aspect as propounded by the theologian Karl Holl. American Luther films propagate the idea of liberation from 'medieval' thought and behaviour or extol the rejection of an exploitative system informed by the doctrine of justice as interpreted by the Catholic Church to mean salvation for righteousness accompanied by good deeds and the overcoming of those teachings through Luther's doctrine of imputed righteousness (salvation 'by grace alone, by faith alone', without personal merit). Luther becomes a pioneer at an intellectual frontier, heading a populist movement. How this doctrinal conflict is visualized in each instance is a core question in dealing with how Luther is represented in film.

All Luther films share the canonical key scenes originally drawn from the motif repertory formulated in illustrated Luther biographies, in history paintings and the theater: Luther entering the Erfurt friary, nailing of the theses, burning the papal bull at the Elster Gate in Wittenberg, his presence at the Diet of Worms, Luther staying incognito as Junker Jörg at the Wartburg and typical Reformation iconoclasm. The dramatic epiphany Luther experienced in a wood near Stotternheim on July 2, 1505 ("Help! Saint Anna, I want to become a monk!") has more than once occupied a pivotal position in these representations (G 1927, FRG 1983, FRG/USA 2003). The sources of each of those topoi will be identified in the present study and the form of, and reasons for, the changes in them will be explained from film to film through comparison of the works.

The 'Luther film phenomenon' should be assigned its proper place in cinematic history. Since the Luther film is a hybrid of the biographical (biopic[15]) and the religious film, two traditions must be examined in this connection. Luther film represents a specifically Lutheran response and substitute to the Jesus film of Roman Catholic provenance, which is *inter alia* expressed in the various elements, some of which are traditional of the 'Christiformitas' (Christ-conformity) with which the Reformer is characterized. In 1908, for instance, the Oberkonsistorium [High Consistory] of the Bavarian Lutheran Church categorically rejected a petition from the Bavarian State Ministry of the Interior for Ecclesiastical and Educational Affairs to permit the life of Christ to be represented in film, although they had approved a film on the Passion.[16] The first Protestant film on Christ was, not surprisingly, initiated by evangelical Christians in the US and was not released in Germany until 1979.[17]

Since "movies have always served as one of the primary sites through which the culture, in process of promulgating that fiction, has also exposed its workings as a mythology"[18], lines of development and change in the way Luther was viewed and shown will be made clear in an overview of all Luther films made between 1911 and 2003, with priority given to analyzing filmic representation. The method used borrows from the system devised by Knut Hickethier.[19] Preliminary work has already revealed that, with two exceptions (1923 and 1964), the Luther film can hardly be said to have ventured into uncharted territory. On the contrary, a traditional form of narrative prevailed. In most of the films, Luther's life is narrated diachronically. Only one film, the 1964 television film, breaks with this pattern by using a retrospective view of Luther's life as he recalls it on his deathbed. The whole story is told in flashbacks. With this single exception, the character Luther always remains the driving force of the narrative, a typical feature of the traditional closed biographical narrative system,[20] which is indebted to both a belief in progress and the cult of genius.[21] As for content 'Luther' as a character is noticeably re-interpreted and redefined.

In this context the question how and why the central topos of the Luther iconography 'Nailing of the Theses' is staged in every film will be discussed in a separate chapter dealing with the visualization of that event. The main section of study is devoted to disclosing the background of each interpretation. The motives for the paradigm shift in the interpretation of the protagonist as well as the differences between the German and the American representations are delineated: the producers approach both in financing and advisory work in Germany and America as well as viewer and reviewer response to the films will be examined. Material from England will be drawn upon for comparison since no Luther films have been produced apart from feature films for television in other countries, which is quite remarkable in the case of the Protestant Netherlands.[22] The study is based on source material on the films collected in the Lutheran Church Central Archives (Zentralarchive der Evangelisch-Lutherischen Kirche) in Nuremberg, Berlin and Elk Grove Village, Illinois (near Chicago), in the archives of the Evangelischer Bund in Bad Bensheim and the film archives in Amsterdam, Berlin, Frankfurt am Main and Washington and the international press.

II. The Luther Film Sui Generis

1. Genre Classification

What demands were made on the genres to which the Luther film should be assigned and what traditions of representation did it uphold? It is astonishing how closely the Luther film follows biographical conventions and that the religious element is subordinate to those patterns. Remarkably, scholars have hitherto ignored the Luther film genre as a whole both as filmic biography and as explicitly religious cinema (e.g. Bible spectacular, Jesus film, hagiography) except in specific cases such as the 1927 and 1953 Luther films. The Luther film is not included in the canon of classic religious film[1] despite the fact that it indubitably meets all the criteria defined for that group.[2] No one can doubt that the idea of God and the concept of the Christian church are at the core of every Luther film.

The Jesus film was the prototype for the Luther film as far as definition, form and treatment of the religious content and subject matter are concerned. With the earliest examples dating from 1897, *La passion du Christ* (Frères Basiles, France), *La vie et la passion de Jésus-Christ* (the Lumière brothers, France) and *La passione di Gesu* (Luigi Topi, Italy)[3], the Jesus film is one of the oldest filmic genres and its tradition remains unbroken down to the present day, despite all the changes it has gone through in the course of its history. Religiously affiliated cinema critics tackled the subject early on.[4] The youthful hero as liberator, miracles, leadership, dialogue with God and the use of Christian iconography and iconology (including the Cross, angels, light imagery) as well as church music are characteristic of the genre.[5] These elements are also found in the Luther film. Nevertheless, it is always clear that Luther communicates with God and desires to follow Christ but cannot be equated with him. Luther's 'Passion' is usually confined to a few moments of self-chastisement, which enable him to recognize God's mercy and love. Therefore, one can speak only of elements and not a wholistic concept of Christ-conformity in the Luther film.

Ultimately, all that is recounted in Luther films is the biography of a human being and not the history of the Redemption. The relative lack of eventfulness that distinguishes a life shaped by intellectual work led to the oft-criticized overemphasis on dialogue in most Luther films—though this is also characteristic of many other biopics.[6] Since they externalize his thinking, it is through these dialogues that the hero is characterized.[7] This occurs most noticeably in the dialogues with Staupitz. However, in Luther's debates with opponents such as Karlstadt and Kajetan the (ecclesiastical) historical context is defined as the source from which the new thinking arises. Luther remains the driving force in this typical feature of the traditional, closed, biographical narrative system[8] committed to both a belief in progress and the cult of genius.[9] Luther's life is usually narrated chronologically in the films. Only one of them, the 1964 television film, breaks with this pattern with a flashback from Luther's deathbed, which is expanded into a narrative frame. Otherwise, the filmic Luther does not "die" even though he faces death in the last part of the 1983 serialised GDR production.

2. Introducing the Hero

In the following analysis, the beginnings of the films will be examined in light of the oft-cited rule that in classic biopics the protagonist is presented in the first minutes of the film as he will continue to be and act throughout:[10] We will determine whether the character 'Luther' is defined at the outset for the whole film, or not. The individual portraits must also be examined in terms of staging and visual language, especially given the near-synchronous presentation of several entirely different solutions in the 1980s. Looking at the Luther films diachronically reveals a certain dialectic: though the choice of beginnings varies, they are interrelated, which shows that the Luther film really is a specific genre that has developed a dynamic of its own.

As indicated above, almost all Luther films begin with a turning point in the hero's life rather than with his birth. Luther's childhood and youth play a role only in the earliest Luther films. The first quarrel with his father when he enters the monastic establishment and the second conflict with him after Martin's first mass are part of every early Luther film. This is a pivotal topos of the biopic, according to which the youthful hero must first assert himself against his own family before he can go out and conquer the world.[11] In the later Luther films, this relationship is usually reduced to Luther's father opposing his son's taking monastic vows. Only in the 1927 and 1964 films a loving mother is depicted as a counterpoint to the harsh father. In 1927 this was a new aspect in the interpretation of Luther's life because scholars did not go in for systematic psychological study of Luther until they were inspired to do so by Erikson's interpretation.[12]

The earliest surviving Luther film that premiered in 1913 as *Die Wittenberger Nachtigall. Martin Luther.*[13] was censored several times and given new titles as well as intertitles. (When the film failed to pass for showing to child and adolescent viewing in 1921, the title was changed to *Der Weg zur Sonne / Martin Luther*.[14] It was ultimately given the agenda-heavy title *Doktor Martin Luther. Ein Lebensbild für das deutsche Volk*, an almost verbatim use of the title of the Georg Buchwald Luther biography.[15]) A 1920s version is in the Bundesfilmarchiv in Berlin under the first title *Die Wittenberger Nachtigall*, and it is the basis for the present study. This copy begins with the intertitle "1ˢᵗ Chapter 1483–1505", and a subsequent intertitle narrates Luther's birth. The first biographical event shown, however, is Luther as a precocious schoolboy driven by strict upbringing at home and harsh schooling to pray before a crucifix: "O God, hear my ardent supplication, deliver me from this grievous pain."[16] The pictorial narrative usually remains, due to the state of technology at the time, illustrative as long-shot tableaux. Still it is remarkable that the beginnings of Luther's profound trust in God are depicted as emerging in his youth and that the reason why Luther wants to change the world in his lifetime is explained as the result of a harsh, uncaring upbringing. That is the dramaturgical structure of the so-called "back-story wound" often used in Hollywood cinema.[17] Luther's relationship with his parents is depicted differently in *Martin Luther: His Life and Time* (1923), in which even Luther's father is shown in a consistently loving, nurturing relationship with his son throughout the relevant part of the film. This innovation is indicated at the outset, when the son's birth is staged like a nativity scene (Luther as the Messiah). Only when the father is mourning his two children who have died he reacts with anger and rejection on hearing his son's plans to enter a monastic establishment. However, by the time Martin officiates at his first mass, reconciliation is possible. A remarkable feature of this film is the way in which Luther is embedded in the historical context: The film starts with the picture of the Reformer, arms outstretched to receive the light. Shots of the humbled Holy Roman Emperor Henry IV barefoot and freezing miserably while waiting at the gates of Canossa in the icy winter of 1077 follow. This event, as is well known, made history as an act of disgraceful submission to the pope. It was still a sore point in the collective German memory as late as 1872, when Reich Chancellor Otto von Bismarck alluded to it at the height of the culture struggle by vowing to the Centre Party in the Reichstag on May, 14: "Do not worry: we will not go to Canossa, neither in body nor in spirit."[18] (The phrase is engraved on a plaque on the Canossa Column in Bad Harzburg and elsewhere.) From the standpoint of many present-day historians, however, Henry IV pulled off a clever move in going to Canossa only to emerge with restored freedom to act and the ability to anticipate the moves of the hostile papal coalitions.[19] In this first Luther film, the Canossa scene is followed by Jan Hus—the classic prefiguration of Luther—burning at the stake. This image of a reform movement being brutally quashed recurs in a quotation at a crucial point of the film: In a scene labeled "Gethsemane" Luther appears at night, after levelling his accusations at the Diet of Worms. God, however, allows the bitter chalice of a death sentence to pass him by. Thus, the Luther biography is embedded in the general historical framework. In no other Luther film is the historical aspect covered so extensively.

An early version of *Luther: Ein Film der deutschen Reformation*, dated December 17, 1927, begins with an act entitled *The Vocation* (*Die Berufung*): Luther is returning home to Mansfeld after taking his MA degree. The link with the previous Luther film, which portrayed Martin as the victim of a proto-Prussian school system, is nonetheless easy to recognize in this film. Thus, Luther appears to be a true humanitarian, teaching the long-suffering Mansfeld schoolboys to conjugate "amare" with kindness instead of blows of the schoolmaster's cane. Here Luther's drive for change without violence is already apparent. Characteristically, in the version of the film with a short title sequence approved by the censors on February 29, 1928 (Prüfnr. 18 288), not a single picture of this sequence is shown. Instead, the film begins with the dramatic vow in the thunderstorm near Stotternheim. The same scene was chosen for the 1993 ZDF television film and the 2003 cinema production.

The 1953 film, however, is emphatically documentary in character from the outset. It begins with close-ups of the Romanesque chapel at the gates of Großkomburg near Schwäbisch Hall, the cloister of the former Cistercian monastery of Maulbronn and the refectory of the former Cistercian monastic establishment at Eberbach, none of which were places that had anything to do with Luther's activities, but in 1952 they were situated in the Anglo-American zone of occupation.

Screenshot of the introduction of "Martin Luther" (USA 1953)
showing the cloister of the former Cistercian monastery of Maulbronn.

The soundtrack of the title sequence is scored with bombastic variations on *A Mighty Fortress is Our God*, played by the Munich Symphony Orchestra. Next the notice appears: "This dramatization of a decisive moment in human history is the result of careful research of facts and conditions in the 16th century as reported by historians of many faiths". This statement is intended to authenticate the historical accuracy of the film. Accordingly, a spoken commentary on maps of Europe around 1500 and a montage of intercut motifs taken from the wood engravings of Albrecht Dürer's *Apocalypse* (1498) and *The Dance of Death* in Hartman Schedel's *World Chronicle* (1493), intended to represent fears of the Last Judgement, lead into the plot of the film itself. Martin Luther is introduced as a dollying camera tracks him on his way to the farewell celebration put on by his fellow students of jurisprudence. He comes fully into view as his friends are welcoming him: The camera shows him in head-and-shoulders close-up and then Luther introduces himself with his valedictory address, in which he indicates the start of a new phase of his life.

A far bleaker, even eschatological mood prevails in the 1964 German television production, which was broadcast in 1965. The economical staging as if for the theater lends the historical material a markedly timeless quality. Luther's world of fears and doubts is scored—still without a picture—with the dissonant strains of a "Mitten wyr ym leben sind / mit dem tod vmbfangen" sung a capella.[20] The camera first shows Luther in his pastoral vestments on a bier, his eyes closed, in bird's-eye view, then in extreme close-up from the side while the narrator relates in a soft voice that Luther died in Eisleben in 1546, a poor man who sought a merciful God all his life.

Screenshot of the first scene in "Der arme Mann Luther" (FRG 1964).

The flashback begins with Luther opening his eyes and Tetzel holding forth in a tirade full of hatred. For the first time in these films, Luther appears as a passive character. Even as the film progresses, he remains more reactive than proactive. However, the externalised interior monologue brings viewers closer to Luther as a man, an effect supported by the camera, which repeatedly zooms in and out in leitmotif-like revealing shots of his face.

The film made from the John Osborne stage play also begins simply with the sound of bells tolling and without major orchestration; a portal opens to reveal the chancel of a church, followed by the inscription "American Film Theater" in German black letter as if after a scene or act in a stage play. Next, it cuts to Luther, about to mount the pulpit when someone enters the church, gradually recognizable as a lansquenet with a dead peasant on a handcart. The knight finally addresses Luther with irony as "Brother Martin" and blames him for the dead of the Peasants War. The actual film follows the title sequence, which is staged as a flashback in this way.

The ZDF television production broadcasted in 1983, which is very closely related to the above film in its choice of locations and its critical view of the Reformer, begins in a far more dramatic manner: the thunderstorm in which Luther vows to become a monk rages before a portal of St. Lorenz in Nuremberg. The main character is shown at a turning point in his life. This dramatic start was also chosen for the 2003 film, in which a fanfare-like bolt of lightning introduces the hero, who then seeks shelter from the elements in a very human way. Soon afterwards, intercutting transfers us to Erfurt, where we see Luther take his monastic vows. The velocity of the narration slows down after this very taut beginning but then grows steadily. The GDR film broadcasted in 1983 in several parts sought an entirely different introduction to the material. After the musical prelude with variations on "A Mighty Fortress is Our God" The first part, "Protest" does not begin with documents or works of art from the period nor with a scene that is played. Instead, it starts with the camera zooming in to focus on a detail of the Werner Tübke painting *The Early Bourgeois Revolution in Germany* (*Frühbürgerliche Revolution in Deutschland*), in which Tetzel, the purveyor of papal indulgences, is depicted.[21] The Tübke painting sets the scene for the action to begin and it does so with the introduction of the antagonist. The camera pans from Tetzel in close-up riding in a magnificent cart to the barefoot members of his retinue. The first message has already been conveyed before Luther even appears: we are in an era fraught with social injustice with participation of the Church.

The French view of Luther in the 1981 Alexandre Astruc television film is politically in the same camp but this film starts on a pronounced documentary note, probably because most of the broader French public is unfamiliar with the Reformer. The first part, *God's Justice* (*La justice de Dieu*) begins with pictures of Luther's coat of arms, "Luther's rose"[22], and the abridged Luther quotation beneath it "When one has the Cross in one's heart, one has one's heart on a rose" ("Quand on a la croix dans le coeur, on a le cœur sur une rose").[23] The phrase quoted by a narrator serves as the device for the narrative (cf. see image on p. 19). The chorale *A Mighty Fortress is Our God* is sung in French (*C'est un rempart ...*) to organ accompaniment as the background music. The main character is now given a face: the celebrated 1520 copperplate engraving by Lucas Cranach the Elder, which depicts the young Luther as an Augustinian mendicant friar. Luther's importance is outlined in a brief account by the narrator: he is a theologian who wanted to return to the wellsprings of Christendom

Bernard Lincot as Luther in the French television film "Frère Martin" (F 1981).

and thus he rebelled against the pope and the Holy Roman emperor. Given that introduction, one might expect to see that the Reformation was accomplished as the work of a single man. However, in the action that follows, the protagonist is at first unidentifiable. He is shown with another Augustinian mendicant friar in the middle distance of a long shot and only from the rear in the fictitious situation of begging for alms, which according to the intertitle took place in Erfurt in 1507. The path of the two friars is crossed by a noble hunting party. The friars' faces are not shown until the following scene. As in the 1983 GDR film, the entrance of the protagonist is delayed, allowing Luther to be shown in the context of social and political relationships.[24]

A completely new opening was chosen for the documentary broadcast in 2007. The 45 minute feature directed by Günther Klein for the ZDF series *Giganten* (*giants*), contains long re-enactments featuring Luther (played by Ben Becker) in his exile at the Wartburg (actually filmed at a castle in Romania). The first scene shows Luther translating the New Testament and struggling with the devil. The scenes are connected with commentaries by the Lutheran theologian Margot Käßmann, at that time also Lutheran bishop, pastor Jürgen Fliege, journalist Peter Hahne and Hermann Glaser, professor of cultural history. Glaser is the first, in such documentaries, to assign a metaphorical meaning to the legendary scenes in Luther's life, for example interpreting the famous scene "Luther throwing the inkpot at the devil" as an image of Luther's strategy to fight the Antichrist with the written word.

The following year another ZDF documentary, *Luther und die Nation* (*Luther and the Nation*) was shown on TV. It starts with the scene 'Luther entering Worms in 1521' in order to give an insight into the political situation of the Holy Roman Empire at the beginning of the 16th century.

Finally, we come to the question of whether, and if so, how the hero develops. For Luther, this means: do the films begin with a Luther who is still Catholic? Do they convey the impression that Luther's teachings develop as a gradual process? The answer to both of these questions is no.[25] In the silent film era, the boy Luther is characterized as a 'puer senex', who precociously possesses all virtues and talents he will later need as the Protestant Reformer. In the 1923 film, Luther is even saved by divine providence—by Christ himself—allowing him to accomplish his mission of liberation in the future. Luther is always a man seeking God who is at odds with himself. He plods on the way he has set out for himself even though a change in course is inspired only by external events (the thunderstorm at Stotternheim, the behavior of the secularized clergy in Rome, Tetzel's trade in papal indulgences, etc). The core Theses of Luther's teaching are thus motivated. They are not shown as the fruit of intellectual investigation of the Bible or debates with Church Fathers. Hence, these filmic representations contradict what is known today about how Luther's theology evolved.

3. Excursus:
The Ninety-Five Theses in Motion Pictures. Text in Film

Written and printed texts play an extraordinary and pivotal role in Luther films, probably because Protestantism defined itself as a religion of writing according to the Luther dictum "sola scriptura". Therefore, the presentation of text in film has to be considered as one of the main characteristics of the genre.

All Luther films reach a first and decisive climax in the scenes showing the composition of the 95 Theses and their publication. As Lutherans see it, the Theses have the status of a first 'constitutional document', despite their orientation towards the indulgence issue. No wonder that the 2003 Luther film was also reviewed in the form of twelve theses.[26] Instead of the question of if or by whom the Theses were nailed to the door of Wittenberg Castle Church, this study considers how the highly abstract content of the Theses is visualized in film and which Theses were chosen. The core problem of representing "the Theses", which were primarily disseminated in print, centers on how this static media could be represented in the moving image even better than on stage, because in its early phase cinema was still viewed as competing against the stage. It is also a question of how the media revolution represented by printing is reflected in Luther films.

First of all, the specifically filmic modes for the visualization of writing as they are used in Luther films must be considered here, because they were subject to change over the course of history. Luther films overlap two eras of cinema history that dealt with language in fundamentally different ways: the silent film and the sound film. Four feature films are known to have been devoted to the life of the reformer before sound films were introduced (c 1929) but only two of them have survived. Textuality plays an important role in silent films in any case, since the intertitles replace the spoken word and the visual narrative is rhythmatized by it. However, the silent film was never really without sound. The musical accompaniment, which has only survived for the last silent Luther film, generated moods, created dramatic effects and also gave sound to the music shown on the screen. This fact is significant, especially where the Lutheran hymn *A Mighty Fortress is our God* is concerned. Although synchronization of sound was common as early as 1904,[27] no evidence of this has yet been found in the early Luther films.

Returning to written language: apart from the intertitles, there are other modes of presenting writing in film[28] that are also found in the Luther film genre. In this context, supertitles at the beginning and end and subtitles will be ignored. Here the focus will be on the "pre-inscriptions" and "in-scriptions" as defined by Joachim Paech.[29] This means we are concerned with the screenplay on the one hand, and with the intertitles and the cut-in "inserts"[30] that is, visualizations of words and intercut texts, both handwritten and printed on the other. As far as I know, the screenplays of only the most recent Luther films are extant. Thus they can only be used for comparison in certain cases. The typography of the inserts is particularly interesting in Luther films. When were gothic letters chosen, when were latin letters preferred? Another question is how such inserts make interior monologues visible. Luther's battle with his conscience is presented in the 1927 film by means of a Menetakel-like inscription "O Ewigkeit Du Donnerwort" that grows larger and larger,[31] accompanied by a visitation of the Archangel Michael[32] clad in armour of the kind Luther himself will soon be wearing. These "inserts" function both as the diegetic part of the visual narrative and as the staging of a quotation. However, inserted texts were rejected by the avant-garde of the silent film era as an infringement against "cinéma pur". One of the pioneering intellectuals of that era, Béla Balász, saw the increasing dependence of Western culture on writing as the reason "why the soul has become almost invisible"[33] whereas film-makers would be able to make humanity perceivable again. He explicitly condemned printing because it had, over time, made the face of man unreadable.[34] Early Luther films, however, do not reveal a critical attitude of this kind. The early Luther films were not concerned with self-reflection qua medium although the 1983 Luther film probably was. Printing is celebrated everywhere as a vehicle for propaganda.

In early Luther films, writing, especially in the scene where Luther is translating the Bible, is also an established visual topos, an unmistakeable iconographic borrowing from the portrait of the Evangelist. The image of Luther with the (German) Bible in his hand, is, after all, a central motif.[35]

This motiv is not even missing from the 2003 Luther film. However, writing

Left: Hermann Litt as Luther in "Doktor Martinus Luther", Germany 1911. Right: Still from the 1927 film used for advertising: Eugen Klöpfer as Luther with his translation of the Bible.

the Theses did not become a subject in its own right until the post-war Luther films.

The end titles can also be counted as "inserts". These are texts containing information on the content and form of representation, which also function as epilogue or afterword. How important these can be for the response to a film is shown by the reaction to the afterword in the 2003 Luther film, in which the number of Christians professing Lutheranism is given as 450 million to emphasize the relevance of the historic events depicted.[36] Moreover, this statement served to reassure the main sponsors of the film on the role their church is playing in the world.[37]

The last category associated with textuality in Luther films, the texts written about the film,[38] wether from the producers of the film or respondents to it, will also be discussed on the basis of individual cases. Since the role played by textuality has never been studied in connection with Luther films, cases will be presented chronologically to clarify developmental trends.

The main character of the Luther film may not be a saint in the narrowest sense of the term yet he is the recipient of a comparable veneration. Nevertheless, the Luther film conveys religious content[39] and many of its motifs have been borrowed from Christian iconography. Although the Ninety-Five Theses do not belong to the Lutheran creed as such, they do contain important arguments about Luther's teachings on grace. However, it was certainly not the sophisticated content of the Theses, which is very difficult to understand for post-medieval laics, but the metaphorical imagery of the blow aimed at the old Church that made this subject irreplaceable in Luther film. A blow which so clearly formed the representation of the event which made the Nailing of the Theses the incident that sparked off the Reformation and, therefore provided one of the most important aspects of specifically Protestant identity. The Nailing of the Theses established the date of Reformation Day. Whether Luther really did nail his Theses to the door of the Wittenberg Castle Church on October 31, 1517 was not a matter of controversy until the mid-20th century, that is, after the rise of the silent film. The date has, of course, never been entirely disproved. Martin Treu's new reading of the sources has nonetheless considerably improved the verifiability of the event.[40] Any hopes of indisputable proof, which could only consist of an eyewitness account or a hitherto undiscovered statement by Luther himself, are likely to be raised in vain.[41] If, therefore, one does assume that the Nailing of the Theses did take place, the question of which version was used still remains a moot point. After all, both the form and the content of the "disputationes" referred to in Luther's famous letter to Archbishop Albrecht of Magdeburg and Mainz on the traffic in indulgences (October 31, 1517) are unknown. According to Klemens Honselmann, the earliest extant printed copies of the Theses are those of the Nuremberg printer Hieronymus Hölzel (Proof A) and the Leipzig printer Jacob Thanner (Proof B).[42] Although a copy from Wittenberg is highly plausible, none has yet been found.[43] This would seem to argue for the Nailing of the written Theses on the Castle Church door as represented in the 2003 Luther film. The text was surely written in Latin, the language used at that time for administration and scholarship. The Theses were not printed in German and in Latin until 1518.[44] The screenwriters dealt with this fact in very different ways, as I will demonstrate.

Luther was not concerned with the public at large, let alone having his Theses disseminated among the populace like a sort of broadsheet. It is more likely that he originally wrote the Theses for a debate in a circle of close colleagues—one that never took place[45]—or that he sent them to the bishops primarily as arguments against the prevailing indulgence praxis.[46] Posting the Theses on the door of the Castle Church, which was also the Wittenberg University place of worship,[47] was the usual practice for starting debates at the university, and these were handled by an officiant. This fact was cleverly alluded to in the 1983 GDR production, which indicated that Luther only had to do the deed himself because the porter was too drunk to hold the hammer in his hand. However, in film the assumed original door is never shown, because this place was transformed into a memorial site by the Prussian King Frederic William IV. The porch is orned since 1850 in the tympanum with painting showing Luther and Melanchthon and since 1858 with the 95 Theses cast in bronze.[48] So the film-makers had to choose others doors: in *Die Wittenberger Nachtigall* they filmed the scene at the the Wittenberg City Church.

Luther nailing the Theses in the *Wittenberger Nachtigall* (Germany 1913/1927 [?]). The scene was filmed at the City Church in Wittenberg (Courtesy of EYE Film Instituut Nederland).

For Luther posting the notice was not meant to make the Theses known to the citizenry of Wittenberg as is represented in nearly all films. Thus was also made for dramaturgic and economic purposes. Advertising for silent film, after all, tended to focus on what were known as mass scenes.

In reality probably there were never any popular revolts involving the Theses. After all Luther himself and also the immediate records surrounding him up to the entry made on the event by Georg Rörer in the early 1540s are consistently silent in this regard.

Nailing the Theses to the door is one of the classic scenes in the Luther iconography with an enormous dramatic potential that was already discovered by playwrights such as August Strindberg.[49] This is equally true for film. The event was excluded only once—when the discussion sparked by Erwin Iserloh was at its height—in the 1964 television play.

Although there are variants of the staging of the event in film the (fee-paying) public has usually been granted the recognition of the traditional iconography. Visualizing the content of the Theses as well as representing and evaluating the medium through which they were disseminated provided more scope for dramatization, however. In particular, the selection of individual Theses reveals considerable differences from film to film and, therefore, also differences in focus.

In the first silent Luther film to have survived, *Doktor Martin Luther. Ein Lebensbild für das deutsche Volk* (otherwise known as *Die Wittenberger Nachtigall*) the Reformation is staged as a media revolution "avant la lettre", the first intertitle runs: "And Master Luft sets nimbly to work since the printing must be done that very day before All Souls".[50] Then we see how printing with movable type is admired by an awe-struck public. Nevertheless a written sheet of paper (rather than printed letters) is shown as product of the procedure.

Screenshot of the "Wittenberger Nachtigall" (1913/1927?): Essek as Luther explaining the Theses (Courtesy of EYE Film Insituut Nederland).

The spectator is able to read the words "95 Theses against Indulgences" ("95 Thesen gegen den Ablaß") painted in large lettering. What mattered here, therefore, was content rather than bibliophile authenticity. Nor did it matter to the film-makers that the original version of the Theses was in Latin. Nailing the Theses to the door is depicted as a revolutionary act: "And now Luther took a step which broke the power of the Pope with brutal force. That same day in the year 1517, he nailed the 95 Theses to the door of the Wittenberg [Castle Church]."[51] What appears on the screen is the celebrated printing of the Theses on a single sheet, an event also used in nearly all later films. Then Luther hammers, nailing the sheet to the door. In the next scene, a few richly clad citizens come to the church without paying much attention to the Theses. Not until a short man climbs up on a stone in order to read the Theses and to carry the message they convey into the church does the public become aware of them. Soon a growing mob of vehemently gesturing people pours from the Castle Church. Luther then steps from the crowd, wearing his monk's habit. Finally, the forces of law and order have to scatter the mob. That closes the second chapter. The next chapter begins with the words: "Like wildfire, it spread to the ear of the Papist Cardinal Messer Cajetan that Luther had taken the momentous step of defying the Pope before the eyes of the world."[52] Then Luther is "struck" by the papal ban. Here, therefore, the act of nailing the Theses to the door is at the beginning of a chain of events. Nothing however, is said of the letter to the Archbishop of Mainz, with which Luther actually informed Church authorities of what he planned to do. The conflict, which continued in fact as a war of words on paper, is reflected in the film by the inserted textuality. Thus the intertitles to the scene of Luther's reaction to the announcement that he will be excommunicated contain not only comments[53] but also the vizualization of his notice "The academic youth is to prepare the faggots for burning on Thursday, December 10, before the Elster Gate at Wittenberg; there the work of the Anti-Christ [...] Martin Luther is to burn."[54] After a comical song on marriage (!) is sung in a rousing chorus, a papal nuntius hands Luther the Bull threatening excommunication: "Martinus Luther, I have been appointed by the grace of the Holy Father to deliver this personally into your hands."[55] The title page of the printed bull bearing the papal coat of arms is focused then in order to prove authenticity and to imitate the position of the protagonist. Therefore camera pans from the title line to the papal arms, thus imitating reading behaviour. In the intertitle, the text is translated into German: "Bull against the heresies of Martin Luther and his adherents." ("Bulle gegen die Irrtümer Martin Luthers und seiner Anhänger.") Then Luther himself is shown reading it, surrounded by friends. He bursts out laughing. "So, to it, students. Set to work! Quickly fan the flames for me."[56] Faggots are brought and piled up accompanied by the text "Because you have destroyed Christ, may the everlasting fire consume you."[57] With a histrionic gesture, Luther hurls the document into the flames. This act is virtually stylized into liturgical officiation at mass by means of the intertitle commentary: "While Luther and the adults departed, the students struck up a 'Te deum' and subsequently a 'De Profundis'."[58] The power of the written word in the guise of the papal Bull threatening excommunication is a discussion point in each of the Luther films. Therefore, also consigning it to the flames is a pivotal scene in every Luther film. In fact, light and fire imagery is used to the fullest both here and in subsequent films; the theses "spread like wildfire"; subsequently Luther is "struck" by the threat of excommunication (literally "ray of banishment" in German) and he burns the Bull conveying the threat.

In the 1923 film however, Luther doesn't use a tool, but his bare fist to affix the Theses to the door of the Castle Church.

Like a 16th-century broadsheet, film has been used since early in the 20th century as a vehicle for the expression of political opinions, often through the portrayal of historic events. *Luther: Ein Film der deutschen Reformation*, which was commissioned by the Luther-Filmdenkmal, Zentralstelle für die Schaffung eines Lutherfilms and directed by Hans Kyser[59] was made at an unprecedented cost. The films featured an all-star cast and accorded even more scope to printing and the individual Theses. In no other Luther film were so many scenes devoted to these subjects. In sound films, especially, this ran counter to the speed of

Wüstenhagen as Luther is standing in front of church door after having affixed the Theses in "Martin Luther. His Life and Time" (Germany 1923).

narration. This last silent Luther film was finished in 1927—the same year in which *Metropolis, Berlin: Symphonie einer Großstadt, Königin Luise* and also *Die Weber* caused a sensation.[60] *Luther*, for which Wolfgang Zeller composed the musical accompaniment,[61] was supposed to link up with history films such as *Fredericus Rex* (*Frederick the Great*), 1921–22, which centred on historic figures drawn from German history. In the Luther films, the portrait of the reformer was an expression of a Protestantism shaped by German nationalism of the type represented by Bruno Döhring, Cathedral Preacher and founder of the *Deutsche Reformationspartei* (German Reformation Party), who advised Kyser in writing the screenplay.[62]

In the 1927 film, writing the Theses was motivated by a horrific description of Luther's sojourn in Rome, which was also consistent with the anti-Catholic thrust of the film as a whole. Tetzel, a character who is also portrayed in each subsequent Luther film as a demagogue and vernacular foe of Luther's "in the street", was characterized in such an exaggerated manner in the 1927 film that the effect is risible. This is very different from the harmless characterization of 1913. The change reflects the influence of Expressionist theater on 1920s cinema. In every Luther film the legendary words about the soul leaping out of Purgatory as soon as the coin clinks in the offeratory box are given to Tetzel.

In the 4th act of the 1927 Luther film, *Die Thesen*, the discussion of the powers of papal indulgences is introduced with a "pronouncement" of Luther that echoes Ecclesiastes 3:7 (A time to rent, and a time to sow; a time to keep silence, and a time to speak): "the time to keep silence is past [...] the time to speak has come!"[63] Karlstadt and Melanchthon support him. The scene ends with a sentence that is pregnant with meaning: "The word has been spoken [...] the time has come."[64] The following act is devoted to the *Way of the Theses* ("Weg der Thesen) as the title indicates. The 43rd and 44th Theses are quoted.[65] Hutten and Sickingen are given the 72nd Thesis.[66] The commentary that follows reflects the views of

Melanchthon presenting the papal bull to Luther and Hutten in the 1927 film.

the nationalist consultant to the film project: "Hence, there is something that is stronger than Rome and all popes: the German conscience".[67] The poet Hans Sachs is assigned the 62nd Thesis.[68] Before the papal Inquisition a verbal skirmish breaks out, which is solely concerned with the published writings: "The papal Bull commands you to burn Luther's writings!". "Burn the papal writings!! Burn Canon Law!"[69] is the reply, which ends in the pronouncement: "If the Pope writes with a Latin goose quill, our Luther will answer with a German eagle plume."[70] This is only surpassed by the fighting words given to Ulrich von Hutten: "You the word—I the sword!"[71]

At the end, the metaphorical flames are invoked once again: "This flame no man can extinguish!"[72]

In no later Luther film are the Theses handled as extensively. There the Theses are very often reduced to the indulgence issue or only the basic tenets of the doctrine of God's grace are addressed. In the 2003 Luther film they are even simplified to the teachings of a religion of love. Like this film the first Luther film shown after the Second World War was an American production, albeit made with German partners. Nevertheless, it was in the tradition of the transatlantic film aesthetic. The 1953 Luther film was made in the US against the background of a general "religious revival".[73] For Lutherans especially, the question of their history and their sources played a pivotal role. In the US, interest in Martin

Luther was greater than it had ever been.[74] It was no coincidence that this was the time that Jaroslav Pelikan edited the first complete translation of Luther's works into English. The Pelikan translation was published in fifty-five volumes between 1955 and 1971. Pelikan was also a consultant for the Luther film that premiered in 1953. The historical introduction to the film gives fear of Judgement Day as the reason for the success of the traffic in papal indulgences, which is represented as the root cause for the Reformation. Critics noted that Theses 36[75] and 62[76] were chosen "not for their theological content but also as examples of anti-papist and anti-Roman polemic".[77] Whether or not it was intended to be polemical, the first half of the film was largely shaped by the indulgence controversy. Given this fact the Nailing the Theses motif was also accorded a pivotal role in this film as well. It is localized in a scene showing the devout who have come to venerate the holy relics: "Among those waiting to be forgiven and blessed, none could know that this document would become one of the most widely read in all history".

Niall McGinnis as Luther is going to leave the scene after having nailed the Theses onto the door in "Martin Luther" (USA 1953).

The expression "widely read" is left out in the German-language version[78], which is probably closer to historical truth. Promulgation of the printed Theses in Latin and subsequently in German, however, is shown on a way that matched the state of Luther research at the time the film was made. The papal Bull threatening excommunication is burnt and Luther utters the ambitious words: "Rome, because you have destroyed the truth of God, let God destroy you in these flames."

The history of viewer response to this film also shows how, even after the Second World War, the Reformation was still viewed from the standpoint of the schism within the Church and this denominational view also informed discussion of the Theses.

In the 1960s, the mainly denominational slant on those events yielded to a psychological interpretation of Luther. This was actuated above all done by Erik H. Erikson's study *Young man Luther*[79], which was published in 1958. It shaped various representations of Luther in film. On the one hand, a play by John Osborne premiered in 1961 entitled *Luther*,[80] which in turn became the basis for the 1973 American film production of the same title starring Stacy Keach with Judy Dench as Katharina von Bora and directed by Guy Green. On the other, a German television film by Leopold Ahlsen, *Der arme Mann Luther*, was broadcast by the German TV channel WDR in 1965. The latter film was conceived as a stage production with minimalist props and scenery. Indeed, it was still performed on stage in 1967 even after it had been shown abroad on television (in Finland, Switzerland and the Netherlands).[81] The main subject of *Der arme Mann Luther* is Luther's personal conflict with the authorities. It is carried out in retrospect in dream-like sequences, looked back on by Luther on his deathbed. Nor is Nailing the Theses rendered as a straightforward relation of events. Instead, following a carnivalesque representation of the trade in indulgences, Luther gives a fiery oration against the "idolaters, priests of Baal and practitioners of simony" ("Götzendiener, Baalpriester und Simonisten"). His Theses are summarised in the following sentence: "I, however, say unto you, through no letter of dispensation, no liturgy, no monkish habit can buy you justification before Him; through love alone, through faith; herein dwells God; I have realized this".[82] The scene changes to reveal Luther as an omnipotent Giant ("Riese-alles-tu") and "The Tower from Eisleben" ("Turm aus Eisleben"), as his alter-ego calls him. Thus, it reproves Luther's hubristic treatment of the Old Order in standing alone on the world stage with his printed Theses.

Indeed, in *Der arme Mann Luther* the reformer is alone in the end, deserted by all former companions and adherents: Karlstadt, Sickingen, Staupitz and Müntzer have doubts about his work. Käthe alone stands by him. The reformer's diabolical alter ego (played by Hannes Messemer) tempts Luther (played by Dieter Zeidler) to recant even in the hour of his death. However, this attempt fails: Luther refuses to recant and trusts in the grace of God.

The three-part French feature film *Frère Martin* (*Brother Martin*) with Bernard Lincot in the leading role was first broadcast in France in 1981 and then shown on ARD in Germany in the Luther Year 1983.

The screenplay is based on a 1950s screenplay by Alexandre Astruc.[83] Astruc, who had attracted attention with a film about Jean-Paul Sartre, interprets Luther, on the one hand, from the history of philosophy angle, as the harbinger of a movement of intellectual and spiritual emancipation and, on the other, from a socially critical perspective as someone who questioned the feudal system. This title, *Brother Martin*, also seems to refer not only to Luther as an Augustinian friar but also as an embodiment of egalitarian principles. The first scene, in which Luther, begging for alms, is nearly knocked over by a furious hunting party, illus-

Hans Dieter Zeidler as Luther with a printer's proof of the Theses in the WDR television film "Der arme Mann Luther" (FRG 1964).

trates the excesses of the "ancien régime". The overthrow of the existing social order—sparked off in Astruc eyes, by Luther—of course did not occur in the early 16th century. Nevertheless, Astruc has succeeded in plausibly demythologising Luther as a hero by juxtaposing a young couple, with which viewers could identify, in a parallel narrative strand that is almost on an equal footing. The model of a parallel action strand "in the midst of the people" was even enlarged in the GDR production. In the Astruc film, Bernard, who, married to Marguerite, has become a father, is among the earliest adherents to Luther's teaching. That is according to Astruc' interpretation of Luther's doctrine primarily the idea of the "freedom of religion" ("liberté de la religion"). Bernard becomes a journeyman printer, thus contributing to the dissemination of the Theses and playing a more active role than simply being a disciple of the reformer. To Bernard's master, however, content is secondary; what matters most to him is business. This aspect was thoroughly discussed in the Luther film shown on ZDF in 1983.

Part 2 of the Astruc film begins with the nailing of the Theses, but this time on the stone wall of a Romanesque (!) church. Moreover, it is not Luther hammering away, but an anonymous messenger from among the citizenry. This crucial action is performed by a person who has played no prior role in the narrative. The Theses are proclaimed out loud in French by Augustinian monks—the use of the vernacular is not singled out for discussion. These are not verbatim translations but rather summaries and free paraphrases.[84] After mass, the anonymous messenger proclaims the content of Theses 86 and 46 to the populace. In response the mob asks "What does this priest actually want"? Oversimplifying Luther's purely theological teachings *On the Freedom of a Christian*, Bernard anticipates the demand for general freedom by answering: "[so] that one may be free" ("Qu'on soit libre"). The representative of the profane world only reads the political and economic advantages in the Theses: no tax to pay Rome and questioning papal authority. Nevertheless Astruc views Luther's deed as a "coup d'état spirituel", one that ends with iconoclasm and anticipates the slogans of the French Revolution: "Death to the Pope and the clergy" ("Mort au pape et aux curés"); "Let us burn down the churches, let us burn down the castles" ("Brûlons les églises, brûlons les châteaux"). An interior of a church is shown in a picture that is a borrowing from the celebrated woodcut *Lament of the wretched persecuted idols and temple images* (*Klagerede der armen verfolgten Götzen und Tempelbilder*), printed *c* 1530.[85] The strong differences in directional impetus and the range of social classes causing the Peasants' War, iconoclasm and Luther's reform movement have been blended here without allowing the different positions to be really articulated. The Theses have been interpreted as a political manifesto.

The Luther Year 1983 led to very different representations of Luther's Theses in the two Germanys: in the GDR as a polysemic historical epic that took over seven hours to narrate, and in the Federal Republic as a parable staged in St. Lorenz in Nuremberg. Thus, the blows of the hammer were given a completely different context in the two states.

The Federal Republic version was based on the Theodor Schübel screenplay and directed by Rainer Wolffhardt. Luther's words, spoken in a study at Wittenberg University "I take the Holy Scripture seriously, nothing else"[86] are the introduction to the nailing scene. It begins in front of the Castle Chapel in Wittenberg, actually of course, St. Lorenz in Nuremberg. The published screenplay reveals that it is "towards noon, mass is being said in the church."[87] Finally hammering is heard in the church. The event does not, therefore, grow out of the action as it does in all other Luther films. Luther leaves the scene as soon as his work is done. As in the 1953 film he does not wait for a reaction. The director deliberately eschewed a long shot of Luther after the deed, a filmic device that is used as a means of heroic stylization in both the 1983 GDR and the 2003 US films.

Next, the problem of a poorly educated populace is staged in condensed form by two women who ask: "What has been hammered on there?", "What is written there?"[88] A student helps with a translation, closely adhering to the Latin text in translating Theses 27 and 28 as well as 43 and 11.[89] That closes the scene. In the next scene, the Archbishop of Mainz shares a princely repast with Staupitz, Tetzel and two canons to the accompaniment of lute music. The squandering of the money paid for indulgences could not have been more pointedly illustrated. Staupitz explains that Luther wants a debate in order to explain the Theses to the archbishop. Schübel lets the archbishop spell out what effect the new medium has: Although the Theses were written in remote Wittenberg, they had immediately circulated in print to a vast readership in the great cities of Leipzig, Nuremberg and Basel. Not until later in the film does Luther explain the content of the Theses in a sermon. In it, he emphasizes that it would be better to give the money paid for indulgences to the poor, and, since man only becomes just through faith, one should do penance and show remorse.

At the time the film was being made in the early 1980s citizen's initiatives were in their heyday. Thus it is surely the reason why the aspect of freedom of speech expressing criticism of the authorities and civic awareness are emphasized so explicitly. This is also the thrust of Luther's speech at the Elster Gate: "One should have no fear of the bigwigs. Let them condemn my writings and consign them to the flames! I can do everything they can" whereupon he hurls the Bull threatening excommunication and the books into the fire.[90] In another scene, against the background of the Luther translation of the Bible, the film advocates the ideal of the emancipated citizen when Luther says: "The people should finally read for themselves what is written. It is much better to see with one's own eyes than with those of another."[91] Luther's connection with the vernacular could not be handled more differently in the two films: what was stylized into an expression of national identity in Kyser's film has in Schübel's screenplay become the means to educating people to think for themselves and exercise (political) emancipation. This also explains the author's partiality for a Müntzer who is represented as a social revolutionary in a fictional debate with Luther. In this discussion, Müntzer criticizes Luther's political inconsistency and ultimately accuses him of being the "Pope of Wittenberg",[92] implying that he has been consolidated into a new religious establishment.

The film, made by the generation that originated the protest movement against the Springer concern, includes many aspects of media criticism. In one particular scene Theodor Schübel portrays the printer Grunenberg[93] as a calculating business man who speaks the following words: "How my business is doing? You're still asking that, Brother Martin? I can't print enough of your writings. Orders are pouring in from everywhere, even Nuremberg, Freiburg and Basel. I hope you'll soon find time to write something again."[94] When Luther gives him the manuscript of *Von der Freiheit eines Christenmenschen*, Grunenberg again offers him a fee, which Luther rejects again. The printer is the one who immediately realises the far-reaching implications of the criticism expressed by Luther: "If I print that—there won't be any place for you in our Church after that."[95] Still, Grunenberg realizes that publicity also brings profits. Schübel shows this in another scene in the printing workshop, which takes place after Luther's appearance at the imperial Diet of Worms, at which he was declared a heretic and an outlaw. Karlstadt says: "He left Worms three weeks ago and he has not yet arrived here in Wittenberg." Grunenberg thereupon remarks to his journeymen: "His writings will be much in demand. And we only have a small stock left! On with it. We'll print *Über die Freiheit eines Christenmenschen* again." One journeyman warns: "Master, that is forbidden!". Grunenberg replies: "Forbidden? Definitely. But it's also good business."[96] The message is that profit-seeking in any case is immoral; it is also conveyed in the dialogue with Brother Gabriel that reveals that the new medium also aids Luther's adversaries: Gabriel: "Although it is strictly forbidden, your books are still on the market. High prices are being paid for them in the cities. However, your printers don't only print your books; they are just as industriously printing books against you." Luther explains tersely: "Printers are businessmen. Why shouldn't they carry on both shoulders if they double their earnings by doing so?" The screenplay adds: "He laughs".[97]

The GDR Luther film does not open with a portrait of the main character. Instead, it portrays his opponent, Tetzel, moving to Jüterborg in 1517. Christina Gärtner, a peasant girl, and Valentin Böhm, a journeyman working for Cranach, are the representatives of the people with whom the audience is supposed to identify. This first part, entitled *Der Protest*, is all about the power of papal indulgences. Five theses are extensively presented by Luther himself to his university colleagues.[98] In the debate that follows, in which he is accused of hating the Church, Luther also encounters acceptance of his views. Johannes Agricola asks "Why isn't the Pope compassionate enough to free souls from Purgatory with one blow since he has the power to do it for money?"[99] A speaker for the legal profession asks "Why doesn't Pope Leo X […], who is heir to one of Italy's greatest fortunes, at least build this one Church of St Peter's with his own money instead of with the pennies of the pious?"[100] Finally, the dean of the university refuses to support Luther since he is responsible for displaying the reliquaries of the All Souls' Chapter [Allerheilgenstift] and proclaiming the related indulgence. Before Staupitz warns Luther once again not to arouse enmity against his order by publishing the Theses, Luther quotes the last Theses to strengthen his own faith in God. Next he reads the 45th Thesis that appeals for charity and social justice: "Christians should be taught whoever sees a needy person in want and does not help him but spends money on indulgences is not buying papal indulgence but is purchasing God's wrath". With the quotation of the 44th Thesis the anti-materialistic impetus is emphasized: "For with a work of love, love grows in a man and he grows better; through an indulgence, however, he does not grow better. He must pay an eternal penalty instead." The 46th Thesis says "Christians should be taught that whoever possesses nothing in overabundance should keep what is necessary for his house and his family and not squander it on indulgences" and the 52nd Thesis warns "Whoever expects salvation from a letter of dispensation, is foolish, even though the commissioner granting the indulgence, even if it is the Pope himself, should pawn their souls for it." With the 50th Thesis Luther avoids insulting the Pope by wisely arguing "Christians should be taught that if the Pope knew that, he would rather see St Peter's Church go up in flames than build it with the skin and flesh and bones of his flock."[101] The last Theses Luther is shown adding to the discussion are Theses 94 and 95, that have to do with trusting in Christ. Not until then is Luther shown dictating his letter to the Archbishop of Mainz and enclosing the Theses. Finally—because the porter is drunk—Luther himself nails the Theses, which have been printed by

Grunenberg (!) to the door of the Wittenberg Castle church. Still he has qualms, especially about their dissemination among the people: "I wanted to debate the Theses with scholars."[102] Luther emphasizes that he merely wanted to point out abuses and did not want to establish dogma, which was his right as a doctor of theology. Luther also advocates the distribution of wealth in accordance with Marxist doctrine. The last part of the film, entitled *Conscience* (*Das Gewissen*) shows Luther struggling with the consequences of the Reformation.

The 2003 Luther film, made by Eric Till, seems almost post-Modern. Based on a screenplay by Camille Thomasson and Bart Carvigan, it presents a Luther who might have stepped out of a Romantic Nazarene painting, a Christ-like Luther who occasionally also works miracles. Luther is shown nailing the Theses in his handwriting to the door. This act is followed by a close-up of his face in worm's-eye view, which enhances the impression that a heroic deed has been performed.

Joseph Fiennes as Luther after nailing the Theses in "Luther" (USA 2003).

It is not Luther himself, but his followers who ensure that the Theses are disseminated: They take the manuscript to the printer. The Theses are reduced to three sentences, and this after Tetzel's demagogic urging has been handled more extensively than in any other Luther film. The criticism that the film contains "little theology" ("wenig Theologisches") does not seem entirely unjustified. Luther quotes his letter to the Archbishop of Mainz: "Christ did not preach indulgences; he preached the Gospel."[103] Students continue to read the 43rd Thesis on the door: "It should be preached to the Christians that he who gives to the poor or lends to the needy is doing better than buying letters of dispensation with it."[104] Finally, the paper is shown in the hands of Tetzel and his comrades. One of those comrades quotes the 82nd Thesis: "If the Pope can teach Purgatory, why does he not do that for love's sake rather than for money?"[105] Here the Theses, the papal Bull threatening excommunication and the translation of the

Bible are the central motifs. Nevertheless, in some scenes textuality is staged in an entirely unfilmic way, for instance when Luther stands for minutes statically with his translation before the Elector. Perhaps the director wanted to refer to the figures of Old Testament prophets on Gothic cathedral portals. The silent films stuck more closely to the content of the Theses when they were quoted verbatim, which was usually the case. This was to convey a more convincing impression of authenticity. In the sound films, by contrast, the Theses are reduced to a few core Theses and accordingly given an epigrammatic turn. There are often not the same Theses. Even though the indulgence theme is always cited, the weighting varies. It ranges from criticism of Rome through the Doctrine of Justification to anticipation of freedoms that are not just religious.

In the silent films, the written language was not just paramount for the dramaturgic handling of the Theses. In the *Wittenberger Nachtigall*, for instance, the rhyming form of the intertitles sought to echo writing for the stage, a medium against which the cinema was still struggling to compete. In addition, the vernacular aspect of the language in which the Theses and the Luther translation of the Bible are couched, as opposed to scholarly language is also a subject discussed in early Luther films. In the 1927 Luther film especially, the emphasis laid on the use of the German vernacular instead of Latin is a leitmotif because of the nationalist thrust of the film.

What all Luther films have in common is that printing, the medium through which the Theses were disseminated, is given a great deal of scope. In the first half of the 20th century, the emphasis in this regard was placed on printing being represented as a "German invention". In the latter half of the 20th century, however, aspects of media criticism are expressed. The press is represented as an instrument for shaping public opinion that is also moulded by economic considerations.

III. The Image of Martin Luther in Motion Pictures 1911–2003

1. Romanticism (1911–1921)

The history of Luther in motion pictures begins in the early 20th century at a time when cinematography was a new, commercially oriented branch of the entertainment industry. Its growth was visible in the explosive multiplication of film theaters. In 1910, there were 480 cinemas in the German Empire, but by 1913 there were an estimated 3000, with most of them concentrated in big cities.[1] Most films on release were feature films; of those, dramas and comedies were the most popular. The Berlin pastor Walther Conradt, who studied 250 films of those on release in 1910 from a combined sociological, ethical and theological standpoint, recorded ninety-seven murders, fifty-one cases of adultery, nineteen seductions, twenty-two abductions and forty-five suicides.[2] It was in this 'environment' regarded by the clergy with such concern that the first Luther film was made. *Doktor Martinus Luther* premiered in Berlin in 1911.

The title of the film, with the inclusion of the formal academic honorific in the spoken form of address, signals that this is to be a serious biography serving an educational purpose. Most later Luther film titles retain that thrust even though they seem less formal and remote without the doctoral title and Latin. At the same time, the explicit use of the words "Life of" in the sub-title or full title made it clear that these films were biographies. The name "Luther" or "Martin Luther" is the dominant element; only once is the name preceded by the attribute coined by Hans Sachs: 'The Wittenberg Nightingale'. The egalitarian *Frère Martin* evidently conformed only with the socially critical concept formulated by the French director of a Luther film.[3]

No copy of the first Luther film seems to have survived even though distribution of it by the *Deutsche Bioscop-Gesellschaft* was not confined to the capital. Just a few stills are extant, showing Hermann Litt, then a celebrated Berlin actor, singer and theater director, in the role of Luther.[4] Advertising for the film promised an authentic representation of Luther's life up to his marriage.[5]

Just two years later, in 1913—the same year that saw *Richard Wagner*, the film biography of another 'great German' released—*Die Wittenberger Nachtigall*, Mar-

Luther at the Diet of Worms and Luther's wedding in the 1911 film.

tin Luther (*The Wittenberg Nightingale, Martin Luther*) premiered in Berlin.[6] Erwin Báron both wrote the screenplay and directed the film. John Edward worked up the manuscript following Johann Mathesius' *Historien von Luthers Anfang Lehr und Leben*. After the censor had declared the film unsuitable for showing to young people, it was cut in 1921 and the title was altered to *Der Weg zur Sonne / Martin Luther* (*Way to the Sun / Martin Luther*)[7] and finally in 1927—revealing changes in the political climate—the film was entitled *Doktor Martin Luther. Ein Lebensbild für das deutsche Volk* (*Doctor Martin Luther. A Portrait of a Life for the German People*). This title borrows closely from that of a Luther biography by Georg Buchwald that had run to numerous editions.[8] Before the last submission to the censors, the producers had changed from Rubin-Film (Berlin and Vienna) to Marg.-Fried-Film GmbH (Berlin), which distributed films for schools.[9] It was also distributed abroad as two copies made in the 1920s show which have Dutch intertitles. [10] These copies were still screened in the early 1930s when Kyser's Luther film was already on the market in the Netherlands.[11] It is clear that the Luther biography was increasingly subject to nationalist prescription by then. The 1913 Luther film has survived only in revised versions of the 1920s. It depicts Luther in Romantic fashion as a wanderer and Latin scholar, who first had to earn a livelihood 'singing at courts',[12] as an ardent reformer and finally as a lusty wooer, smoothing the way for a new era. An unusual amount of narrative space is devoted to the life story of Katharina von Bora, which is told in parallel.

Astonishingly, Luther's wife is only a marginal figure—if she appears at all—in subsequent films.[13] However, in *Doktor Martin Luther: Ein Lebensbild für das deutsche Volk*, the relationship between Katharina von Bora and Martin Luther is stylized into a romantic love-story, with its roots in Luther's Erfurt student days. The leading role was played by Rudolf Essek (1885–1941), who was already much in demand as a stage actor by the time he made his film début in 1913 in *The Wittenberg Nightingale*.[14] The subsequent roles Essek played show that he was above all an actor at home in romantic or sentimental comedy. In the same way he approached his role in *The Wittenberg Nightingale*. "Luther set a good example in wooing Katharina von Bora"[15] runs a caption of the 1920s version of the film, the intertitling of which is considerably more extensive than the intertitling of the *Wittenberg Nightingale*.

Luther's proposal to Katharina in "Die Wittenberger Nachtigall".

The wedding scene logically forms the final shot of the film, in order to promote the Luthers as role models for the German parsonage. Finally, the expectations of a predominantly female cinema audience must surely have been met by capitalizing on emotional values.

2. The Nazarene (1923)

Martin Luther, completed in 1923,[16] has a totally different bias, a theological one. Drawing an analogy between Luther's biography and the Life of Christ has lent the life of the Reformer redemptive qualities, with light imagery playing a crucial role. Even the intertitles are framed by a representation of a brightly lit church window on the left, boasting Luther's coat of arms (the rose) at the top,[17] and a candle in front of a book on the right that can only be meant to represent the Bible. This film was produced by Lutherfilm GmbH for the Lutheran World Congress (Lutherischer Weltkongress) in Eisenach. The director was Karl Wüstenhagen (1893–1950), who also played the leading role.[18]

Left: Karl Wüstenhagen as Luther in „Martin Luther. His Life and Time" (Germany 1923), first scene. Right: Karl Wüstenhagen as Luther, first scene, subsequent shot.

The film was shot at historical sites in Erfurt and the Wartburg. The screenplay, written by the Berlin pastor Walther Nithack-Stahn (1866–1942), was thoroughly revised by P. Kurz. Nithack-Stahn had made a name for himself in 1910 with *Das Christusdrama* and had already written two plays about Luther for the stage.[19] In the 1923 Luther film, which seems to have survived only in versions made for distribution outside Germany, Luther appears as enlightened—literally—right from the outset. He is first depicted standing in shadow beneath a Gothic arch and—in an obvious allusion to John 12,46: "I am come a light into the world, that whosoever believeth on me, should not abide in darkness."—and light ultimately shines down on him from above. He stands in this scene looking upwards with his hands crossed. This gesture is in the tradition of humility gestures familiar from representations of the Virgin before the Christ Child in the manger at Bethlehem.[20] Luther's birth is accordingly interpreted in the film intertitle as follows: "The world had slumbered through a night of many centuries; the Dark Ages were ended. God said: 'Let there be light; and there was light'". It was staged as a birth longed for by Christendom: "Oh Lord, deliver us and restore unto us Thy truth"; "The Lord heard — On November

10, 1483, in the little town of Eisleben, there was born to the humble miner Hans Luther, and his wife Margaret, a son". Today it is known that Hans Luther was not a miner but was the foreman in a copper smelter. Martin Luther's father first leased a smelter from Count Mansfeld and, as his income grew, succeeded in leasing more copper mines and smelters. Hans Luther, therefore, belonged to an aspiring middle class able to afford university studies for their male progeny.[21] However, the topos 'to be of modest origin' is often used for identification in image building.[22]

In the film, Luther's mother is then shown with her child in a room that corresponds with 16th-century representations of the virgin birth. However, this room is not unequivocally the room in the house (now a museum) where Martin Luther is thought to have been born.[23] Then Luther as a baby is shown once again in a close-up. Luther's childhood is described quite extensively in this film, although not much is known about it. Presumably, this was meant to appeal to a youthful audience like candidates for confirmation. A parable was even invented for this film that takes up quite a lot of narrative space: The child Martin is terminally ill and the physician (the embodiment of scientific rationality) prescribes that he is to be given no water to drink. A nun (personifying the Old Church) prays a rosary for his salvation, sprinkles holy water on him and places a sculpture of Virgin and Child with St. Anne beside the sick child's bed. After everyone has left for Vespers, the boy, despite the ban on water, stumbles out of bed, drawn as if by magic to the jug of water that the nun had placed at a safe distance, and thirstily finishes it in three gulps. The scene is interpreted in an intercut dream image: Christ appears, handing the Samaritan woman a similar water jug in front of an altar-like structure. The appropriate Bible quotation from John 4,14 is inserted: "But whosoever drinketh of this water that I shall give him, shall never be more athirst [sic!]; but the water that I shall [sic!] give him shall be in him a well of water, springing up into everlasting life."[24] It would remain for a later era in cinematic history to depict Christ himself giving a thirsty supplicant water to drink.[25]

In the 1923 Luther film, a clear distinction is still drawn between biblical history and human biography. The young Luther recovers and, on his return, the physician speaks of (divine) "providence" in view of the miraculous healing. The stylization into what is virtually a Jesus scene suggests that it was based on a popular model, perhaps drawn from a devotional image given as a confirmation present.[26] That the student in this film succeeded in taking his doctorate in 1505 rather than his MA, as has been verified,[27] might be due to a translation error. Another element of Christ-conformity in this film is the character of Luther's fictitious female friend named Magdalen, who has to renounce her wedding plans when Luther enters the friary. The film's image Luther as a mendicant friar might have been inspired by an 1892–93 Eduard Kämpffer painting of him as a mendicant friar begging in the streets of Erfurt.[28] This is a reference to the fact that OESA (Ordo Eremitarum Sancti Augustini) was founded as a mendicant order.[29]

Luther the student is portrayed as eager to learn and surrounded by books. However, he ignores one book, with "ARIS" written in huge letters on its spine. It is a malicious reference to the pagan philosopher Aristotle, whom Luther despised.[30] The composition of the scene refers to Gustav König's engraving "Luther entdeckt in der Erfurter Universitätsbibliothek eine lateinische Bibel" (finished in 1847) that shows Aristotle's name completely.[31] In the film, the presentation of a Christian author is entirely different: Saint Paul appears in person in order to point the pivotal verse (Romans 3:28) to Luther for exegesis.

As in every Luther film, Luther's visit to Rome is a central scene. The secularisation of the papal court and the lives of the clergy are invariably described in drastic terms, with cliché-ridden jibes at ultramontanism.

The impression that Luther was disappointed in what he saw in Rome is enhanced as viewers follow Luther and his companion on their arduous trip across the Alps. Throughout the journey, Luther's steadfast gaze is directed towards Rome, another motif taken from art historical models.[32] Luther's experience of Rome was not made a symbol of protest against Rome's claim to universal power. Neither was it stylized into the myth of German particularism that appeared first in the Thomas Mann essay *Betrachtungen eines Unpolitischen* (*Reflections of an Unpolitical Man*) finished in 1918. In fact, Luther's journey did not, as far as is known, represent a turning point in his life: a pious young friar at the time, he visited the places that were still holy to him.[33] A remarkable feature of the 1923 film is the original footage of the Forum Romanum, which at the same time represents pagan antiquity. In later films, there would be no such striving for authenticity in depicting the city.

In the 1923 film, papacy is portrayed in a manner strongly reminiscent of Thomas Couture's huge history painting with moralizing overtones, *Les Romains de la décadence* (*Romans in the Decadence of the Empire*), finished in 1847, now in the Musée d'Orsay in Paris. In addition, a flattering insincerity is still attributed to Roman clerics. They are shown reclining so very much at their ease that they quickly stroke a cat—symbol of falsity—before Luther enters to convey his messages.

Despite the intellectual and spiritual resistance he demonstrates, Luther remains a pacifist in this film. This may be attributed to the way the character was conceived in the scenario as it was originally presented by the openly anti-war Nithack-Stahn. Similarly, Luther is not shown hammering the Theses to the Castle Church door. Instead, he sticks them on with his bare fist in a way that is not explained. This lack of overt aggressiveness is not only apparent in the way Luther is made to confront the iconoclasts but is also demonstrated in the fictitious situation of hare coursing, in which Luther, disguised as Junker Jörg, is forced to participate. Luther is not actually shown taking part but instead giving shelter to the hare in his lap in order to save it from the staghounds. This has an authentic source: In one of his letters, written at the Wartburg, Luther describes such a scene. In the ZDF documentary, this event was depicted even more dramatically and interpreted as a metaphor for Luther saving Christendom from the antichrist (the pope). In yet another scene in the 1923 film, Luther is also shown as an animal-lover—like St Francis—feeding the pigeons at the Wartburg. This serves as an image for his search for peace and harmony in the world. In the 1927 film, by contrast, Luther will be characterized entirely different, with far more martial behaviour.

In his appearance before Karlstadt and Eck at the Leipzig debate—which actually sealed Luther's break with the Church of Rome as an institution—the Augustinian friar is made to resemble Christ among the Doctors. The twig in Luther's hand with its white flowers, underscoring his innocence, was not part of the traditional Luther iconography.[34] "The start for Worms", is also clearly linked with the iconography of Christ: Before the gates of a town along the way, crowds greet Luther by waving branches as is familiar from representations of Christ's Entry into Jerusalem according to John 12,12f. and Matthew 21,1–11, especially 9 ("Blessed is he that cometh in the name of the Lord"). Like his triumphal entry into the city, the staging of Luther's appearance before the Diet of Worms belongs to the classic motifs of Luther iconography.[35] It may not be missing from any Luther film like the famous quotation "Hier stehe ich, ich kann nicht anders, Gott helfe mir, Amen" ("Here I stand. I cannot do otherwise. God help me. Amen"). This is a German summarized version of the closing words of the speech Luther gave in Latin, added by the editor of the printed version.[36] Luther actually said in Latin: "and as long as my conscience is held captive by God's word, I am neither able nor willing to recant anything since it is neither safe nor right to act against conscience. God Help me. Amen."[37] In another analogy to the Passion, the previous scene that depicts the time granted to Luther to consider recanting is literally designated "Gethsemane" in the intertitle. Here Luther uses his break creatively and relaxes by penning A Mighty Fortress, which appears in the English version. The Diet of Worms is annotated—probably only in the American version—with an evaluation of the events by the Scottish essayist and historian Thomas Carlyle (d. 1881), who also translated Luther's song Ein feste Burg into English in 1831:[38] "The Diet of Worms, Luther's appearance there on April 17, 1521, may be considered the greatest scene in modern European history, the point, indeed from which the whole subsequent history of civilization takes its rise."[39] This is a reference to the fact that reception of Luther outside Germany took place largely through Anglo-Saxon channels.

In his 1841 lectures On Heroes, Hero-Worship, and the Heroic in History of 1841,

Carlyle devoted an entire chapter to Luther and John Knox under the aspect of the "Hero as Priest".[40] Carlyle, who was not a Luther scholar, advanced a very essayist line of reasoning without access to source material on Luther. He characterized the heroic type he attributed to Luther as a "spiritual Captain of the people," as a "Prophet shorn of his more awful splendour; burning with mild equable radiance, as the enlightener of daily life,"[41] even as a "Christian Odin".[42] He assigned the Protestant Reformer to the ranks of such variously assorted heroes as Odin, Muhammad, Dante, Shakespeare, Samuel Johnson, Rousseau, Robert Burns, Cromwell and Napoleon. Oddly enough, Christ is missing from this pantheon.

The end of the biographical narrative—as in the 1953 and 2003 films—was the Confessio Augustana (1530). It pronounced the "final victory of Martin Luther and his teachings", since "The principles for which he stood are embodied in it, as the first great Protestant symbol and proclaimed to an enlightened world."

The final scene shows the protagonist at the head of 'his' people, which is approaching him in eurhythmic movement. At the climax of the scene, Luther's followers reach out their arms to him.[43] It is unmistakably an allusion to Moses leading the Children of Israel out of Babylonian captivity to the Promised Land and thus to Luther's central reforming treatise, *De captivitate ecclesiae babylonica* (1520), in which he described the condition of the Church at that time as a Babylonian captivity. The last intertitle proclaims: "My people! My people! The gateway of freedom is open unto you; enter and stand fast in the liberty where-with Christ hath made you free!" This final scene seems to anticipate Siegfried Kracauer's 1927 thesis that mass is ornament (published in English as *The Mass Ornament*).[44] However, in this Luther film, the mass has not yet mutated into the 'faceless sign' described by Kracauer,[45] because individuals are recognizable in advance. One man speaks to Luther seeming to formulate the Reformer's obituary: "Thou man of ages! Thou hast conquered the forces of darkness and opened the gateway to a new and better world." The gestures of the followers point to the leader and repeat the filmic leitmotif, the Gothic arch (see p. 87).

A Gothic arch also frames the final scene, the whole of which is religiously transfigured by the light imagery.

However, the Gothic arch was not merely regarded as an element of the 'Luther style'[46] but rather as symbolizing German culture as such. This stands in contrast to the Roman(esque) round arch, because the Romans were to be portrayed as decadent parasites. Already in this film, the aim was prevalent in Germany not just to film the life of a reforming ecclesiastic but also to stage Luther as a 'Great German' in the mould of Frederick the Great in *Fridericus Rex*. I will address this point in more detail in the next chapter. However, this image of Luther did not inform the concept of the 1923 film as strongly as it would later films. Hence, the 1923 film could be shown abroad, especially in countries where Lutheranism represented one of many denominations, including Protestant ones, in the interests of consolidating personal faith. When it was screened at the Concordia Seminary in St. Louis in January 1925, Dean Fritz declared: "No Lutheran can see these pictures without being strengthened in his faith."[47] Of course, there, too, Luther was given the role of leader yet, in this case, it is defined purely in the religious sense. In a contemporary description of the film published in the *American Lutheran* Luther is interpreted as a second Moses who leads his people safely to the Promised Land: "The awakened Luther, near-martyr, man, and ever the leader, is then carried into enforced exile at the Wartburg, where he makes his other great contribution to religious freedom, the translation of the New Testament into the language of the people. He leaves the protection of the Wartburg to stem the tide of iconoclasm, and leads his people into safer channels of worship and public order."[48] *Martin Luther, his Life and Time* attracted 12,167 viewers in the first two months it was running in the New York metropolitan area.[49] Between October and December 1925, 70,000 to 90,000 people a month are said to have seen the film.[50] The film was re-released in 1970, this time with the title Rebel Priest, in an attempt to build on its earlier success. However, by that time the silent film could no longer compete with the 1953 production.

3. German Nationalist Hero (1927)

The next cinematic treatment of Luther on a grand scale, *Luther: Ein Film der deutschen Reformation*, commissioned by the society "Luther-Filmdenkmal – Zentralstelle für die Schaffung eines Lutherfilms", was an extremely expensive production.

Boasting an all-star cast, it was directed by Hans Kyser and made history as a "Lutheran Annunciation film".[51] This silent Luther film, for which Wolfgang Zeller composed the musical accompaniment,[52] was steeped in German nationalist tinged Protestantism as represented by the Cathedral Preacher Bruno Döhring, who, as I will explain in chapter V.2.2, had a great deal of influence on the spirit of the screenplay. In this film, the Reformer embodies the triumph of a Protestant German intellectual culture over Roman Catholicism. Key scenes in it are Luther's horrifying experiences in Rome, which is depicted as the "Whore of Babylon".

This representation is obviously modelled after the story *Laocoön* by the Naturalist playwright August Strindberg, an extremely provocative account of the experiences of an "Augustinian friar" in the Holy City during spring 1503 that was first published in German in 1908.[53] It was a kind of commentary on Strind-

On Luther's way to Rome: Scenes of Idolatry and Rome shown
as an oriental marketplace.

berg's very popular play *Näktergalen i Wittenberg* (1903), that premiered 1914 in German as *Luther* and had 47 showings in Berlin during winter 1914/1915. The last scene of the play was dedicated to Luther's sojourn at the Wartburg castle and ends with the nationalistic statement. Luther remarks "Look, there is daybreak in Thuringia now" and Dr. Johannes [Faust] corrects him: "in Germany"[54]. The Luther film instead ends with iconoclasm as a revolutionary inferno that must have reminded viewers of the events of 1918. The 1928 *Illustrierter Filmkurier* vividly recounts this scene: "There, in the midst of a fanatical onslaught raging around him, Luther appears alone in the pulpit. The knight's armour he wore on the Wartburg still shimmers through his vestments. As if an angel of wrath himself were descended unto us, his appearance works a miracle. His powerful oration compels all to their knees in pious humility. Through the church interior, which is so still that not a breath is heard, reverberates Luther's great battle hymn of the Reformation, *A Mighty Fortress is Our God*, played by an elderly organist."[55] This chorale will also shape the music of the sound films. The use of music plays a very important role for the emotional response to a film. As the brain researcher Wolf Singer showed, all sensations have a deeper impact on us when they are supported by music.[56] In the Luther films, the chorales arouse the situation of a service, which strengthens the corporate identity of the Lutheran spectators. An image of the Wartburg with the verse "Ein feste Burg ist unser Gott" has adorned many editions of Protestant hymn-books since the late 19th century.[57] Luther's hymn appeared in the earliest songbooks of the 16th century like the "Klugsches Gesangbuch".

Eugene Klöpfer played the Messianic figure of Luther described in the *Illustrierter Filmkurier*. A famous stage and screen actor at that time, Klöpfer had the title of a State actor since 1934 and, since 1936, was the director of various Berlin theaters. He also appeared in several Veit Harlan films, including the notorious *Jud Süß*.[58] In the Luther film, Klöpfer dominates the screen from the outset. His performance leaves no doubt about the power of ideas of reform to assert themselves. The pope and the Holy Roman emperor are made to look like nonentities enmeshed in the conventions of their stations. They are powerless to offer any resistance to the man from Wittenberg. Casting the comic actor Jakob Tiedtke in the role of Johann Tetzel, the Dominican friar and papal commissioner of indulgences, was also part of the unmistakable polemic against Roman Catholicism. It also had a revanchist component: it was easy to equate Peter's Pence with the hated reparation payments imposed at Versailles.[59]

The Nuremberg screening of December 17, 1927 elicited vehement protests from Catholics, and the film had to be subjected to censorship several times.[60] The third, greatly abridged version submitted to the censor on March 22, 1928 was finally approved.[61] Despite the earlier controversy, the film was praised with gushy euphoric overtones after its official premiere at the Ufa-Palast am Zoo in Berlin in 1928: "Luther's life is really genuine material for a film, which is important above and beyond the aspect of contemporary history. It will encounter enthusiasm from Protestants, who are, after all, not confined to Germany".[62]
In that day, however, some critics voiced profound doubts about the suitability of representing Luther on film. Otto Eckert, a pastor, declared a filmic Luther impossible for Protestants, because it showed a lack of respect for the Reformer's historic stature. Luther could not be dragged inside a cinema.[63] The film was on release in a fourth version, once again abridged to accommodate the censor,

when Lutheran work on film was discontinued in Germany in 1939.[64] With its nationalistic interpretation of Luther's character, this film was perfectly suited for inclusion in the 'Great Germans' series of films produced under the National Socialist regime. The series included *Friedrich Schiller. Der Triumph eines Genies* (*Friedrich Schiller: The Triumph of a Genius*). The Luther film therefore, is an important bridging chapter in the annals of the biographical history film. No structural break is discernible in the genre during the 1930s and 1940s. On the contrary, there is absolute continuity, so there can be no talk of a renaissance of the genre during that period either.[65]

What is astonishing is that the film was distributed abroad, where it was mainly handled via Lutheran channels—in the US through Reformation Films Inc., New York. It was advertised in the US Lutheran journal *American Lutheran*.[66] The occasional problems with US censors were incorporated in the marketing strategy. Thus, the American Lutheran ad appeared with the following journalistic sub-title appended to the title of the film *Freedom: An Epic of Reformation*: "The Picture The New York Censors Tried To Stop". The reviews in the *National Board of Review Magazine* were entirely positive. Klöpfer's portrayal of Luther was described as a solid achievement, even though the reviewer's idea of Luther revealed no intellectual aspects: "Luther himself, as acted by Eugen Kloepfer, in a large gallery of performers, is least actor like. His plain peasant heritage, his embodiment of the faith which he preached, the contrast between his spiritual humility and his forceful reaction when called upon to act in situations requiring courage and decision are most ably portrayed."[67] As late as 1955 the campaign against the then new Luther film was recalled in a British review: "The people who started or encouraged the circulation of this silly rumour may have had in mind the fate of the pre-war German film *The life of Martin Luther*, which was banned in Germany and was heavily cut in Britain."[68]

4. The First American Luther Film (1953)

The post-war years, that were shaped in Germany by denazification and integration into the Western economic community, and in the US by fear of communism, were also informed by a mentality that sought a return to Christian values.[69] That attitude united the two countries in the Cold War. Six Lutheran churches in the United States joined forces to commission a Luther film in collaboration with the EKD (the German Protestant Church). It recounts the biographical events from Luther's entry in the Augustinian friary in Erfurt in 1505 to the convention of the Imperial Diet in Augsburg in 1530. This was the era of the grand Hollywood spectaculars about the Bible and early Christianity, which began with *Samson and Delilah* (1949) and was followed by *Quo Vadis* (1951), *The Robe* (1953), *The*

Ten Commandments (1956) and culminated in *Ben Hur* (1959).[70] Thus, it is not surprising that the Lutherans also wanted to get back to their roots. Moreover, it was deemed important to cinematographically update the image of the historic sites and the mission. The Luther of this film also embodies something that was typical of the post-war mentality and recurs in the great Bible spectaculars. This was a stance that defied authority, expressing a will to resist arbitrary abuse of power, even when the situation seemed hopeless (because the main character represented a powerless minority).[71] The staging of the Diet of Worms scene is appropriately memorable: "… the dramatic peak is reached as Luther gives his "Here I stand" speech. To underscore the intensity and emotion of the scene, the camera moves ever closer to Luther, and at the moment when he says, "Here I stand, I cannot do otherwise. I cannot, I will not recant," a large close-up of Luther's intense face fills the screen."[72] Luther thus symbolizes religious liberty. A primary goal of the film was to make that clear to the public.[73]

Whereas in the biblical films, Christians have to hold their own against the heathens, it is the band of 'true Christians' who protest in Luther films against the errors of Christian Rome. In the Luther film, the persons of Luther and his family exemplify the middle class virtues, with which the (Protestant) middle classes in both America and Europe could identify: uprightness, self-control (moderation in all things), faith in God, courage and family values (in contrast to debauchery, greed and deceit). In political terms, this meant democracy instead of hierarchy and monarchy.[74] Nevertheless, this dramatization of Luther's life does not present a real antagonist. Even Fryer—who was in general very gentle with the object of his research—had to admit that the criticism advanced by Joseph Lortz, a Roman Catholic professor, was not completely wrong in his criticism, that the film lacked an antagonist. Fryer correctly pointed out that there is indeed an antagonist, but he is "underdeveloped"[75]; but also the filmic Luther always reacts in such a self-controlled manner that his character recedes behind his ideas. However, Roy Ringer called this effect "conviction": "McGinnis succeeds always in investing Luther with conviction, but the script permits him to go no further. We are left with only the one-dimensional portrait, and that a severe one."[76] (Nonetheless, from his writings we know Luther was a man not just of intellect but also of passion.)

On the other hand, no other character in the 1953 film gets a chance to defend himself, because Luther is always talking: "Niall Mac Ginnis begins talking almost at the start and either he or someone else is talking, virtually talking all the time, right to the end"[77]. Luther's dominance of the dialogue as well as the techniques used to present the other side make him seem invincible. Eck, for example, was filmed at "the most violent angle of all: the jarring tilt up. Carlstadt, who in Luther's absence has usurped his pulpit, who catches in grotesque perspective the words and grimaces of a false prophet tumbling down over the lip of the pulpit at an orphaned congregation"[78]. Since a hero never ages, Luther does not age on the screen: he has that same youthful face through twenty-five years that looks of a twenty-two year old man.[79] Luther's youth, which was given quite a lot of narrative space in the silent films, plays virtually no role in this film or in subsequent Luther films. Niall McGinnis fits into the Hollywood type-casting tradition, according to which a good hero must also have a handsome face.[80] Behind that casting principle stands a long tradition of philosophical reflection as well as a pernicious misinterpretation of the ancient pseudo-science of physiognomy.[81]

A scene to which much attention was paid in making the film, and one that is also emphasized in the 1973 and 2003 films, depicts Luther officiating at his first mass and almost failing to cope. Before consecrating the host, Luther as celebrant is overcome by such horror that he is left speechless. In other films, he spills the wine and has difficulty in keeping up with the liturgy or even finishing the divine service. In his *Table-talk*, Luther reported in retrospect that he almost died at that moment because he felt himself so alone with his sins.[82] In film, the scene exemplifies Luther's doubts about his faith and his vocation as a priest.[83]

The topical scene "Luther nailing the thesis to the door of the Castle Church in Wittenberg" was part of the classic hagiography of the Reformer. In the American film, it is interpreted as an act of universal historical relevance as the commentator in the film explains: "Among those waiting to be forgiven and blessed (They were waiting for the 'Heiltumsschau', the presentation of relics), none could know that this document would become one of the most widely read in all history". The promulgation of the thesis first in Latin then in German in the print media is shown without the national pathos we know from the German films. What is remarkable is the sentence that accompanies the burning of the papal Bull at the Elster-Gate: "As you corrupted God's truth, so shall you be destroyed by these flames".

The concept of this traditional filmic biography was *a priori* supplemented by a documentary film,[84] made by Curt Oertel as both director and cameraman. Oertel was also head of his own production company in Wiesbaden (Curt Oertel Film-Studiengesellschaft m.b.H.). The film agent for the German Lutheran Church, Werner Hess, advised on the screenplay *Der gehorsame Rebell (The Obedient Rebel)*. It is a black-and-white film (82 minutes running time) with an economical soundtrack, consisting of more music than speech, and a character resembling a slide lecture.[85] It premiered in Hanover on July 27, 1952 at the Annual Conference of the Lutheran World Federation in anticipation of the feature film *Martin Luther*. Commissioned by Lutheran Film Productions, Inc., shooting of *Der Gehorsame Rebel* began at the original historic sites in East and West Germany in autumn 1951. Remarkably, the project was also supported in the GDR by DEFA (Deutsche Film AG [German Film Corporation]), the

East German Film Institute. One may wonder why this help was not accepted or offered for the feature-length film as well, since Germans were responsible for the content of this film project. Evidently, the aim was to retreat to neutrality after the experience of 1927.[86] However, the number of screenings of the two films between 1955 and 1957 reveals that the documentary circulated far less widely than the feature film.[87] The collaboration between Lutheran Film Associates and Luther-Film GmbH lasted until 1971.[88]

5. Luther Psychoanalyzed

5.1. Leopold Ahlsen (1964)

The Leopold Ahlsen television play *Der arme Mann Luther* had an entirely different thrust; for the first time the cliché of the immaculate hero was abandoned. It was broadcast by WDR television in 1965 with Hans Dieter Zeidler in the leading role.

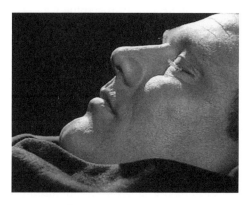

Screenshot of the first scene in "Der arme Mann Luther" showing Hans Dieter Zeidler as Luther on his deathbed in the WDR television film "Der arme Mann Luther" (FRG 1964).

Der arme Mann Luther was inspired by Erik H. Erikson's psychoanalytical work *Der junge Mann Luther* (first published in German in 1964).[89] Ahlsen ventured on a psychological interpretation of the Reformer's character. Luther's fear of a punishing and judging God came from his relationship with his father, which was shaped by a mercilessly authoritarian upbringing. Thus, Luther saw his father's face in the figure of the pope. Luther's mother was also portrayed as a punishing goddess, who beat her son black and blue because of a single little yellow nut. The same incident had already figured in the first scene of Strindberg's play, *Luther*.[90] The play may also have inspired Ahlsen with with the declension of "hic haec hoc" in its opening scene, as I will discuss later. However, the television play has a different structure: Mainly fictitious meetings between Luther and his contemporaries are inserted in the framing plot that deals with the hour of the Reformer's death. In these scenes, Luther must justify himself. In one verifiable episode, Justus Jonas and Michael Cölius ask their teacher on his deathbed: "Reverend father, dost thou wish to die firm in the Christian faith and doctrines as thou hast preached them?"[91]

Infused as it is with psychology, the Ahlsen scenario seems to anticipate the results of Elisabeth Kübler-Ross's research, which would not, however, be made known to the public at large until 1969 (*On Death And Dying*). The phases of dying that she calls "bargaining" and "acceptance" seem to be enacted in the film. The friar within Luther, played by Hannes Messemer as a Mephistophelian alter-ego, tries to tempt the Reformer to recant his life's work but does not succeed in doing so. The concept and the title of Ahlsen's television screenplay were the lines written by Luther on February 16, 1546 shortly before his death. With the words "We are mendicants; that is true" ("Wir sind Bettler: hoc est verum") Luther expressed his humility before God's creation and the esteem for the life's work of other men, especially of other thinkers.[92]

In the narrative frame, Luther is shown arguing with his alter ego as he did with his opponents. Sometimes his alter ego assumes the stance of the Catholic Church, for instance in the interpretation of sin (according to Lutheran doctrine, remorse and insight are sufficient for God's forgiveness; Catholic doctrine requires absolution through the Church as representing Christ on earth followed by remorse). The effect of Luther's works and other interpretations of them are often incorporated in the Ahlsen scenario.

In this film, only Luther's wife Katharina, played Madonna-like by Margarete Carl, finds words of approbation for him. His adversaries call him a "renegade, apostate and heretic". Thomas Müntzer curses him for his half-heartedness. Franz von Sickingen is portrayed as finding his hopes of a German national Christendom disappointed by Luther.[93] Luther's confessor, Staupitz, misses the solemnity of the Roman Catholic mass. Dieter Zeidler most memorably plays the long, tortured struggles endured by poor Luther, who in the hour of his death asks "Shall I find a God who is merciful to me?"[94] Franz Peter Wirth staged the television film like a theater play, virtually without historicizing props and scenery, and with a large, stepped podium as the main set. In the imagined conversation between Charles V and Luther at the close of the film, the Reformer is assigned his historic role, which at best sees him as the catalyst for a development. Thus, the Holy Roman emperor exonerates the Reformer by saying: "The Middle Ages were dead by the time you came along".[95] The associative intercutting of some events in the television film might in certain cases be viewed as an adroitly handled device for heightening the content. For instance, when Tetzel appears in the midst of the Carnival festivities in Rome and sells his letter of indulgence with the familiar "As soon as the coin sounds in the offertory, the soul leaps out of Purgatory into Heaven"[96]; a well-known apocryphal epigraph.[97] However, towards the close of the film, the same style of intercutting has the effect of greatly falsifying the historical facts. The papal bull threatening excommunication is shown reaching Luther during his marriage ceremony, which is much too late. Further, the Reformer in fact never fraternized with the peasants during the Peasants' War as he is shown to do in the Ahlsen film. The highly sophisticated content of the dialogues—which are over-rich of quotations from the Bible and Luther's most important writings (such as *De servo arbitrio* and the proemium to the Latin writings), not to mention allusions and references—would presuppose that viewers had a profound knowledge of theology. Hence, in an episode that refers to the opening scene of Strindberg's Luther, a quarrel between Luther and his father over the correct declension of the Latin pronouns might superficially be interpreted as a struggle against authority. However, what is actually at stake is the correct form of the genitive, which is in turn an allusion to the genitive in the Epistle to the Romans 3, 21 (the righteousness of God) as a genitivus subjectivus or a genitivus objectivus.[98] Nor would laymen be familiar with Luther's doctrine of the "Deus absconditus", the hidden God, which is also handled here in condensed form.[99] Luther's dispute with Cajetan on the authority of the Church to interpret the Bible had a very relevant contemporary background in the Second Vatican Council.[100] A controversy that long informed the Lutheran-Catholic dialogue is the concept of sin, which after all was fundamental to the issuing of papal indulgences.[101] In the Ahlsen film, it is fought out between Staupitz and Luther. The density of content, which lasts for the entire duration of the film (over two hours) and is couched in remarkably exciting, even brilliant performances by the actors, evidently tallied with an educational mission that was taken very seriously indeed by German state television. It would have been unthinkable in a film made for general release to cinemas.

Most critics were disconcerted by the psychoanalytical approach to the characterization of Luther.[102] *Der Reformator*, a documentary film with re-enacted scenes that was shown three years later by ZDF channel, lacked this aspect entirely.[103] The goal of Guenther Sawatzki, who wrote and presented the later German television production, was to instruct his audience. He did it in the style of a television educational seminar with a description of the events of 1517 and 1530 that was based upon the most current Luther research and presented in a way that was as objective as possible. As in the 1953 film, some of the scenes were shot in the former Eberbach monastery. In the leading role, Christian Rode appears as a reticent, primarily intellectual Luther. Rode later described his approach to the role: "The idea was almost to play against the usual Luther. So no heroic champion of God but instead a man in a really agonizing striving towards a merciful God."[104] The combination of documentary and feature-film scenes, however, failed to convince some critics.[105]

5.2. John Osborne (1965–1973)

The first Luther film in colour was produced by Ely Abraham Landau at the Shepperton Studios in England. Landau based the script on a play by John Osborne (1929–1994), written in 1961 and first performed at the Theater Royal in Nottingham on June 26, 1961, by the English Stage Company.[106] That was "the new English theater movement's first effort to bring history on to the stage in contemporary terms."[107] Inspired by Bert Brecht's theater theory, a knight plays the part of the narrator who explains the historical background. He links the scenes and breaks the illusion of the play according to Brecht's theory. The choice of an episode from German history was perhaps an attempt to avoid the stage censorship operated by Lord Chamberlain's Office until 1968, because Osborne's play does not conceal its lack of respect for the authorities. The text was translated into several European languages; the German version was published in 1963. In the same year, Richardson's Royal Court Production of Osborne's *Luther* was reproduced at the St. James Theater in New York.[108] The performance there was quite successful: *Luther* with Albert Finney as protagonist ran from September 25, 1963 to March 28, 1964 and Osborne won the Tony Award as well as the New York Drama Critics' Circle Award for the Best Play.

John Osborne's three-act play was then filmed twice for television by the BBC. In 1965, it was featured as the "play of the month" and in 1968, with a different director and cast, it was shown in the pre-Christmas programme. This second *Luther* production was also broadcast once on ABC in the US.[109] The first of the two productions was savaged by the London *Times* critic[110] and that might explain why it was dropped. The second version met with a more positive, albeit short-lived, media response.[111] Consequently, the continuing popularity of the material in Osborne's interpretation is remarkable indeed. As the enthusiastic descriptions indicate, the British playwright's Luther was—as anti-authoritarian rebel—exactly in tune with the times and all the various protest movements.

In 1973, Ely Abraham Landau chose Osborne's *Luther* as a script for The American Film Theater.[112] Landau's enterprise was intended as a reaction to the wave of movies that gave priority to sex and crime. His idea was: "You will not see filmed plays. You will see real movies with all of the technological advances that implies. All of the original language will be left intact, which means adult theatrical fare in many cases, but no nudity or pornography."[113] Ely Landau had raised $11.5 million through sponsors to produce eight films of modern plays and hoped that he would be able to cover costs by touring with the whole programme to three hundred US cities. There was a great deal of scepticism about whether his concept, which ran counter to all Hollywood commercial conventions with his eschewal of 'sex and crime', might not end in a fiasco after all.[114] The success was duly moderate. The film was not distributed internationally although

Landau was able to attract Broadway and Hollywood stars. Stacy Keach played the lead in *Luther* and Judy Dench was cast as Katharina von Bora.

What was radically new about this film was the idea of staging Luther's life and work from 1506 to 1530 in the setting of a Gothic church.[115] This location served, albeit unintentionally, as a metaphor for medieval society. In 1983, this plurivalent motif was cited again when Rainer Wolffhardt staged his Luther film in St Lorenz's in Nuremberg.

Landau was the first to break with the 'handsome Luther' tradition by employing Stacy Keach, an actor whose face is marred by a cleft lip.

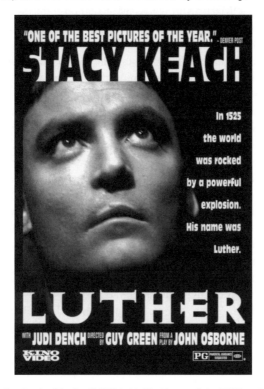

Stacy Keach as Luther in "Luther" (USA 1973), Cover of the DVD published in 2003.

This breach with the traditional image went further and was already noticeable in the very first seconds of the film, even before the title appeared. The knight who is disappointed at Luther's commitment to opposing the Peasants' Revolt, stains Luther's white robe with a dead rebel's blood. This scene is repeated at the end and thus creates a frame for the whole biopic. The contrast of white and red as a sign of guilt and pretended innocence is a leitmotif in the film that was also used to characterize Cardinal Cajetan. He is shown standing in his red robe next to a bunch of white lilies, symbols of purity, when Luther enters the room.

In Green's production, Luther's life as a father plays an important role and gets much more space than in previous film productions. For the first time the image of Luther holding a baby appeared on a poster made to advertise the film.

The effects of 1960s "sexual liberation" (permissiveness) are conspicuous in the scene in which Luther takes his vow; he is shown receiving his monk's habit while almost naked. Theoretically, this aspect also informs Luther's quarrel with his father, when the hero is reminded of his biological origin and limits as a human being: "Martin you would like to pretend that you made yourself, that is you who made you—and not the body of a woman and another man."[116] Martin defends his free will and in doing so he shows a very modern concept of individuality: Full of doubts and soul-searching. Twice in the film, the conflict with the subconscious is so overwhelming that Martin faints in agony. These 'seizures' underscore the difference between Luther and his brothers, who have lapsed into the monastic routine. Thus, the whole play is a psychodrama initiated by the knight's accusation. Luther's apology is the narration of his biography, expressed in dialogues not in action. The exterior intrudes only once, with the violence of the peasants war.

Although the film follows the script very closely, there are some notable omissions, for example, in Act 2, scene 5. However, more significant is the omission of expressions tinged with emotive British nationalism, such as Luther's statement from the last act: "Now then! If your peasant rebelled against that Word, that was worse than murder because it laid the whole country waste, and who knows now what God will make of us Germans!" and the knight's answer: "Don't blame God for the Germans, Martin!", laughs, "Don't do that! You thrashed about more than anyone on the night they were conceived!"[117]

Following Osborne's text, director Guy Green did not show Luther nailing his theses to the portal of Castle Church in Wittenberg. The episode is only mentioned by the knight. Perhaps the scene was eliminated because it is not part of the collective memory of an English audience. Nonetheless, Green staged the burning of the papal bull at the Elster Gate as an expression of disobedience and protest against the authorities. The response to the film was very reticent. Only a few articles in cinema journals praised the acting, and the public seems not to have noticed this film.

The 1986 *Motion Picture Guide* states that the film—apart from the excellent acting—exemplified the fact that some of the best plays are by their very nature unsuitable for filming.[118] Although it was not distributed internationally, the entire American Film Theater series has been available on DVD since 2003.

6. Frère Martin (1981)

In 1983, West German ARD television showed the two-part film *Bruder Martin*, made and produced by TF-1 Paris French television in 1981 in collaboration with Taurus Film in Munich and the Bayerischer Rundfunk. Jean Delannoy, who directed the film, had already proven his affinity with Protestant thinking in his choice of subject matter for other film productions,[119] which may also have been due to his being of Hugenot descent. This interest was evident in his 1981 Luther film. The action begins in 1507 in Erfurt. Luther, a mendicant friar, begs for alms from peasants and begins to doubt about the justification for thus exploiting such poor people. Nevertheless he is characterized as a rather more sensitive and self-controlled figure than Thomas Müntzer, who is portrayed as a revolutionary shouting "Vive la liberté". The plot ends with Luther's return from the Wartburg to Wittenberg in 1522, where he finds the churches empty and religious art destroyed. The final scene, which permits more than a glimmer of hope, shows Luther, still clad as Junker Jörg, ringing the bell to summon Christians back to the churches. Luther's later life, including his marriage and family, are left out. Alexandre Astruc, who had written the screenplay in 1950 for a cinema audience that evidently did not exist at the time in France, characterized his interpretation of Luther as follows: "His thinking contains the first seeds of the Enlightenment and the French Revolution—in brief, Luther is, in my eyes, one of the most important intellectual and spiritual champions of the Modern Age. In this film, however, I wanted first and foremost to show Luther as a man [...]. In contrast to Calvin, that tortured ascetic of a reformer, Luther was—after he had arrived at the realisation that what counts most is the trust placed in God—a very liberated, very vigorous man and bursting with life. [...] A person of great boldness, who used to say: 'Pecca fortiter—Sin bravely.'"[120]

7. The Double Feature: Luther in East and West-Germany (1983)

For the Luther Year 1983, television in both Germanys strove for productions of their own. With the support of Studio Barrandov in Prague, the DEFA Studio für Spielfilm (Feature Film Studio) produced *Martin Luther*, a five-part feature film for GDR television. The ZDF channel in the Federal Republic came up with a two-part film with the same title. In the GDR, Kurt Veth, director and author of the screenplay, chose to shoot as close to the original historical sites as possible. Rainer Wolffhardt's film for the ZDF was based on a screenplay by Theodor Schübel and was shot almost entirely in and in front of St Lorenz's in Nuremberg.[121] Thus Luther's cause was shown as literally inseparable from the ecclesiastical context. The Reformer was even disputing with Müntzer from the pulpit in the nave of the church, and the attic of St. Lorenz was the setting for the hanging of peasants who had participated in the uprisings. Wolffhardt, who was borrowing from the American Film Theater production of the Osborne stage play, maybe unconsciously linked his film with the theological—and iconographic—tradition of envisioning the church building as Ecclesia itself, a tradition that originated in Early Christian times.[122] As Wolffhardt explained it in 1983, the challenge of choosing a church as his film location consisted in "subjecting it to a continual metamorphosis; from the establishment of medieval Catholicism to the calling into question of all the values embodied in it and the establishment of Protestantism, which in turn was also increasingly questioned in the course of politicisation and institutionalization."[123] A critic characterized it as a "symbolic universal theater".[124] The director (who had once worked with Bertolt Brecht at the Munich Kammerspiele), is still convinced today that objectivity is impossible. One may at best approach historical truth, and in so doing, one must be selective. In the case of Luther, Wolffhardt said he had omitted the anti-Semitic aspect, which earned him a great deal of criticism.[125]

Lambert Hamel played the Reformer vigorously and passionately as both preacher and father of a family, who at the end is sustained by a realisation: "had [I] all the faith in the world so that I moved mountains yet had I not love, I would be as nothing."[126]

Lambert Hamel as Luther in "Martin Luther" (FRG 1983).

The five-part film GDR epic starring Ulrich Thein had a running time of more than seven and a half hours. It represents the largest monument erected to the Reformer in film. The scriptwriters were advised by members of the national "Luther Committee" of the GDR. This committee, appointed to coordinate the celebrations of Luther's anniversary, included members like the historians Prof. Dr. Adolf Laube and Dr. Gerhard Brendler. According to Detlev Urban "The SED had officially declared 1983 as Karl Marx Year, but no expense was

Ulrich Thein as Luther in "Martin Luther" (GDR 1983).

spared by the comrades for Martin Luther and his five hundredth birthday". The film was not only one of the most elaborate contributions to the GDR national commemoration of Luther,[127] it also redefined the Reformers role in relation to Thomas Müntzer.[128] Preparations for it began in 1978. The GDR film met with a positive response on all sides. In 1983, it had an audience of 2.34 million viewers. The only criticism of the impressive characterization of Luther was that there were so many lengthy passages played with Luther in a bellicose grumpy mood. Klaus Hilbig summed it up by asking: "Why must Luther bellow?"[129] Thein portrayed Luther as a fighter enmeshed in self-doubt who occasionally wrestled with the Devil but always won. This film was seen early on as part of, and reflecting, the new evaluation of the figure of Luther in GDR historiography. In the words of Eckart Kroneberg: "Luther is not whitewashed; he fails because of his limitations. Nevertheless, he is rehabilitated. The former betrayer of the people is today an early bourgeois revolutionary. The film omitted to impute political motives to him rather than theological ones. It no longer had to do that. With this film, the GDR has claimed Luther for itself. He is to be part of the national self-awareness."[130] Nevertheless, Luther's final words had an obvious political cast to them against the background of international rearmament: "As long as I live, I shall beseech God—Germany shall have no hardship through war [...]."[131]

Furthermore, as a complement to this feature the DEFA produced a three-part documentary on behalf of the national television station DDR 1. The first part treated the youth of Martin (*Ein Schüler aus Mansfeld. Die Jugendjahre Martin Luthers* [27 min.]), and the second addressed his exile at Wartburg Castle (*Der die Zeit beim Worte nahm. Martin Luther auf der Wartburg* [28 min.]). The final installment, entitled *Bürger Luther 1508–1546 (Citizen Luther)*, was the longest (45 minutes running time) and covered the decisive periods of Luther's life. It was also screened in cinemas and, at a later stage, adapted for educational purposes in the GDR.[132] When he saw the first version on May 4, 1982, Professor Adolf Laube, the vice director of the Central Institute for History at the Academy of

Sciences (Zentralinstitut für Geschichte der Akademie der Wissenschaften), suggested adding a sentence that would refer to Erich Honecker's speech about Luther. This addition should highlight two specific aspects: Luther's class-affiliation, and what Honecker regarded as the tragedy of Luther's life: Luther having initiated a revolutionary process, could not prevent it from turning into slaughter of men.[133] Both aspects were expressed in the later filmic feature.

As a minor contrasting program, the DEFA Trickfilmstudios (studio for animated cartoons) produced a short animated cartoon film, *Copyright by Martin Luther*, which presented the Reformation with sly humour as a media revolution.[134] After the decline of the GDR, Lew Hohmann also produced the documentary with re-enacted scenes *Martin Luther. Ein Leben zwischen Gott und Teufel* (*Martin Luther: A life between God and the devil*), which was embedded into a complete history of Middle Germany and broadcast only on the regional channel MDR on November 16, 2003.[135] The feature shot at the castles of Kriebstein and Rochlitz, in Eisleben, Wittenberg, Dessau and Erfurt, presents Luther (Matthias Hummitzsch) as a breaker of taboos whose words resulted in war and death on the one hand and hope, freedom and self-determination on the other. In this way, Luther became a "revolutionary against his own will" and eased the birth of a new age. It is obvious that the image of the GDR hero as the protagonist of the early bourgeois revolution was transformed into a Post-Communist hero of Middle-Germany, who represents liberal christian-democratic values.

8. New Emotionalism (2003)

The year 2003 saw the completion of a new Luther film that was produced with an international cast of stars and cost 21 million dollars. Marketing spin-offs worth nearly $10 million included screensavers and a gambling game. This was probably the most commercial version of the subject ever brought to the screen.[136] Like the 1953 production, the 2003 Luther film was funded mainly by Lutheran organisations in the US. The German Lutheran Genossenschaftsbank and the Lutheran aid organisations AAL/LB (Aid Association for Lutherans/Lutheran Brotherhood) were responsible for the production from the start. Canadian Eric Till directed it. In writing the screenplay, Camille Thomasson and Bart Gavignan did not draw on the John Osborne play for the stage, which would have meant following the Anglo-Saxon tradition of the 1973 film.[137] Instead, they were inspired by the American 1953 production. However, in 2003 the film could be shot on the original historical sites. This film also has a far more emotional thrust that occasionally dissolves into hagiographic kitsch. The filmmakers tapped all the topoi of the classic Luther iconography, but added a new scene, namely the hunt with the slaying of a boar. The hunt is an allusion to the *Exsurge domine* imagery of the papal bull issued in Rome on July 24, 1530 threatening Luther with excommunication. The bull was authorized by Pope Leo X while he was hunting boar and contains the words "A raging boar seeks to root it [the Lord's vineyard] up".[138] The 1569 epitaph of Paul Eber in the Wittenberg Stadtkirche, painted by Lucas Cranach the Younger, depicted Luther metaphorically in a vineyard and the scene was thus absorbed into the Luther iconograpy. However, in the 2003 film the intercutting was such that even uninformed members of the audience would relate this scene to Luther.

In interviews, director Till emphasized that previous characterizations of Luther had lacked sensitivity and passion, the very values that should be imparted to audiences today.[139]

Joseph Fiennes, who played the lead, had received the accolade "the hand-some Luther" ("Der schöne Luther") even before the official German premiere of *Luther* on October 30, 2003.[140] He is depicted as a figure of suffering, long accompanied by Johannes Staupitz, played by Bruno Ganz as a caring father figure. This Luther quarrels, specifically with the papal legate Girolamo Alean-dro, played by Jonathan Firth as a power-mad intriguer, and Cardinal Cajetan, intelligently accounted for by Mathieu Carrière. The rebel friar is under the protection of Frederick the Wise (Frederick III, Elector of Saxony), played in a quirky rendition by screen legend Peter Ustinov, whose Frederick seems senile on the surface, but is secretly sly and resourceful. As Ustinov explained in an interview, the Elector of Saxony had learnt from Luther to have the courage of his convictions. Accordingly, what could be learnt from Luther above all was belief in oneself.[141] Further, Ustinov stated: "Luther was too good a Catholic to remain a Catholic. [...] he was so critical of some of the habits of the clergy [...] he was [...] scandalized by this commercialization [...] he took action against it and started the Reformation. [...] It [the film] does speak of the independence of the human being to think and to think deeply."[142] That Ustinov has been engaged here to provide a Luther exegesis tallies with the concept of the film. Rather than being intellectual, it was primarily intended to affect the emotions. This slant that was conveyed chiefly via the star of the film, who was the prime vehicle for eliciting viewer sympathies. Consequently, Joseph Fiennes also had to explain Luther and his era in the bonus material marketed with the DVD. Fiennes did not interpret the film and his role as a historian or a theologian who was merely expected to read out Luther's Catechism. He states: "I think it is very much about the minority and the suppressed [...] it's about the control the Catholic Church had on the masses during that time through language and interpretation [...] you can't keep man down and you can't control [...] sooner or later he will gain knowledge and through knowledge, power to be liberated in freedom of [...] conscience. [...] As he starts out he is an innocent man who gets driven by a clause [...] an argument in the Testament which, in the interpreta-tion of the Catholic Church, amounts more or less to a debit and credit account

[...] Martin Luther very much saw [...] it is a gift [...] that one doesn't need to buy [...] one's way into heaven. [...] As an actor [...] I tried to identify [...] one hundred per cent [...] and be believable [...] that's really the challenge of this project: to bring it into a modern context [...] I tried to play Martin with doubt as much as knowing what's right [...] it's a very human condition [...] he is [...] a genius who invented a lot of the German language [...] brought Rome down. [...] I like the idea that he is still human and pursued by doubts [...]." In this film, however, the Reformer usually acts on his own; the leitmotif of the film is a close-up of his face. Melanchthon and other contemporaries of Luther play only a marginal role in the events of the Reformation, for example in the cursory treatment of Luther's quarrel with Karlstadt about the iconoclasm unleashed by the Peasants Revolt. The historical background is scarcely intelligible to the average viewer. Given the self-confident rhetoric of such scenes, it may be too harsh to jugde Luther here as an "anxiety-ridden neurotic" ("ängstlicher Neurotiker") or "mediocre douche bag" ("mittelmäßiges Weichei") as Susanne Hermanski put it.[143] Nevertheless, Fiennes' eternally youthful face and the equally lovely Claire Cox as Katharina von Bora unquestionably reveal that emotional values were given priority in this film and these values are the vehicle for communicating a hagiographical image of the Reformer. Luther makes a lame girl walk again and is venerated like a saint, although he rejects such devotion as a sign of his humility. Is Luther here "alter Christus" or is this the expression of the "new Lutheran emotionalism" ("neue evangelische Emotionalität"), defined by Matthias Drobinski?[144] For the sake of the emotional impact they provoke familiar scenes such as Nailing the Theses are repeated in this film while the political interests that played a role in consolidating the Reformation are simply ignored. Another disruptive feature that manifests in this film more than in earlier ones is the great number of anachronisms. These can be found not just among the props and sets, like the 19th-century-style stained glass windows that are smashed by the iconoclasts or the Baroque foot of the cross that Luther replaces on the altar, but also in the anachronistic behavior of the main character: Luther, who after all believed in the Resurrection of the body, buries a suicide by vandalizing the graves of the dead. The act is patently absurd. Nor did the historical Luther preach in the style of a college lecturer, sauntering down the rows of pews with a Bible tucked under his arm. Such anachronistic features impair the plausibility of the representation.

Nevertheless, the critics, whether Catholic or Protestant, meted out relatively mild treatment to the work, despite the fact that, as Susan Vahabzahdeh critically noted, "everything that isn't fun" has been excised from Luther's teachings, especially the aspect of atonement.[145] If Luther's doctrines have been thus reduced to a minimum, what is left over for viewers—only the image of a man courageously standing up for his ideals?

Dirk Blothner accordingly attempted a sociological interpretation of the film's success: "*Luther* found in autumn/winter 2003 an unexpectedly large audience. One reason for this may be the social reforms the Federal Republic is about to embark on. People suspect that many things will have to change but as yet they have no concrete ideas of what this might entail. The film makes it possible to envisage a process of change with all concomitant promises, risks and consequences."[146] It is doubtful whether the multilayered historical process that was the Reformation, in which so many foreign policy factors play a role, can be compared at all to domestic reforms undertaken under the auspices of a parliamentary system. It is indeed highly unlikely that social reforms (to a democratic system) could trigger a civil war today. Younger viewers of the 2003 Luther film were usually left with the impression of a colourful history film steeped in period atmosphere with Joseph Fiennes playing the lead as a man who bravely and resolutely challenges the powers that be.

It is obviously part of the dialectics of Luther films that the next production was a documentary centered on a German film star in the action scenes and reduced nearly to one place, the Wartburg Castle. The lesson-length feature (45 minutes) was directed by Günther Klein and commissioned by the ZDF for the series *Giganten* (*Giants*) in 2007, which contained features about other great Germans who "changed the world", like: Ludwig van Beethoven, Alexander von Humboldt, Johann Wolfgang von Goethe, Sigmund Freud and Albert Einstein. Luther's perspective on the world from his exile frames this dramatization of his life, which is shown in flashbacks. This sojourn of 300 days is thus stylized as the crucial period of his life. The viewer sees Luther mainly as squire George in his secular garment, and not as the more familiar Augustine monk. Perhaps this secularization of his appearance was intended to reduce the distance to the modern spectator. However, the myth of Luther's birthplace (a complete reconstruction made after 1693[147]) is repeated. Whereas theologians (Margot Käßmann and Jürgen Fliege) are the main commentators for these scenes, the next documentary with re-enacted scenes broadcasted in 2008 was dominated by historians. It was produced by the ZDF for the series *Die Deutschen* (*The Germans*). Despite the emphasis on history, the feature has the tendency to fall back to the old patterns, as revealed first by the title *Luther und die Nation* (*Luther and the Nation*). Reformation seems to be the work of a single person. The 71 minutes film is dedicated primarily to the response to Luther's writings and deeds. The biographical narrative is subordinated to this purpose. Especially in the statements of Heinz Schilling and Luise Schorn-Schuette, the documentary explores the importance of Luther's translation of the Bible for the written German language and the consequences of the foundation of a new church for German history, as well as the resulting Thirty Years War (1618–1648). Thus, the character of the protagonist—played in short scenes by Georg Prang—did not get its own profile. Despite their differences, these two documentaries both use the classical strategies of infotainment, namely aestheticisation, dramatization, personalization and emotionalization.[148] It is also clear that the length of each was reduced to a minimum, a common cost-saving practice since the 1990's.[149] Nevertheless, it is remarkable that Martin Luther is still used as model to represent the changes in the 16th century, a subject that is uncommon in history programs on German television: The 16th century accounts for only about 0.7% of of all history films on German channels.[150]

IV. Gender Roles

1. The Concept of Masculinity

There is no doubt, that film plays an eminent role in the construction of role models by reflecting ideals and giving visual commentaries. Given the change in image found in the Luther films, the question arises to what extent would this hold true for the representation of the protagonist as a male character, as well as for the female characters?[1] Because masculinity can only be shaped in comparison with femininity, the aim of this chapter is also to define the female positions in Luther films and their changes.

Hitherto, gender research into films has concentrated on Hollywood productions.[2] Biopics, on the other hand, have not received the attention that they should.[3] Nevertheless, the biopic genre is a particularly rewarding field in which to examine the relevance of the by now universally accepted concept of "hegemonial masculinity" as developed by Connell.[4] Martin Luther, a "dead white middle-class man"[5] who was also emphatically Christian and heterosexual by inclination,[6] can be regarded as a classic case as far as this issue is concerned, especially since modern "hegemonial masculinity" has even been credited to Luther.[7] At first glance, the Reformer embodies all the traditional middle-class ideals of masculine virtue as he stands up for his idea against the world, leading his supporters to success while simultaneously revealing moral integrity and conveying a sense of responsibility. The crucial aspect of this, however, is that Luther does this not by using physical force, but through his speeches and writings. This kind of intellectual proceeding does not really belong to the concept of "hegemonial masculinity" although it is often a concomitant phenomenon[8] and, above and beyond that concept, traditionally connotes 'masculinity'.[9] Even in the 1927 Luther film, which depicts Luther as a Christian knight, sword in hand, as a stylized icon of Protestant nationalist propaganda, Ulrich von Hutten emphasizes: "You [are] the word—I [am] the sword!" Here we find physical force legitimated as fostering the power of the Protestant logos. This refers also to Luther's doctrine of the Two Kingdoms (two reigns). However, violence in the form of iconoclasm contesting the divine order is repudiated later in the film.

This raises the question of whether the traditional gender construct is infringed anywhere in the films. The "crisis of hegemonial white males", which is dated by various scholars to around 1900,[10] cannot be discerned in the earliest Luther films. In *Wittenberger Nachtigall* (1913), Martin Luther makes a conquest of Katharina early on, freeing her from the nunnery, making a romantic declaration of love on bended knee and marrying her in the Castle like the prince in Grimms' Fairy Tales. Similarly, in the 2003 film, Luther marries for love. In the 1913 film, he is the active force in bringing about the marriage. The eroticisation of the 'Luther' character was part of the concept underlying both films. It is surely no coincidence that Joseph Fiennes, who had caused such a furore as 'Shakespeare in love' in the 1998 film of that title, was chosen for the leading role.[11]

In the eighty years between the 1913 and the 2003 film, Luther films barely dealt with intersubjective feelings. This holds true for the 1923 film, even though Luther founds a family and the final shot shows him in the family circle gathered round the Christmas tree; the focus is on his public deeds. Nithack-Stahn's concept of a pacifist Luther definitely had to do with the collective experience of the First World War and must also be read as a response to the failure of striving for power through martial prowess.[12] This Luther is a messianic, charismatic character imbued with a great deal of tenderness, one who disapproves of all physical violence; hence, even wild animals trust him. The post-war American filmic Luther, on the other hand, acts pragmatically rather than charismatically. He lives for his idea of reformation alone and is never led astray by personal feelings. Even Katharina, who embodies the ideal woman of her times as far as the emotions are concerned, must reason with Luther and convince him that it would be sensible to marry her in order to set an example for the new Protestant world. In this, the character also meets the standards applied to a "Hero of Modernity", although the ideal man of the time (according to the then prevailing cinematographical typology), would otherwise have been embodied by physicians, scientists and inventors.[13] The ideal of the perfect, complete hero is not overthrown until Osborne's interpretation: his Luther is racked with self-doubt and beset with controversy in his own time, an approach that humanises the characterization. This interior world is also revealed in the film made in 1963 for ARD, the German television channel. In it Luther's traumatizing conflict with his father is also a struggle with the masculine role which Hans Luther, a citizen aspiring to higher social status, is trying to impose on his son. Martin chooses the role of the monk cloistered from the world, which his father views as feminine, but then seeks to justify his choice by ambitiously pursuing his chosen career. His mother's strictness in this film merely mirrors the father's rigidity. By contrast, the warm-hearted mother in the silent Luther films made in 1923 and 1927 represents the opposite pole of the father in the classic dichotomy, and is the wellspring of the love that the son will in turn give to the world (rather than to a woman). In these films, the paternal harshness is continued in Luther's teachers, and the Reformer counters it with his concept of mercy and forgiveness.

In Green's 1973 production for the American Film Theater (based on the Osborne play), Luther as father plays a more important and emotionally charged role. The image of Luther holding a baby appears on the screen for the first time.

2. The Presence of Femininity

The opposite of this form of masculinity, which is defined by asceticism, the Word (biblicism) on the part of Luther and often—by his adherents—the sword (willingness to defend a principle), can be found in almost all Luther films: The portrayal of the papacy and its representatives as a decadent society. It includes also the Holy Roman emperor, who is usually portrayed as youthful, even effeminate, and thus disparaged. Already in the staging of Strindberg's *Luther* (premiered 1914 in Berlin) the only part performed by a woman was that of Charles V.[14] The stereotype of feminine southern European males, all of them cut from the same block, is usually reproduced. Rome was originally also the place where, in the 1927 Luther film, sexuality was portrayed in the guise of prostitutes (although this was cut by the censor). Not until 1964 does this motif reappear, now in carnevalesque attire, on the television screen. In the 1964 film, too, Luther is again a character who has no desire beyond a merciful God.

Apart from the early Luther film *Die Wittenberger Nachtigall*, which advertised itself with a feminine title ("nightingale" is a feminine noun in German), there has not been much scope for women in this genre. Even in documentaries, the experts were exclusively male until 2007, when the history professor Luise Schorn-Schütte and the Lutheran theologian Margot Kässmann gave statements on Luther's actual importance and his position in history.[15]

One reason for the absence of women in Luther films also lies in Luther's own biography: since he spent most of his life as a monk, this fact was then distilled into the pictorial narratives. Nevertheless, they never examine the sexual issues raised by celibacy as related to Luther; at best they resort to showing members of the Roman clergy cavorting with prostitutes. Only the GDR film stages Luther's awkwardness as an 'ex-monk' forced to instil in the liberated nuns the biblical injunction to "bring forth fruit and multiply" (Gen 1, 22) by finding suitable partners in marriage. This also underscores the puritan asceticism of a hero who has sacrificed his life to his ideals. Not until the 2003 feature film and in a scene from the 2008 ZDF German television documentary is this image of 'purity' and 'virginity' on hagiographic lines briefly suspended by Katharina seducing Martin.

Another reason for the scant presence of women in Luther films is that representing Luther with pacifism and artistic talents also leaves scope for many components viewed as feminine. Thus, women are not needed for the special purpose of embodying them as role models for viewers to identify with.[16] Apart from the character of Luther's mother, women first enter the foreground when Katharina appears.

When the filmed biography ends, as it does in the 1927 film, with the marriage, the public is at least given a hint that the hero can be charmed by the opposite sex, meaning that he is heterosexual by inclination. In a fictitious scene with Luther disguised as Junker Jörg and playing the lute, the role of the page listening to him with such admiration is given to a woman so that the whole scene is made to appear "en tête à tête". However, the image of the Lutheran Redeemer with an awareness of German nationalism had no room for a woman at his side. Nor does the complete intertitle text from the silent film on the earliest censor card of December 17, 1927 hint in any way that the character of Katharina von Bora or allusions to her have been deleted in the prescribed cuts.

Katharina von Bora after all, is indisputably assigned the leading female role in Luther films. For a long time she was depicted solely as a charming creature in a supporting role, helping Luther to fulfil his mission and thus contributing to the Reformation. She had been interpreted dramaturgically in plays for the stage since the 19th century[17] on the familiar patriarchal principle "Men act; women are acted upon".[18] Not until 1983 was Katharina given more scope in a play and allowed to show more self-assurance. This may also have been due to the publication of Christine Brückner's *Ungehaltener Reden Ungehaltener Frauen* (*Speeches by angry women that were not given*)[19] in which a speech is assigned to Katharina that would become a source for a feature film in its own right.

Be that as it may, the ZDF German television production in 1983 presents Katharina as assertive and active, the manager of a large household constrained by a very low budget meant to feed numerous children and students. For this, she earns her husband's respect; he addresses her, as documented in Luther's letters to Katharina, as "Herr Käthe" (Sir Kath)[20], as if she ruled over her realm as a man (and a man of higher social rank).

In the silent film, specifically in *Doktor Martin Luther. Ein Lebensbild für das deutsche Volk* (or *Die Wittenberger Nachtigall*), the interpretation of the character of Katharina as Luther's female opposite number and helper is a late echo of dramatic models such as the early 19th-century romantic tragedy *Martin Luther, oder Die Weihe der Kraft* (*Martin Luther, or The Sanctification of Power*) by Friedrich Ludwig Zacharias Werner, published in 1807. Here the core message is the abolition of clerical celibacy by the Reformer. In that play, Katharina is given the supporting role of the nun who has converted to Protestantism for love of Luther and she becomes his wife to lead a life of "strength, faith, freedom and God". Such are the values proclaimed at the end of the play.[21] In the 1913 film, historical facts were even modified to highlight Katharina in this role as soon as possible. Hence, while he is still a student in Erfurt, bonds of love already exist between Luther and Katharina, as the intertitle explains: "Vis à vis above the window of his room dwells a lovely maid. Kathrein von Bora was her name. So industrious was the studio[sus] that he did not suspect her cheeks reddened whenever he showed himself at the window."[22] Viewers' sympathies are aroused by the sight of Katharina languishing seated at her spinning wheel.

Margot von Hardt as Katharina von Bora with Rudolf Essek as Luther in the background in "Die Wittenberger Nachtigall", Germany 1913/1927 (?).

The intertitle gives the explanation for this situation in even more touching words "The maid was sore at heart. Her harsh father had determined that she should take the veil and enter Nimbschen [Cistercian] convent."[23] Katharina casts another yearning gaze at the industrious Martin: "Melancholy, she confides her suffering to her old nurse. Since she first saw Martinus Luther, it has become ever more difficult for her to bid farewell to earthly things."[24] Katharina's entry to Marienthron, the Cistercian convent of Nimbschen, is made to follow on Luther's taking his monastic vows. Thus the film creates a connection between Katherina's and Luther's life that becomes a leitmotif. After Luther has accepted the appointment as professor of theology at Wittenberg University and confessed to Staupitz also his uncertainty about his vocation, Katharina's doubts about convent life are mentioned, even though they are differently motivated: "Käthe, too, rebelled against her destiny. The Studio [sic!] picture of the young man refused to fade from her soul." The novice nun is shown praying fervently before a crucifix. Another nun tries to console her, but the image of Luther appears to her in a vision in an insert shot.[25]

The romantic literary topos of the vision is probably a borrowing from the play *Martin Luther, oder Die Weihe der Kraft*. In it, Martin Luther meets Katharina von Bora very dramatically in a sort of religious epiphany as an "archetype": "I must take heart—I must indeed / To the Saviour himself confess!—I love Luther—He is the archetype I long for."[26]

Katharina reappears in the last "chapter" (1522–1525), just as the flight of the

Katharina as a Cistercian nun dreaming of Luther in "Die Wittenberger Nachtigall", Germany 1913/1927 (?).

nuns is deemed the result of the impact made by the "new spirit". From there, Luther's "first way" leads to Torgau, to find "a home" for the nuns: "Kathrein von Bora he brought to Wittenberg, to the house of Philipp Reichenbach, later mayor, who would almost have liked to have kept her, so much did he love her. Liking for the lovely maid began to grow strongly in Martinus."[27] Finally, the situation comes to a climax in the Wittenberg iconoclasm. In the film, even these events assume a personal tinge, albeit with religious qualities. After Luther has prevented the iconoclast Karlstadt from committing the worst offences, Katharina encounters him, saying: "You [...] look as if it were a dream. In Luther, she believes she has seen a saint when he gently led her to the door of the church."[28] Here the images foreshadow the happy ending of the romance. The intertitles attest its reforming effect: "To make a clean break with the old customs, the clergy now began to abolish celibacy. Luther set a good example in wooing Katharina von Bora."[29] The courtship is one of the longest and most sentimental in all films about Luther: "When storms are raging outside, my home, ordered by solicitous loving hand must be my refuge. Do you, Kathrein, wish to help me to found this home, let us be joined together before God and man in honest union!"[30] It is only consistent that the wedding scene is the final scene in the film so that the married Luthers can be proclaimed as role models for the German parsonage.

This notion of marriage and, concomitantly, the image of women projected in the film are summed up rather coarsely in a drinking song sung by the reformer's colleagues shortly before Luther burns the Papal Bull threatening excommunication: "A spouse must be patient and not keep his wife like a pig. A housewife must be reasonable. Learn carefully a man's ways. God will then give His grace that the union is happy."[31] Even though this representation has little to do with historical veracity, it is nonetheless typical of the way in which Katharina and

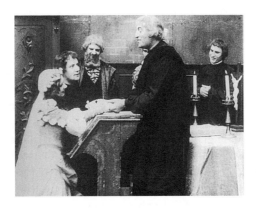

Luther's wedding in "Die Wittenberger Nachtigall.

Martin were celebrated as the model German couple, as they so often were in 19th-century literature.

In the 1953 film, Luther's wife, played by Annette Carrell, appears in only three scenes: in conversation before the wedding, in which Katharina utters monosyllabic replies to the suggestions made by Martin Luther, in the nuptials that follow and in a dialogue with her husband set in 1530. This last scene is staged in a setting reminiscent of a 19th century genre painting. The conversation carried on by the married couple serves merely as a vehicle for conveying historical events; Katharina encourages her husband, who is awaiting the results of the Diet of Augsburg at home in 1530, with the words "half Germany is on his side" and assures him that Johann, Elector of Saxony, and Philipp, Landgrave of Hesse, support him. Katharina is then 'enlightened' by Martin that those princes support him primarily for reasons of power politics. In this film Katharina von Bora is still portrayed as a tender and beautiful yet not particularly resolute woman, who supports her husband in a rather naïve way but is certainly not his equal. German cinema audiences objected that Katharina was not "nun-like", whatever that term might imply, perhaps 'unwordliness': "Luther's Katie seems to have come from Hollywood rather than a nunnery."[32] This appraisal was also included in the handbook for Protestant cinema when the film was billed as the "Best film of the month of March 1954".[33] Nevertheless, the traditional role models in the 1953 film did not correspond at all to post-war society in Germany. There was an enormous surplus of women, forced to organize their lives without men's help. That meant that they had to work in the years of reconstruction as rubble women and to replace men in the factories. At home, they often had to support their disabled husbands.[34]

That Katharina's film portrayal also differed from the state of historical knowledge at the time is shown by an evaluation of her by Pastor Werner Hess, then

Lutheran film commissioner for Germany, who also had a hand in the scenario of the documentary *Der gehorsame Rebell*, produced in 1952. Hess still defined Katharina's role by her relationship with Luther but was the first to empathize with what initially must have been unusual for both parties about being married: "Brother Martin finds learning how to be a husband difficult. He approaches his young wife with a blend of shyness and emotional warmth. She, on the other hand, soon develops a talent for practical skills and begins to build up a household from nothing. No money, everything shabby and ruined, every day friends and transients who are expected to eat at the Doctor's table. The most basic cookware is missing from the kitchen, the rooms are bare, the stalls empty, the garden overgrown. Within a year, however, everything has changed. Not only in courtyard and garden but also in her hesitant husband, who happily has his little son Hans in his arms."[35]

The television play *Der arme Mann Luther* broadcast by the West German channel WDR in 1965 (based on a screenplay written by Leopold Ahlsen in 1962–63) characterizes Luther's wife, played by Margarete Karl, as her husband's faithful helpmate. However, the wedding scene at the close of the film, which recalls a painting by Pieter Brueghel the Elder and seems to be linked with the Diet of Worms, conveys no insights into the character and role of Katharina. The Günther Sawatzky docudrama, *Der Reformator*, broadcast only a few years later (1968) by the ZDF channel, focuses on the years 1517–30. In it, the issues relating to the marriage of Katharina, played by Andrea Dahmen, are not examined. The tableau of Luther's wedding at the close of the film serves to finish off the usual hagiography or, as Klaus Hamburger put it: "Incidentally, however, this overdrawn pre-Raphaelite figure progressed unchanged, untouched through crucial stages in life—a romanticised Reformer, to whom, albeit with a twinge of conscience, a bit of what a certain sector of the popular press classifies as 'human interest' is granted, belatedly, at the end of the play, that is: the domestic idyll with Katharina von Bora."[36]

In the 1973 American Theater Luther film, modelled after the 1961 John Osborne play *Luther*, Katharina, played by Judi Dench, appears only in the last scene of the third and last act and by then she is already married to Luther. Surprisingly, when one bears in mind the considerable change that has taken place in the interpretation of Luther as a character in the meantime, even this work clung to the traditional image of Katharina, allowing her no scope for individual development.[37] Accordingly, Osborne has his Luther remark on 'Kath', who only figures as a cipher based on clichés: "It's a shame everyone can't marry a nun. They are fine cooks, thrifty housekeepers, and splendid mothers. Seems to me there are three ways out of despair. One is faith in Christ, the second is to become enraged by the world and make its nose bleed for it, and the third is the love of a woman."[38] Apart from the repugnant male chauvinism Osborne imputes to Luther, the playwright has utterly ignored the historical burden weighing down both Luther and his wife, namely that a liaison between a monk and a nun was viewed by their 16th-century contemporaries as the Devil's work.

It was not until 1983, when thirty-five productions on the occasion of the 500th anniversary of the Reformer's birth were broadcast in 1983 (solely by West German television channels),[39] that a feature was devoted to "Luther and women". The author devoted herself to Katharina von Bora and not just in her functional capacity as model pastor's wife. She also attempted to go beyond the purely economic significance of Katharina in Luther's household, a quality that can be read in the sources. The author points out in an essay on her broadcast: "On the other hand, he [Martin Luther], who usually signed letters to his wife 'Your dearly beloved' or 'Your loved one', commissioned her to deal with printers; he imparted to her the outcome of theological disputes—for instance in Marburg—and he also felt she was capable of giving intelligent advice on appointing a pastor."[40] This is probably the first scholarly indication of the fact that Katharina's entrepreneurial acumen was not atypical for the time.[41] Research into the social history of the early modern era had up to then made no impact on the way the Luther family has been portrayed in mass media. However, in the Luther biography broadcast by ZDF in 1983, Katharina, played by Brita Fischer,[42] already appears in the wedding scene as a thrifty housewife who stops her husband from refusing a present of money. The only comments on the marriage itself are here provided by onlookers: they reflect the judgement of Luther's contemporaries, who viewed the marriage of a monk with a nun as "Devil's nuptials".[43] There is no discussion of the personal fears that probably long tortured the newlyweds. Katharina is not shown again until the depiction of Luther's family life in 1543. Here, too, the sequence lasts for only a few minutes. The familiar picture of the faithful provider and thrifty housewife again predominates: Katharina is shown bringing her sick daughter home, emptying her apron of apples and urging insistently that roof tiles be ordered while her husband is preoccupied with answering various queries. Finally, she hastens to bring out his boots and cloak when the visit of a papal legate is announced. The fact that she does not overlook a showy chain—a present to him from the Elector—while clothing her husband for the visit, is probably intended to show her class-consciousness. Moreover, a degree of diplomatic skill is imputed to Katharina when she is shown advising her husband to go up to the papal legate to greet him. She herself leaves when his arrival is announced. Viewers glean most items of information on Katharina from the conversation that follows between the legate and Luther. The latter opens it with the provocative query whether the visitor might like a beer brewed by his wife in order to ascertain whether the legate knows that he has married: the Reformer praises her domestic qualities in the words "My Katie has brought order into my life."[44] Luther explains that she takes care of everything: she plants orchards and vegetables, keeps chickens and pigs and takes care of children and guests alike. Luther's justification for a pastoral marriage follows: With an allusion to a passage from the letters of the Apostle Paul follows he points out that even the Apostles married. Katharina is not shown as capable of being more deeply interested in the content of the conversation. After the papal legate has left she returns and inquires only briefly what he was concerned with, only to finish by asking her husband whether he has fulfilled his duties as host. Luther sarcastically replies that he has done so, addressing his wife as "Sir Kath", and goes on to share his worries about the war he expects and his despair at the lack of understanding shown by his contemporaries. Katharina does try to show sympathy and calm his fears, but she does so without advancing any objective line of reasoning. When the collaborators on the Bible translation enter the room, Käthe also leaves; she must pay the rent.[45] The image of Katharina as the perfect domestic economist is finally rounded out, when she commissions her husband to tell the butcher to come the following morning to slaughter the pigs. Katharina's historically verified entrepreneurial qualities, which went far beyond her role as housekeeper, are not conveyed. Even though an attempt has been made to do this more thoroughly than in the other Luther films at least, she is once again portrayed as the solicitous housewife who subordinates her interests to those of her husband and family and has no share in the theological discourse or the discussion of church politics going on in her home.

Films made at the occasion of the Luther-year 1983 such as *Der Reformator. Luther wandelt seine Zeit* (*The Reformer: Luther Changes his Era*)[46] and *Martin Luther. Stätten und Stationen seines Lebens*: Part 3. *Eine feste Burg* (*Martin Luther – Places and Stages of His Life: Part 3. A Mighty Fortress*),[47] which were also designed for use in West German classrooms, again leave little scope for characterizing Katharina von Bora. The latter film at least explains the social and historical reasons for Katharina living in the convent. This same film ends with the suggestion that Katharina was a very energetic woman who exerted a strong influence on her husband. All the other West German films made for the Luther Year 1983, such as Frank Burckner's *Luther ist tot*,[48] concentrate on Martin Luther as a person. They reveal no new approaches and have not been dealt with here because the focus is on feature films about Luther, not on documentaries or theatre plays. In *Die Wittenbergisch Nachtigall*, a film first shown in 1984 by Südwestfunk television in a series of broadcasts called *Notenschlüssel* (*Clef*), Katharina von Bora is merely introduced in a scene in which she agrees with Luther's ideas on music. When footage from this film was recycled a year later to make a roughly half-hour broadcast entitled *Frau Luther und ihr Martin*, it, too, was mainly concerned with showing a model Lutheran parsonage.

By contrast, the WDR channel produced a film of its own with a running time of about 20 minutes, entitled *Der Morgenstern von Wittenberg*, which was one of the epithets Luther applied to his wife, probably with the meaning "morning star". Here Katharina von Bora is introduced with Christine Brückner's words on *Speeches that were not given*[49]. The question that follows, "Who was this Katharina who saw to it that all had enough to eat at the great Reformer's table?"[50], is answered with a biography that is intended to call into question the traditional image of Katharina as a "devoted housewife and mother". The supposedly "unworldly nun" ("weltfremden Nonne"), who had learnt how to work efficiently on a regular basis as well as pray at the cloister, in this film, as Luther's wife, became a "hands-on women, who had the confidence to tell workmen what she wanted and give orders to her domestic servants."[51] Moreover, emphasis is laid on the fact that "her realm extended far beyond the household to encompass leasehold land and later even an estate of her own."[52] The reason why such a distorted image of Katharina arose is explicitly investigated and ascribed chiefly to the way women are portrayed in Luther's own writings. According to the film, that image called a subordinate female role in the family and the state. Luther's statements on marriage are verifiably not at all so one-sided,[53] because that image of women and of Katharina in particular long conformed to the image prevailing at any given time, it continued to be widely accepted.

Martin Luther, the film broadcast by GDR television in 1983, which had an overall running time of 7 hours and 45 minutes, could have given more scope to configuring the character of Katharina. However, the Reformer's marriage is not discussed until the last part of the film. Much of what is addressed in this connection is covered in a debate with Melanchthon, who voices vehement criticism of Luther for marrying when the Peasants' War was going on and at a time when Luther himself was being so aggressively attacked. Luther, played by Ulrich Thein, here defends his decision as the only logical outcome of his reforms as applied to the private sphere. His wish was that at the end of his life nothing would recall his time as a monk and that he could be as God created him. Katharina herself, played by Barbara Schnitzler as a delicate, elfin creature, hardly appears at all.

She is permitted to introduce herself briefly in the circle of runaway Nimbschen nuns and offer herself to the Reformer as the remaining candidate for marriage. Compared to her husband, who is not shown as racked with doubts and battling fears until towards the end of the film, the character of Katharina remains incongruously colourless, obedient and devoid of personality.[54] The image of Katharina sketched in another screenplay broadcast that same year by GDR television is similarly without contours.[55] Three documentary films on the life of Martin Luther were produced by DEFA for GDR television in the Luther Year 1983. They were revised in 1991 by the Institut für Film in Wissenschaft, Unterricht und Bild (Institute for Film in Science, Teaching and Pictures) into

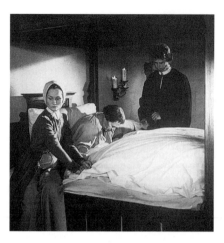

Barbara Schnitzler as Katharina Luther and Ralf Kober as Melanchthon at Luther's bedside in "Martin Luther" (GDR 1983).

a four-part serial for teaching purposes. In the part entitled *Citizen Luther in Wittenberg (Bürger Luther in Wittenberg)*, Katharina's life was documented in pictures, notably in the form of 19th and 20th century genre pictures. However, in the commentary, her role is cursorily defined as only that of a nun who has fled the veil,[56] who managed Luther's household with "a strong will" and a "strict regimen". No mention is made of Katharina's commitments as the manager of a landed estate, a beer brewer, etc. Instead, the focus is on Luther's own work in his garden as a vehicle for the transition to the celebrated Cranach allegory *Die Reformatoren im Weinberg des Herrn (The Reformers Labouring in the Vineyard of the Lord)* as a device to heighten the portrayal of Luther. As in the 1953 Luther film, the focus is on the fact that Katharina was one of the nuns who fled the cloister and were protected by the Reformer. Thus, she is again assigned the role of the one leftover nun whom Luther actually married only because there was no one else. Luther quotations on the subject of marriage are intended to explain his views on the matter, but they are not backed up with a portrayal of his own marriage. Katharina's viewpoint, whatever it might have been, plays no role at all in this film.

Even after that, the first Lutheran pastor's wife was still not made the subject of a film. In 1996, a 20-slide show of paintings, photos and montages was made, dealing with the various verified and conjectural stages in the life of Luther's wife. Since then, this slide show has been distributed by the Evangelische Zentralbildkammer in Bielefeld for teaching purposes, with the promise that it does not portray "Katie Luther as a dull little housewife" ("biedere Käthchen Luther").[57] The texts are based on the Martin Treu biography of Katharina,[58] emphasizing her entrepreneurial achievements with reference to the chronic financial straits in the Luther household, which forced Katharina to manage it firmly and efficiently. The deaths of some of Luther's children, a subject which is ignored in most of the films, is addressed here for the first time. However, the presentation only vaguely hints at Katharina's flight, caused by plague and war. Another slide show comprising 12 pictures was produced to commemorate the 500th anniversary of Katharina von Bora's birthday. The motifs assembled for it are directly related to her life or are associated with the history of the response to her. The focus is the Luthers' house in Wittenberg and how Katharina furnished and decorated it. As far as marital relations between Katharina and Martin Luther were concerned, the author comes to the following conclusion: "The enormous burden of work resting on Luther explains why he left shaping their domestic life entirely to his wife. However, behind that was the Reformer's basic conviction of the equality of men and women as prescribed in the Bible. Their spheres of activity were different ones. A husband was active outside the house; the wife's realm was the home. [...] Bearing in mind the scale of the household, it is definitely appropriate to speak of a division of labour based on equality."[59] That her areas of responsibility, including the acquisition and leasing of land and the selling of produce, often brought Katharina out in public, does not, however, contradict this archetype, which was evidently so overriding that it was resurrected for the 2003 film. Katharina, played by Claire Cox, does appear self-assured and even seductive, but the extent of her share in the Reformer's success is not revealed. At least a third of the 2003 MDR-produced film (a documentary with feature film elements) was dedicated to Katharina as the proprietor of a small enterprise. Maybe this subject will finally appear in the movies on the occasion of the 500th anniversary of The Nailing of the Thesis in 2017.

V. Church as Film Maker

1. Lutheran Church and Cinema

As early as 1910, Walther Conradt, a Lutheran pastor, challenged his Church in his book *Kirche und Kinematograph. Eine Frage*, to give the public some resources as aids to interpretation and to take the lead in producing quality films. However, the first efforts made by the Lutheran Church hierarchy to create a constructive relationship with film and to establish an 'official' body of theory did not take place until 1922. In that year the regional Churches amalgamated to form the German Protestant Church Union (Deutscher Evangelischer Kirchenbund), and established a cinematography department under August Hinderer, the director of the Protestant Press Association for Germany (Evangelischer Preßverband für Deutschland). By about 1927, the Regional Press Associations (Landespresseverbände) had begun to set up their own film offices and so called Picture Chambers (Bildkammern). The first chamber at Berlin served as the temporary headquarters for all Protestant film work in Germany between 1922 and 1928. As early as 1925, Pastor Julius Kelber had established a Protestant Film Chamber in Nuremberg for Bavaria (Evangelische Bildkammer für Bayern) modelled after the Berlin Bildkammer. The Nuremberg chamber also functioned as a distributor for the Lutheran film offices in Baden, Württemberg and the Palatinate. Hinderer also wanted to found an institute for cinematic research but was unsuccessful; instead, his efforts contributed to the marginalization of cinema in the eyes of the Church authorities. The First Lutheran Film Congress (Erster Evangelischer Filmkongress) did not convene until 1931, at which time the proper representation of Jesus was among the issues addressed. Unlike the Catholic Church, which had been producing its own films since 1917 in collaboration with, among others, Leo-Film AG (which had grown out of Legendenfilm GmbH), the Lutheran Church almost invariably commissioned other firms to produce their films until after the Second World War. Almost all of the Lutheran productions released were proselytising films or representations of Church institutions and facilities, and most of these can be classified as documentary films. Altogether only 130 Lutheran films were produced between 1922 and 1933.[1] In America, criticism of Hollywood productions as amoral[2] led to the "Production Code", which the film industry was willing to submit to voluntarily. In 1935, the US National Lutheran Council issued "A Statement on Motion Pictures", in which it appealed to its congregation not to support any form of immoral film whatsoever, indeed to combat them with all legal means.[3] As elsewhere, a constructive approach to film (other than official Church productions) does not seem to have developed in the US until later. However, the first major works on film theory often read like practical instruction manuals for dealing generally with film and were mainly addressed to 'secular cinema'. They were supposedly not published until about 1970,[4] that is, at a time when the traditional cinema was already crisis-ridden while the importance of television was increasing.

2. Featuring a German Protestant Hero

"Luther films" have yet to be evaluated in depth as source material for studying the Protestant mentality, although such films were used as a medium for teaching the history of the Reformation even during the first phase of their widespread distribution, which began in 1911.

The time span to be studied in this chapter, which goes up to 1930, encompasses the silent film era, whose dramaturgy was shaped by the use of intertitles. Staging and acting styles were modelled after theatrical praxis. It should be emphasized first and foremost that silent films were never entirely without sound. The musical accompaniment, which has only survived from the last silent film on Luther, enhanced the visualized moods or underscored dramatic effects and made the performance of music shown on screen audible.

As previously indicated copies of only two of the four silent films on Luther are extant; most of these, however, are not of the original version. Censorship of all films shown publicly in the Weimar Republic was mandatory under the terms of the "Reich Motion Picture Regulation" (Reichslichtspielgesetz) that went into force on May 29, 1920.[5] The censorship documents are often the only reliable source for the original content of the films because the intertitles that has survived in them at least allows inferences to be drawn about the lost visual material.

The paradigm shift in the way the reformer is presented shows up clearly in the 1920s Luther films: from Romantic aesthete in the 1913 *Wittenberger Nachtigall* (*Wittenberg Nightingale*) to the "German Reformation" hero in the 1927 film. In two of the three Luther films made up to 1927 (the films made in 1911 and 1913), the reasons for making the films in the first place can no longer be clarified. The situation is different with the film *Luther. Ein Film der deutschen Reformation* (*Luther: A film on the German Reformation*), which was finished in 1927; the history of its inception and making and of viewer response to it is well documented. This film has been briefly and variously discussed, both under the auspices of Lutheran cinematic involvement and in the context of the history of the Protestant League (Evangelischer Bund). Still, the intentions of the production company created by the Evangelische Bund and those of its then president, Bruno Döhring,[6] who submitted an outline to be used in writing the script, have yet to be defined. A study of those intentions would reveal crucial aspects of the film's significance for religious history.

The silent Luther films were made in Berlin, Munich and Babelsberg. The locations were, however, the original historic settings, which were incorporated into the film as much as possible. One reason for this practice was the desire to give the new medium film a higher profile compared to theater. Location source material was gleaned from illustrated biographies of Luther, 19th-century history paintings and pieces written for the theater,[7] from which the canon of scenes selected for the film can be shown to derive (Eisleben, Erfurt, Stotternheim, Elstertor, Worms, Wartburg etc).

2.1. Kaiserreich

Doktor Martinus Luther, the first film known to have been devoted to the reformer's life, premiered in Berlin in 1911 consisted of eighteen scenes and the reel of film was 600 metres long. Therefore, the running time cannot have been much more than 20 minutes. Nothing is known about the screenplay. No copy of this film seems to have survived[8] although it was distributed by the Deutsche Bioscop-Gesellschaft and not just in Berlin. In Düsseldorf, its authenticity was emphasised as its chief selling point: "True to life—strictly objective—entirely free of attacks on members of other faiths" ran the marketing slogan.[9] The film depicted Luther's life, including his marriage, and what "a happy family life" he led.[10] In this respect, it was based on a concept similar to the basis for the subsequent Luther film. Only a handful of stills from that first Luther film have survived. They show Hermann Litt, a well-known Berlin actor, singer and stage director in his day, in the role of Luther holding the Bible like one of Dürer's Apostles, defending his writings at the Diet of Worms and marrying Katherina von Bora.[11]

Soon afterwards, in 1913, *Die Wittenberger Nachtigall. Martin Luther* (*The Wittenberg Nightingale: Martin Luther.*) premiered in Berlin at the Admiralstheater.[12] The title and the intertitles of the film were changed several times: In 1921, it was censored under the name *Der Weg zur Sonne: Martin Luther* (*The Way to the Sun: Martin Luther*).[13] Evidently in keeping with political requirements, the film was ultimately entitled *Doktor Martin Luther. Ein Lebensbild für das deutsche Volk* (*Doctor Martin Luther: A Biographical Portrait for the German People*),[14] an almost verbatim borrowing from the title of the Georg Buchwald Luther biography, which had run through many reprints.[15] Nevertheless, the starting credits purport that the screenplay, written by John Edward, was based on Johann Mathesius' *Historien von Luthers Anfang Lehr und Leben*, the earliest known comprehensive biography of Luther. The criticism that the film lacked historical authenticity, a slur against which the director Erwin Báron defended himself unsuccessfully in 1913,[16] was also the pivotal criterion on which the censors based their decisions in 1912. In 1913, advertising had still boasted that the film "was approved for children".[17] Furthermore, the Magdeburger Zeitung reported that "this highly instructive film [...]" was to "be shown to pupils at Berlin educational institutions in special showings."[18], but in the same article the enormous cost of the production with its cast of 600 actors[19] was highly exaggerated. Katharina von Bora, played by Margot von Hardt, appears in several mass scenes even though the script has her still residing in the Cistercian convent at Nimbschen.

2.2. Weimar Republic: The Paradigm Shift

On March 24, 1921 the censors argued for banning the film *Der Weg zur Sonne* (alias *Die Wittenberger Nachtigall*).[20] About a month later, on April 20, 1921, only a ban on showing it to young people was upheld.[21] Not without justification do the findings contain the following criticism: "The creator of the film has evidently only informed himself to a slight extent about the historical sources which are available to all educated people. It is worth mentioning, for instance, that, in the present film, Martin Luther is characterized as the son of a carpenter, joiner or cooper." This item of information has been corrected in the introductory intertitle in the version preserved in the Berlin Bundesfilmarchiv, in which Luther's father is referred to as a "slate miner" ("Schieferhäuer"). The visual side, however, has not been altered to match the change in the intertitles. For instance, a scene in the film shows Luther's father working on a wine cask when Luther has a meeting with him while fleeing the authorities. Other examples of the criticism in the censors' report are "that Katharina von Bora had already met him in her youth, and developed a liking for him as a young girl. Moreover, on the occasion of his stay on the Wartburg the event of the Bible translation is not mentioned".[22] Even though Luther had been previously shown studying the Bible, his Bible translation is only mentioned in the corrected intertitles. Surprisingly, the final decision taken by the censors reveals an astonishingly sharp distinction drawn between religious and historical awareness: "The object was to be examined whether this representation, which is incidentally free of improprieties, was liable due to its historical inaccuracy and whether the related flattening characterization of one of the greatest German folk heroes could be objected to the terms of § 1 Motion Picture Regulation. [...] According to this appraisal report [what is meant is the finding of March 24], the film is liable to grossly offend the religious feelings of Protestant circles. This finding could not be agreed upon. Since the figure of Martin Luther belongs to history but is not part of the Lutheran faith. Consequently, it cannot be an infringement of religious feeling, but rather one of [...] historical integrity. Therefore, it had to be examined whether such an infringement [...] might endanger peace. This query was answered in the negative."[23]

The film indeed characterizes and portrays Luther in a very romantic manner. His childhood is dealt with more extensively here than in any other Luther film. The scenes in which he has to earn a livelihood by "singing motets in courtyards"[24] in the Currende are nothing if not touching. The Reformer is passionate; he is smoothing the way for a new era. An intertitle is used like a leitmotif in the 1913 version, according to the censor card, in every act. In the version that has survived in Berlin, however, this occurs only twice: once in a quotation from Revelation 21:5 in a forward-looking German translation that only slightly alters the meaning. Further, the text does not begin with "Ecce" (Behold) as it does in the Vulgate: "Ego nova facio omnia !!" (I make all things new).[25]

What is remarkable is the effort made to stage the action in the original settings. Most of the film was shot in Wittenberg. The conversation with Staupitz was moved to the inner courtyard of the Luther House. However, the decision was made to film the scenes taking place inside the Wartburg in the nearby Moritzburg in Halle. At the Elster Gate the scenery is obviously painted. As in later Luther films, all key scenes from Luther's biography are shown. That means nailing the Theses to the door, the confrontation with the Worms Reichstag, the feigned kidnapping on Luther's return, his stay at the Wartburg, etc. Some of the scenes are unmotivated in context and the action has been unnecessarily drawn out. To take one example, Luther is shown on his flight taking a moment to meditate on a skull. This scene seems to have been inspired by representations of the saints (St Jerome and St Frances, for example).

The back-story of Luther's marriage is elaborated as in no other Luther film. In *Doktor Martin Luther. Ein Lebensbild für das deutsche Volk* (once *Die Wittenberger Nachtigall*), the relationship between Katharina von Bora and Martin Luther is stylized into a romantic love story which begins back in Luther's student days in Erfurt, as it is discussed in chapter IV. The film ends with the score of the chorale "A Mighty Fortress is Our God", which was probably quoted in the piano accompaniment and is also audible in later films with sound.

The next Luther film was definitely not instigated by the German film industry. Rather, the idea came in 1922 from Freiherr von der Heyden-Rynsch, then Dezernent (Head of the Administrative Department) of Art, Sports and Tourism of the city of Eisenach, in anticipation of Lutheran World Congress, which convened on August, 21, 1923. He addressed the top Lutheran authorities, who fostered his project and ultimately distributed the film through the Evangelische Bildkammer. Freiherr von der Heyden-Rynsch wanted to link up with the history-film tradition as exemplified by Fridericus Rex (Frederick the Great: 1921–22),[26] which was centred on historic figures from German history. The Lutheran authorities' stated aim was a "historically faithful picture without the embroideries of legend".[27] During the planning phase, it was even suggested that Karl Holl should collaborate on the film as theological adviser.[28] Holl had inaugurated what is known as the Luther Renaissance with his research into the Doctrine of Justification,[29] which is also the ideological groundwork from which the Luther film developed as a genre. Holl had been teaching ecclesiastical history in Berlin since 1906, his ideas influenced several generations of theologians,[30] a factor that was just as significant for the film that followed.

Under the title *Martin Luther*, with Karl Wüstenhagen playing the leading role and directing, the film publicly premiered in 1923 at the Wartburg[31] following a press screening in Munich, where the producers, Luther-Film GmbH., (most likely incorporated expressly for the purpose of making the film,) were based.[32] Distribution, however, was regulated by the Evangelische Pressverband (Protestant Press Association) in Berlin.[33] Only copies for the foreign market seem to have survived. In Germany the censors' card of June 28, 1923, which permits the film to be shown to children and adolescents, a description of the film published by the Evangelische Bildkammer and the first script by Walther Nithack-Stahn, which was sent to the Kirchenbundesamt in Berlin to be monitored,[34] are preserved. The scholarly value of this script as the decisive outline for the film cannot, therefore, be overestimated even though it was considerably shortened and the language was altered for the screenplay by P. Kurz. Nithack-Stahn (1866–1942),[35] had been reverend at the Kaiser-Wilhelm-Gedächtniskirche in Berlin since 1906 and had published several novels and plays. He also authored a play about Martin Luther for the 1921 celebration in Breslau, which commemorated the 400th anniversary of the Diet of Worms.[36]

The plot of Nithack-Stahn's script does show motifs that were taken up again in later Luther films. For example in the 1927 Luther film, the Dance of Death as the memento mori motif and the visitation of the Archangel Michael were used.[37] However, the scene showing the Luther family under the Christmas tree only appeared in the 1923 film, and some scenes were not adopted from Nithack-Stahn's script even for the scenario of the 1923 film for reasons of both content and technique.[38]

Examination of the film description by the Evangelische Bildkammer (see p. 85) and the American version of the film reveal that the movie was restricted to the life of Luther and eschewed places of minor interest to German Reformation history such as Münster in 1535.

Nor was any reference made to the political consequences of the schism, including ultimately the Thirty Years War.[39]

LUTHER = FILM

Berlin-Steglitz, Datum des Poststempels.
Beymeſtraße 8

Jn der Weltgeſchichte ſtehen wie einzelne Wahrzeichen von beſonderer Wucht überragende Perſönlichkeiten, die über ihre Volksgrenzen hinaus der Menſchheit von allgemeiner Bedeutung ſind. Die Größe ihres Lebens, ihres Denkens und Wirkens gibt immer wieder Anreiz zu erneuten Schilderungen von anderen Geſichtspunkten aus.

Martin Luther iſt ein Menſch von ſolcher Bedeutung. Sein Bild zu zeigen, wie es heute vor uns ſteht, war erſter An= ſtoß zu unſerm Filmwerk. So wurde nicht einfach übernommen, was als Dichtung und Wahrheit über dieſen Heros der Menſch= heitsgeſchichte vorlag. Zu Grunde gelegt wurde das Ergebnis neueſter Forſchungen, und ſo entſtand ein geſchichtlich treues Bild, ohne legendäre Arabesken. Beſonders über die Jugend Luthers wird eine neue, rührende Poeſie von innerlicher, dramatiſcher Wirkung ausgeſtreut. Die heldenmütige Standhaftigkeit des Mannes wird gleichſam ſchon durch das Jugendbild des Knaben Martin vorhergekündet. Schwere Schickſalsbürde laſtet auf den ſchwachen Schultern des auserwählten Kindes. Krankheiten, mit viſionärer Bilderwelt durchſetzte Träume, ergreifende Empfänglichkeit für die Leiden der Menſchheit, kraftvolle Zuverſicht und trotziger Wille, leiden zu wollen zum Heile der Welt, rollen als ergreifende, rührende, aufrüttelnde Bilder an uns vorüber. Um ihn herum der Kreis der Seinen: Der Eltern wechſelvolles Geſchick, ihre peinigende Angſt und leiſe Zuverſicht, der Freunde und Feinde teils ſtützende, teils untergrabende Mit= und Gegenarbeit; hier der feinſinnige Geiſt Melanchthons, dort als Gegenbild der phantaſtiſche Kopf des Bilderſtürmers Karlſtadt uſw. Von Akt zu Akt türmt ſich das Schickſal. Wie eine Naturnotwendig= keit entwickelt ſich der Prozeß, gipfelnd in der machtvollen, weltgeſchichtlichen Stunde: Worms! Zwei Tage unerhörter Anſpannung aller ſeeliſchen und phyſiſchen Kräfte, und dazwiſchen eine Nacht in furchtbarem Seelenkampf. Der Sieg und die reifende Frucht des durchgekämpften Streites auf der Wartburg; ſeine mittelalterlich=wahren Teufelsbegegnungen, das Einſetzen mit der ganzen Wucht ſeiner großen Perſönlichkeit für das Glaubenswerk ergänzen und ſchließen das Werk. Als ein ewig Lebender und lebendig Wirkender ſoll er uns am Schluſſe in der Seele verbleiben. — Einem Stoff von dieſer Bedeutung mußte eine typiſche Form gegeben werden. Eine Art Prologbild kündet ſie an. Luther bricht die erſtarrende lateiniſche Welt — angedeutet durch einen r o m a n i ſ ch e n Bogen — und erweitert ſie himmelwärts mit einer Gebärde des Glaubens zum Herzen hin. Er erſchließt das Tor der Freiheit, für das nunmehr die g o t i ſ ch e Formenwelt die ſymboliſche Linie gibt.

Propaganda material for the 1923 film (Courtesy of LAELB).

In visual terms, Nithack-Stahn explicitly referenced the work of such exemplary exponents of history painting as Wilhelm von Kaulbach and Karl Lessing. Moreover, he composed scenes from well-known allegories and motifs taken from Christian iconography.[40] Even contemporary art was quoted, for example the painting "Lichtgebet", the 'icon' of the German Reform movement, by Hugo Karl Johann Höppner, whose pseudonym was Fidus.[41]

Hugo Johann Höppner, Das Lichtgebet (first version 1908).

Allegory figures prominently in the film, as the advertising text promised: "[H]e [Luther] is to remain at the end in our souls as one who shall live eternally and work as when alive. Material of such significance had to be given a typical form. A sort of prologue scene announces it. Luther breaks down the rigid Latin world suggested by a Romanesque arch and expands it heavenwards with a gesture of faith to his heart. He opens up the gate to freedom, for which from now on the Gothic world of forms give the symbolic line."[42]

Although classification of this kind is far away from any art historical scholarship, it is firmly anchored in the tradition of Christian medieval typology, which was rediscovered in the 19th century and often referred to. For example, the Rogier van der Weyden triptych with the Adoration of the Kings known as the Columba Altarpiece (c 1450), is well known to feature both architectural styles,

Karl Wüstenhagen as Luther preaching in the 1923 film.
Crowd responding to Luther's sermons first and last shot.

the Romanesque and the Gothic, and this can be interpreted as references to the Old and the New Covenants.[43] According to this interpretation, the Romanesque style used to render the shabby manger in Bethlehem is deprecatingly contrasted with the radiant Gothic of a new church. In addition, the Gothic style had attained the status of the German national style in the early 19th century, a valuation based on Goethe's *Von deutscher Baukunst* (1772). Hence, the use of this motif in the 1923 Luther film should surely also be interpreted as revanchist in spirit and motivation.

It is not recorded when the subtitle *The Struggle of his Life (Der Kampf seines Lebens)* was added to the film nor by whom it was added. It does, for instance, appear on an advertising flyer distributed inter alia by the Evangelische Bildkammer.

In that text, elements of the Christiformitas are emphasized in the description given of the Reformer: "Illnesses, moving receptivity to the sufferings of mankind, forceful confidence and defiant will, the desire to suffer for the salvation of the world, roll past us as affecting, touching, stirring images."[44]

Between October 24, and November 7, 1926, the film was shown eleven times. Screenings took place mostly in Nuremberg (five times in churches and six times in halls), but also in Munich (twice), in Ansbach and other communities. The German Protestant Circle of Companion (Deutsch-evangelische Weggenossenkreis) organized showings in Augsburg.[45]

What is remarkable is that even then, cuts were made by the parties who leased the film and the Inner Mission in Bavaria.[46] The public did not give the film a positive rating everywhere it was shown.[47] Professional film critics also made negative comments such as "un-Lutheran tepidity" ("unlutherische Lauheit"). They pointed out that this first work by Luther-Film GmbH strove purely toward religious and nationalistic purposes: "If, for reason of inner quality, the comparison were not blasphemy, one might say [...] Brilliant fulfilment—brimming with the ineffable—is lacking here of course. One must assume, however, that the intention was good. The script may be irreproachable in both the religious and the ecclesiastical sense, but as a film, it doesn't work. Not because it merely presents an attractive series of images instead of [possessing] dramatic structure but because it presumes too much and then leaves gaps in important places."[48] Regarding the new film in the pipeline at the Lutherfilm-Denkmal society, in November 1926, Dean Schiller described his disappointment which convinced him that the subject of the "sacred psychomachy of a soul wrestling with God" ("heiliges Ringen einer Seele mit Gott") could not be filmed at all. Further, he expressed fundamental scepticism about the medium as such. This reflects the basic problem associated with religious films,[49] which is shown in the following as a variant of the classic iconographic issue:

"I find my views definitely confirmed, my fears even surpassed. The performances were preceded by extensive advertising. Day after day Luther's head looked out of tram windows. Announcements were printed in newspapers with reports from other cities, like Magdeburg, that promised something very powerful; particularly since it also reported on the participation of high-ranking, even top-ranking clerical dignitaries. The public thronged to the showings. What was actually offered was wretched rubbish. A few silly childhood scenes, abortive attempts at representing Luther's psychomachy, the big scenes unimpressive [...] I am only too happy to admit that something far better might be made than this film, which was served to us here and has disgusted not just me[,] but many others as well. The masses, of course, enjoyed it as they do any sort of rubbish. [...] It [the film] has, on the contrary confirmed for me that it is a dubious undertaking to film a story which at its core is the story of an inner life. Anyone who undertakes to do that has either no clear idea of the possibilities the cinema has for expression or he has no feeling of how repellent it is when pose, gesture and histrionic miming are to make the sacred wrestling of the soul for and with God into effective theater. That is the main reason why I assume a radically negative stance towards any and all Luther films. [...] It is in the nature of film that it promotes superficiality. The images rush past on the flickering screen, a stimulus for the eye but not the

Advertisement for the 1923 film, recto and verso.

Martin Luther

Der Kampf seines Lebens

In der Weltgeschichte stehen wie einzelne Wahrzeichen von besonderer Wucht überragende Persönlichkeiten, die über ihre Volksgrenzen hinaus der Menschheit von allgemeiner Bedeutung sind.

Martin Luther ist ein Mensch von solcher Bedeutung. **Sein Bild zu zeigen, wie es heute vor uns steht, ist die Aufgabe des Films, der hier am Orte in den nächsten Tagen zur Vorführung gelangt.** Ein geschichtlich treues Bild als das Ergebnis neuester Forschungen. Die heldenmütige Standhaftigkeit des Mannes wird gleichsam schon durch das Jugendbild des Knaben Martin vorhergekündet. Krankheiten, ergreifende Empfänglichkeit für die Leiden der Menschheit, kraftvolle Zuversicht und trotziger Wille, leiden zu wollen zum Heile der Welt, rollen als ergreifende, rührende, aufrüttelnde Bilder an uns vorüber. Von Akt zu Akt türmt sich das Schicksal bis zu der machtvollen, weltgeschichtlichen Stunde: Worms! Zwei Tage unerhörter Anspannung aller seelischen und physischen Kräfte, und dazwischen eine Nacht in furchtbarem Seelenkampf. Der Sieg und die reifende Frucht des durchgekämpften Streites auf der Wartburg; seine mittelalterlich-wahren Teufelsbegegnungen, das Einsetzen mit der ganzen Wucht seiner großen Persönlichkeit für das Glaubenswerk ergänzen und schließen das Werk. Als ein ewig Lebender und lebendig Wirkender soll er uns am Schlusse in der Seele verbleiben.

Vaterländische Verlags- und Kunstanstalt, Berlin SW 61.

Lutherfilm (handwritten)

Evangelische Elternvereinigung
Nürnberg-Gibitzenhof

Sonntag, den 24. Oktober 1926, abends 6 Uhr
in der Turnhalle, Gibitzenhofstraße 127

Großer Eltern-Abend

zu Gunsten armer bedürftiger Schulkinder
der Evangelischen Schule Gibitzenhof.

Vortrags-Folge:

1. „Leih aus deines Himmels Höhen" von W. v. Gluck
(Posaunenchor Gibitzenhof)
2. „Lobe den Herrn" (5. Klasse der ev. Schule Gibitzenhof)
3. a. „Das Erkennen" (vorgetragen von H. Harz, 4. ev. Klasse)
b. „Maria bei der Großmama" (vorgetragen von K. Schmidt, 4. ev. Klasse)
4. „Celesta", Konzertfantasie für Zither von Kollmaneck
Solist: Herr Zithervirtuose und dipl. Verbandslehrer Horn aus Erlangen
5. „Seppl und der Schultheiß", (vorgetragen von G. Horter, 4. ev. Klasse)
6. „Der liebe Gott" (vorgetragen von O. Grüner, 4. ev. Klasse)
7. „Die Kapelle" (Posaunenchor Gibitzenhof)
8. Ansprache von Herrn Pfarrer Gloßner
9. „Erhalt uns, Herr, bei deinem Wort" (Ev. Kirchengesangverein Gibitzenhof)

— Pause —

10. Luther-Film in 5 Akten

Die Pausen zwischen den einzelnen Akten werden durch Vorträge
von dem Evangelischen Kirchengesangverein, dem Posaunenchor
und einem Kinderchor ausgefüllt)

11. Gemeinsamer Gesang: „Ein' feste Burg ist unser Gott".

Eintritt 50 Pf. mit Steuer. :: Saaleröffnung 5 Uhr.

Max Müller, Nürnberg.

Evening program for the screening of the 1923 film.

object of observation and thought. Should we educate people—I'm thinking of children especially—to look at serious, indeed sacred things in such a way?—One of the greatest delusions from which those who advocate films such as the Luther film suffer is that the people can thus be made accustomed to watching good, valuable films rather than bad[,] harmful films. Far from it, I fear that the Church, in cultivating film, is teaching people to like film who would not otherwise go to the cinema. You will now understand that I am opposed to your undertaking. I am glad that my colleagues share my point of view."[50]

The criticism did not fail to make an impression on the distributors. Dean Kelber from the Landesverein für Innere Mission (State Inner Mission Association) wrote to a colleague on November 4, 1927: "I am not entirely enthusiastic about the Luther film and very much hope that the new historical Luther film from the Protestant League will be better. After all, many valuable scenes are indeed missing [in it] from Luther's life. Hence, we have not recommended this Luther film all too much and are waiting for the one to come."[51] Finally, he decided cease showing the 1923 Luther film.[52] As one might imagine, the new film project was awaited with high hopes.

Luther. Ein Film der deutschen Reformation was accordingly an elaborate production. It was commissioned and produced by the *Luther-Filmdenkmal, Zentralstelle für die Schaffung eines Lutherfilms* (Central Office for Producing a Luther film), which was founded in Berlin on July 6, 1926.[53] This film cost a great deal to make[54] and featured an all-star cast directed by Hans Kyser. It was intended to make cinematographic history as a "Protestant Annunciation film" ("evangelischer Verkündigungsfilm").[55] The Luther-Filmdenkmal association was affiliated with the Protestant League (Evangelischer Bund) and had concluded a contractual agreement with Cob-Film GmbH concerning the form that the League influence would take.[56] At the same time, the League committed itself "not to approve the making of any other Luther film for the duration of three years".[57] Cob-Film-GmbH guaranteed distribution to cinemas in Germany and abroad. This indicates that, unlike previous productions of a similar kind, this film was targeted to a much wider audience that went beyond just the clerical public. The producers were counting on the Protestant grass roots being enthusiastic in any case. The appeal made by the Association to the public to support the production financially by signing share certificates demonstrates that what was at stake was a large-scale missionary undertaking under the supervision of the top Church authorities:

"Lutheran associations are the expression of Lutheran feelings of community. It is their task to nurture and promote what is quintessentially Lutheran […] 1. Our film will not be a usual film like any other but will symbolise the great ideas of the Reformation in a way that grips hearts. It will be shown in every cinema that fills the masses who go to the cinema, but who probably do not to church with religious, Lutheran ideas. It will, therefore, have a proselytising effect to an extraordinary extent. 2. You are aware that Rome is making the greatest efforts to reconquer Germany, the land of the Reformation. Thus […] in the time span from 1913 to 1925 the number of male members of monastic orders has risen from 6430 to 11,250, the number of female members of monastic establishments from 63,078 to 77,646 (including 5926 novices). Would not all Protestants uniting to make a Luther film be a worthy and impressive protest? 3. We are not requesting donations but a loan that will be paid back and also will represent a share in the profits. 4. The design of the film and the management will be supervised by a committee to which a commissioner from the highest-ranking German Church authority, the Deutsche Evangelische Kirchenausschuß (German Protestant Church Commission), belongs. The film will be made with the most perfect and modern artistic and technical facilities. This really does represent a warranty that the film will be designed so that it will be worthy in every religious, ecclesiastical, scholarly and technical respect and that the business will be handled in a refined and unobjectionable way. It seems to us to go without saying that in a Lutheran matter of such overriding importance, your association [what is meant is the Landesverein für Innere Mission] should not stand aside. We are confidently counting on you! With Lutheran greetings Luther-Filmdenkmal. Zentralstelle für die Schaffung eines Lutherfilms E.V. [endorsed with the signature stamps of the members of the board of governors, Freiherr Curt von Gillhausen (Chairman), Werner Wilm (Director) and D. Repsold (Treasurer)]."[58]

Whereas the first appeals made in early 1926 merely emphasized that collecting donations from members of the Lutheran congregation meant independence from other donors ("And you, German Protestant folk must stand up in the place of Big Capital!"[59]), an explicitly anti-Jewish thrust now surfaced in an internal paper during the last phase of funding: more endorsements were desired so that it would "be possible to avoid under all circumstances support from the Big Capital side of film, which is eagerly proffered but usually not Protestant."[60] The irony of history was that less than 50 years later, the American Jewish producer Eli Landau initiated the creation of one of the most ambitious Luther films.

However, it is safe to assume that in the 1920's none of those who lent money, most of whom were low earners, ever drew profits from the film. As late as 1930, complaints were being voiced that donations had neither been reimbursed nor had interest been paid.[61] A reply to such complaints issued by the League emphasizes that not enough revenue had yet been earned from the film to even cover the costs of making it.[62]

For all the difficulties incurred, the silent film, shot in Babelsberg and followed with great public interest since late August 1927,[63] premiered in December 1927.

Luther-Filmdenkmal.
Zentralstelle für die Schaffung eines
Lutherfilms E.B.

Evangelische!

Ein Luther-Filmdenkmal? Was soll das bedeuten?

Wohl in jeder größeren Stadt Deutschlands mit evangelischer Bevölkerung erhebt sich ein Denkmal Luthers aus Erz oder Stein, um zu den nachkommenden Geschlechtern von der gewaltigen Geistestat dieses Größten aller Deutschen zu reden. Aber wer liest ihre Sprache, und wer kann sie verstehen? Das ruhelose Geschlecht unserer Tage hat keine Zeit, solche Denkmäler in Muße zu betrachten und ihrer stummen Sprache nachzudenken.

Bilder bilden. Bilder aus dem Leben eines Großen bilden in dem Beschauer feste und sichere Vorstellungen und lassen ihn eindringen in die Welt seiner Taten, Gedanken und Empfindungen.

So ist ein Lutherfilm das eindruckvollste und wirksamste Luther-Denkmal.

Ein solches Luther-Filmdenkmal wollen wir schaffen, aber nicht auf dem bei einem gewöhnlichen Film üblichen Wege der Zusammenarbeit mit dem doch immerhin lediglich auf geschäftliche Interessen eingestellten Großkapital, sondern in Gemeinschaft mit innerlich interessierten evangelischen Kreisen, damit unser Luther-Filmdenkmal aus den Herzen herauswachse und in den Herzen immer und immer wieder die Liebe und Dankbarkeit zu unserem Luther erwecke und wachhalte.

Freilich, eine Vorbedingung muß ein solcher Film erfüllen: **er muß den höchsten Ansprüchen genügen.**

Das Manuskript für unseren Lutherfilm schreibt Herr Hofprediger D. Doehring-Berlin, die Ausführung erfolgt unter Zuziehung erster Künstler und der erfahrensten Fachleute und wird durch das Präsidium des Evangelischen Bundes in allen Einzelheiten überwacht. Welche Bedeutung die höchsten kirchlichen Stellen unserem Unternehmen beimessen, geht aus dem umseitig abgedruckten Schreiben des Deutschen Evangelischen Kirchen-Ausschusses und aus zahlreichen Zuschriften anderer kirchlicher Stellen mit aller Deutlichkeit hervor.

Und an die Stelle des Großkapitals sollst du treten, deutsches evangelisches Volk! Um jedem Evangelischen die Möglichkeit eigener Beteiligung zu geben, stellen wir Anteilscheine über 50.— Mk. aus. Sie werden aus den Erträgnissen des Films zurückgezahlt und erhalten einen erheblichen Anteil am Reingewinn. Das alles unter der ständigen Kontrolle des Präsidiums des Evangelischen Bundes.

Es erscheint uns der Sache nicht angemessen, große Versprechungen zu machen; wir glauben aber zu der Annahme berechtigt zu sein, daß die Anteilscheineigner auch in materieller Beziehung durchaus zufriedengestellt werden dürften, zumal da der Lutherfilm auch in Nordamerika, England nebst Kolonien, Schweden, Norwegen und Dänemark die denkbar besten geschäftlichen Aussichten hat und niemals veraltet. Schon seit Jahren wird gerade von Amerika aus die Schaffung eines würdigen Lutherfilms in Deutschland, dem Lande der Reformation, angeregt.

So wenden wir uns vertrauensvoll an alle evangelischen Kreise Deutschlands mit der Bitte, uns zur Seite zu stehen. Wer selbst Anteilscheine zeichnen möchte, oder wer uns dafür in Betracht kommende Persönlichkeiten nachweisen kann, wolle sich sofort mit uns in Verbindung setzen. Er hilft dadurch ein großes Werk der evangelischen Christenheit mit erbauen, ein herrliches, würdiges

Luther-Filmdenkmal!

Mit deutsch-evangelischem Gruß

Luther-Filmdenkmal.
Zentralstelle für die Schaffung eines Lutherfilms E.B.
Der Vorstand:

Berlin W 50, Kurfürstendamm 14/15
Fernsprecher: Bismarck 571.

Frhr. von Gillhausen   Wilm
Wirkl. Geh. Rat,   Schriftführer.
Vorsitzender.

Subscription forms for the 1927 film.

Zeichnungsschein.

An
„Luther-Filmdenkmal, Zentralstelle für die Schaffung eines Lutherfilms e.V."
BERLIN W 50.
Kurfürstendamm 1415.

i. W.: _____ Mk.

Hierdurch zeichne ich den Betrag von _____

als ein „Luther-Filmdenkmal, Zentralstelle für die Schaffung eines Lutherfilms
e.V." zu Berlin W 50, Kurfürstendamm 1415, gegebenes Darlehn unter den mir
bekannten, umseitig abgedruckten Bedingungen und verpflichte mich zur Zahlung auf
Anforderung.

Ort und Datum: _____

Wohnung: _____

Vor- und Zuname: _____

Stand: _____

Um genaue und deutliche Angaben wird gebeten.

Zeichnungsschein.

An
„Luther-Filmdenkmal, Zentralstelle für die Schaffung eines Lutherfilms e.V."
BERLIN W 50.
Kurfürstendamm 1415.

i. W.: _____ Mk.

Hierdurch zeichne ich den Betrag von _____

als ein „Luther-Filmdenkmal, Zentralstelle für die Schaffung eines Lutherfilms
e.V." zu Berlin W 50, Kurfürstendamm 1415, gegebenes Darlehn unter den mir
bekannten, umseitig abgedruckten Bedingungen und verpflichte mich zur Zahlung auf
Anforderung.

Ort und Datum: _____

Wohnung: _____

Vor- und Zuname: _____

Stand: _____

Um genaue und deutliche Angaben wird gebeten.
Für eine Exemplare ist für Sie bestimmt, das andere wollen Sie uns einsenden.

Abschrift.

Deutscher
Evangelischer Kirchenausschuß

K.-A. Nr. 280/26.

Berlin-Charlottenburg, den 22. März 1926.
Jebenstraße 3

Aus Ihrem an den hiesigen Evangelischen Oberkirchenrat
gerichteten und an mich weitergegebenen Schreiben vom
3. Februar 1926 habe ich mit Interesse Kenntnis genommen,
daß Sie die Herstellung eines Martin Luther-Filmes planen.
Es bedarf keiner Versicherung, daß jedes Unternehmen, das
geeignet ist, das Leben und Wirken unseres Reformators den
Evangelischen unserer Zeit näherzubringen, bei den deutschen
evangelischen Landeskirchen Förderung finden dürfte, wenn es
sich um eine würdige Darstellung handelt, die nicht nur in
ästhetischer und technischer Form, sondern auch in wissenschaftlicher, ethischer und kirchlicher Beziehung befriedigt.
Unter diesen Voraussetzungen bin ich auch gern zur Förderung
Ihres Unternehmens im Rahmen der bevorstehenden Arbeit bereit.
Ich habe die Referenten in Filmangelegenheiten, Herren
Konsistorialrat Troschke und Oberkonsistorialrat Scholz
ermächtigt, sich Ihnen zur Beratung bei der Herstellung des
Films, soweit die sonstigen Dienstgeschäfte es erlauben, zur
Verfügung zu stellen.

Der Präsident
gez. Kapler

Teil der Rundschauleser bei der Atelierführung zum Lutherfilm in Neubabelsberg
1. Klöpfer als Luther, 2. der Regisseur Hans Kyser

"Fan tourism" to the film-studios at Babelsberg in 1927.

In this year history films such as *Königin Luise* and *Die Weber* had already caused a furor, but *Luther* was more than that. The pointedly nationalistic thrust had been given to the film by the cathedral preacher Bruno Döhring. Döhring (b. 1879 in Mohrungen, East Prussia; d. in 1961 in Berlin), who had attended university in Halle, Berlin and Königsberg, had had a meteoric career by the time he became Court and Cathedral Preacher in Berlin in 1914, and ultimately taught practical theology at the university there (1923–1953). Döhring's importance was further enhanced by his being President of the Evangelischer Bund from 1924 until 1927. He was also politically active and a Member of the Reichstag for the Deutschnationale Volkspartei, DNVP (German National People's Party) from 1930–1933.[64] Döhring championed the nationalist position in numerous writings, most of which had originally been either sermons or addresses he gave as chairman of the Protestant League, and he also edited such treatises written by others. Radicalized by the First World War, Döhring presented his extremist nationalist view of Reformation history with a great many martial rhetorical flourishes[65]—as late as 1952, he was still speaking of Luther in his autobiography as the "General Pastor of his Beloved Germans" ("Generalseelsorger seiner lieben Deutschen") and the "German Prophet".[66]

The denial issued by the producers, Lutherfilm-Denkmal, and disseminated by the Protestant Press Association, that Döhring had exerted any influence whatsoever on the screen play[67] was evidently a defensive measure adopted when the reaction to the anti-Rome polemic in the film centred on Döhring.[68] In addition, the Protestant League, which supported the film producers, evidently wanted to put some distance between itself and Döhring after Döhring declared his withdrawal from the film on January 29, 1927[69] and proceeded to go his own way. However, the denial contradicted the announcements made previously by the League[70] as well as the advertising published by its film association, in which Döhring was always named as a guarantee for the quality of the film.[71] As early as November 28, 1926, when a press release was issued, the Evangelischer Bund, of which Döhring was still chairman, was explicitly designated the "intellectual originator" ("intellektueller Urheber"). It also reported that Döhring was occupied in writing the screenplay;[72] moreover, Döhring himself issued a statement on the mission and concept of the Luther film, in which he emphasized the proselytizing aspect.[73] However, since Döhring, like Nithack-Stahn before him, was concerned with Luther's work as well as his biography, he also wanted "the most important aspects of the effect exerted by the Reformation to the present day to be emphasized in it."[74] The appearance of Gustav Adolf, inspired from Nithack-Stahn's script for the 1923 Luther film, was accordingly inserted in the 26th scene of the last act of Kyser's film. In this scene A Mighty Fortress is Our God is stylized into a "battle hymn" ("Kämpferlied") to the "martyrs in the cause of the Protestant faith" ("Märtyrer des evangelischen Glaubens"): "Gustav Adolf died a hero's death at Lützen with the hymn on his lips".[75] Although (as was later stated), Döhring had only written the first script whereas the screenplay was by Hans Kyser, Döhring's intellectual authorship is indisputable.[76] Döhring, who would found the Deutsche Reformationspartei (German Reformation Party) in 1928,[77] definitely wanted to win over a wider public to this political cause.

The particular significance of the film from the viewer-response angle is also indicated by its lengthy run in cinemas. It continued to be shown—in a version that was shortened once again after passing the censors for the fourth time—until Protestant involvement in film ended in Germany in 1939.[78] However, it was evidently shown less and less frequently during the 1930s after the introduction of motion pictures with sound.[79] In 1935, it was allegedly "virtually no longer in demand".[80] Still the effect it had on one generation's idea of Luther cannot be underestimated. After all, the screening was designed to be an "hour of religious consecration" ("zu einer religiösen Weihestunde"), which "included choirs performing chorales". Programming was sent to cinemas and other institutions that screened it (cf. evening program for the screening of the 1923 film on p. 91).[81] Finally and most importantly, this work is recognizably referenced and invoked the later Luther films.

In it, the reformer embodies Protestant German intellectual and spiritual culture triumphing over Roman Catholicism: "I have written against the papists because they are bleeding the German people white with the traffic in indulgences"[82].

The final scenes represent the visitation of the Archangel Michael. The Archangel was the patron of the German army and his image was often used thus in militaristic propaganda since 1871.[83] In the film he appears with the quote "O

Ewigkeit Du Donnerwort" ("O eternity, you word of thunder") referencing to J. S. Bach's cantata.[84] The Archangel is clad in armour of the kind Luther will soon be wearing. Luther's terrifying experiences in Rome, which is depicted as the "Whore of Babylon", are also shown. The representation is recognizably borrowed from Laokoon, a story by the Naturalistic dramatist August Strindberg, which was first published in German in 1908 and is a highly provocative visualisation of the experiences of an "Augustinian friar" in the Holy City in spring 1506.[85] The closing scenes in the film also convey the message formulated by Bruno Döhring. Still caught up in the rhetoric of the cultural struggle on the occasion of the 1923 Reformation Day, he stylised the Church of Rome into a "danger to the world", which, in his view, consisted "in the endangering of the German folk soul. Its temporal and eternal relationships"[86] were even worse than Bolshevism because, as he saw contemporary history, "It can no longer be denied that purely Protestant parts of the country, Prussia especially, are being covered over with a network of Roman colonies so that they will be subject to the Pope, who reckons in terms of long time spans."[87] According to Döhring, however, Luther appeared "in the midst of the German people as a fighter with the sword of God's spirit against the spirit of the times".[88] A year later, on September 1, 1924, Döhring formulated what is a vision on an apocalyptic scale at the 28 General Assembly of the Evangelischer Bund in Munich: "Germany is only then fully defeated when the Luther in it has been slain with his gospel of the free grace of God which creates characters against which the Devil with his thousand crafty intrigues endeavours in vain."[89] As the chairman of the Protestant League, Döhring even calls this group Luther's "Sturmtrupp" (storm-battalion).[90] The Evangelischer Bund (est. 1886) was founded with the chief aim of combating Ultramontanism and was a forum for discussing the issue of apolitical representation for Protestantism on the lines of a Centrist Party, which inter alia found its response in forming the quite unsuccessful Christlich-sozialer Volksdienst (CSVD).[91] In 1925, Döhring made the looming worst-case scenario seem even more acute by speaking of "German Protestantism in self-defence" ("deutschen Protestantismus in der Notwehr") and contending "that through the Bavarian Concordat, non-German right has crept into the sphere of German legal sovereignty." As he puts it, Rome was not willing "to come to terms with the independence of the imperial and popular circumstances of a nation"; after all, he rants, "the Roman invasion [...] since the Jesuit law was revoked in 1917 has, however, set in since the Revolution on a much stronger scale."[92] Finally, he notes, representatives of the Curia spoke the language of the Antichrist, but with Luther the return to Early Christendom had been achieved.[93]

In the film, Luther's vision of Wittenberg as the new Rome is introduced by a vision of a cross of light growing ever larger,[94] which stylises the reformer into a second Emperor Constantine in the sense of "in hoc signo vinces" (In this sign shall you conquer). The rest of the plot is simply a success story. After showing the Theses being nailed to the door and continuing on through the stay at the Wartburg, the plot ends with iconoclasm as a revolutionary inferno that must have been intended to remind viewers of the events of 1918. Nevertheless, this presentation was seen by critics as a defamation of the peasant's cause, which meant to them "Germany's only great revolution" ("die einzige große Revolution der Deutschen").[95] The following scene, Luther appearing alone in the pulpit wearing knightly armour, achieved what it set out to do. H. Zappe described the effect it had on him as follows: "The image powerfully grips the soul, this final scene from Wittenberg, where Luther, his armour gleaming beneath his black preacher's robes, stands in the church pulpit and calls the raging iconoclasts to reason, to soul-searching."[96] The scene before that is also of crucial significance. Still set at the Wartburg, it shows how Luther, who is already in armour, is holding up a sword with the sign of the Cross on the pommel. This image was also circulated in the form of a series of picture-postcards.

Luther as "Junker Jörg" (Knight Jörg) in the 1927 film.

Cinema audiences were familiar with the motif from the Fritz Lang film *Die Nibelungen*, Part 1: *Siegfried* (1922–1924). There the main character also holds the sword that has just been forged in the same pose before setting out into the world (canto 1, time code 8.35).[97] The message conveyed by the filmic quotation is clear: Luther as liberator.

This Luther as a messianic figure was played by Eugen Klöpfer, in his day a well-known stage and screen actor and, according to the advertising circulated by Lutherfilm-Denkmal, probably the "most important character actor in Germany".[98] Following a glimpse of Luther's Bible translation with the verse

"That Word above all earthly powers" ("Das Wort sie sollen lassen stahn") from A Mighty Fortress is Our God, the last image is a view of Wittenberg with the monument to the reformer in the foreground.

The film was passed by the censors in Berlin on December 17, 1927 on condition that cuts were made. A day later it premiered in Nuremberg; twenty thousand people are said to have seen it in the first fourteen days after the premiere.[99] Approval of the film elicited sustained protest from the Catholic side;[100] the film was repeatedly subjected to censorship.[101] The criticism that the Protestant League was continuing the 1870s culture wars, now also supported by a film, was surely not unjustified; the reasoning, however, was no less polemical for that.[102] The battle raging in the press was even commented on in *Der Stürmer*.[103] The Protestant League at first reacted rather casually: indignation was hypocritical. After all, Catholics need not watch the film.[104]

The film was dropped from the bill by UFA in Berlin, where it had first been shown at the Ufa-Palast am Zoo on February 16, 1928. The Bavarian state government wanted to have it banned in Bavaria, which led to an injunction being sought and enforced by the office of the Commissioner of Police in Munich. Representatives of the Lutheran Church protested against such action.

For them it was a basic question of their status as a religious minority. The Lutherans did not want to bow to "one-sided power politics" ("einseitigen Politik der Macht"), wrote Dean Weigel, chairman of the Landesverein für Innere Mission, in a letter to Hippert, an MP in the Bavarian State legislature on February 23rd, 1928.[105] He also emphasized his stance in an article, published in the *Allgemeine Rundschau* of February 27, 1928, headlined "Protestant Part of the People Resists Roman Tyranny" ("Der evangelische Volksteil wehrt sich gegen die römische Willkür"). That same day the Protestant League called for "fiercest resistance to the [economic] boycott of the Luther film and demanded "active defence of German Protestant interests wherever and however an opportunity should be afforded".[106] Neither side was willing to discuss the true nature of the conflict.[107] Protests were unleashed internationally against the "hounding by Roman Catholicism" ("Hetze des römischen Katholizismus") since an attack on Luther, "the greatest hero in the history of God's Kingdom since Paul and Augustine" ("den größten Heros in der Geschichte des Reiches Gottes seit Paulus und Augustinus") and his work represented a "blow aimed at all Protestantism".[108]

Not until more cuts were made did the censors pass the film on March 22, 1928.[109] However, even on the Lutheran side, doubts about the general suitability for filmic treatment of Martin Luther were voiced again.[110] Dean Johannes Kelber of the Evangelische Bildkammer attempted to counter them in a long essay entitled "Basic ideas about the Luther Film" ("Grundsätzliches zum Lutherfilm"). In it, he emphasized, on the one hand, that the film was the ideal vehicle for reaching non-churchgoers. On the other, history films were almost invariably fiction but nevertheless could reveal historical truths, as in the Luther

Deutsch-Evangelische Korrespondenz

Mitteilungen des Evangelischen Bundes

27. Jahrgang	Berlin W 10, den 29. Februar 1928	Nummer 9

Fernsprecher: Amt Lützow 294 und Nollendorf 1767 — Postscheck: Berlin 18124 — Zu beziehen durch die Post.

Die Deutsch-Evangelische Korrespondenz erscheint wöchentlich in einem Umfange von je 4 Seiten, zum Preise von vierteljährlich 100 Reichspfennigen. Sie ist, wie bisher, durch die Ortspostanstalt zu bestellen. — Für das Ausland erfolgt die portofreie Versendung durch den Verlag zum Preise von vierteljährlich 9,50 Reichsmark.

Der Verlag des Evangelischen Bundes, Berlin W. 10, Friedrich-Wilhelmstraße 2 a.

So spricht Dr. Martin Luther:

Alii dii exigunt a nobis opera nostra, non operantur in nobis, quemadmodum solet deus noster.

(Andere Götter verlangen von uns unsere Werke, wirken aber selber nicht in uns, wie unser Gott zu tun pflegt.)

Deuteronomion Mosi cum annotationibus 1525.
W. A. XIV. 609, 2 ff.

Zum Sonntag Okuli.

„Wer nicht mit mir ist, der ist wider mich". Luk. 11, 23.
„Wer nicht wider uns ist, der ist für uns". Luk. 9, 50.

D. E. K. Mit dialektischer Schärfe hat Jesus seinen Gegnern klar gemacht, daß über ihn und sein Werk nur ein doppeltes Urteil möglich sei: es ist entweder von Gott oder vom Teufel. Und indem er sie selbst zu der Erkenntnis zwingt, daß dämonische Kräfte bei und in ihm nicht wirksam sind, stellt er sie vor die letzte, klare Entscheidung: für mich oder gegen mich, denn „wer nicht mit mir ist, der ist gegen mich".

Klare Entscheidung, entschiedenes Christentum, das ist's, was Jesus auch in der Gegenwart und die Gegenwart selbst von uns verlangt. Es bedeutet nicht „mit ihm sein", wenn wir nur Namens-Christen, Taufschein-Christen, Kirchensteuer-Christen sind. Es ist kein Eintreten für ihn, wenn wir nur ein bedauerndes Schweigen haben gegenüber all den Angriffen und Anfeindungen, denen heute das Christentum und die Kirche von allen Seiten ausgesetzt sind. „Mit Jesus sein", das heißt ein Mensch der Tat, des Opfermutes und des freudigen Bekenntnis sein: „Wer nicht mit mir ist, der ist wider mich."

Seltsam, daß wenige Verse zuvor derselbe Herr das scheinbar widersprechende Wort sagt: „Wer nicht wider uns ist, der ist für uns". Und doch kein Widerspruch! Das ist ja das Wundervolle an Jesus, daß sich in ihm mit der klaren Entschiedenheit immer auch die weitherzigste Milde vereint. Wo er nur einen Funken glimmen sieht, da hofft er noch auf hell auflodernde Feuer. Freilich, für Jesu Weltherzigkeit ist niemals Schwäche. Wenn der Funke sich nicht anfachen läßt, wenn er nicht weiter wirkend ergreift, was sich ihm als entflammende Nahrung darbietet, wenn er sich ersticken läßt unter der Asche der Lauheit und Gleichgültigkeit, dann ist es aus mit ihm; dann ist über Menschen dieser Art, die höchstens Funken sind und niemals Flammen werden, das Gericht ausgesprochen: „Weil du aber lau bist und weder kalt noch warm, werde ich dich ausspeien aus meinem Munde."

So einen sich beide Worte und stellen dich und mich vor die größte Entscheidung unseres Lebens und Sterbens: Für ihn oder wider ihn!

Erklärung des Präsidiums des Evangelischen Bundes.

D. E. K. Gegen den Lutherfilm Hans Kysers hat eine lebhafte katholische Protestaktion eingesetzt, an der sich außer den Pfarrerkollegien in München, Nürnberg und Berlin auch die Fuldaer Bischofskonferenz durch eine Eingabe des Fürstbischofs Bertram an die preußische Staatsregierung beteiligt hat. Die bayerische Staatsregierung, insbesondere der bayerische Innenminister Stützel, fordert die vollständige Zurückziehung des Films. Soweit die Proteste sich gegen einzelne Szenen des Films richten,

muß immer wieder darauf hingewiesen werden, daß der Film auch nach der Ansicht katholischer Sachverständiger bei der Darstellung der doch nun einmal historisch und aktenmäßig feststehenden Zustände jener Zeit durchaus schonend verfährt. Aus der ganzen Art dieser Proteste, die übrigens zum Teil schon vor der Fertigstellung des Films einsetzten, und aus den sie begleitenden Kommentaren der römisch-katholischen Presse, ganz besonders aber aus der Begründung des katholischen Innenministers, er wisse nicht, ob er mit der Beanstandung einzelner Teile des Bildstreifens den Anschauungen der katholischen Kirche gerecht werde, geht indessen klar hervor, daß der Vorstoß sich nicht mehr gegen diese oder jene einzelne Szene, sondern gegen die Darstellung Luthers und der deutschen Reformation überhaupt richtet. Damit wird klar, daß es sich jetzt nicht mehr um den Lutherfilm allein handelt. Es geht jetzt vielmehr darum: Hat die evangelische Mehrheit in dem Deutschland von heute noch das Recht, sich an ihren besten und größten Erinnerungen zu freuen, sich zu ihnen zu bekennen, sie sich gegenwärtig und lebendig zu halten, oder hat sie es nicht? Die verletzende Tendenz liegt für die römisch-katholische Welt nicht so sehr im Film, als vielmehr in der Reformation, in Martin Luther und denen, die seines Geistes Kinder sind. Das unterdrückt werden soll, ist nicht so sehr der Film, als die Wahrheit der Geschichte, der Reformator, das Glaubenserlebnis der Reformation und der Protestantismus, dem die neueste Papstenzyklika „Mortalium animos" vom 6. Januar 1928 ausdrücklich und unmißverständlich die Existenzberechtigung als christliche Religionsgemeinschaft abspricht, und dessen Unterwerfung unter die römisch-päpstliche Lehre und Leitung sie verlangt.

Das ganze Verfahren läuft also darauf hinaus, daß in unserm zu ⅔ evangelischen Lande die deutsch-evangelische Geschichte nur mit römisch-katholischer Genehmigung dargestellt werden dürfe, und daß sich insbesondere auch eine protestantische Darstellung der Reformation der katholischen Auffassung anzupassen habe. Hiergegen legen wir allerschärfste Verwahrung ein. Dem deutschen Volke stehen Luther und die Reformation zu hoch, als daß es gewillt wäre, die Erneuerung ihres Andenkens auch durch die Gewalt des Films sich von unduldsamem katholischen Einspruch verbieten zu lassen. Es wäre ein unerhörte Unparteilichkeit, wenn etwa die zuständigen Behörden sich von jener Seite geäußerten Ansprüch gefügig zeigen würden, während gleichzeitig evangelische Belange, wie etwa bei der Abhaltung der oftentalich in vorwiegend evangelischen Städten abgehaltenen römisch-katholischen Fronleichnamsprozessionen nur zögernd und mangelhaft vertreten werden. Die durch das gesamte katholische Vorgehen verursachte, täglich stärker werdende Erregung im evangelischen Volksteil ist nur allzu berechtigt.

Unser Einspruch würde sich gleichzeitig auch gegen die vereinzelten, von römisch-katholischer Seite besonders gern angeführten protestantischen Stimmen richten, die im angeblichen Interesse des konfessionellen Friedens sich dafür einsetzen zu müssen glauben, daß der Film, da er doch nun einmal katholisches Ärgernis errege, zurückgezogen werde, wenn diese Stimmen nicht gar zu bedeutungslos wären. Im übrigen verrät diese Begründung einen höchst bedauerlichen Mangel an protestantischem Ehrgefühl und Sachkenntnis, der angesichts der neuesten Papstenzyklika völlig unverständlich ist.

Wir weisen die evangelische Bevölkerung Deutschlands mit allem Nachdruck auf die grundsätzliche Bedeutung hin, die infolge des katholischen Vorgehens die Angelegenheit des Lutherfilms

888

Responses to the Catholic propaganda against the 1927 film in the newspaper "Deutsch-Evangelische Korrespondenz" in February 1928.

nunmehr gewonnen hat. Welche Formen dieses Vorgehen annimmt, beweist der bereits hier und da von römisch-katholischer Seite verbreitete wirtschaftliche Boykott wegen der beabsichtigten Vorführung des Lutherfilms. Ein solcher Terror verlangt die allerschärfste Abwehr. Wir fordern nun umsomehr alle Evangelischen auf zu erneutem Treubekenntnis zu Luther und der deutschen Reformation und zu tatkräftiger Wahrung der deutsch-protestantischen Interessen, wo und wie immer sich Gelegenheit dazu bietet.

Berlin W 10, den 27. Februar 1928.

Das Präsidium des Evangelischen Bundes.

D. Scholz.   D. Lang.

Besfg.   Dr. Ebart.   Fahrenhorst.

„Wartburg"-Versicherungsverein a. G. des Evang. Bundes.

D. E. K. Der Versicherungsverein a. G. „Wartburg" des Evang. Bundes ist von den Aufsichtsbehörden genehmigt. Die Arbeit ist seitens der Haupt- und Zweigvereine aufgenommen, zahlreiche Versicherungen sind schon abgeschlossen. Die Organisation des Evang. Bundes gibt passende Möglichkeit, durch Vertrauensleute innerhalb des Zweigvereins für diesen rein evangelischen Versicherungsverein tatkräftig zu werben.

Gegen die römische Siedlungspolitik in der Grenzmark.

D. E. K. Es geht uns folgende Entschließung zu: „Die Grenzmarksiedlung in Berlin — Leiter Dr. Kurig, Schwiegersohn des Zentrumsführers und Reichskanzlers Dr. Marx — beabsichtigt, evangelische Güter in rein evangelischer Umgebung, z. B. Domslaff im Krs. Schlochau und Tschartsberge im Krs. Dt. Krone — teilweise oder sogar gänzlich mit katholischen Siedlern zu besetzen. Das widerspricht

1. der Bestimmung in § 25 b des Reichssiedlungsgesetzes vom 11. 8. 19 und 7. 6. 23, wonach „bei der Ansetzung nachbarlicher Zusammenhang mit einer Bevölkerung gleichartigen religiösen Bekenntnisses gewahrt werden" soll.

2. den elementarsten Forderungen vernünftiger und sparsamer Finanzwirtschaft, denn bei einer gemischten Besiedlung, wie z. B. in Domslaff vorgesehen ist (21 evang., 22 kath. Stellen), müssen natürlich für die neu entstehenden Gemeinden von je 120—160 Seelen doppelte Schulen und Kapellen errichtet und unterhalten werden;

3. dem für unsere Zeit und unsere Provinz so besonders wichtigen Gebot der Wahrung des konfessionellen Friedens. So wenig wir evangelischen Siedlungen in katholischer Umgebung verlangen, so sehr müssen wir mit allem Nachdruck fordern, daß unsere rein evangelischen Gebiete nicht durch katholische Einbruchstellen zerrissen werden.

Da die bei der Grenzmarksiedlung in Berlin — die übrigens mit staatlichen Mitteln arbeitet — in dieser Angelegenheit unternommenen Schritte erfolglos geblieben sind, erheben wir noch einmal in letzter allerschärfster Stunde Einspruch gegen die durch ihre Maßnahmen drohende Störung des konfessionellen Friedens in unserer Provinz.

Dt. Krone, den 23. Februar 1928.

Der Zweigverein Dt. Krone des Evangelischen Bundes."

Das Urdatum des Evangelischen Bundes.

D. E. K. Daß die in Erfurt 1886 erfolgte Gründung des Evangelischen Bundes zur Wahrung der deutsch-protestantischen Interessen, die Frucht einer Besprechung war, die Anfang 1886 in Rom zwischen Professor Benrath, Professor Beyschlag und Botschaftsprediger Roennecke stattfand, war bekannt. Nicht aber stand der Tag dieser Besprechung fest, der als das Urdatum des Evangelischen Bundes anzusehen wäre. Dem Pfarrer Roennecke an der Bartholomäuskirche in Halle a. S. ist es jetzt gelungen, auch den genauen Termin dieser Aussprache ausfindig zu machen. Nach dem Tagebuche seines Vaters, des Botschaftspredigers Karl Roennecke, vom Jahre 1886 fand diese folgenschwere Besprechung zwischen den Genannten am Abend des 12. April 1886, einem Montage, statt.

Burg Normannstein für die Allgemeinheit gerettet.

D. E. K. Die oberhalb der Stadt Treffurt malerisch an der Werra gelegene Burg Normannstein, die in Folge einseitiger Belegung durch die römische Jugendorganisation Neudeutschland,

die bekanntlich unter jesuitischer Leitung steht und eine Pflanzstätte des Ordensgeistes auf den höhern Schulen ist, der Allgemeinheit verloren zu gehen drohte, ist — laut „Leipziger Neuesten Nachrichten" vom 17. Februar 1928 — von der Stadt Treffurt zur öffentlichen Bewirtschaftung auf 30 Jahre gepachtet worden. Die Stadt wird demnächst einen neuen Burgwart einsetzen und dafür Sorge tragen, daß die Burg wieder allen Wanderern und Besuchern in allen ihren Teilen zugänglich ist.

Römischer Boykott der höheren Schulen Dresdens.

D. E. K. Wie planmäßig und energisch man auf katholischer Seite dahin arbeitet, auch das höhere Schulwesen konfessionell umzugestalten, beweist u. a. ein Anschlag im Vorraum der katholischen Hofkirche zu Dresden, in dem katholische Eltern, die ihre Kinder auf eine höhere Schule zu geben gedenken, nachdrücklich darauf hingewiesen werden, daß für sie das Benno-Gymnasium in Dresden die einzig in Betracht kommende Anstalt sei. Mit diesem Boykott gegen alle übrigen Dresdener höheren Lehranstalten ist zugleich das Benno-Gymnasium als die katholische höhere Lehranstalt der Zukunft gekennzeichnet.

Die Hetze gegen den Lutherfilm.

D. E. K. Angesichts des tiefen Eindrucks, den der neue Lutherfilm bei denen unwillkürlich hinterläßt, die ihn wirklich gesehen haben, selbst wenn sie der Filmkunst gegenüber grundsätzlich kritisch eingestellt sind, angesichts weiter der außergewöhnlich günstigen Presse, die dieses Spiel von der deutschen Reformation so ziemlich auf der ganzen Linie bis weit in die Linke hinein gefunden hat, geht die Hetze in der römisch-katholischen Welt gegen das Unternehmen mit verstärkter Kraft weiter. Die römischen Blätter schweigen geflissentlich die günstige Aufnahme tot und fälschen sie — einzelne kritische Sätze, die sich in jeder Besprechung zu finden pflegen, aus dem Zusammenhang reißend und sie für das Ganze ausgebend — in das Gegenteil um. Der Vorsitzende der Fuldaer Bischofskonferenz, Kardinal Bertram, hat, ohne den Film selber zu kennen — bei den zuständigen Stellen Protest erhoben unter Berufung auf einen evangelischen Außenseiter in Nürnberg und einen evangelisch nennenden notorischen Psychopathen, der fälschlich als „evangelischer Theologe" ins Treffen geführt wird. Diese Kronzeugen beweisen übrigens, wenigstens im Falle des Nürnberger Pfarrers, schlagend, wie man durch Kritiksucht und nichtgenügende Selbstdisziplin sich wider Willen zu einem Schädiger der evangelischen Sache werden kann. Ebenfalls ohne den Film gesehen zu haben, hat das Zentralkomitee der Münchner Katholiken am 11. Januar gegen eine „etwaige Vorführung" Einspruch erhoben. Die Polizeidirektion München hat — rechtlich offenbar ganz unzulässig — den von der Zensurstelle genehmigten Bildstreifen verboten und schließlich hat das Innenministerium im Konkordatsstaate Schritte getan mit dem Ziel, den Lutherfilm zu unterdrücken.

Angesichts dieser von der Gegenreformation vorgetriebenen Phalanx muß festgestellt werden: Es geht jetzt nicht mehr um den Lutherfilm! Den kann man in der Auseinandersetzung ganz bei Seite lassen. Es geht jetzt darum: Hat die evangelische Mehrheit in dem Deutschlands von heute noch das Recht, sich an ihren besten und größten Erinnerungen zu freuen, sich zu ihnen zu bekennen, sie sich gegenwärtig und lebendig zu halten, oder hat sie es nicht. Darüber besteht kein Zweifel: Die verletzende Tendenz für die römische Welt liegt nicht im Film, sondern in der Reformation, in Martin Luther und den Söhnen seines Geistes selber. Woran man sich stößt, ist nicht, was der Film darstellt, und wie er es tut, das Fatale für das römische Gemüt liegt darin, daß diese zahm und schonend gezeigten Dinge wahr sind. Was verschwinden soll ist nicht so sehr der Film als die Wahrheit der Geschichte, der Reformator, das Geisteserlebnis der Reformation und die Protestanten, die Exultata Mortalium animos ausdrücklich und unmißverständlich auffordert, römisch-katholisch zu werden.

Der „Vorwärts" steht bestimmt nicht im Verdacht „evangelischbündlerisch" zu sein, und doch schreibt er am 21. Februar 1928 und hat damit:

„In katholischen Kreisen verstärkt sich die Tendenz, nichtkatholische Meinungen und Werturteile als Staatsverbrechen anzusehen. Die

Demokratie gibt der katholischen Kirche Freiheit, für ihre Anschauungen zu werben und zu kämpfen — sie gibt aber auch ihren Gegnern die gleiche Freiheit.

Es ist Mode geworden in katholischen Kreisen, gegen antikatholische Meinungen nach Zensur und Staatsgewalt zu rufen. Hohe katholische Geistliche haben gegen die Aufführung des Luther-Films von Hans Meyer in Berlin protestiert, sie fordern von der preußischen Staatsregierung Widerruf der Genehmigung des Films. Also Zensur. Es gibt immer noch viel zu viel Zensur in Deutschland (manchmal auch nicht.). Mißbrauch der Zensur im Dienste einer religiösen Anschauung — das wäre sehr undemokratisch, mittelalterlich und sehr unklug."

Hoffentlich begreift das evangelische Volk, daß es hier um mehr geht als um einen Film, nämlich um ein Prinzip, um das Recht der Protestanten, in Deutschland auch noch da zu sein! Und hoffentlich begreift der Protestantismus auch das andere, daß das Bild der römischen Welt in dieser Sache doch ein recht klägliches ist. Wie unsicher muß eine Kirche sich fühlen, ein wie schlechtes Gewissen muß sie haben, wenn ihre Kardinäle, Bischöfe und Erzpriester nach der Staatsgewalt schreien, weil sie — Angst haben nicht nur vor dem Qnos ego! des lebendigen Reformators und Gottesboten, sondern schon vor seinem blassen Schattenbilde, das doketisch über die Leinwand wandelt!

Warum der einfache Katholik gegen den neuen Lutherfilm ist.

D. E. K. Die berühmte römische Volksseele kocht. Sie wirft beträchtliche Blasen. Der Versuch, Martin Luther im Lichtbild heranzubringen an den Menschen der Gegenwart, dünkt ihr unerträglich. Unanständigkeit, Kitsch, alles mag hingehen, aber Martin Luther? Nein! Was hat der „einfache Mann aus dem Volke", aus dem katholischen natürlich, gegen die Sache? Die „Märkische Volkszeitung" vom 26. Februar 1928 gibt darauf die Antwort, indem sie dem genannten „einfachen Manne" das Wort erteilt. Dieser spricht also: „Luther-Film! Wer kennt nicht die Reklame! Luther ist doch in der Gelehrtenwelt längst erledigt! Seinen Glauben kann doch kein denkender Mensch verdauen, sein Glaube ist doch viel schwerer als der katholische. Es ist hier nicht der Platz, darauf näher einzugehen. Gibt es wohl heute noch einen Protestanten, der das glaubt, was Luther lehrte! Und doch muß es ein Luther-Film sein! Sie können es nicht lassen! Sie müssen diejenigen von sich stoßen, die allein noch an Christus festhalten, festhalten auf's eben und Tod! Die Welt ist verdreht!" Die Anima candida (die reine Seele) des „einfachen Mannes aus dem Volke" ist bei weitem ehrlicher, als die Eingaben der Hochmögenden seiner Kirche. Er sagt es schlicht, was sie verstecken, was mir nicht paßt, ist: Martin Luther, ist: der Protestantismus! Noch ein zweites aber lehren diese so rührend törichten Zeilen, die die „Märkische Volkszeitung" der Ehre der Öffentlichkeit für wert hielt: Es führt kein Weg von Rom nach Wittenberg, nachdem es in jahrhundertlangem Mühen die ewige Kirche gelang, zwischen beiden zu befestigen das unergründlich tiefe Meer der Ignoranz!

Verletzung des religiösen Empfindens durch Bildstreifen?

D. E. K. Die „Märkische Volkszeitung" vom 8. Februar 1928 bringt einen Artikel aus der Praxis der Film-Oberprüfstelle, geschrieben von dem natürlich römisch-katholischen Leiter derselben. Der Artikel beschäftigt sich mit der „Verletzung des religiösen" d. h. natürlich römischen „Empfindens" durch Bildstreifen in Ausführungen, die für jeden völlig unbegreiflich sind, bei dem sich gesundes, religiöses Empfinden noch nicht in religiöse Pimpelei aufgelöst hat. Nachdem darauf aufmerksam gemacht worden ist, daß auch der Papst schon Gegenstand der Darstellung auf einer Bildstreifenreklame war (bei dem römischen Film: „Aus dem Dunkel der Katakomben zu den Wundern des Vatikans"), wird voller Beziehigung festgestellt, daß es einen sonst einwandfreien Darstellung die Oberprüfstelle die Verwendung des Plakates mit folgender Begründung verboten hat: „In Ausübung der der Prüfstellen nach dem Lichtspielgesetz obliegenden Wirkungsprüfung kann bei der Prüfung der Bildstreifenreklame an der Tatsache nicht vorbeigegangen werden, daß es sich gemäß § 5 Abs. 2 dieses Gesetzes um eine Reklame an den Geschäftsräumen und öffentlichen Anschlagstellen" handelt. Das geltende Lichtspielgesetz bietet

keine Handhabe, die Art der Verwendung von Reklamebildern vorzuschreiben oder einzuschränken. Der Sachverständige hat bekundet, daß es für einen Katholiken unerträglich sei, wenn das Bild des lebenden Papstes als Reklame benutzt und etwa auf einer Litfaßsäule neben der Darstellung einer Tänzerin oder neben der Ankündigung einer Revue angebracht werde. Unter diesen Umständen hat die Oberprüfstelle das Vorliegen des Verbotsgrundes der Verletzung des religiösen Empfindens, trotz der an sich einwandfreien Darstellung des Papstes, bejaht." (Urteil vom 31. Oktober 1925.)" Wie gesagt, man begreift es nicht. Der Herr Christus darf in eigener Person als Reklame — leider — auf die Litfaßsäulen geklebt werden. Hundertfach hat man's zu sehen bekommen. Da ging er neben „der Darstellung einer Tänzerin und neben der Ankündigung einer Revue." Daran hat sich der römische Sachverständige nicht gestoßen und das eigenartig konstruierte religiöse Empfinden der Katholiken fand es nicht unerträglich. Aber: Der glorreich regierende lebende Papst! Da ist die Sache ganz anders. Zwar heißt es Matthäus 10: „Der Jünger ist nicht über seinen Meister, noch der Knecht über den Herrn. Es ist dem Jünger genug, daß er sei wie sein Meister und der Knecht wie sein Herr." Nach „authentischer Auslegung" und dem bewußten religiösen Gefühlspimpelei, sowie obigem Urteil scheint die Sache nicht zu stimmen. Da ist der servus servorum dei und vicarius (Stellvertreter) Christi seinem Herrn offenbar ganz gewaltig über.

„Wenn du katholisch gewesen wärest . . ."

D. E. K. Im Amtsblatt Nr. 32 des badischen Ministeriums des Kultus und Unterrichts am 3. Dezember 1927 werden die Namen derjenigen bekannt gegeben, die die Prüfung als Zeichenlehrer bestanden haben. Neun gingen in die Prüfung, sechs bestanden. Unter den Letzteren erregte es einiges Befremden, daß die, welche als künstlerisch besonders veranlagt galten und auch von den Professoren für tüchtige Schüler gehalten wurden, von dem Herrn Vertreter des Ministeriums als nicht bestanden erklärt wurden. Es sind dies die drei einzigen Evangelischen. Eine Äußerung über den Eindruck dieses Prüfungsergebnisses aus den Reihen der bestandenen Kandidaten wirft ein besonderes Licht: „Wenn du katholisch gewesen wärest, hättest du auch die Prüfung bestanden."

Minister „Becker über das Konkordat und andere römische Lieblingswünsche.

D. E. K. Der preußische Kultusminister Dr. Becker, bekannt durch den Eifer, mit dem er sich die Wahrung einseitig römisch-katholischer Interessen angelegen sein läßt, hat bei der Beratung des Kultusetats im Hauptausschuß des preußischen Landtages wieder Ausführungen gemacht, die ganz in der bei ihm gewohnten Linie liegen. Sehr bezeichnenderweise hielt er eine besondere katholische Akademie für katholische Lehrerinnen — das Zentrum will sich nicht dazu verstehen, daß, wie es auf evangelischer Seite üblich ist, Lehrer und Lehrerinnen an derselben Akademie ausgebildet werden — für wünschenswert. Über die Verhandlungen mit der Kurie erklärte der Minister nach der „Täglichen Rundschau" vom 21. Februar 1928, daß diese Verhandlungen aus dem Stand der Vorbesprechungen bisher nicht herausgekommen seien. Es hätten nur bisher solche Vorbesprechungen stattgefunden, aber das Staatsministerium sei mit der Angelegenheit bisher nicht befaßt worden. Bei dem gegenwärtigen Stande der Vorbesprechungen werde die Angelegenheit auch den Landtag in absehbarer Zeit nicht beschäftigen. Diese Erklärung des Ministers steht in recht merkwürdigem Widerspruch zu der Erklärung der Fuldaer Bischofskonferenz vom 10. August 1927 zur Konkordatsfrage, die aus undurchsichtigen Gründen in der gesamten Zentrumspresse Weihnachten 1927 noch einmal der Öffentlichkeit als das Neueste vom Neuen aufgetischt wurde. In dieser Erklärung nämlich sprechen die Bischöfe ganz unmißverständlich von „Verhandlungen, die zwischen dem Vertreter des päpstlichen Stuhles und der Staatsregierung über Neuordnung der katholischen Kirche in Preußen eingeleitet sind." Am Ende der Erklärung wird noch einmal von der „Natur und Notwendigkeit des schwebenden Verhandlungen" gesprochen. Darnach scheinen in den beiden Lagern verschiedene Auffassungen schon über die Natur der gepflogenen Verhandlungen zu herrschen, wenn

film.[111] However, acceptance of the film—especially by viewers who were well-disposed towards it—was not usually based on the cogency and coherence with which the historically verified facts were presented, but rather the extent to which viewers encountered their own projections of a heroically transfigured Luther. It was not, as critic Wolfgang Loeff contended, that even "the most ahistorical [...] even the most un-Lutheran [...]" had "a couple of firmly established, inalterably clear fundamentals [archetypes] of the way Luther and the quintessence of the Reformation were perceived."[112] What mattered was how individuals' personal variants of those basic perceptions shaped response behaviour. Rolf Brandt, for one, wrote enthusiastically about the way the leading role was interpreted: "Klöpfer, who plays Luther, has a very large share in the success. It is as if he were one with the character, so that it is no longer a role but rather a part of his humanity: Not a single histrionic gesture, always an undertone of suffering by a person who is basically cheerful and robust, who knows the demons of the soul. Always farewell and always victory."[113] H. Zappe was another who confused the planes on which the actor and the part he played operated: "Eugen Klöpfer as Luther has found the monumental line. He was a champion, patiently bearing a conflict of conscience."[114] Fritz Olimsky, on the other hand, did not find the reformer portrayed as sufficiently strong-willed and heroically heightened.[115] Yet another Berlin critic, by contrast, found that was exactly what had been achieved: "Luther is just the symbol, living expression of that movement (the Reformation), called upon from a destiny laden with sorrows to be the driving force and the leader guiding it to its goal. This birth of folk, time and space, which defines the essence and necessary importance of all great men in history, has been perfectly conveyed in visual terms by director Hans Kyser. The experience he gained in collaborating with Murnau on the Faust film is much in evidence [...]."[116]

Other critics understood the message only as related to the current political situation, as it is summed up in the title "Luther and our Times: On Screening the Luther Film" ("Luther und unsere Zeit. Zur Aufführung des Lutherfilms"): "Luther secured the national individuality for the Germans. He secured for all mankind the right of personal intellectual freedom and he also gave each individual his intellectual property in freeing him from the herd. [...] His word was deed. He secured German liberty for us. Let us ensure that we never lose it again. And even were the world full of devils!"[117] This last quote clearly shows that Döhring's sermon had been understood even though there were certainly also Protestants who did not agree with the nationalist interpretation of Lutheran teachings.[118] In 1930, Döhring, for his part, defended his own specifically Protestant approach to nationalism against being appropriated by the thinking promulgated by Hitler's party.[119] Essentially, this meant that Döhring and the National Socialists were using the same vocabulary but advocating two different causes. A flyer issued by the Evangelisch-Sozialen Preßverband in the province of Saxony begins as follows: "[The] Luther Film. The struggle for freedom engaged in by the German conscience. We all call today for a great leader who will put an end to German suffering. We do not yet know whether he will come but we do know that in the past outstanding figures were given to our people, from whose strength of soul and courage of their convictions we are still drawing vital substance. A leader of that kind was our Central-German compatriot, D. Martin Luther. A film has set itself the task of showing what he was like [...] At the end he stands alive before us. Luther is not dead; his spirit lives on in us."[120] In the line of reasoning adopted by the film, the term "conscience" is of pivotal importance, albeit in a nationalistically biased way, when Hutten and Sickingen staunchly pronounce: "So there is something that is stronger than Rome and all popes. The German conscience".[121] It is only logical, therefore, that the following act, which promises that this "resistance movement" will come to fruition, should bear the title "The Way of Conscience" ("Der Weg des Gewissens"). In this, Karl Holl's interpretation of Luther's idea of religion and God as a "religion of conscience" is still visible, but it is also clear that it had been corrupted by nationalism.

The commotion stirred up by the film and probably also the failure to pay back money lent to the producers, meant that it was long impossible to arouse any enthusiasm for a new Luther film project. Hence, a press release on a new Luther film series in 1931 was greeted with a great deal of scepticism.[122] Nor was the plan ever realized.

3. The Americanization of Luther in Film

3.1. Lutheranism in the United States

Lutheran spirituality has been part of American mindset since the 1620's when Scandinavian, Dutch and German Lutherans first settled along the Hudson River.[123] German communities were especially influential in the 18th century.[124] Lutherans have never been religious extremists and always respected the government according to Luther's doctrine of the two reigns, in brief, that God rules the world on the one hand through secular as well as ecclesiastical government by law and order and on the other hand through grace and the gospel. Lutherans thus integrated very quickly into the American society. Nevertheless, they were very often ignored as contributors for the formation of the American mentality. In a recent study about Protestantism in America, they don't even appear.[125] The process of the historization of Luther's image in the United States was also not systematically investigated unto the late 20th century. Hartmut Lehmann's "Martin Luther in the American Imagination", published in 1988, was the first monograph that called attention to the "Public view of Luther"[126] in the United

States. Even Lehmann did not include the medium of film, because he limited his studies "from the era of American independence to the First World War"[127]. He showed that in the Puritan tradition of the early 17th century, the Reformation was the starting point for the history of salvation and Luther played the role of "the man who pulled down the Pope" in the words of the contemporary commentator John Norton.[128] In the 18th century, Luther was seen as an ascetic reformer, for example by Benjamin Franklin.[129] Others like George Washington or Alexander Hamilton simply did not mention him,[130] because the question of religious liberty was a political one, to be solved by the separation of state and church in the constitution. According to Lehmann, the situation at the end of the 18th century was as follows: "The great political decisions concerning the state of religion in America in the era of the Revolution were taken without historical reference to the Reformation."[131] Unitarianism and a growing knowledge and intense discussion of Luther's works in the 19th century changed his image. A turning point was the commemoration of Luther's four hundredth birthday in 1883. It was indeed the first time that it was celebrated in America. In 1783 almost no one noticed a "Luther-year", but in 1883 Luther "became American",[132] he was stylized as "the humble miner's son, who was born on St. Martin's eve, and who became the leader of one of the most important movements in human history".[133] Robert C. Winthrop, at that time President of the Massachusetts Historical Society, even described Luther as an "instrument of God".[134]

In the 20th century, Luther was still seen as a hero. However, even the Lutherans had problems dealing with the supposedly 'medieval', in the sense of irrational, character of the Reformer.[135] In 1917, the fact that he was a German became an obstacle for veneration. Furthermore, that year also saw the publication of Klara Hofer's *Bruder Martinus: Ein Buch vom deutschen Gewissen* in Stuttgart and Berlin by Cotta'sche Buchhandlung, which also held the copyrights for the United States. The book, which addresses Luther's history to 1517, is full of racist and chauvinistic elements expressed in an elliptical and awkward language that is nearly incomprehensible to Germans.[136] It is very likely that this publication encouraged American animosities. The quite moderate biography *Wittenbergisch Nachtigall* by Wilhelm Kotzde, published in the same year also in Stuttgart by F.J. Steinkopf, was not written for an American readership. Of course, the increasing 'national Protestantism' in Germany did not help to make Luther more popular in America. So it is not surprising that the title *Luther: Ein Film der deutschen Reformation* (1927) was changed in America into *Freedom: An Epic of Reformation*. Unfortunately, there are not many sources that record the response to this film in America.

There was apparently no move to make an American Luther film prior to the 1950s. In the 1950s, the United States were in the throes of a "religious revival".[137] Even President Eisenhower stated in 1952 that government made

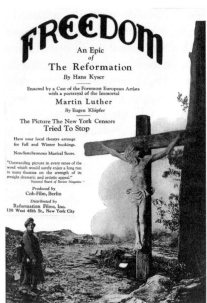

Left: Stills from the 1927 film in Filmkurier No. 810 showing the index of the actors and the scene of Luther's decision to become a monk. Right: Advert for the 1927 film renamed as "Freedom" in North America.

no sense unless it was grounded in religious faith of some denomination.[138] Nevertheless, days of Protestant predominance by number and influence in American society were over. By 1953 the percentage of Protestants in the total population was 35.1, of Catholics 19.8[139]: In 1952, they numbered 53,000,000 Americans. The Lutherans were the third largest group with 6,500,000 members after Baptists (17,000,000) and Methodists (12,000,000).[140]

Many of the immigrants during the Second World War were Jews and Catholics, so Protestants felt that they had to define their own position. It is not surprising that in 1950 Lutherans in the United States began discussing the possibility of producing a film about the founder of their church. They wanted to tell the story of his challenge to the Church establishment partly as a way to combat the subtle defamation of him (and other reformers of his day) on the part of specific religious groups. As a sector of Protestant denominations represented in the United States during the 1950s, Lutheran groups also wanted to acknowledge a new appreciation for the work of their Church.

At the time the first American Luther film was prepared, Jaroslav Pelikans edition of the translation of Luther's works in English was about to be published; it appeared in 55 volumes from 1955 to 1971. That was perhaps the most important step for the academic appropriation of Luther's theological heritage in America, and it fostered a greater inclination toward objectivity in the 1953 Luther film in which production Pelikan was involved as a consultant. Other fundamental texts were also published in these years: in autumn 1952, the National Council released the "Revised Standard Version" of the Bible, of which the first edition was sold out immediately.[141] This was the era of a wide-ranging attempt at 'moral rearmament' in the media launched by the Lutheran Church. In 1951 the United Lutheran Churches are said to have commissioned a film that would be entitled *Like a Mighty Army* (a quotation from the 19th-century hymn *Onward Christian Soldiers*, sung both in 1941 on the battleship HMS Prince of Wales when the Atlantic Charter was drawn up and at Dwight D. Eisenhower's funeral). The hymn was not only martial, but also associated with anti-establishment protest and civil disobedience. The film was to be produced by Cathedral Films and would have depicted Lutheran life in a Midwestern town. In addition, the Protestant film commission planned thirty more films for the following two years: five on democracy, seven on spiritual health and the remainder on missionary activity, international relations, Christian education, Christian family life and the Bible.[142] The Luther film made an unmistakable ecclesiastical-historical point in the Marian year 1953/54, inaugurated by Pope Pius XII in preparation for celebrating the centenary of Pope Pius IX's definition of the dogma of Immaculate Conception in 1854.

3.2. The Making of the 1953 Film

The production history reveals a lot about the interest groups who wanted to create a new cinematographic image of the first protestant. Robert Samuel Fryer's 1964 master's thesis contains a lot about its facts[143], but his focus was on the film itself, namely its aesthetic values. Fryer was not interested in contextualizing the specifically American image of Luther, partly because he considered *Martin Luther* to be a prime example of the semi-documentary film[144] and thus to be highly objective. This is an interpretation I do not share; for many reasons it is a conventional movie with a happy ending. The narrative elements dominate and there is no space for a specialist discussion of Luther's theology or his place in history. Fryer's statement also reveals a rather uncritical attitude about the use of original documents where his definition of "documentary" is concerned.[145] Moreover, the scene he cites as an example of the semi-documentary style, the meeting of Pope Leo X and Archbishop Albrecht of Mainz, is complete fiction. This encounter never took place, although there is evidence of the discussion between the representatives of the Pope and the Archbishop about the fine the Archbishop should pay for his rampant accumulation of offices (simony). The director Irving Pichel was quite aware that he was caught up in the dilemma of having to choose between dramatizing biography and staying as close as possible to the historical sources.[146] According to Pichel, the solution to this problem "can be approached only on the level of the imagination, informed by documentation and brought to intense vividness by the desire to communicate with a contemporary audience".[147] Consequently for him documentation could only be the basis for a film, but not its content.

Fryer's research (confirmed by records in the ELCA) indicates that in 1950, the Lutheran Churches of North America (Augustana Lutheran Church, the Evangelical Lutheran Church, Lutheran Church-Missouri Synod, the United Lutheran Church in America), the National Lutheran Council and the Lutheran Church of Canada started planning a film biography of Martin Luther.[148] The aim was to create an educational film for a mainly Lutheran audience.[149] The six Lutheran bodies elected Paul C. Empie of the Lutheran Council as chairman of the Lutheran Film Production.

The script was written by a committee of scholars; among them were Jaroslav Pelikan, Theodore G. Tappert, Allan Sloane and Lothar Wolff.

By then the earlier German Luther films of the 1920s that had been shown in the US quite successfully under the titles *Martin Luther: His Life and Time* and *Freedom: An Epic of Reformation*[150] seemed to have been forgotten. No reference to them can be found in the surviving sources of the 1952 production.

The script was sent to a group of readers with a questionnaire on March 24, 1952.[151] In the questionnaire, Henry Endress explained that the viewer should learn about the biography of Luther in its historical context and realize the relevance of the reformer's work for his own life. Because it would be limited to a Lutheran audience, the film was supposed to be released in 16mm. The format excluded the distribution by commercial film rental services.

3.2.1. Fund Raising and Administrative History

The National Lutheran Council (NLC) took the lead in coordinating efforts to produce the film and contributed $200,000 to the film's budget. The NLC approached American Lutheran churches and asked if they could provide supplemental funding. They proposed forming an incorporated production board comprising representation from organizations or churches that would be proportional to the amount of money that each group contributed to the film's production. Participating churches and organizations would also receive rental income from the film in proportion to their contributions to financing the film. In 1951 Lutheran Church Productions, Inc. (LCP) registered as a corporation comprising representatives from the Augustana Evangelical Lutheran Church, the Evangelical Lutheran Church, the National Lutheran Council, the American Lutheran Church, the United Lutheran Church in America, and the Lutheran Church—Missouri Synod. Dr. Paul Empie, Executive Director of the NLC, was chosen as its chair.

The film had a budget of $500,000, at that time the largest amount ever spent on a production funded by church organizations.[152] LCP realized that American dollars would buy more German "sperrmarks", marks that were for restricted use,[153] as opposed to marks in unrestricted circulation. To be able to exchange dollars for sperrmarks, it was necessary to establish a corporation in Germany, the Luther Film Gesellschaft m.b.H., through which the film could be financed with the restricted-use marks. After a series of legal maneuvers—required because "sperrmarks" could not be used on items marked for export restricted-use marks—, Luther Film Gesellschaft m.b.H. was able to produce the film and release it in both Germany and the United States.

As the film began to attract attention, LCP decided not to cede responsibilities for distribution to a commercial distributor and created its own distribution network instead. LCP established a sales department that created a press book for the film which complied with the standards of Protestant churches as applied to theater promotion. Church stewardship policies were followed in that there were no fund-raising campaigns. Only a few weeks after the publicity drive was launched, 1,200 cities had booked the film. LCP sent specially trained church workers to serve as liaisons between the church and the theaters and to help organize groups of moviegoers from churches and church organizations to see the film. LCP churches that had financed the film were given discounts of 25% on tickets. Congregations were given twice as many tickets as they had members in order to help promote the film. Even though the film was heavily promoted to Lutheran congregations, 30–50% of tickets were allocated to regular cinemagoers, a marketing practice known as "off the street sales".

3.2.2. Production

Producer Louis de Rochemont was chosen from an international field of candidates. LCP selected de Rochemont because he was familiar with shooting historical films on location and because it considered him to also have the ethical convictions necessary to make the film. He suggested the film to be shot in Germany in order to be as close as possible to the historic settings of the various events in Luther's life, and in some cases to use them. LCP hired Allan Sloane to draft the script. He and Lothar Wolff spent about eighteen months researching and writing the first draft. Even though the initial idea was to film a biography of Luther, the decision was made to limit the subject matter to the religious issues involved in Martin Luther's break with the church. LCP hired Irving Pichel to direct the film and Mark Lothar to compose the music.

The director Irving Pichel, a former professor of English at Stanford University and Wisconsin University, had been in the film business since 1930 and acted in over 40 films. In *Martin Luther* he played Chancellor Brueck, who read the Confessio Augustana.[154] For Pichel, "the theme of spiritual freedom was the most important"[155] aspect of the production. The making of *Martin Luther* was a crucial point in Pichel's directing career; after that film he made another religious movie, this time on the life of Christ. He died shortly after the completion of this second religious film. Nevertheless, the obituaries indicate that he was mainly noted for *Martin Luther*.[156]

Joseph C. Brun (1907, Paris–1998, Florida), who was responsible for the photography, earned an Oscar nomination for *Martin Luther*.[157]

3.2.3. The Quest for Authenticity

The fact that academics were collaborating on the production should guarantee that the script had a sound historical basis.[158] In March 1952, it was sent to an inner circle of readers with a questionnaire in order to find out if it would "result in a successful motion picture for the special audience", made up primarily of "non-Catholic Americans".[159] The participants appreciated mainly the "historical accuracy".[160] Some of the comments were: "It is a remarkable piece of semi-documentary reconstruction; even a good deal of the dialogue is based on historical documents, and (leaving aside that Luther's own rude personality has been somewhat varnished over, and that Erasmus has been made an Oxford man) it is a most careful and accurate account of Luther's life".[161] However, the same critic also noticed "increasing tedium". Only a few critics claimed that the political context was missing, for example "It will be noted that this film confines itself to the religious conflicts only. The political upheavals of 16th-Century Germany, of which the religious struggles were a part, are wholly neglected. So are many of the personal and family facts about Luther that influenced his psychology."[162]

Even the choice of black-and-white-photography was celebrated as "wonderfully 'in period' ".[163] The casting was also based, apart from the need for good acting and mastery of the English language, on the idea that actors had to resemble figures in the paintings and woodcuts of the day.[164] In an advertisement in the *New York Times* of August 23, 1953, the main characters are directly compared with the historic models; photographs of them are juxtaposed with historic woodcuts and paintings.[165] The aim is obviously to convince the audience of the "authenticity" of the cast. Such typecasting still predominates in the production of biopics: Thus, a director like Oliver Stone had to justify his choice of Anthony Hopkins for Richard Nixon.[166]

Nevertheless for *Martin Luther*, a "mid-Atlantic" English was supposed to satisfy both American and English audiences. Moreover, the source documents were translated into English.[167] Niall McGinnis, a "distinguished English actor"[168], was chosen for the leading role, because he was said to "look like Luther"[169]. A Swiss source reveals that he was not the first choice. In 1951, Alfred Flückinger mentioned that the Danish actor Ib Schønberg should play the part.[170] Annette Carell, an immigrant from Germany who had American citizenship, was cast in Germany at the Bavaria Film Studios for the part of Katharina von Bora. Apart from Aleander and Eck who were acted by Egon Strohm and Heinz Piper only the bit parts were played by Germans. This was also necessary in order to use the "Sperrmark"[171]. With principal actors cast and a revised script, filming began in August 1952.

There is no evidence of any discussion about seeking the permission to film on the other side of the 'Iron Curtain'. Only one critic—a former citizen of Wittenberg, who fled to England in 1937, questioned the wisdom of this omission and combined it with criticism of the idealized image of Luther: "I do not know whether the producers tried at all to get permission from the authorities of the Soviet zone to film in East Germany and were refused through fear of spies. One could imagine that the orthodox Marxist version of Luther's life would have been on the side of the revolutionary peasants against whom Luther wrote a merciless pamphlet which is not mentioned in the film."[172] Filming in Western Germany meant to the producer that filming locations were already as close as possible to the places where Luther had lived. Most parts were filmed in the monasteries at Eberbach and Maulbronn, hence the 95 Thesis were nailed onto a stage-door in the monastery of Eberbach; the Diet of Augsburg "took place" in Regensburg's Town Hall and other scenes were shot in the AFIFA studios in Wiesbaden. Wittenberg was reconstructed in the form of a model. The costumes came from the theater in Kassel or were "made in a simplified design"[173]. The historic Gutenberg printing press was filmed in the Gutenberg Museum in Mainz.[174]

As indicated above, the original idea was to make a 16mm-film to release to churches. However, when LCP saw the results of preliminary filming, it realized that Martin Luther was a film that would appeal to a wider audience. Consequently LCP decided to distribute it to cinemas as a 35mm black and white film with a running time of 1 hour 45 minutes.

Filming was finished on October 11, 1952[175] and production ended in January 1953, but LCP could not find a theater that would show the film. This reluctance was partly due to what was perceived as its controversial nature and subject matter. Finally, LCP rented the Lyceum Theater in Minneapolis, Minnesota, and premiered the film on May 4, 1953. After a successful four-week run at the Lyceum, LCP premiered the film in Houston, Texas, partly to see if it might appeal to a broader audience as well as Lutherans since Houston was not perceived as a center of Lutheranism. LCP also chose to show the film in the small town of Hickory, North Carolina, also to see if it might have broader commercial appeal outside major urban centers.

The British premiere of *Martin Luther* was on August 23, 1953 at the "Seventh International Festival of Music and Drama" in Edinburgh. It opened the film section of the festival, which comprised two hundred films from thirty countries.[176] On September 9 and 15, previews were screened in Chicago for clergymen of all denominations, and commercial screening began on September 25.[177] September 9 marked the official start in New York.[178]

Advert for "Martin Luther" (USA 1953) at Times Square in New York City.

3.3. Merchandizing

The iconography of the advertising is very revealing for Luther's image in the US: Unlike the adverts in 1926 for the film *Martin Luther: His Life and Time*, which featured Lucas Cranach's portrait of Luther and seemingly appeared only in Lutheran newspapers,[179] the 1950s advertising campaign focused on the actor playing the leading role. For example, on September 6, 1953, the *Los Angeles Times* ran a photo of Niall McGinnis with the caption "British actor Niall McGinnis is shown as Martin Luther in film on life of the 16th century monk ...".[180] The monk seemed more likely to attract larger audiences than professor Luther, especially in a largely Catholic city. The accompanying story follows this lead with these opening words: "The original Gutenberg press on which the first Bible was printed, was used in making 'Martin Luther'."[181] Needless to say, it was definitely not one of the presses on which the "Ninety-Five Thesis" were first printed. But it appears that some kind of relics were deemed necessary to make the film attractive to the American audience. Edwin Schallert's review in the *Los Angeles Times* finally concedes that the film deals with "the tempest of religious reform striking Europe at the beginning of the 16th century".[182]

After the first wave of enthusiastic reviews, there was enough text material to integrate into the advertising logo, which was based mainly on a still of Niall McGinnis portraying Luther. The actor's face was obviously considered to be more attractive, perhaps because it was better known than historic paintings of Martin Luther's face. The portrait of Niall McGinnis was first inserted into the letter "L" in "Luther"[183] like a modern adaptation of medieval manuscript illumination, and later put on top of the "L" like an inverted exclamation mark.[184] Sometimes the portrait was also inserted in a ring joining McGinnis' face to the Name "Luther".[185] Since advertising always uses mnemonic repetition for both immediacy and long-term recognition, only slight variations on these patterns occur in the newspapers.

Martin Luther had to compete for attention, not only in the advertising sections of the newspapers, but against other religious dramas, for example *The Robe*. In this film, a Roman soldier (Richard Burton) converts to Christianity after being in charge of the crucifixion of Christ.[186] *The Robe* was a strong rival in business: It was the first motion picture in CinemaScope and also fascinated its viewers with its colors. However, *Martin Luther* and *The Robe* shared the misfortune of inciting racial discrimination, as will be discussed below.

Martin Luther was translated and synchronized for the foreign market, a taxing procedure, especially where the Spanish version was concerned.[187] In these countries, Twentieth Century-Fox also distributed promotion material in Spanish. There the face of Niall McGinnis was also the dominant feature: it was framed by quotations of the film such as "No puedo … No quiero … retractarme", "Estoy en lo firme" and comments as "Una gran personalidad en un drama colosal" or "El hombre que alteró el mundo".[188]

TV commercials were also broadcast and special radio transcripts were intended to promote the film.[189] In 1958 a marketing plan for broadcasting the film was developed that contained lists of markets to be targeted by specialized, organizational and direct selling.[190]

As in 1923, the Evangelische Bildkammer LCP also distributed stills and information sheets of "ideas for speakers" which contained the most important facts on the production.[191] Later, Louis de Rochemont offered professionally crafted packages entitled "The Showman's Manual of Promotion for *Martin Luther*."[192]

Alternatively, "The All-Important Church Promotional Plan" was offered to anyone interested in showing the film. It contained a step by step explanation of how to organize the show, a contact check list, sample invitation cards, evaluation sheets, addresses for books, bookmarks and other materials.[193]

When a showing on television was scheduled, LFA distributed sheets with "Suggestions for Women's Groups (Adult and Older Youth)" containing 10

Cover of "The Showman's Manual of Promotion for 'Martin Luther'".

points for preparing a screening, which ranged from placing posters to discussing "the need of a more effective Protestant witness through radio and television". Viewing the film was to be a guided "group study experience" based on prepared questions. Remarkably, the questions lead from the history shown in the film to the situation of the actual ban on the film (see chapter 3.4.3): "Are the teachings as shown in this film Biblical? Is the film historically accurate? What distinctly Protestant beliefs are portrayed? [...] What great contributions did Martin Luther make to the Christian religion? What are the dangers today to freedom of religious expression? What can we in Chicago do to preserve freedom of religious expression?"[194] Unfortunately, the answers to those questions have not been preserved in the extant records.

3.4. Reviews and Reactions

3.4.1. Response in the US and Canada
No film of the early 1950s provoked such controversial reactions as *Martin Luther*: hero-worship on the one hand, passionate rejection on the other.

BUT THIS FILM HAD TO BE SHOWN

BECAUSE its religious truths are embraced by men all over the world. . . .

BECAUSE its challenge to fight for freedom is needed by today's half-free civilization. . . .

BECAUSE men must learn to stand fast in the liberty God gave them. . . .

BECAUSE its story of courage in the cause of truth and conscience can be a mighty bulwark for all free and honest men. . . .

BECAUSE men need inspiration to seek freedom of conscience and to find complete faith in God.

AND SO determined amateurs ignored the warnings of the "experts" and set out, not just to bring this vital film story to the people, but to make it the biggest public showing in motion picture history.

THIS IS HOW IT WAS DONE—

THE MINNEAPOLIS STORY OF THE "MARTIN LUTHER" PREMIERE

Propaganda material defending the 1953 film.

"It has been hailed, in America, as a great film. [...] This film deserves high marks for historical accuracy"[195] and "it could hardly be surpassed"[196] exemplify the enthusiastic responses. Fryer even judged it to be "the most extraordinary audience-appeal motion picture of the 1950's"[197]. Its success was really unexpected. During the first six months it played to audiences totalling more than 1.5 million in 170 screenings. A year later it had been seen by approximately 7 million people in the US and 3 million in Canada. Finally more than 20 million Americans went to the performances of *Martin Luther*, which had been distributed in twenty-seven foreign countries and translated into twelve foreign languages.[198]

Nevertheless or perhaps just because of its popularity, this film provoked about as much disapproval in 1950s America as the 1927 film had in Germany. It was especially criticized by Catholics, even though it was phrased "Separately Classified" on the September 1953 Legion of Decency List. The verdict was quite sedately phrased: "This picture offers a sympathetic and approving representation of the life and times of Martin Luther, the 16th century figure of religious controversy. It contains theological and historical references and interpretations which are unacceptable to Catholics".[199] The film was, however, condemned by the Catholic press on the whole as it is shown by the title of Lon Francis' article in *Our Sunday Visitor Press*: "The Martin Luther Movie, unhistorical, unbiblical, unfair"[200]. The *Philadelphia Catholic Standard and Times* of October 30, 1953 stated: "Practically every event recorded is a distortion of the truth". The main criticism was that the intention of the film was to argue against the Pope and the Roman Catholic faith. Indeed half the film is taken up with the question of the papal indulgences, but that issue was—and this is undisputed—what sparked off the Reformation and that fact had to be explained to the modern American audience. The reviewers even criticized the selection of Theses presented.[201] But the Theses cited, Thesis 36 ("Every Christian who feels true repentance for his sins has perfect forgiveness of both punishment and sin without the need for indulgence") and Thesis 62 ("The true treasure of the Church is the most sacred doctrine of the glory and grace of God") are very general and do not attack the Pope explicitly as so many other Theses do.

Some aspects of the discussion remind us of the German "Kulturkampf", the controversy that broke out again in 1927–28 when Kyser's Luther film was released. We should also bear in mind that *Luther: Ein Film der deutschen Reformation* was forbidden and frequently censored because the Catholic Church protested. In 1927 also Catholic involvement in the work of the High Church Ecumenical Federation in Germany was prohibited at the first Faith and Order Conference at Lausanne[202]; consequently, both Catholics and Protestants adopted a hard line in the interdenominational dialogue. Broadcasting *Martin Luther* on TV was at first forbidden in America because of the protests voiced by the Catholic Church. This will be covered in more detail below. The Second Vatican Council (1958–1959) was still far away and Luther was still the "archetypal heretic"[203]. Finally, the history professor Albert Hyma wrote a new history of reformation in order to indicate all the errors begotten by the film.[204]

Otherwise, the film *Martin Luther* met with critical and commercial success. Among the critical accolades it received, the National Board of Review named it as one of "The Year's Ten Best Films of 1953". The film also garnered two Academy Award nominations from the Academy of Motion Picture Arts and Sciences, for best art direction for a black and white film and for best black and white cinematography. Its commercial success was evident in the number of viewers, which topped the one million mark after the first six months. After running at cinema theaters, the film was distributed in 16 mm prints that were sold directly to private users.

3.4.2. Martin Luther against Racism?

"Church Cracks Ban" was the first newspaper headline to serve notice that Lutheran Pastors would boycott the national premiere in Washington if "members of colored races were barred from attending"[205]. This stance fostered the hope that it "may have helped crack the century-old 'color-bar' in Washington's amusement places."[206] As we know, the film premiered in New York, which didn't solve the problem at all, because there were many other cities that didn't admit "colored people" as well.[207] The film was finally shown in Washington on October 21, 1953 at the Dupont cinema, which "in 1947 pioneered in opening its doors to members of all races"[208] (this was reported without mentioning the scandal).[209] That the wish to attend a screening of a film on Luther could incite racial discrimination was a peculiarly American phenomenon at a time when "[n]one of the Negro theaters are yet equipped with the wide screen necessary to show the new religious films"[210]. In Louisville, people were still protesting in December that they were not allowed to see *Martin Luther*. Among the refused were also theologians for example Charles Johnson, a Liberian student at Louisville Presbyterian Theological seminary, and a major in the Army chaplain corps stationed at Ft. Knox and the College of the Scripture (a non-denominational seminary).[211] The upshot was that the three requests that African-Americans should be permitted to view the films *The Robe* and *Martin Luther* were turned down by the theaters managements on December 5: "The decision was based on a long-standing policy of racial segregation". The laconic explanation was that "under Kentucky law a theater has the right to refuse admittance to anyone and return their money."[212]

3.4.3. Ban on Luther Film

3.4.3.1. Quebec 1953

Shortly after the film was selected as one of the best films of 1953[213] and a series of approving articles had been written[214], the "Quebec Film Censorship Board" banned *Martin Luther* because "it would antagonize the people of this predominantly Roman Catholic province"[215].

Board chairman Alexis Gagnon "denied prejudice on the board's part" by refering to other previous decisions: "other films have been banned in Quebec because of objections from non-Catholics"[216], but he did not explain which scenes had provoked such a decision. The Protestant side reacted immediately;[217] not only Lutherans expressed disapproval, but "The Association of Civil Liberties" mounted also the "strongest possible protest"[218]. "The Canadian Church Press association", an organization to which various Protestant editors belonged, claimed that screening should at least be permitted in Protestant churches and schools in the Montreal area, because there were 400,000 persons of Protestant faith living there.[219] Finally, representatives of the Montreal District of the Presbyterian Church protested against the Quebec Provincial Governement's ban, but the answer was only a stereotypical repetition of the argument that showing the film in the predominantly Catholic province "would cause undue antagonistic sentiments".[220] The controversy that had been stirred up by the ban was only a prelude to the protest against showing the film on TV in 1956. It took nine years that the ban was lifted in Quebec.

Canadian premiere of "Martin Luther" (USA 1953).

In this conflict, the ban was castigated as a "dictatorial" act "in the tradition of Communist-dominated Countries"[221]. In the political atmosphere that spawned the almost hysterical persecution of communists under Joseph McCarthy, it was the most severe reproach that could have been voiced. The headline "Luther Biographer Admits He Was Red" only a few months later[222] must, therefore, have shocked American Lutherans even more than it did the rest of the world. There must have been a great relief on their part, when Allen E. Sloane confessed that he was only a Communist from March 1943 to July 1944.[223] To make this statement, he appeared voluntarily before a closed session of the House Un-American Activities Committee in January 1954. Presumably this was the best way for him to stay in the business of writing for radio and television.

3.4.3.2. Cancellation on WGN-TV 1956
Two days before the slated WGN-TV showing, the film was cancelled because the station did not want to be "a party to the development of any misunderstanding or ill will among persons of the Christian faith in the Chicago area".[224] The station denied that it had acted under pressure of the Catholic church, but it was clear that the ban had such a background, because a Catholic spokesman

confirmed "that the 1,800,000 Catholics in Chicago could not be blamed if they spoke up in protest against something which was an obvious insult to them".[225] Some did not understand why the story of Luther should be more offensive in this medium than in others.[226] Chicagoans seemed to be split into advocates and opponents of the ban[227]; it provoked the largest response in letters and telegrams in WGN-TV's history.[228] A committee of Protestant ministers and rabbis was immediately formed to protest against "de facto censorship" that "violates the principles of civil and religious liberty as defined in the First Amendment".[229] They also expressed their fears that this case would set a precedent for arbitrary censorship by private groups over the public media.[230] Other groups and individuals concurred, including Glenn L. Archer, executive director of "Protestants and Other Americans United for Separation of Church and State", who denounced this act as being un-American and sent letters to the "House Committee on Un-American Activities" and to the "Federal Communications Commission" (F.C.C.).[231]

Finally, in February 1957 the "Action Committee for Freedom of Religious Expression", organized in Chicago by representatives of the "Church Federation of Greater Chicago", the "Lutheran Council of Greater Chicago", the "Midwest Region of the National Association of Evangelicals" and forty other religious organizations, submitted a petition to the F.C.C. that urged government action against the ban. It was signed by 150,000 Chicagoans.[232] The petitioners also stressed that the ban clashed with America's mission as an ambassador of freedom in the world: "Freedom of religious expression is an unquestioned right; and this means that no man may prohibit another from expressing his own religious beliefs. The heritage of our nation is the freedom of man. It is the duty of all Americans, Catholic, Protestant and Jew, to guard their heritage and to exploit it to the maximum for the betterment of mankind in a troubled world". As a benevolent Catholic statement, the article "'Martin Luther' in Chicago", that appeared on February 15, 1957 in *Commonweal*, was attached. The author even blamed Catholic activism: "No matter how good their intentions, they have damaged the fabric of our democratic society; they have damaged the Catholic Church; and they have damaged relationships between Catholic and Protestant in this country." It is obvious that this campaign was only partly for freedom of expression. It also coincided with the tradition of anti-Catholic sentiment that had been widespread in America since the day the Mayflower landed in Massachusetts, a bias that was not just cultivated by Calvinists, contrary to what Hochgeschwender assumed.[233]

After another period of hostilities (including counterattacks against Jesuit licenses for TV[234]), in which only a few moderate voices could be heard,[235] the Committee abandoned the strategy of exerting pressure on WGN-TV[236] to show the film because "Community Builders", a Chicago civic organization, purchased the rights and two hours broadcasting time at another Chicago TV-station, WBKB, in March 1957.[237] So WGN-TV did not have to revoke the cancellation and the film was eventually shown by WBKB on April 23, 1957. After that vehement and polemical controversy on both sides, with comments going as far as to call the film a "hate provoking movie"[238], the advertisement sounds rather cynical: "Without any religious motive and only in the spirit of brotherly love, Community Builders presents *Martin Luther*.[239]

During the controversy that triggered an 'avalanche' of newspaper articles, the content of the film and its alleged "errors" or offending parts were hardly discussed at all.[240] Only a few statements deal with it, for example a "Point-by-Point Clarification" in the *Alamo Register*[241], an early discussion of the main criticisms by Robert Bainton, who emphasized that the film was authentic, fair and biblical[242], a statemenet by Robert Welch[243] and the book by A. Albert Hyma[244]. In order to better understand the agitation on both sides, it is useful to look at Welch's crucial points. Father Welch of the Diocese of Davenport, who was attached to the Catholic Student Center at Iowa State University, had already criticized the film in 1953. He repeated his polemic as well as his most important factual arguments in 1957: "We object because the film is unfair from the beginning to the end; that it not only mistreats history but does so with blatant cynicism; that it is designed to perpetuate known falsehoods which were blasted out of even the careless histories years ago. The falsifications and distortions do not touch merely the Church [...] too much has been added that is fictitious"[245]. His main criticism of the film concerns the way it handles the theology of indulgences: he emphasizes that the Church did not promise forgiveness by selling indulgences without remorse or confession; penitents had to be absolved of their sins "as a necessary condition for receiving the indulgence"[246]. That is true of most of the indulgences, but not for Tetzel's. The indulgences for the benefit of the construction of St. Peter did not need repentance and the trade in indulgences would not have been as successful as it was in general, if people had not believed more in the salutary powers of those letters than in confession and remorse. Apart from that, there was no biblical basis for indulgences. Welch further criticizes a crucial scene in the film, Luther's release from his monastic vows. Welch emphasizes correctly that Staupitz could never have released Luther from his vows because only the Pope had the right to do so, a right that could be delegated but was not in Luther's case. As Luther himself reported, Staupitz released him with the words "Absolvo te ab oboedientia mea et commendo te Domino Deo"[247]. Luther himself interpreted it as his exclusion from the Augustinian order: "me absolvit ab observantia et regula ordinis".[248] Of course, this interpretation was never confirmed by the Church. Another point of Welch's critism was that the translations of the Bible into German before Luther were not mentioned. Although this is true, but none of those translations was officially accepted and authorized for liturgy or even for the use of the laity, and preaching was always done in Latin. Welch also criticizes the way Leo X is portrayed ("his love of pleasure is overdone") and states that the response of the Apostolic see to Luther is not adequately presented in the movie. Both points are correct; the story is told from the Lutheran perspective. At the same time, many critics have complained that the narrative is already overloaded with historical facts, as has already been pointed out.

3.4.2. Response in Germany and Great Britain

Nevertheless, the film had a successful career. In June 1954, Twentieth-Century Fox announced that *Martin Luther* would be released in thirty-eight countries, including France, Italy, Spain, Brazil, Argentina, Israel and Japan.[249] It was not coincidental that Twentieth-Century Fox was interested in the distribution of the film in foreign countries: The company produced most of the biopics between 1927 and 1960, 63 films exactly (that was 22% of all biographical movies).[250]

A comparative analysis of viewer response in these countries is actually a desideratum that can't be fulfilled in this study, which is focused on the German and American reception. But it seems that the reactions to the film were nowhere as passionate and antagonistic as in America and Germany, even though it was banned more or less officially in some of the other countries.[251] However, it is remarkable that in India the government required some small cuts showing scenes of iconoclasm.

In 1954 the film premiered in Germany: on March 4 in Hanover and on March 5 in Nuremberg. Regional bishops Lilje (Hanover) and Meiser (Munich) had assumed the patronage, which turned the showing almost into an ecclesiastical event. Lilje explained in an unofficial letter that he saw the film as a means to portray the church as "Church of the Reformation" by appealing to "as broad a public as possible in a positive and effective way."[252] The Lutheran Bishops' Conference realized the film's potential for conflict and recommended that 'the scenes with the pope and the mendicant friar' should be toned down. Some actually expected the "storm" that later ensued.[253] The first assessments, however, tended to be lenient on both the clerical and non-clerical sides. They only deplored the lack of historical context for the events and the motives for supporting Luther as well as his opponents (and that these were unnconvincingly characterized). Katharina von Bora's marginalized role also displeased the clergy. Ultimately it was concluded that scholarship on Luther's life and work was more advanced than indicated by the film.[254]

"Vicarages have become the box office for worldly cinema. The catchword was disseminated: 'This film is our thing!' Even someone who otherwise never goes to a film must see *Martin Luther*!" recalled Günther Dehn as late as 1982. Commenting on the rumours never verified (that made the rounds while the film was on general release) that the Irish Catholic lead actor McGinnis converted to Protestantism while the film was being made, Dehn asked: "Should the step he took set a precedent?"[255] Ultimately, four million Germans saw *Martin Luther* in the first six months after it went on general release. By 1956, 60 million people around the world had seen it.[256] Nevertheless, no mass conversions took place. In Germany, however, *Martin Luther* sparked vehement reactions that are hard to understand today, since the Reformer was not represented as a demagogue in any way. "Luther's head was torn of a film poster in a big south-western German city."[257] In the German Democratic Republic's CDU journal *Union-Pressedienst*, the film was condemned as "horrifyingly irreligious" ("schauerlich irreligiös"), with Luther allegedly as embodiment of naivety. The criticism that the film was intended to instigate anti-Catholic sentiments was expressed in varying degrees of shrillness in the journal of the Association of Catholic Priests of Bavaria and the Palatinate *Klerusblatt*, in *St. Heinrichsblatt* (a Sunday paper for the Catholic family) and by the archiepiscopal Vicar-General's Office (Generalvikariat) in Cologne.[258] The mouthpiece of the Catholic Film Commission for Germany criticized the "outdated theological representation of Luther's image".[259] Finally, the Lutheran theologian Gerd Albrecht, in his doctoral dissertation *Film und Verkündigung* (published 1962), much of which was devoted to the critical reception of the Luther film, tried to show that theology had been falsified as a consequence of dramatization. Luther's Theses 36 and 62 had been selected, according to Albrecht, "not for their theological content but also as exemplifying anti-papist and anti-Roman polemic".[260] Ultimately Luther's christology came off badly in the process.[261] On the whole, Albrecht accused the film of "manipulating history/the story".[262] Even before the film premiere in Germany, an attempt had been made to have it shown only in narrow film stock—not in the format usual on general release to cinemas—in order to shield the Catholic public at large. In some locations, posters had to carry the additional notice "A Protestant film" ("Ein evangelischer Film"). Werner Hess, a Frankfurt pastor, defended the film at that time in his capacity as film agent (Filmbeauftragter) for the Protestant Church in Germany: "On the German side in particular there are fears that a film on *Martin Luther* by the American Lutheran churches will not avoid the risk of false glorification of the hero. The result was all the more surprising. The finished film makes such a powerful spiritual statement and is concomitantly informed by such a sustained inner dramatic tension that it may be viewed as a superb achievement in the field of the religious feature film taken as a whole."[263] The Protestant Film Guild (Evangelische Filmgilde)[264] nominated the work as the "Best Film of the Month" even though they noted that "as we see it, the roles of Käthe Luther and Charles V were not suitably cast and the confirmation scene was not well played."[265] The South-West German regional Board of Film Classification (Filmbewertungsstelle der Länder) in Wiesbaden was only willing to concede the rating "worthwhile" ("wertvoll"). Nevertheless, until the Luther Year 1983, the film was uncontested as 'the' film about Luther to be shown to West German schools and congregations. It had a lasting influence in shaping the way candidates for confirmation and pupils saw Luther.

In the US, too, it continued to be distributed "for educational use" in 16 mm-format. In 1970 Lutheran Film Associates produced a half-hour version that showcased the highlights.[266] It was even shown once again on television in the US to mark the Luther Year 1983. The television actor David Soul[267] introduced the telecast in the following words: "There is a lot of fear in our world today [...] and I believe that Martin Luther's legacy translates into hope and courage and stand-fastness for humanity. In the face of rebuke and rejection and condemnation by 16th-century authorities, he took his stand on conscience. His story speaks to me and I hope it will to you too. That's why I am so pleased to invite you to watch this movie full of lingering overtones for our own time—the celebrated film *Martin Luther*." Finally, the year 2003 saw the production of a jubilee edition. In the DVD bonus material, Robert E. A. Lee, former executive of Lutheran Film Associates, presented the "biography of the film" as a story of pure success according to which the film gave rise to boundless euphoria unless there was resistance against the showing of the film. The evaluation of the American sources has shown that this is an euphemistic description. The pictorial narrative of this "biography" does, however, give the impression that the team of consultant scholars headed by Lothar Wolff helped the world to rediscover the Reformer through this film.

In Great Britain, *Luther*, which was distributed by the venerable British Lion Film, provoked mostly moderate and factual criticism.[268] An odd exception is the polemical song *Martin Luther's Bawl* ....[269] It was inspired by *Martin Luther*, a leaflet written by Fr. James Broderick SJ and issued by the Catholic Truth Society (CTS). Hundreds of copies were distributed to viewers of the film.[270] They exerted a great deal of influence on commentators from *The Catholic Herald* and *The Universe*. Only a few churchmen in Britain believed in the religious and missionary qualities of the film despite the claims made for it by the Reverend F.P. Copland Simmons from the Free Church Federal Council: "I hope you will not only got to see this great film yourself, but arrange to take coach parties from your Church to see it. In these days when Revival is in the air and the Protestant Church in our land is growing, it is essential that we should know what we believe and where we stand. *Martin Luther* is a film which most of us will want to see more than once, so that the glory of our Protestant faith and tradition may come home to our minds and hearts with conviction."[271] Norman Potton emphasized the aspect of Protestant self-awareness in the film: "At a time when Romanism is challenging our Reformed position, and the unscriptural doctrines of salvation through sacraments are being so widely propagated, it is well to remember that Luther taught the New Testament doctrine of justification by faith alone."[272] Arnold Craigmore took a similar stance (but with nationalistic overtones): "We have great heritage of Protestant faith which has moulded this country and given us a glorious freedom of thought and spirit which is not to be found in foreign countries of a different faith."[273] Astonishingly, although this may be a postcolonial phenomenon, a similar religious reaction can be noted in Australia, where J. A. Friend wrote: "In these days when there are such strong forces arrayed against the Gospel of Christ, it is good to have this reminder of the truths for which it stands. We hope that this film will have the large audiences it deserves."[274]

Although it was such a great financial success in America that it was heralded by the British press as "one of the top box-office grossers in the States, *Martin Luther* has broken one money making record after another"[275], British distributors considered the film as "uncommercial", an attitude which was deplored by Scottish Presbyterians especially.[276]

In the US the film was also integrated into celebrations of the 440th Anniversary of the Reformation in 1957. It was shown in a hundred Lutheran Churches in the Los Angeles area that day.[277] The positive response to the film in America made a TV showing there seem viable, so a study of several pictures and their acceptance was conducted.[278] As a consequence the TV premiere of the film was scheduled for December 21, 1956 on WGN-TV in Chicago.[279]

Although the second half of the 20th century saw the Luther film produced by the American Film Theater in 1973, the 1953 film was almost the only Luther film used in the catechetical praxis in the US.[280] It took 50 years before the efforts for a new church production on Martin Luther were made.

3.5. Picturing Luther in the 21st Century

In the 21st century, American historians like William Naphy have stressed the political consequences of the Reformation and called it "The Protestant Revolution". Naphy pointed out that "When Martin Luther nailed 95 criticisms of the Catholic Church to the door of his local church in 1517 he sparked not just a religious Reformation, but an unending cycle of political, social and economic change that continues to this day. By challenging the authority of the Pope, Luther inadvertently unleashed a revolutionary force: the power of the individual to determine his or her own thoughts and actions. Over four centuries later, the Protestant minister Martin Luther King Jr. was acting on the same revolutionary principle when he rejected racial discrimination and spearheaded the US Civil Rights Movement."[281] This was also a very American message of the 2003 film, and a justification for an American production. Naphy's interpretation may also be a sign that secularization has continued to advance in the Protestant denominations.[282] Furthermore, the discrimination against black people who wanted to see the film in 1953 showed that the Lutheran "civil rights" movement was not all that effective–and one should be very careful with analogies between Martin Luther and Martin Luther King.

2003 was advertised as an official Luther Year that should be celebrated with a new biographical movie of the reformer.[283] Although the administrative structures that had served to finance the first American Luther film still existed in 2001[284], another financing method was used for the new movie. One reason for this change may have been that the film relased in 2003 had cost $20 million and the marketing budget had swallowed another $10 million. This was too much for a branch of the church administration to pay. Unfortunately, nothing is yet known about the person or persons who first conceived of the film. No reports are yet available that address the decision-making process that led to the Thrivent Society financing the main part of the film. In the end, 50% (over $10 million) of the funding came from the American insurance company, Thrivent Financial for Lutherans. Other partners were the German NFP (Neue Filmproduktion, Berlin), the official producer of the film, and the Protestant Church of Germany (EKD), which contributed only 2%.

Thrivent Financial for Lutherans is one of the largest benefit societies in the United States. Its history goes back to the early 20th century. The company's 'autobiography' as it is published on the internet reveals a certain self-stylization as a religiously founded society.[285] Unfortunately, the archives of Thrivent corporate have not yet opened the files of production of *Luther*.[286]

Not much is known about the research that might have been done for the film or any literary sources that Camille Thomasson and Bart Gavigan might have used for their script, but we do know that it was not based on John Osborne's play as many newspapers have claimed and only few have denied[287]. Luckily, we have an interview with the director Eric Till (born in 1929).[288] Till was chosen because he had successfully staged another Protestant hero, Dietrich Bonhoeffer. For Till, Luther was also a character who rebelled against the religious and political establishment and acted on his own convictions.[289] In line with Till's aesthetic creed, the film had to look like a painting by Vermeer, with a palette featuring lush dark tones and emphasising contrasts of light and shade.[290] Unfortunately Till doesn't explain why he didn't take medieval or early modern paintings as coloristic models. Concerning Luther's image, he emphasized that he didn't want Luther preaching from the pulpit; instead he was to be seen in the midst of his congregation during the service.

Despite its predominant educational content *Luther* was rated PG13 which means "Parents are strongly cautioned" because it has scenes of mob violence and bloodshed.

This film has met with a response that is entirely different from the reaction shown in the 1950s. Newspapers devote to this *Luther* only a tenth of the coverage they had lavished on reviews of the first American *Luther* film. Moreover, reviews this time were centred on the stars of the production: Sir Peter Ustinov and Joseph Fiennes. Ustinov was singled out for praise: "Now, at 82, he is back in someone else's clothes in Eric Till's 'Luther', a study of Martin Luther, the

German priest and scholar who touched off the Protestant Reformation".[291] In Stephen Holden's review, Fiennes is credited with bringing glory to Luther: "The handsome, fact-filled historical epic, in which a fiery-eyed Joseph Fiennes portrays the father of the Reformation"[292]. Apart from that Holden didn't find many positive qualities in the film. His main criticism was that there was too much history teaching and unmotivated hokum: "When the historical details become too clogged, the movie shamelessly overcompensates by wallowing in cheap sentimentality".[293] Even the most sympathetic reviewer had to admit that the film had a "clumsy narrative theology".[294] Nevertheless, defenders of the film like Susan Boettcher emphasized the fact that in the mission context, "historical or theological precision may actually hinder the film's task of sketching a Luther figure that can take the historical heritage of Lutheranism to broader groups into the future"[295] and admits that "the film shows no sympathy with the church as a political or administrative institution".[296] However, Catholic protests were quite moderate, even in Germany (see chapter III.8).

Many critics preferred to focus on the revolutionary thrust of Luther's work. Jean Oppenheimer, for example, argued that "The Protestant Reformation not only changed the course of Western religious history, but also paved the way for radical shifts in political and economic thought."[297]

3.6. "Martin Luther" as American Biopic

As the subject of a biographical picture, Luther was initially supposed to be the presentation of a 'great German' like Frederic the Great or Ferdinand Sauer-bruch. Such a concept would not work in America, so the protagonist was transformed into a champion for freedom against abusive and autocratic authorities based on Christian values. A similar transformation of a national hero can be noticed in the case of Joan of Arc. She also served as a symbol of standfastness and moral integrity based on Christian belief and personalizes a democratic force against the corrupt political system of monarchy and church. However, the inner structure of her image also changed: After the Second World War it shifted from a role model that "redefined female heroism as a retreat from battle and a return to conventional roles"[298] to an androgynous medium of supernatural forces in the late 1990s.[299]

The post-war image of Luther in motion pictures was never so much a part of the commercial revival of medievalism as it was the representation of St. Joan. This is because the Protestant church as the driving force behind the films didn't have financial issues as its primary aim, but rather religious, missionary, and self-affirmative intentions (though the latter were never explicitly expressed). Within Protestant iconography especially the 'christiformitas' of the last presentation in 2003 shows that the character of Luther serves as a kind of substitute for Jesus, and therefore the Luther film itself may be a substitute for the Jesus film, a Catholic domain, Protestants always harshly criticized (also because of their scruples of picturing 'the saint').[300] Apart from that, the two American productions in 1953 and 2003 were remarkable expressions of Lutheran self-assurance. Jews and Protestants allied against Catholics when the television showing of the film was cancelled in 1956. Such an alliance is a specific American phenomenon, unthinkable even in post-war Germany.

What did the Luther film contribute to the history of its genre, the biopic? Is it typical? The most important difference between the typical biopic and the Luther films is that: none of them is a classic Hollywood production. That may be the reason that the Luther film was totally ignored by scholars, who dedicated their work to the biopic genre. However, when it was decided that a Luther film should not be presented in 16mm it was clear that it had to compete against the other biopics and history films on the market. In 1953, the Biblical epic film *The robe* was the main rival for *Martin Luther*. Aesthetically the American Luther films in 1953 and 2003 were geared to the standards of Hollywood. This is even more clear, if we compare the 1953 *Martin Luther* with the biopic of another revolutionary monk: Rosselini's *The Flowers of St. Francis*, released in Italy 1950 and in the US in 1952. This neorealistic biography transposed the idea of a post-war anti-hero, living with the poor and preaching peace. This film was realized with non-professional actors, mainly actual monks. Nevertheless, it was based on hagiography, namely a version of the "Actus beati Francisci et sociorum eius", known under the title "Fioretti di San Francesco", written at the end of the 14th century. The American title of the film refers to this source, but in Italian it was *Francesco, giullare di Dio*, which means "Francesco, God's Jester" and stresses the idea of Francis's life as a provocative counterpart to the existing ethical and social system. The title change makes it clear that this subversive concept could not be sold on the American movie market. *Martin Luther*, which was made for a middle class audience, did not break with conventions. On the contrary, it showed an example of the heroic struggle of the individual for progress in human science and society as *The Story of Louis Pasteur* (1936) did for medical science and *The Life of Emile Zola* (1937) did for politics.[301] Moreover, *Martin Luther* stands for the early modern period and the idea of liberation. This is also typical for the genre, in which the hero always transcends the deeds of the individual.[302] Another characteristic element of a biopic is the staging of the "big break". In Luther's case, it is the nailing and the proclamation of the 95 Theses and a scene in court,[303] in which the hero must defend his ideas. Luther does this at the Diet of Worms.

According to Custen's theory on biopics, it was Hollywood that created history. Instead, reseach on Luther films proves first, that it was not just the film industry that used the illusion of a biopic to visualize a hero, and second, that images cannot be created without tradition. There is a history of veneration, secondary literature and imagination that paves the way for the moving image. This tradition guarantees the producer the acceptance of his product. Filmmakers have always used existing patterns and hyperbolized certain features.

Conclusions

The Luther film genre, which originated in 1911 as an expression of an ongoing Luther renaissance reveals a paradigm shift in the way Luther was perceived within the time span of only a few decades: from romantic aesthete in the 1913 *Wittenberger Nachtigall* to hero of the "German Reformation". The paradigm shift was not triggered by the discovery of Luther as a national hero; that had happened much earlier.[1] Instead, it can be traced to the intentions of each set of producers, which were at first probably commercially oriented. That may also have been the reason why sentimentality was first given priority, but the thrust became increasingly clerical. The examination of church involvement has clearly shown how in the last silent film a particular interest group, the Evangelischer Bund, determined what image of Luther was to be conveyed.

Even though the response to the earliest Luther films of 1911 (*Doktor Martin Luther*) and 1913 (*Wittenberger Nachtigall*) was ambivalent and partly also motivated by critical opinions voiced in the media, those films did shape the canon of scenes that would be used in the cinematic Luther iconography. The focus changes, however: The biographical narrative of Luther's marriage that characterizes the early silent films nearly disappears in the later films until it is taken up again after the Second World War, when an attempt was made to invest the religious hero with more human qualities.

Serious involvement on the part of the Lutheran Church cannot be verified until the 1923 Luther film. The suggestion for this film was made by the head of the Eisenach municipal administrative department for Art, Sport and Tourism with a view to the Lutheran Wold Congress held in Eisenach on August 21, 1923. In this case, the top-ranking Church authorities only promoted the project by advising on the screenplay and eventually having the film distributed by the Evangelische Bildkammer. Opinions were, however, divided on the film. The reasons for this were weaknesses in performances and fundamental doubts about whether the medium of film could do any justice to this religious subject matter. The production of *Luther: Ein Film der deutschen Reformation* (1926-1927) was far more professional and sophisticated. This film was another expression of the "Kulturkampf" against the Roman Catholic Church in a medium quite new to the church at that time. It served the propaganda supported by the Evangelischer Bund, on whose initiative the corporation responsible for the production was based and whose head, the Berlin cathedral pastor and university instructor, Bruno Döhring, had a paramount influence on the screenplay. Responsibility for the film, which was in circulation until 1939, was assumed by the Evangelischer Bund after Döhring withdrew. The work was intended to continue the cultural struggle and win over the masses to the Lutheran cause. It led to severe conflicts between Lutherans (as well as between Lutherans and Roman Catholics) that the tradition of the Luther film in Germany ended for the time being.

It was not until after the Second World War that the next big Luther film project would be realized in West Germany, under American supervision and commissioned by the American Lutheran Film Production. The film *Martin Luther*, which premiered in Minneapolis in 1953 and was not released to West German cinemas until 1954 (at first in Hanover and then in Nuremberg), was a motion picture with sound. Entirely different intentions informed it; the group that commissioned it was not interested in stylizing the reformer into a German national hero. Rather it moved toward demythologizing the figure of Luther by portraying the Reformer as an introverted intellectual rather than as a superhuman being. To do so, the canon of scenes prescribed for a Luther biography did not have to be changed. However, critical aspects were omitted. There followed several quite ambitious interpretations of the material intended solely for television. It was not until 2003 that cinema once again linked up with the sentimental beginnings of the Luther film, albeit not intentionally. However, this film, made for a worldwide cinema audience was not merely intended to affirm Lutheran belief, but also to appeal to the emotions so as to have a missionary effect.

In no other medium can the change in the Lutheran mindset during the past century be so clearly read as in film. In this mass medium scholarship, whether in respect to psychology or the interpretation of the Reformation as a media reformation, was popularized on a grand scale. Nevertheless, Luther films fairly consistently adhere to the positive image of the hero. Other important historical figures from the Reformation who also influenced Luther, such as Melanchthon, are thrust into the background so that the impression remains that 'great men' always 'make history' on their own. Whereas the view of Luther in German films increasingly emphasized the nationalist element until 1927, the Anglo-American tradition has placed the emphasis on the theme of emancipation from conventional thinking, liberation from the authorities of the Middle Ages, and on new beginnings.[2] This Anglo-American image of Luther replaced the German one and became the basis for all later filmic representation. Therefore, it is legitimate to speak of an Americanization of Luther in film. This should not be underestimated, because film has always been the main medium of Americanization in Western Europe since the late 1920s.[3] The success of the 1953 Luther film disproves Heide Fehrensbach's thesis that "throughout the 1950s,

West German films and German rereleases from the Weimar and Nazi periods surpassed imports in popularity".[4]

Nevertheless, some main aspects of Luther's image can be seen in both the European and the American traditions: the omission of Luther's late hostility against Jews, and a more or less obvious justification of his adversarial attitude towards the peasants' cause and his tolerance for the bigamy of Landgrave Philipp I. von Hessen for political reasons. Life with his family is given increasingly greater scope in the presentation beginning with the film adaption of John Osborne's play in 1973, but the illnesses of his later years, his six children and the death of his daughter Magdalene are not mentioned until the TV productions of 1983. However, one can discern a paradigmatic shift in the image of Luther from Europe to America:[5] His image mutates from the German national hero to a champion of freedom of thought and a rebel against traditional authorities. In this sense, Luther corresponds to the American role model of the pioneer at the intellectual frontier who breaks down institutional barriers und promotes spiritual freedom. Nevertheless, Luther remains a member of the bourgeoisie and thus gives mainly middle-class audiences a chance to identify with the Reformer as a role model. Luther also personifies the Protestant church and its values, so the recent scepticism towards Luther films is not justified. Since the representation of his individual faith does not eliminate the idea of the Christian community, the cinematic Luther is not even the "anti-ecclesiastic character" described by Werner Schneider-Quindeau.[6]

Moreover, viewer response to the Luther film has shown itself to be an indicator of the degree of secularisation in a society. It also shows whether and if so, how strongly, links to a particular religious affiliation are perceived at a given time. There was a change between 1953 and 2003 from an emotionally charged reaction expressed in extreme polemics by those who were for or against particular films, to moderate commentary. The bias of the 2003 film, with theologians excluded from interpreting Luther's life work and this task instead being left up to the actors, reveals a phenomenon described, remarkably, as long ago as 1962 by Hermann Gerber: "that a good bit of conveying the message has shifted from theologians to laymen."[7] What has been called secularisation has evidently not eliminated religion;[8] instead, it has changed the way it is handled. The German actor Ben Becker, who played Luther in the television documentary 2007, says that he would not expressly call himself a Christian since he is not rooted in the Christian faith, but he is also not a 'non-Christian' and the Bible raises many questions for him. Nevertheless, he helped to officiate at divine service on the NDR television channel with Margot Käßmann, at that time Lutheran bishop, on Reformation Day, 2008 and recited passages from the Bible.[9]

Since a feature film, which has an average running time of 80 minutes, can never explain everything and must inevitably focus on certain points, must always remain unintelligible and unexplained as far as characterization is concerned.

Moreover, in interpreting a tradition that is full of gaps, which in respect to Luther is especially true of the Nailing of the Theses, so many solutions, even filmic ones, are possible that there will have to be more Luther films! As new icons emerge from each era, which are invariably also personified in the figures of the old heroes, it is not surprising that a new Luther film is planned for 2017.[10]

Acknowledgements

The present study of the image of Martin Luther in film goes back to 1998 when I was commissioned by the Luther Memorial Foundation of Saxony-Anhalt (Stiftung Luthergedenkstätten in Sachsen-Anhalt) to study viewer response to the image of Mrs Luther in film. This study was planned on the occasion of the 500th birthday of the Reformer's wife, Katharina von Bora, which was about to be commemorated. In the following years I continued to work with the Luther film that was to serve as the primary source. During this process, the field of related questions continued to expand and the number of known films increased. It finally became necessary to amalgamate the various parts of the study. For the purpose of this book, it became necessary to represent the whole with a view to film theory by assigning the Luther film to a complex genre of its own.

For so kindly supporting my project, I owe a considerable debt of gratitude to Professor Dr. Christof Mauch at Ludwig-Maximilians University in Munich. My work has benefited greatly from the lively exchange of ideas on theology and on the history of religion with Dean Dr. Reinhard Brandt of the board of directors of the Luther Society (Luthergesellschaft e.V.) as well as with Dr. Stefan Rhein and Dr. Martin Treu at the Luther Memorial Foundation of Saxony-Anhalt in Lutherstadt Wittenberg. Without the generous support provided by the members of the film archives in Frankfurt, Berlin and Washington, the archives of the Lutheran Churches in Nuremberg, Berlin and Elk Grove Village, IL as well as the Evangelischer Bund in Bad Bensheim, this study could never have been undertaken and completed. The translations into English were done by Joan Clough, Castellack, Penzance, with her usual professionalism. I am very grateful to my dear friends Professor Dr. Robert Paslick and his wife Professor Dr. Erica Kurasch-Paslick in Ann Arbor, MI and Dr. Heather McCune Bruhn in Pennstate College for polishing the text.

The donation of the Lasky Center for Transatlantic Studies in Munich helped me to disburse the copyright fees.

Notes

I. Introduction

1   After the dissertation written by the Lutheran theologian Gerd Albrecht, in which the 1953 Luther film was discussed as a case study (*Film und Verkündigung. Probleme des religiösen Films*, Gütersloh: Bertelsmann, 1962 [Neue Beiträge zur Film- u. Fernsehforschung 2], 61–106), Heiner Schmitt, an historian, devoted himself to the early Luther film: "'Luther. Ein Film der deutschen Reformation' im Widerstreit der Konfessionen", in *Aus der Arbeit des Bundesarchivs. Beiträge zum Archivwesen, zur Quellenkunde und Zeitgeschichte*, Boppard 1977 [Schriften des Bundesarchivs 25], 499–510, reprinted in Johannes Horstmann (ed.), *Martin Luther. Zum Wandel des Luther-Bildes in der Geschichtsschreibung und im Film*, Schwerte: Kath. Akademie 1983 (Veröffentlichungen der Katholischen Akademie Schwerte, Dokumentationen, 8), 51–61. This first collection of essays comprises introductions, essays and reprints of reviews written on the Luther films known up to 1983. A brief survey of them in François Traudisch, "Das Lutherbild in deutschen Filmen", ibid. 37–45. The contributions by West German television channels commemorating the 1983 Luther year have been annotated and documented in Margret Trapmann and Fritz Hufen (ed.), *Martin Luther. Reformator – Ketzer – Nationalheld. Texte, Bilder, Dokumente in ARD und ZDF, Materialien zu Fernsehsendungen,* Munich: Goldmann, 1983; a comprehensive evaluation of GDR productions is provided in the following collection of essays: Horst Dähn / Joachim Heise (ed.), *Luther und die DDR. Der Reformator und die Medien anno 1983*, Berlin: Ed. Ost 1996.

2   Esther Wipfler, "Katharina von Bora in den audiovisuellen Medien des 20. Jahrhunderts", in *Katharina von Bora, die Lutherin*, Wittenberg: Stiftung Luthergedenkstätten in Sachsen-Anhalt 1999, 318–334; Esther Wipfler, "Das Luther-Bild im Spielfilm", in Volkmar Joestel and Jutta Strehle, *Luthers Bild und Lutherbilder. Ein Rundgang durch die Wirkungsgeschichte*, Wittenberg: Stiftung Luthergedenkstätten in Sachsen-Anhalt 2003, 85–89; Esther Wipfler, "Vom deutschnationalen Titan zum Herzensbrecher: Neunzig Jahre Luther-Film. Zur Geschichte des Luther-Bildes in Kinematographie und Fernsehen", in *Luther* 75 (2004), H. 1, 17–28. Esther Wipfler, "Luther im Stummfilm. Zum Wandel protestantischer Mentalität im Spiegel der Filmgeschichte bis 1930", in *Archiv für Reformationsgeschichte* 98 (2007), 167–198. Esther Wipfler, "Luthers 95 Thesen im bewegten Bild. Ein Beispiel für Schriftlichkeit im Film", in Joachim Ott and Martin Treu (ed.), *Faszination Thesenanschlag – Faktum oder Fiktion*, Leipzig: Evangelische Verlagsanstalt 2008, 173–197.

3   Herfried Münkler, *Die Deutschen und ihre Mythen*, Berlin: Rowohlt 2009, 181–196.

4   Cf. Heimo Reinitzer, *Biblia deutsch. Luthers Bibelübersetzung und ihre Tradition*, Exhibition catalogue Herzog August Bibliothek Wolfenbüttel 1983, 13.

5   On this: Thomas Kaufmann, "Die Bilderfrage im frühneuzeitlichen Luthertum", in Peter Blickle at alii (ed.), *Macht und Ohnmach der Bilder. Reformatorischer Bildersturm im Kontext*

der europäischen Geschichte, München: Oldenbourg 2002, 407–451; Esther Wipfler, "Götzen-bild oder Adiaphoron – Positionen protestantischen Bildverständnisses", in Marianne Stößl (ed.), *Verbotene Bilder. Heiligenfiguren aus Rußland*, Munich: Hirmer 2006, 41–48.

6   For example: *Johannes Calvin – Berufen zum Reformator*, documentary (DVD: Hänssler Verlag, 2008, 60 min).

7   For instance, Alfred Flückinger, *Protestantismus und Film*, Zurich: Wanderer-Verlag 1951.

8   There is no doubt that Cranach initiated Luther's iconography with his portraits: Martin Warnke, *Cranachs Luther: Entwürfe für ein Image*, Frankfurt a.M.: Fischer Taschenbuch Verlag 1984.

9   For example the pure documentary *Luther und die Juden* (ZDF, Nov. 12, 1983); on this the author of the film: Paul Karalus, "Erstlich, dass man ihre Synagoge oder Schule mit Feuer anstecke …", in Trapmann, *Reformator*, 223–240. Only one documentary with feature film elements mentions Luther's hostility towards the Jews, the production commissioned by the MDR that was broadcast in 2003.

10   Martin Steffens, *Luthergedenkstätten im 19. Jahrhundert. Memoria – Repräsentation – Denk-malpflege*, Regensburg: Schnell & Steiner, 2008, 15–25, 32–58, 325–350 (Review by Esther Wipfler in *Kunstchronik* 62 [2009], H. 5, 224–229); Wolfgang Flügel, *Konfession und Jubi-läum. Zur Institutionalisierung der lutherischen Gedenkkultur in Sachsen 1617–1830*, Leipzig: Leipziger Univ-Verlag, 2005.

11   *Martin Luther und die Reformation in Deutschland*, Exhibition catalogue Nuremberg 1983, Frankfurt a.M.: Insel-Verlag 1983, 222; cf. on this also: Henrike Holsing, *Luther – Gottes-mann und Nationalheld: sein Image in der deutschen Historienmalerei des 19. Jahrhunderts*, Cologne University doctoral dissertation 2004, online-resource: URL: http://kups.ub.uni-koeln.de/volltexte/2007/2132/, 19, n. 41.

12   Cf. Bernd Möller, "Thesenanschläge", in Joachim Ott, Martin Treu (ed.), *Faszination Thesenanschlag – Faktum oder Fiktion*, Leipzig: EVA 2008, 11.

13   Henry McKean Taylor, *Rolle des Lebens. Die Filmbiographie als narratives System*, Marburg: Schüren 2002 (Zürcher Filmstudien, 8), 378.

14   Cf. ibid., 93.

15   For biographical film, the term Biopic has been used since 1951. The Biopic had its classical period from 1927 to 1960, for that period Custen counted 300 films; George F. Custen, *Bio-Pics: How Hollywood Constructed Public History*, New Brunswick, NJ: Rutgers University Press 1992; for the latest tendencies see: Sigrid Nieberle, *Literarhistorische Filmbiographien: Autorschaft und Literaturgeschichte im Kino. Mit einer Filmographie 1909–2007*, Berlin: de Gruyter 2008 (Media and Cultural Memory / Medien und kulturelle Erinnerung, 7).

16   Heiner Schmitt, *Kirche und Film, Kirchliche Filmarbeit in Deutschland von ihren Anfängen bis 1945*, Boppard am Rhein: Boldt 1979 (Schriften des Bundesarchivs, 26), 29.

17   Its beginnings go back to 1950: at that time, Bill Bright, founder and president of the organisation Campus Crusade for Christ, was already planning with proselytising intent to have a film of the life of Christ made. The project did not have sufficient financing until 1978. The producer was John Heyman, who had qualified in the genre by filming Genesis. The Jesus film was shot at the historical sites in Israel. This film is still used for mission purposes with a soundtrack in innumerable languages: http://www.jesusfilm.org.

18   Steven Cohan and Ina Rae Hark (ed.), *Screening the Male: Exploring Masculinities in Hol-lywood Cinema*, London u.a.: Routledge 1993, 3.

19   Knut Hickethier, *Film- und Fernsehanalyse*, 4th updated and enlarged ed., Stuttgart: Met-zler 2007. The method developed by Johann Hahn, which is to be supported by Caftani, a dedicated software programme, is, in my view, a system that is too rigid to do justice to the individual features of each film since all elements are dealt with in the same way (see: Johan G. Hahn, "A Methodology for Finding the Filmmaker's Weltanschauung in Religious

Films", in John R. May [ed.], *New Image of Religious Film*, Kansas City: Sheed & Ward 1997, 213–234).

20 Cf. McKean Taylor, *Rolle des Lebens*, 139.

21 Cf. ibid., 167.

22 There is only a small number of TV productions known that treat Luther exclusively, for exampel the musical *Maarten Luther, De jonge Luther* screened in 1983, the four part documentary *Maarten Luther* screened in 1991 (part 1: *Luther: De briljante student*, part. 2: *De zoekende monnik*, part. 3: *De rebelse bekeerlin*, part 4: *Luther de energieke reformator*), and the two part documentary with re-enacted scenes *Maarten Luther* screened in 2005 (part 1: *Op zoek naar waarheid*, part 2: *Rebel tegen wil en dank televisie*).

II. The Luther Film Sui Generis

1 See for instance the choice of films in Peter Hasenberg (ed.): *Spuren des Religiösen im Film. Meilensteine aus 100 Jahren Kinogeschichte*, Mainz: Matthias-Grünewald-Verlag 1995, 27–249.

2 The concept, originally usually applied to Bible spectaculars and devotional hagiographic films has been widened since the 1960s to include the films of I. Bergman and L. Buñuel, which discuss issues related to the search for meaning and world-views. A major share in this discussion in Germany has been carried by: Stefan Bamberger und Franz Everschor, *Religion im Film. Ein Beitrag zu Geschichte, Funktion und Gestaltung des religiösen Films*, Düsseldorf: Verlag Haus Altenberg 1963, 30–32. Today the term often used is "spiritual film" or one speaks of the "spiritual aspect" that is included in the religious tenor of the film. Hence Hasenberg defines films very generally as religious if they possess a "spiritual dimension" as Frits Tillman understands it, that is, life as aiming at transcendence although need not be defined in Christian terms (ibid., 11–17; cf.: Frits Tillmann et al [com.], *Religion im Film. Lexikon mit Kurzkritiken und Stichworten zu 1200 Kinofilmen*, 2nd ed., Cologne: Katholisches Institut für Medieninformation 1993, 10).

In my study, however, the term "religious film" is used in its original sense, that is, as applied to films about religion, i.e., man's relationship with God (cf. the definition of the term religion in *Religion im Film. Lexikon*, 10), even though what is chiefly concerned here is religious history.

3 Melanie Helm, "Jesusfilme in Geschichte und Gegenwart ", in *Stimmen der Zeit. Zeitschrift für christliche Kultur*, March 2005, 161–170, here: 161.

4 There is only space here to mention the most important works of the past ten years: Reinhold Zwick and Thomas Lentes (ed.), *Die Passion Christi. Der Film von Mel Gibson und seine theologischen und kunstgeschichtlichen Kontexte*, Münster i. W.: Aschendorff 2004. Reinhold Zwick and Otto Huber Otto (ed.), *Von Oberammergau nach Hollywood:Wege der Darstellung Jesu im Film*, Cologne: Katholisches Institut für Medieninformation 1999. Georg Langenhorst: *Jesus ging nach Hollywood*, Düsseldorf: Patmos-Verlag 1998. Peter Malone: "Jesus on our Screens", in John R. May (ed.), *New Image of Religious Film*, Kansas City: Sheed & Ward 1997, 57–71. Gerald E. Forshey, *American Religious and Biblical Spectaculars*, Westport CT: Praeger Publishers 1997, 83–121. Robert Hodgson and Paul A. Soukop, *From One Medium to Another. Basic Issues for Communicating the Scriptures in New Media*, Kansas City: Sheed & Ward 1997. Manfred Tiemann, *Bibel im Film. Ein Handbuch für Religionsunterricht, Gemeindearbeit und Erwachsenenbildung*, Stuttgart: Calwer Verlag 1995. Bruce Babington and Peter Williams Evans, *Biblical Epics: Sacred Narrative in the Hollywood Cinema*, Manchester, etc.: Manchester University Press 1993.

5 More extensively on these references: Peter Hasenberg, "Der Film und das Religiöse:

Ansätze zu einer systematischen und historischen Spurensuche", in Peter Hasenberg (ed.), *Spuren des Religiösen im Film,* 14–17.

6   McKean Taylor, *Rolle des Lebens,* 308.

7   Cf. ibid., 162.

8   Cf. ibid., 139.

9   Cf. ibid., 167.

10   Cf. ibid., 247f.

11   Cf. ibid., 102.

12   Roland Bainton, "Luther und seine Mutter: [on the psycho-analytical interpretation of Luther's youth in the Erikson book *Der junge Mann Luther*]", in *Luther* 44 (1973), 3, 123–130; Roland Bainton, "Luther und sein Vater. Psychiatrie und Biographie". Translated from the American by Elisabeth Langerbeck, in *Zeitwende* 44 (1973), 393–403.

13   Gerhard Lamprecht, *Deutsche Stummfilme 1913–1914,* Berlin: Druck V. Magdalinski 1969, 180.

14   See the censors' findings of March 24, 1921 (Filmprüfstelle Berlin Tgb. Nr. 1673) and April 20, 1921 (Film-Oberprüfstelle B.29.21: banned for youth [Jugendverbot]) at the Dt. Filminstitut Frankfurt am Main (Film-Oberprüfstelle B.29.21: finding of April 20, 1921, 3).

15   Georg Buchwald, *Doktor Martin Luther. Ein Lebensbild für das deutsche Haus.* Mit zahlreichen Abbildungen im Text sowie dem Bildnis Luthers in Heliogravüre nach einem Gemälde von Lucas Cranach zu Nürnberg 1. Aufl. 1902; völlig umgearbeitete Auflage mit zahlreichen Abbildungen im Text und auf 16 Tafeln nach Kunstwerken der Zeit [With numerous illustrations in the text and a portrait of Luther in heliogravure after a painting by Lucas Cranach in Nuremberg 1st ed. 1902, 3rd entirely revised ed. with numerous illustrations in the text on 16 plates after art works of the time], Leipzig and Berlin: Teubner 1916.

16   The original intertitle is as follows: "Oh Gott erhöre mein innig Flehen, erlöse mich aus dieser schweren Qual".

17   Michaela Krützen, *Dramaturgie des Films. Wie Hollywood erzählt,* 2nd edition Frankfurt am Main: Fischer 2006, 25–50. Normally the back-story wound is a traumatic experience for the main character in his childhood or youth that occurs before the action or narrative and is going to be revealed during the film.

18   "Seien Sie außer Sorge: Nach Canossa gehen wir nicht, weder körperlich noch geistig."

19   See the discussion about the interpretation of this encounter up to this point: Johannes Fried, "Der Pakt von Canossa. Schritte zur Wirklichkeit durch Erinnerungsanalyse", in Wilfried Hartmann and Klaus Herbers (ed.), *Die Faszination der Papstgeschichte,* Köln: Böhlau 2008, 133–197; *Canossa 1077. Erschütterung der Welt. Geschichte, Kunst und Kultur am Aufgang der Romanik,* Exhibition catalogue Paderborn 2007, Vol. 1: Essays, Munich: Hirmer 2006. On the visual strategies in the "Kulturkampf": Friedrich Gross, *Jesus, Luther und der Papst im Bilderkampf 1871 bis 1918. Zur Malereigeschichte der Kaiserzeit,* Marburg: Jonas Verlag, 1989.

20   The song derives from a processional first recorded in the 11th century (Walther Lipphardt, "Media vita in morte sumus [Deutsch]", in *VerfLex* 6 [1987], Cols. 271–275) and has remained to the present day part of the Lutheran hymnal as *Mitten wir im Leben sind mit dem Tod umfangen* (EG, No 518). The first verses are taken over from the 1456 Salzburg version; the last verses are all Luther's own. The hymn was arranged as a chorale by Johann Walter in 1524. An abridged version is also printed in *Lieder für den Friedhof.* The first verse in Luther's translation is also included in the Catholic hymnal (GL No 654), followed by a modern translation of the text by Lothar Zenetti.

21   For the film shooting only the first version in faithful detail (1979–1981) was available. The enlarged version, ten time its original size, was painted in 1983–1987. The canvas for this version measured 1.722 square metres and the work was placed in a specially-built

round structure at Bad Frankenhausen. Although there were some initial disagreements with the artist, it was regarded as the official GDR history painting. Even today scholarly opinion is divided on its interpretation: Eduard Beaucamp, „Die Macht der Erinnerung: Geschichtsphantasie und Geschichtsreflexion im Werk Werner Tübkes" in Mosheh Tsukerman (ed.), *Geschichte und bildende Kunst*, Göttingen: Wallstein 2006 (*Tel Aviver Jahrbuch für deutsche Geschichte*, 34), 293–308; Harald Behrendt, *Werner Tübkes Panoramabild in Bad Frankenhausen: zwischen staatlichem Prestigeprojekt und künstlerischem Selbstauftrag*, Kiel: Ludwig 2006 (*Bau + Kunst*, 10).

22   This coat of arms consists of a heart with a cross in the center of a rose. In the film Luther's rose appears chiseled in stone in about 1540 at the so-called Catherine's porch at Luther's house in Wittenberg (see Steffens, *Luthergedenkstätten*, fig. 14).

23   See the statements Luther himself made about his coat of arms, which he wrote to Lazarus Spengler in 1520: WA B, Vol. 5, p. 444f., No. 1628.

24   Cf. McKean Taylor, *Rolle des Lebens*, 254.

25   Cf. the results achieved by Albrecht with the 1953 film (Albrecht, *Film und Verkündigung*, 91).

26   Hans-Martin Barth, "Luther – der Mann und der Film. Zwölf Thesen", *Evangelische Orientierung: Zeitschrift des Evangelischen Bundes* 2003, H. 4, 13.

27   Thomas Elsaesser, *Filmgeschichte und frühes Kino. Archäologie eines Medienwandels*, Munich: Ed. Text + Kritik 2002, 22.

28   Hans-Edwin Friedrich and Uli Jung (ed.), *Schrift und Bild im Film*, Bielefeld: Aisthesis-Verlag 2002 (Schrift und Bild in Bewegung, 3).

29   Joachim Paech, "Vor-Schriften – In-Schriften – Nach-Schriften", in Ernst Gustav (ed.), *Sprache im Film*, Vienna: Wespennest 1994, 23–39.

30   Hans-Edwin Friedrich and Uli Jung, *Schrift*, 10f.

31   Cf. Cantata BWV 20, 1, Chorus: "O Ewigkeit, du Donnerwort, O Schwert, das durch die Seele bohrt, O Anfang sonder Ende! O Ewigkeit, Zeit ohne Zeit, Ich weiß vor großer Traurigkeit Nicht, wo ich mich hinwende. Mein ganz erschrocken Herz erbebt, Dass mir die Zung am Gaumen klebt."

32   Angels as personifications of communications media also figure in more recent cinematic history, for instance in Wim Wenders Der Himmel über Berlin (1986/87); cf. Joachim Paech, "Die Szene der Schrift und die Inszenierung des Schreibens im Film", in Hans-Edwin Friedrich und Uli Jung: *Schrift*, 70.

33   Béla Balász, *Der sichtbare Mensch oder die Kultur des Films*, Vienna 1924, reprint Frankfurt am Main: Suhrkamp 2001, 17; cf.: Béla Balász, *Der Geist des Films*, Halle an der Saale: Knapp 1930.

34   Balász, *Der sichtbare Mensch*, Col. 16.

35   It is also the most widespread type of Luther's portrait in Lutheran Churches: Harry Oelke, "Ein Bild von einem Reformator. Darstellung Martin Luthers als Identitätsfaktor des Protestantismus durch die Epochen", in *Einsichten: Berichte zur Forschung an der Ludwig-Maximilians-Universität* 2003, H. 2, 33–37, here: 34f.

36   For example Joachim Schmiedl wrote "A final observation relates to the 540 million people throughout the world who today profess to Martin Luther's Reformation as mentioned in the film trailer. If that means all non-Catholic and non-orthodox Christians, the number is correct. However, it obscures the theological and pragmatic differences between the 145 member churches and independent congregations of the Lutherischer Weltbund, which currently number 65.4 million worldwide, and the Reformed churches with some 80 million members as well as the many free churches, which profess an allegiance to the Protestant rather than Orthodox or Catholic tradition." (Joachim Schmiedl, "Luther – Der Film zur Reformation", in *Info: Informationen für Religionslehrerinnen und Religionslehrer, Bistum Limburg* 32 [2003], 248–249).

37   Fifty percent of the financing for the film, which cost $30 million to make, came from the American insurance company Thrivent Financial for Lutherans. Other partners were NFP (Neue Filmproduktion, Berlin) and EKD (the Union of German Protestant Churches) with 2%. Thrivent Financial for Lutherans is one of the largest companies of its kind in the US. Some of the founding fathers of the company were German Lutherans. The company homepage presents, not without a touch of self-stylisation, the history of Thrivent as a pioneering achievement: "Shortly after the dawn of the 20th century, two grassroots groups — one made up of German Lutherans in Appleton, Wisconsin, and the other of Norwegian Lutherans in Minneapolis — were concerned about the security and well-being of their fellow Lutherans. Each group was determined to start a fraternal benefit society that would help Lutherans protect their families with life insurance. Aid Association for Lutherans was chartered for business in 1902, but only after years of effort by the dedicated founders Albert Voecks, Gottlieb Ziegler, William Zuehlke and John Grupe. Lutherans throughout much of eastern Wisconsin were canvassed to sign up the 500 members required for the new organization to obtain its state charter. […]" quoted in http://www.thrivent.com/aboutus/history/index.html [November 26, 2007]

38   Paech defined it as "Nach-Schriften" (Paech, *Sprache*, 36–39).

39   A brief summary of the content of the Theses is given in Jens Wolff, "Disputatio pro declaratione virtutis indulgentiarum," in *Lexikon der theologischen Werke*, Stuttgart: Kröner 2003, 238.

40   Cf. for the state of scholarship Martin Treu, "Der Thesenanschlag fand wirklich statt. Ein neuer Beleg aus der Universitätsbibliothek Jena", *Luther* 78 (2007), 140–144; Manfred Schulze, "Thesenanschlag", in *Religion in Geschichte und Gegenwart*, 4th entirely new and revised ed., Vol. 8, Tübingen: Mohr Siebeck, 2005, 357f.

41   On the doubts: Volker Leppin, "Geburtswehen und Geburt einer Legende", in *Luther* 78 (2007), 145–150.

42   Klemens Honselmann, *Urfassung und Drucke der Ablaßthesen Martin Luthers und ihre Veröffentlichung*, Paderborn: Schöningh 1966, 12 and 15.

43   On this see Cf. Bernd Möller, "Thesenanschläge", in Joachim Ott, Martin Treu (ed.), *Faszination Thesenanschlag – Faktum oder Fiktion*, Leipzig: EVA 2008, 9–31.

44   Honselmann, *Urfassung*, ibid., 19.

45   Thus Heinrich Bornkamm, *Thesen und Thesenanschlag Luthers. Geschehen und Bedeutung*, Berlin: Töpelmann 1967, 40.

46   So Honselmann, *Urfassung*, 87–89.

47   Treu, *Der Thesenanschlag*, 142f.

48   Steffens, *Luthergedenkstätten*, 271–274.

49   Strindberg in a letter on the 6th Dezember 1903 to Emil Schering: "… 'Luther' ist so intim, so kühn, so neunaturalistisch, dass es als ‚Moderne Kunst' gelten kann. Das Beste ist, die Volksscenen zu streichen. Zum Beispiel das Kirchentor in Wittenberg wird so kolossal gemalt, daß es den ganzen Hintergrund einnimmt, also kein Raum für Volk bleibt. Denken Sie, welche Wirkung: der einsame Mann mit seinem Hammer und den drei Nägeln! (Ich sehe ihn jetzt vor mir, zwei Nägel im Munde, während er den ersten einschlägt!)" (*Strindberg*, Luther, [92f.]).

50   The original intertitle: "Und Meister Luft macht hurtig sich ans Werk, da schon am Tage, der vor Allerheil'gen lag, der Druck vollendet sein gesollt."

51   "Und nun tat Luther einen Schritt, der mit gewaltiger Kraft die Macht des Papstes brach. Am selben Tag Anno 1517 schlug der die 95 Thesen an das Tor der Wittenberger [Schloßkirche]".

52   The original intertitle: "Flugfeuer gleich war an das Ohr des päbstlich [sic!] Kardinal Herrn Cajetan die Mär gedrungen, daß Luther den gewalt'gen Schritt getan, vor aller Welt dem Papste Trotz zu bieten."

53 Translated intertitles "Since Luther was informed that the Bull was to be handed to him by December 10, he made up his mind quickly." ("Da Luther wurde hinterbracht, daß schon am 10. Dezember man ihm die Bulle reichen wollte, war schnelle sein Entschluss gefaßt"); "The day before a treatise by Mr Luther was prominently displayed at street corners in Wittenberg." ("Des Tages vorher sah man an den Strassenecken Wittenbergs ein Schriftstück von Herrn Luther prangen.").

54 The original intertitle: "Die akademische Jugend solle am Donnerstag d. 10. Dezember vor dem Elstertor zu Wittenberg den Scheiterhaufen richten, da brennen soll das Werk des Antichrist [...] Martin Luther."

55 "Martinus Luther dies Dir auszuhändigen, bin ich beauftragt durch des heilgen Vaters Gnaden."

56 "So denn her Kommilitonen. An's Werk! Schnell schüret mir den Brand."

57 "Weil Christus du verstöret hast, verzehre Dich das ew'ge Feuer."

58 "Indessen Luther und die Alten sich entfernten, die Studiosi stimmten ein 'Te deum' und alsdann ein 'De Profundis' an".

59 The year before – in 1926 – Kyser had already succeeded with his script for Friedrich W. Murnau's *Faust* (Lotte H. Eisener, *Die dämonische Leinwand* [1st ed. *l'écran démoniaque* 1952], 2nd rev. ed. Frankfurt a. Main: Fischer-Taschenbuch-Verlag 1980, 301. Curt Riess, *Das gab's nur einmal*, special ed. Gütersloh: Bertelsmann 1957, 269).

60 On the era: Wolfgang Jacobsen, *Geschichte des deutschen Films*, 1st updated ed. Stuttgart: Metzler 2004, 39–98. On German cinema 1924–27: Jerzy Toeplitz, *Geschichte des Films*, vol. 1: 1895–1928, Repr. of the German edition, Berlin: Henschel 1992, 420–426.

61 The Deutsches Filmmuseum in Frankfurt am Main owns a score that was used at the showings.

62 On Döhring's role in making the film see chapter V.2.2.

63 "Die Zeit des Schweigens ist vergangen [...] die Zeit zum Reden ist gekommen!"

64 "Das Wort ist gesprochen [...] die Zeit ist erfüllt."

65 The exact wording of the quotation is: "43rd Thesis: One must teach Christians that whoever gives to the poor or lends to the needed is doing better than if he wanted to receive indulgence [...]" ("43. These: Man lehre die Christen, daß wer den Armen gibt oder dem Bedürftigen leiht, besser tut, als wenn er Ablaß lösen wollte [...]"); 44th Thesis: "Through works of love, love grows and man improves [...]." ("44. These: Denn durch Liebeswerke wächst die Liebe und der Mensch wird besser [...].")

66 "Whosoever stands guard against the wanton and impertinent speeches of the preachers of indulgences, may he be blessed [...]." ("Wer gegen die mutwilligen und frechen Reden der Ablaßprediger auf der Wacht steht, der sei gesegnet [...].")

67 "So gibt es also doch etwas, das stärker ist als Rom und alle Päpste: Das deutsche Gewissen!"

68 "The true treasure of the Church is the most sacred Gospel of the glory and grace of God." („Der wahre Schatz der Kirche ist das allerheiligste Evangelium der Herrlichkeit und Gnade Gottes.")

69 "Des Papstes Bulle fordert Euch auf, die Schriften Luthers zu verbrennen!", "Verbrennt die päpstlichen Schriften!! Verbrennt das kanonische Recht".

70 "Schreibt der Papst mit einem lateinischen Gänsekiel, wird unser Luther mit einer deutschen Adlerfeder antworten."

71 "Du das Wort – ich das Schwert!"

72 "Diese Flamme kann keiner mehr löschen!"

73 Hugh McLeod, "Religion in the United States and Europe – The 20th Century", in Hartmut Lehmann (ed.), *Transatlantische Religionsgeschichte. 18. und 20. Jahrhundert*, Göttingen: Wallstein-Verlag 2006, 132. See also chapter V.3.

74　For the American idea of Luther up to the First World War: Hartmut Lehmann, *Martin Luther in the American Imagination*, Munich: Fink 1988.

75　"Every Christian who feels true repentance for his sins has perfect forgiveness of both punishment and sin without the need for indulgence". In the German version of the film, the quote is rendered as follows: "Jeder Christ, der wirklich bereut, hat Anspruch auf völligen Erlass von Strafe und Schuld, auch ohne Ablaßbrief". Excerpts from the screenplay are printed in Robert E. A. Lee, *Martin Luther. The Reformation Years. Based on the film Martin Luther*, Minneapolis: Augsburg Pub. House 1967. The English texts are reproduced from these quotations; the German translations were quoted from the dubbed version of the film.

76　"The true treasure of the Church is the most sacred Gospel of the glory and grace of God." ("Der wahre Schatz der Kirche ist das allerheiligste Evangelium von der Herrlichkeit und Gnade Gottes.")

77　Gerd Albrecht, *Verkündigung*: 104f.: "… nicht wegen ihres theologischen Inhalts, sondern ebenfalls als Beispiele antipäpstlicher und antirömischer Polemik".

78　Cf. the German version: "Keiner der auf Vergebung und Segen wartenden Menschen konnte wissen, daß dieses Dokument einmal eines der bedeutendsten Schriftstücke der Geschichte werden würde".

79　Erik Homburger Erikson, *Der junge Mann Luther. Eine psychoanalytische und historische Studie* (Young Man Luther. A Study in Psychoanalysis and History, New York 1958, translated into German by Johanna Schiche), Munich: Szczesny 1964.

80　On this: Dietrich Schwanitz, "John Osborne: The Entertainer – und John Osborne, the entertainer", in Heinrich F. Plett (ed.), *Englisches Drama von Beckett bis Bond*, Munich: Fink 1982, 100–117, here 110.

81　Friedrich Kraft, "Die bösen Bälge", in *Luther als Bühnenheld*, Hamburg, Lutherisches Verlagshaus 1971, 82.

82　"Ich aber sage Euch, durch keinen Ablasszettel der Welt, keine Litanei, keine Möncherei erkauft Ihr, daß Ihr gerechtfertigt seid vor ihm, allein durch die Liebe, allein durch den Glauben, hier lebt Gott, ich hab's erkannt."

83　"Interview mit Alexandre Astruc", in Trapmann, *Reformator*, 152. The author of the interviews is not named.

84　"The Christian who, seeing his neighbour in poverty, leaves him in that wretchedness in order to buy indulgences is purchasing not the indulgence of the Pope but rather God's anger" ("le chrétien qui voyant son prochain dans l'indigence le laisse dans la misère pour acheter des indulgences ne s'achète pas l'indulgence du Pape, mais l'indignation de Dieu"), cf. Theses 43 and 45; "How could the Pope have been able to convert the soul of an enemy of God with money?" ("Comment le Pape aurait-il pouvoir de changer avec de l'argent l'âme d'une ennemie de Dieu?"); "May all those prophets vanish who say of Christ to the people: 'peace, peace'. They do not give peace." ("Qu'ils disparaissent tous ces prophètes qui disent au peuple de Christ: 'la Paix, la Paix'. Ils ne donnent pas la paix"); cf. Thesis 92; "If the Pope knew what the preachers of indulgence exact, he would prefer that St Peter's basilica should crumble into ashes." ("si le Pape connaissait les exactions des prêcheurs de pardon il aimerait mieux que la basilique de Saint Pierre tomba en cendres plutôt"); Thesis 50; quoted from the film itself.

85　*Luther und die Folgen für die Kunst*, Exhib. Cat. Hamburg 1983/1984, Munich: Prestel 1983, Cat. no. 1.

86　"Ich nehme nur die Heilige Schrift wichtig, nichts sonst" Theodor Schübel, *Martin Luther*, Munich: Droemer Knaur 1983, 28.

87　"Gegen Mittag. In der Kirche ist Gottesdienst" (Ibid.). This "screenplay", however, is different in some respects to the texts as spoken in the film (see the comparison in the following footnote). On Schübels book in the context of 20th-century literary writings on

Luther: Martina Fuchs, "Martin Luther – Protagonist moderner deutscher Literatur", in *Lutherjahrbuch* 73 (2006), 171–194.

88   "Was ist denn da angeschlagen?", "Was steht da?" (cf. Schübel, *Luther*, 28: "Warum hat er das da angeschlagen).

89   "Those who continually say that the soul will be free as soon as the coin clinks in the offertory box are preaching the work of man" ("Menschenwerk predigen die, die beständig sagen, dass die Seele frei werde, sobald die in den Kasten geworfene Münze klinge"); cf. Theses 27 and 28 in the original: 27. "Those who say that the soul flies up [out of Purgatory] as soon as the coin clinks in the offertory box..." ("Menschenlehre verkündigen die, die sagen, dass die Seele [aus dem Fegefeuer] empor fliege, sobald das Geld im Kasten klingt.") 28. "Certainly as soon as the money sounds in the offertory box, earnings and greed grow but the intercession of the Church stands on the will of God alone" ("Gewiss, sobald das Geld im Kasten klingt, können Gewinn und Habgier wachsen, aber die Fürbitte der Kirche steht allein auf dem Willen Gottes"); 43. "Christians must be taught that whoever gives to the poor or lends to the needy is doing better than if he should purchase indulgences" ("Man muss die Christen lehren, dass wer dem Armen gibt oder dem Bedürftigen borgt besser handelt als wenn er Ablässe erkauft"); 11. "The weed of converting a Church punishment into a sentence to Purgatory seems to have been sown when the bishops were fast asleep." ("Jenes Unkraut, eine kirchliche Strafe in eine Fegfeuerstrafe zu verwandeln, scheint gesät worden zu sein, als die Bischöfe fest schliefen."); the published screenplay, however, gives only a shortened quotation of thesis 11 as follows: "All preachers err who say that man will be freed of all punishment and be blessed through indulgence" ("Es irren alle Prediger, die sagen, daß durch den Ablaß der Mensch von allen Strafen befreit und selig werde. Dieses Unkraut ist gesät worden, während die Bischöfe geschlafen haben."); ibid., 28.

90   Ibid., 57f.: "Man darf vor den großen Hansen keine Furcht haben. Sollen sie meine Schriften verdammen und ins Feuer werfen! Was sie können, kann ich auch".

91   Cf. ibid., 68: "Das Volk soll endlich selber lesen, was geschrieben steht. […] Es ist viel besser, mit eigenen Augen zu sehen als mit fremden."

92   Cf. ibid., 94.

93   The name of a printer, verifiably active in Wittenberg, who, however, has not been associated with printing the theses; cf. Honselmann, *Urfassung*, 15.

94   "Wie mein Geschäft geht? Das fragen Sie noch, Bruder Martin? Ich kann von Ihren Schriften gar nicht genug drucken. Von überallher kommen Bestellungen, sogar von Nürnberg, Freiburg und Basel. Hoffentlich finden Sie bald die Zeit, wieder etwas zu schreiben." (Cf. Schübel, *Luther*, 51)

95   "Wenn ich das drucke – danach wird für Sie in unserer Kirche kein Platz mehr sein." (Cf. ibid., 52)

96   "[…] er hat Worms vor drei Wochen verlassen – und hier in Wittenberg ist er nicht angekommen."; "Das wird eine große Nachfrage nach seinen Schriften geben. Und wir haben nur noch geringe Vorräte! Vorwärts! Wir drucken noch einmal 'Über die Freiheit eines Christenmenschen'."; "Das ist verboten, Meister!"; "Verboten? Gewiss. Aber auch ein Geschäft." (Cf. Ibid., 66).

97   "Obwohl es streng verboten ist, sind deine Bücher noch immer auf dem Markt. In den Städten werden dafür hohe Preise bezahlt. Deine Verleger drucken allerdings nicht nur deine Bücher, sie drucken mit dem gleichen Eifer Bücher gegen dich." (ibid., 68).

98   45. These: "Man soll die Christen Lehren, wer einen Bedürftigen darben sieht und ihm nicht hilft und Geld für Ablass ausgibt, der kauft nicht den Ablass des Papstes, sondern handelt sich den Zorn Gottes ein. [44. These:] Denn durch ein Werk der liebe wächst die Liebe im Menschen und er wird besser, durch Ablass aber wird er nicht besser. Er hat bloss ewiger Strafe zu verbüssen. [46. These:] Man soll die Christen lehren, wer keinen Überfluss

besitzt, soll das Notwendige für sein Haus und seine Familie behalten, und keinesfalls für Ablass verschwenden. [52. These:] Wer von einem Ablassbrief das Heil erwartet, ist töricht, auch wenn der Ablasskommissar, ja der Papst selber ihre Seelen dafür verpfändete. [50. These:] Man soll die Christen lehren, wenn das der Papst wüsste, er liesse lieber die Peterskirche in Flammen aufgehen, statt sie mit Haut und Fleisch und Knochen seiner Schafe aufzubauen."

99 "Warum ist der Papst nicht so barmherzig, mit einem Schlag die Seele aus dem Fegefeuer zu befreien, wenn er doch die Macht hat, es gegen Geld zu tun."

100 "Warum baut Papst Leo X., […], Erbe eines der grössten Vermögen Italiens, nicht wenigstens diese eine Kirche St. Peter von seinem eigenen Geld, statt mit den Groschen der Gläubigen?"]

101 The quotation in the film are: 45th Thesis: "Man soll die Christen lehren, wer einen Bedürftigen darben sieht und ihm nicht hilft und Geld für Ablass ausgibt, der kauft nicht den Ablass des Papstes, sondern handelt sich den Zorn Gottes ein"; 44th Thesis: "Denn durch ein Werk der Liebe wächst die Liebe im Menschen und er wird besser, durch Ablass aber wird er nicht besser. Er hat bloß ewiger Strafe zu verbüßen."; 46th Thesis: "Man soll die Christen lehren, wer keinen Überfluß besitzt, soll das Notwendige für sein Haus und seine Familie behalten, und keinesfalls für Ablass verschwenden." 52nd Thesis: "Wer von einem Ablassbrief das Heil erwartet, ist töricht, auch wenn der Ablasskommissar, ja der Papst selber ihre Seelen dafür verpfändete." 50th Thesis: "Man soll die Christen lehren, wenn das der Papst wüsste, er ließe lieber die Peterskirche in Flammen aufgehen, statt sie mit Haut und Fleisch und Knochen seiner Schafe aufzubauen."

102 "Ich wollte mit einigen Gelehrten über die Thesen disputieren."

103 "Christus befahl nicht den Ablass zu predigen, sondern das Evangelium."

104 "Den Christen soll gepredigt werden, dass der, der den Armen gibt oder dem Bedürftigen leiht, hierin besser tut als darin Ablassbriefe zu kaufen."

105 "Wenn der Papst das Fegefeuer lehren kann, warum tut er das dann nicht um der Liebe willen, sondern für Geld?", cf. Thesis 82: " … For instance: Why does the Pope not clear Purgatory for the sake of the holiest Love and the extreme sufferings of souls – for a really sound reason – since he ransoms innumerable souls for the sake of building a church with this unholy money – than for a very shabby reason?" ("zum Beispiel: Warum räumt der Papst nicht das Fegefeuer aus um der heiligsten Liebe und höchsten Not der Seelen willen – als aus einem wirklich triftigen Grund –, da er doch unzählige Seelen loskauft um des unheilvollen Geldes zum Bau einer Kirche willen – als aus einem sehr fadenscheinigen Grund?").

III. The Image of Martin Luther in Motion Pictures 1911–2003

1   Schmitt, *Kirche und Film*, 21.

2   Walther Conradt, *Kirche und Kinematograph. Eine Frage*, Berlin: Verlagsbuchhandlung Hermann Walther 1910, 32.

3   This corresponds to the categories Ia, Ic and II from the eight title classes compiled by Henry McKean Taylor (ibid. pp. 295–298). This shows how little willingness to experiment with titles for Luther films there was throughout an entire century; the intention was ensure that such a film would be instantly recognizable as a Luther biography.

4   They are owned by the Litt family. I am indebted to Stefan Litt for so kindly placing the photographs at my disposal for this study.

5   *Der Kinematograph* No. 239, July 26, 1911.

6   Gerhard Lamprecht, *Deutsche Stummfilme*, 180.

7   See the censorship findings of March 24, 1921 (Filmprüfstelle Berlin Tgb. [Minutes] No. 1673) and April 20, 1921 (Film-Oberprüfstelle B.29.21, Jugendverbot [banned for youth]) quoted and discussed in chapter V.2.2.

8   See chapter V.2.1., note 15.

9   According to the censor card, the examined version *Doktor Martin Luther. Ein Lebensbild fürs deutsche Volk* is 2107 meters long, the format was 35mm, 1:1.33, the film was silent and black-and-white. The film was adjudged „Jugendfrei" („suitable for showing to young people"); Zensurkarte No. B.16455, 29-AUG-27; cf. Schmitt, *Kirche und Film*, 340.

10   The EYE Film Instituut Nederland owns two copies of the Dutch version, a complete one (2055 m) and a fragment (213 m). The film bore the titles *Het Leven en Strijden van Dr. Maarten Luther* and *De macht van het lied*. The last title emphasized the side story of the 'conversion' of Graf Eberhard von Erbach to Luther's cause. The Dutch intertitles differ greatly between the complete version and the fragment, which only contains the first chapter and a part of the second chapter. Elif Rongen-Kaynaksçi, silent-film specialist at the EYE Film Instituut Nederland, detected that some of film material was inserted into the complete copy can be dated into the early 1930s. This indicates that the film was still in use at that time.

11   The 1927 Luther film was available in the Netherlands since 1928 (see for example *Nieuw Weekblad voor de Cinematografie* 7, 1928/1929, No. 6, Nov., 9: Advertisement published by Filmverhuurkantor "Monopole", Rotterdam); for the history of censorship of this film in the Netherlands see: *Nieuw Weekblad voor de Cinematografie* 6, 1927/1928, No. 31, May, 4.

12   Thus the 11th title of the 1913 version, quoted according to the censor cards (28814/19) in the Bundesarchiv-Filmarchiv, Berlin.

13   See chapter IV.2.

14   His appearances on the screen decreased over the years. His other, later silent films include *Fluch der Schönheit* and *Die Rache der Banditen*; he again appeared in films from the 1930s in numerous minor roles. The most important motion pictures with sound in which he has acted included *Der Mustergatte*, with Heinz Rühmann in the leading role (premiere: October 13, 1937 in the Gloria-Palast in Berlin); other films with Rudolf Essek are listed in Index Stummfilm by Thomas Staedeli (www.cyranos.ch/smesse-d.htm [3.3.2009]).

15   "Mit gutem Beispiel Luther ging voran, als er um Katharina von Bora freite."

16   The film shown in Germany had five acts and, according to the censor card of June 28, 1923, was 1961 metres long (Schmitt, *Kirche und Film*, 333). However, the film has only survived in copies made for the foreign market: an American copy *Martin Luther: His Life and Time*, 1925, preserved in Washington, Library of Congress, Motion Pictures Division, may be complete: It is on 8 reels, 16mm, b&w, si., 2550 ft., 84 min (LC Call Number: FAA 6034–6041 [reference print], Harmon Foundation Collection).

17   The Luther rose was used as the introductory motif in the 1981 French film; on this see: chapter II., note 22 and 23.

18   At that time his career was still before him; it would culminate in an appointment as director of the Deutsches Schauspielhaus in Hamburg during the Third Reich: Jutta Gutzeit, "Staatliches Schauspielhaus 1932–1945. Die Intendanz Karl Wüstenhagen", in *100 Jahre Deutsches Schauspielhaus in Hamburg*, Hamburg, etc.: Dölling & Galitz 1999, 48–61. After the Luther film he was in the cast of another history film *Helena – Der Untergang Trojas (Helen – The Fall of Troy)*, 1923–1924, directed by Manfred Noa.

19   *Luther in Oppenheim*. Geschichtliches Schauspiel in einem Aufzuge von Walther Nithack-Stahn, Halle: Fricke 1920. Walther Nithack-Stahn, *Luther – Festspiel in sechs Handlungen*, Breslau: Verlag der Evangelischen Zentralstelle 1921.

20   For instance in the Baldung Grien painting in the Alte Pinakothek in Munich. There the light radiating from the Christ Child emanates from the ground to 'illuminate' the Virgin from below (Martin Schawe, *Altdeutsche und altniederländische Malerei*, Ostfildern: Hatje

Cantz 2006 (Alte Pinakothek, 2), 82f.; on the acceptance of the image of the Virgin in (early) Protestantism: Sibylle Weber am Bach, *Hans Baldung Grien (1484/85–1545). Marienbilder in der Reformation*, Regensburg: Schnell & Steiner 2006 (Studien zur christlichen Kunst, 6), 19–49.

21   Martin Brecht, *Martin Luther. Sein Weg zur Reformation*, Stuttgart: Calwer 1981 (Martin Luther, Vol. 1), 15–18. This is also confirmed by the evaluation of the most recent archaeological finds in Mansfeld: Harald Meller (ed.), *Luther in Mansfeld. Forschungen am Elternhaus des Reformators*, Halle an der Saale: Landesmuseum für Vorgeschichte 2007, 184; *Fundsache Luther. Archäologen auf den Spuren des Reformators*, Exhibition Catalogue Halle 2008/2009, Stuttgart: Konrad Theiss 2008.

22   Simon Wendt, "Massenmedien und die Bedeutung von Helden und Stars in den USA (1890–1929)", in Daniela Münkel and Lu Seegers (ed.), *Medien und Imagepolitik im 20. Jahrhundert: Deutschland, Europa, USA*, Frankfurt/Main etc.: Campus-Verlag 2008, 201 and 202.

23   On Luther's birthplace, its reconstruction and the story of how it came to be a museum: Steffens, *Luthergedenkstätten*, 59–91 and fig. 43 (the room declared as Luther's birthplace after 1917).

24   Cf. The King James Version of the Bible: "But whosoever drinketh of the water that I shall give him shall never thirst; but the water that I shall give him shall be in him a well of water springing up into everlasting life." (*The New Testament of our Lord and Saviour Jesus Christ, Translated out of the Greek: Being the Version Set Forth A.D. 1611, Compared with the Most Ancient Authorities and Revised, A.D. 1881 and A.D. 1901*, New York: T. Nelson 1901).

25   This is the case in a scene of the 1959 film *Ben Hur*. When Judah Ben Hur, who has been condemned to force labour on the galleys, is the only person in his group on the march through the desert to whom the burly overseer refuses a drink of water, Ben Hur implores God for help. His supplication is heard and Christ himself, shown only from behind, gives him plenty to drink.

26   This field of Protestant printmaking has hitherto only been partially studied; see for instance: Martin Scharfe, *Evangelische Andachtsbilder. Studien zu Intention und Funktion des Bildes in der Frömmigkeitsgeschichte vornehmlich des schwäbischen Raumes*, Stuttgart: Müller & Gräff 1968 (Veröffentlichungen des Staatlichen Amtes für Denkmalpflege Stuttgart: Volkskunde 5); Bruno Langer, *Evangelische Bilderwelt. Druckgraphik zwischen 1850 und 1950*, Bad Windsheim: Verlag Fränkisches Freilandmuseum 1992; on the context: Andrea K. Thurnwald, *Weil ich Jesu Schäflein bin. Kinderleben und Kinderglauben im evangelischen Franken*, Bad Windsheim: Verlag Fränkisches Freilandmuseum 1995.

27   Brecht, *Martin Luther*. Vol. 1, 43.

28   The painting is in Erfurt Town Hall; it was, therefore, accessible to reception (Holsing, *Luther – Gottesmann*, fig. 128).

29   Kaspar Elm, "Augustiner-Eremiten", in *LMA*. 1, 1980, 1220f. Cf. Willigis Eckermann, "Augustiner-Eremiten", in *LThK*, 3rd ed., Vol. 1, 1993, 1233–1237.

30   "Aris" is a small herb mentioned in Pliny. It may be "Arum arisarum", for which the English common name is "Mouse Plant" or "Friar's Cowl", but the German translation according to K. E. Georges's dictionary is „Natterwurz" that means literally translated "Viper Root" (Karl Ernst Georges, *Ausführliches lateinisch-deutsches Handwörterbuch*, Vol. 1, 8th ed., Hanover and Leipzig: Hahnsche Buchhandlung 1913, col. 573). Luther said of Aristotle: "I regret in my heart that damned, arrogant, knavish heathen has seduced and deceived so many of the best Christians with his lying words" ("Es thut mir wehe in meinem hertzen, das der vordampter, hochmutiger, schalckhafftiger heide mit seinen falschen worten soviel der besten Christen vorfuret und narret hat") (WA 6, 458) but he did appreciate some Platonic thinking. On individual aspects of the multilayered Luther-Aristotle controversy:

Theodor Dieter, *Der junge Luther und Aristoteles. Eine historisch-systematische Untersuchung zum Verhältnis von Theologie und Philosophie*, Berlin etc.: de Gruyter 2001.

31   See Steffens, *Luthergedenkstätten*, 198, fig. 93.

32   The "Luther Looks Towards Rome" motif was represented as early as about 1872 by Ferdinand Pauwels (Holsing, *Luther – Gottesmann*, fig. 134).

33   Norbert Mecklenburg, "Luther in Rom. Zur literarischen Fabrikation eines deutschen Mythos", in Conrad Wiedemann (ed.), *Rom – Paris – London. Erfahrung und Selbsterfahrung deutscher Schriftsteller und Künstler in den fremden Metropolen*, Stuttgart: Metzler 1988 (Germanistische-Symposien-Berichtsbände, 8), 321–334.

34   On this: Holsing, *Luther – Gottesmann*, 405–425.

35   The 1923 filmic representation of Luther's speech seems to have been inspired by a frontal perspective in a church-like hall with Romanesque round arches as depicted in the 1893 Waldemar Friedrich painting entitled *Ich bin hindurch* (*I have gone through*), that hangs in the Melanchthon Gymnasium in Wittenberg; architecturally, the film scene borrows from the classic representation of the scene in 1864 by Hermann Freihold Plüddemann exhibited in the Luther House in Wittenberg (Holsing, ibid., figs. 228 and 190). On the entry into Worms: ibid., 448–468.

36   Eike Wolfgast, *Die Wittenberger Lutherausgabe. Zur Überlieferungsgeschichte der Werke Luthers im 16. Jahrhundert*, Nieuwkoop: B. de Graaf, 1971, Col. 122 and n. 656.

37   Cf. the Latin text: WA 7, 838; German translation: Brecht, *Martin Luther*, Vol. 1, 439;

38   *Thomas Carlyle's Works. The Standard Edition*, Vol. 6: *Critical and Miscellaneous Essays*, London: Chapman and Hall 1904, 1–6 (Luther's Psalm [1831]).

39   *Thomas Carlyle's Works. The Standard Edition*, Vol. 4: *Sartor Resartus and On Heroes, Hero-Worship, and the Heroic in History*, London: Chapman and Hall 1904, 110; cf. also: "… I need not deny that Protestantism was a revolt against spiritual sovereignties, Popes and much else. Nay I will grant that English Puritanism, revolt against earthly sovereignties, was the second act of it; that the enormous French Revolution itself was the third act, whereby all sovereignties earthly and spiritual were, as might seem, abolished or made sure of abolition. Protestantism is the grand root from which our whole subsequent European History branches out" (ibid., 102).

40   On Luther: ibid., 95–118.

41   Ibid., 95.

42   Ibid., 106.

43   Here the influence of "rhythmnic gymnastics" or "Eurhythmics" as developed by Émile-Jaques Dalcroze (1865–1950) and refined by him, his employees and pupils into what was known in German as "Ausdruckstanz" (expressive dancing: Modern dance) is clearly apparent (cf. for instance the "plastische Übung", ca 1912, or the choral study on the "Gleichstrebend" theme: Hedwig Müller and Patricia Stöckemann, '… *Jeder Mensch ist ein Tänzer'. Ausdruckstanz in Deutschland zwischen 1900 und 1945*, Gießen: Anabas-Verlag 1993, illustrations on p. 13 and p. 21, top). This method of movement was practised and further developed from 1911–13 at the educational facility in Dresden-Hellerau Garden City in seminars and performances, at first with lay performers and semi-professional dancers. The performers sought a new body language and explored the laws of movement since they believed that the forms of classical dance were unsuited to expressing what was experienced and felt. Rhythm functioned here as a pivotal referential category of what was both a physical and emotional experience that was to lead to a holistic feeling for life. The Swiss theatre reformer Adolphe Appia (1862–1928) developed abstract stage spaces for this in the theatre hall at the Hellerau educational facility based on stepped podiums and geometric light rooms, after which the film set is also palpably modelled. On the outbreak of the First World War, Dalcroze and Appia as Swiss nationals had to leave Germany for political reasons so that the experiment in Hellerau was abruptly ended.

However, Dalcroze's approaches were further pursued during the First World War by an employee of his, Rudolph von Laban (1879–1958), notably in summer courses in Switzerland at Monte Verità, a centre of the Reform movement. Laban regarded classical ballet – with its lexis of specifically defined figures, steps and positions – as a historically frozen form. He countered it with the idea of dance as expressive of psychic experience that developed out of improvisation and individual configuration rather than a prescribed arsenal of movements. Out of his work with lay dancers grew the choral movements that were also introduced in the 1920s workers' movement and also influenced the choreographies of mass movement staged by the National Socialists (notably at the 1936 Berlin Olympic Games). Laban also worked at the same time during the 1920s with professional dancers (with or without classical training). Finally, his female pupils developed Ausdruckstanz (Modern Dance) in Germany from the 1920s into an autonomous art form in dance thea-tre. The two most influential representatives of Modern dance in German in the first half of the 20th century were Mary Wigman (Karoline Sofie Marie Wiegmann, 1886–1973) and Gret Palucca (Margarete Paluka, 1902–1993), a pupil of hers; cf. *Jeder Mensch ist ein Tänzer*, 1–54; Gabriele Brandstetter, "Ausdruckstanz", in Diethart Kerbs (ed.), *Handbuch der deutschen Reformbewegungen, 1880–1933*, Wuppertal: Hammer 1998, 451–463.

44   Siegfried Kracauer: *Das Ornament der Masse*. Essays. Mit einem Nachwort Karsten Witte, Frankfurt am Main: suhrkamp 1977 (suhrkamp taschenbuch, 371).

45   Thus Kracauer: "Mass movement represents mute nature without any superstructure; rhythmic gymnastics also, in its view, captivates the mythological upper classes, thus consolidating the reign of nature all the more. It exemplifies many other equally hopeless attempts to arrive at a higher life from the masses." (ibid., 63).

46   The Neo-Gothic style was also used in the 19th century for the reconstruction of Luther memorial sites such as the birthplace. Architects and designers imitated thereby the late gothic style of Luthers life time: Steffens, *Luthergedenkstätten*, 340–342.

47   "The Life of Martin Luther in Motion Pictures", *American Lutheran* 8, March 1925, 8.

48   Ibid., 7.

49   Ibid., 8.

50   J. E. Nickelsburg, "A Sucessful Publicity Tour", *American Lutheran* 9, Feb. 1926, 8f.; quoted in Kahle/Lee, *Popcorn and Parable*, 85.

51   *Lexikon des Internationalen Films*, völlig überarbeitete und erweiterte Neuausgabe [entirely revised and enlarged new ed.], Reinbek bei Hamburg: Rowohlt 1995, Vol. 5, 3529.

52   The manuscript of the score in the Deutsches Filmmuseum in Frankfurt am Main.

53   August Strindberg, *Historische Miniaturen*, Historska miniatyrer <deutsch>, ed. by Roland W. Pinson, Essen: Magnus-Verlag [1985], 181–199 (revised edition after the first German edition of 1908).

54   "Luther: Seht, jetzt geht der Tag auf über Thüringen! Dr. Johannes: Über Deutschland" (August Strindberg, *Luther: die Nachtigall von Wittenberg*; [deutsche Historie in 10 Bildern]; Näktergalen i Wittenberg [1903] übersetzt von Emil Schering, München: Müller 1915, 88); In a letter to the translator Emil Schering written in 1903 Strindberg explained that he wanted to present Luther's story as an example of a national triumph over Rome, not as part of church history (letter on November 22, 1903: "Ich habe Luther zum Deutschen gemacht, zum Waibling gegenüber Rom, dem Welfen. Das ist die Stärke des Stückes! Und dadurch vermied ich die Theologie, die gefährlich und langweilig ist. [...] Ich habe nach Merle d'Aubignés Geschichte der Reformation [full title: Jean-Henry Merle d'Aubigné, *Geschichte der Reformation des sechszehnten Jahrhunderts. Aus dem Französischen übertragen von Dr. Martin Runkel*, 5 volumes, Stuttgart: Steinkopf 1848–54] gearbeitet." ibid., 91]).

55   "Da mitten in dem Sturm des Fanatismus, der ihn umtobt, erscheint, unerwartet allen, Luther auf der Kanzel. Unter seinem Predigerkleid schimmert noch die Ritterrüstung, die er auf der Wartburg getragen hat. Als ob ein zürnender Erzengel selbst hernieder gestiegen

ist, wirkt seine Erscheinung Wunder. Seine gewaltige Rede zwingt alle zu gläubiger Demut auf die Knie nieder, und durch den atemstillen Kirchenraum schallt, von einem greisen Organisten gespielt, Luthers großes Kämpferlied der Reformation: Ein feste Burg ist unser Gott.", *Illustrierter Filmkurier* 1928, No 810, [6] (unnumbered page).

56 Wolf Singer, *Der Beobachter im Gehirn Essays zur Hirnforschung*, Reprint Frankfurt am Main: Suhrkamp, 2004 (Suhrkamp-Taschenbuch Wissenschaft 1571).

57 Examples: Martin Hoberg, *Mit und ohne H.Vogler. Das Bremer Gesangbuch 1917 und die Gesangbuchillustration des 20. Jahrhunderts* (HosEc, 13), Bremen: Hauschild 1982, 179; Otto Lerche, *Druck und Schmuck des deutschen evangelischen Gesangbuchs im 20. Jahrhundert*, Berlin: Eckart-Verlag 1936, fig. 60 und 83.

58 Knut Hickethier, "Veit Harlans Film Jud Süß und der audiovisuell inszenierte Antisemitismus", in *Jud Süß*, Frankfurt am Main etc.: Campus-Verlag 2006, 221–244.

59 Here the political message of the film is clear: the 1918 revolution in Germany and the Republic that grew out of it called for a political leader, who, like Luther, would counter the chaos of the Peasants' War (cf. Johannes Horstmann, "Kritik-Nr. 24 354", in *film-dienst* 36 (1983).

60 Cf. Schmitt, *Luther*. In the petition of February 24 submitted by the *Erzbischöflicher Kommissariat Nürnberg-Fürth* to the Film-Oberprüfstelle in Berlin to ban the film throughout Bavaria, one comment runs: "the film [reveals] such an aggressively anti-Catholic bias […] that showing it would most grievously offend Catholic sensibilities, disturb the religious peace and evoke incalculable prejudices." ("der Film [zeige] eine derart aggressive, von rein geschichtlicher Darstellung weit abweichende antikatholische Tendenz […], dass seine Aufführung das katholische Empfinden aufs schwerste verletzen, den religiösen Frieden stören und unabsehbare Unzuträglichkeiten heraufbeschwören würde.")
The history of the censorship of this film in the 1920s can be easily traced through documents–some of which are published online–in the Deutsches Filminstitut in Frankfurt: Zensurentscheidung v. 17. 12. 1927: Filmprüfstelle Berlin B. 17622, length of film: 3308 m, approved; 10 Jan. 1928: Filmprüfstelle Berlin B. 17863, length of film: 3220 m; approved: 24 Feb. 1928 (Zensurdokument, Bayerisches Hauptstaatsarchiv); March 22, 1928 (Oberprüfstelle O. 204, length of film: 3117m; approved; appealed and partly banned; excised: 93.35m, Zensurdokument und Protokoll [Censorship document and minutes] in the Bayerischen Hauptstaatsarchiv.

61 The following scenes are among those abridged: "the first Roman monastic cell in which various monks are seen feasting [….] Scene of brawl at Tetzel's indulgence celebration [….] the scene in which Tetzel is shown dancing with a wench [….] the scene in which Tetzel in person taps a large cask of beer [….] Scenes from the iconoclastic movement and the destruction of altars [….] Scenes showing burning at the stake" (Protokoll [Minutes] of the Verhandlung über den Antrag der Bayerischen Staatsregierung auf Widerruf der Zulassung des Bildstreifens "Luther" [Proceedings on the petition submitted by the Bavarian state to have the approval of the feature film Luther revoked] of March 22, 1928, p. 8 in the Bayerisches Hauptstaatsarchiv, Munich)

62 *Kinematograph* No. 1096, Feb. 12, 1928: "Luthers Leben, das ist schon ein echter Filmstoff, der über die Zeitgeschichte hinaus Bedeutung hat und bei der protestantischen Menschheit, die sich ja nicht nur auf Deutschland beschränkt, auf Begeisterung stoßen wird."

63 Luther und unsere Zeit: Zur Aufführung des Lutherfilms, in *Deutsche Tageszeitung* of March 6, 1928; Presseausschnittsammlung [Press cuttings collection] in the Bundesarchiv-Filmarchiv, Berlin.

64 Schmitt, *Luther*, 60.

65 Thus Harro Segeberg, "Die großen Deutschen. Zur Renaissance des Propagandafilms um 1940", in Harro Segeberg (ed.), *Mediale Mobilmachung* I, Munich: Wilhelm Fink Verlag 2004, 267–291.

66 See for instance: *American Lutheran* 12, June 1929, 27 [715]

67 *National Board of Review Magazine* 3, No. 10, October 1928.

68 Kenneth J. Robinson, "Martin Luther", in *The Church of England Newspaper*, 16 Sept. 1955.

69 In Germany of course the renaissance of religion might almost be viewed as a reaction to the Nazi neo-paganism; a prime example of this "new" perspective on civilization is the 1956 exhibition "Werdendes Abendland an Rhein und Ruhr" in Essen, which showed the (Roman) Christian basis of European culture. This religious revival also materialized in the long period of government of the Christian Democratic chancellor Konrad Adenauer (1949–1963). The ideology of the "Christian Orient" was almost created in a Catholic milieu, whereas the Protestant Church used more the idea of Europe in order to express an supranational concept (Heinz Hürten, "Der Topos vom christlichen Abendland in Literatur und Publizistik nach den beiden Weltkriegen", in Albrecht Langner (ed.), *Katholizismus, nationaler Gedanke und Europa seit 1800*, Paderborn u.a.: Schöningh 1985, 131–154; Axel Schildt, *Zwischen Abendland und Amerika. Studien zur Westdeutschen Ideenlandschaft der 50er Jahre*, München: Oldenburg 1999; Richard Faber, *Abendland: ein politischer Kampfbegriff*, 2nd ed. Berlin etc.: Philo-Verlag-Ges. 2002 (Kulturwissenschaftliche Studien, 10). One of the first statements that should define the Lutheran position in the culture of postwar Germany was given by Helmut Thielicke, *Kirche und Öffentlichkeit. Zur Grundlegung einer lutherischen Kulturethik*, Tübingen: Furche-Verlag 1947.

70 On the political interpretation of religious films, especially during the Cold-War era in the US: Gerald E. Forshey, *American Religious and Biblical Spectaculars*, Westport CT: Praeger Publishers 1997, 27–54.

71 Cf. Forshey, *Biblical spectaculars*, 28.

72 Kahle/Lee, *Popcorn and Parable*, 31.

73 Roland Bainton, *Roland Bainton speaks on the Martin Luther motion picture*, New York: Lutheran Church Production 1954, 17f.

74 Forshey has made clear that the "righteous nation" theme is already anticipated in *Quo vadis*. Through Christianity, the righteous nation would be able to overcome the precarious state in which society found itself (ibid. 28; on the Christian virtues: ibid., 29). However, since victory was won by force of arms in the Second World War and not through Christian love for one's enemies, the reasoning was reversed, as it was for the Crusades, to imply that a Christian nation per se was doing God's will (in 1095 Pope Urban II clamoured for the liberation of Jerusalem with the words „Deus lo vult!"): "Having destroyed the Axis war machine, Americans believed that their success was the result of divine approval of American goals and values" (ibid., 33).

75 Fryer, *Guide*, 29.

76 Los Angeles Daily News of Sept. 11, 1953.

77 Thus Bosley Crowther in the *New York Times*, Sept. 10, 1953; cf. Fryer, *Guide*, 37; compare the anonymous statement in *To-Day's Cinema*, Oct. 18, 1954: "Practically the whole acting burden falls on Niall McGinnis as Luther. He is seldom off the screen, and he dominates the whole production. With burning sincerity and superb emotional power he brings Luther to live as a man not stern but steadfast, humorous, kindly, and invincible."

78 Fryer, *Guide*, 45.

79 Cf. ibid. 36.

80 Cf. Peter Fraser, *Images of Passion: The Sacramental Mode in Film*, Westport, CT: Praeger Publishers 1998, 169f.

81 As a key to the vast body of publications on the subject, two studies on Lavater are mentioned here: Gudrun Swoboda, "Lavater sammelt Linien: Zu seinem Versuch einer universalen Klassifikation linearer Ausdruckscharaktere im Anschluss an Dürer und Hogarth", in Benno Schubiger (ed.), *Sammeln und Sammlungen im 18. Jahrhundert in der Schweiz.*

Akten des Kolloquiums Basel, 16–18 October 2003, Geneva: Slatkine, 2007 (Travaux sur la Suisse des Lumières, 10), 315–339; Wilhelm Voßkamp, "Semiotik des Menschen. Bildphysiognomie und literarische Transkription bei Johann Caspar Lavater und Georg Christoph Lichtenberg", in Matthias Bickenbach (ed.), *Korrespondenzen. Visuelle Kulturen zwischen früher Neuzeit und Gegenwart*, Cologne: DuMont 2002 (Mediologie, 4), 150–163. The transference of particular models to filmic representation of heroes and villains was recognized early on, probably first by Béla Balász: Claudia Schmölders, "Physiognomik und Film. Ein Literaturbericht", in *literaturkritik.de*, No. 5, Mai 2003 (http://www.literaturkritik. de/public/rezension.php?rez_id=6000 [18.11.2008]).

82 "fere mortuus essem quia nulla aderat fides" (WA TR 4, p. 180, No. 4174). He was so appalled at the words "Aeterno vivo vero Deo" that he wanted to run away from the altar and the prior of the covent had to persuade him not to (WA TR 2, p. 133, No. 1558 [May 20, 1532]).

83 The scene in the 1953 film has been extensively described and criticized from the theological standpoint by Albrecht (Albrecht, *Verkündigung*, 87f.). As he sees it, the film equalizes the Protestant theology on the Sacrament with Catholic concept of Holy Communion.

84 The discussion of defining the two genres cannot be gone into here (see for instance McKean Taylor, *Rolle des Lebens*, 75–82); it is taken as a given, however, that each filmic work, no matter how many elements of reality it may contain, is always an art product informed by subjective experience.

85 On the content Albrecht, *Verkündigung*, 107–111.

86 Johanna Haberer and Julia Helmke, "Das bewegte Lutherbild im Wandel der Zeit – Durchsicht der Filme von 1927 bis zur Gegenwart", in *Amt und Gemeinde. Theologisches Fachblatt* 55, H 3/4, 2004, 55–63; here 59 (first printed in *Arbeitshilfe für den evangelischen Religionsunterricht an Gymnasien*, Folge II, 2003, 13–25).

87

	Der gehorsame Rebell	Martin Luther
1955:	69 (7001)	559 (54,159)
1956:	21 (1990)	555 (229,033)
1957:	4 (845)	478 (47,750)

(EZA Bestand 2, No. 2800, Statistical material and figures accompanying the 1957 *Jahresbericht* [*Annual Report*]).

88 Letter of October 11, 1971 from Robert E. A. Lee, Lutheran Film Associates, to Dr. Johannes Stuhlmacher, Luther-Film GmbH: Luther Film Associates gives up its shares in Luther-Film and leaves them to the Hilfswerk (ADW, HGSt 7077).

89 Erikson, *Der junge Mann Luther*.

90 Strindberg, *Luther*, 18. Nevertheless, this treatment is verified: Brecht, *Martin Luther*, Vol. 1, 18. Brecht, however, depicts Luther's parents in a milder light as having brought up Martin very strictly but not immoderatly so. After all, it was a big family with four or five sons and four daughters, of whom one daughter and two or three of the sons died young (ibid., 19). Further, Luther left Mansfeld at the age of fourteen; from then on other people were the dominant influences on him (cf. ibid., 20).

91 "Reverende Pater, Wollet ihr auff Christum und die Lehre, wie ihr die gepredigt, bestendig sterben?" (WA 54, 492); according to Brecht, Schubart's study on this is still valid: Christof Schubart, *Die Berichte über Luthers Tod und Begräbnis. Texte und Untersuchungen*, Weimar: Böhlau 1917; cf. Martin Brecht, *Martin Luther. Die Erhaltung der Kirche 1532–1546*, Stuttgart: Calwer 1987 [Martin Luther, 3], 368 and n. 2).

92 WA 48, 241 as well as WA TR 5, 168, No. 5468. Extensively on the context of that statement: Heinrich Bornkamm, *Luthers geistige Welt*, 1st ed. 1947, 4th ed. Gütersloh: Mohn 1960, 310–314.

93 Sickingen and Hutten are shown in an extremely negative light, probably as a reflection

on National Socialist demagogy, which wanted to establish a national church against the Roman Catholic Emperor.

94 "Finde ich einen Gott, der mir gnädig ist?"

95 "Das Mittelalter war schon tot, als Du kamst."

96 "Sobald das Geld im Kasten klingt, die Seele aus dem Fegefeuer in den Himmel springt."

97 It has hitherto been impossible to verify that Johann Tetzel used those words in his sermons, which Luther then included in the 27th of his 95 Theses. However, similarly formulations occur in earlier writings, for instance in a popular German version of the *Summa abbreviata* of Johann von Freiburg (late 13th century), which was still being printed in the late 15th century: „Und also möchte auch ein Papst von seiner Allmächtigkeit eine Seele aus dem Fegefeuer lösen und für sie geben und gelten Ablaß aller Pein und Schuld und sie zu den Himmeln senden." (Nikolaus Paulus, *Geschichte des Ablasses im Mittelalter*, 2nd ed. Darmstadt: Wiss. Buchgesellschaft 2000, Vol. 1, 245). The *Instructio summaria* of Archbishop Albrecht of Mainz and Tetzel's (excerpts) sermons are printed in Walther Köhler, *Dokumente zum Ablassstreit von 1517*, Tübingen: Mohr, 2nd revised ed. 1934, 104–124 and 124–127.

98 For instance Ps 51, Ps 90; "Der heilige Geist wehet, wo er will" after John 3,8 ("The winde bloweth where it listeth"); cf. CA 18: "De libero arbitrio. [...] Sed non habet vim sine spiritu sancto efficiendae iustitiae Dei seu iustitiae spiritualis" ("Of free will [...] but without the mercy, aid and effect of the Holy Spirit, man cannot please God" "Vom freien Willen [...] aber ohn Gnad, Hilfe und Wirkung des heiligen Geists vermag der Mensch nicht Gott gefällig zu werden"), BSLK, Vol. 1, Göttingen: Vandenhoeck & Ruprecht, 1930, 70; cf. *De servo arbitrio*, WA 18, 600–787, *Lateinisch-Deutsche Studienausgabe* 1, Leipzig: EVA 2006, 219–661); "Ich haßte Gott" (cf. Proemium to the Latin writings of 1545: WA 54,186, 14; "Wie sehr ich einst das Wort Gerechtigkeit Gottes abgrundtief gehasst habe" ("How profoundly I once hated the word God's justice"), *Martin Luther. Lateinisch-Deutsche Studienausgabe*, Vol. 2: Christusglaube und Rechtfertigung, edited and introduced by Johannes Schilling, Leipzig: EVA 2006, 507.

99 On this issue frequently debated in Luther scholarship: Volker Leppin, "Deus absconditus und Deus revelatus. Transformationen mittelalterlicher Theologie in der Gotteslehre von 'De servo arbitrio'", in *Berliner Theologische Zeitschrift* 22 (2005), H. 1, 55–69.

100 See the dogmatic Constitution *On Divine Revelation "Dei Verbum"*, Chap. II, 10 of November 18, 1965: "But the task of authentically interpreting the word of God, whether written or handed on, (8) has been entrusted exclusively to the living teaching office of the Church, (9) whose authority is exercised in the name of Jesus Christ." Complete text online in English at the Vatican website: http://www.vatican.va/archive/hist_councils/ii_vatican_council/documents/vat-ii_const_19651118_dei-verbum_en.html

101 Most recently: Reinhard Brandt, *Lasst ab vom Ablass. Ein evangelisches Plädoyer*, Göttingen: Vandenhoeck & Ruprecht, 2008, 51–55.

102 "The author seems instead to have borrowed from modern psychoanalytical attempts at explanation in placing Luther's relationship with his father dangerously close to his question about God and also returns to it at the moment the pope is burnt in effigy." (translated from German), Martin Elze, "Einführung zu Leopold Ahlsen, Der Arme Mann Luther", in Horstmann, *Wandel*, 103; "The Freudian view of the father complex – although conceived by the author as strongly poetic in thrust and played by Hans Mahnke with relentless intensity – seemed embarrassing." (U. J., "Der arme Mann Luther. Zum Fernsehspiel von Leopold Ahlsen", in *epd, Kirche und Fernsehen*, No. 3 of 23 Jan. 1965, printed in ibid., 104f.); "Dieter Zeidler convincingly portrayed a Luther who was tortured by doubts, who hated yet believed. Noteworthy: Ernst Fritz Fürbringer as Charles V." (Eugen Netenjakob, "Eine dramaturgische Leistung", in *Funk-Korrespondenz*, No. 5, Jan. 28, 1965, 17f. reprinted in Horstmann, *Wandel*, 106f.).

103 "Christian Rode as the Reformer: a figure idealized in the Nazarene manner, in whom, of course, virtually no trace could be found of what more recent Luther scholarship has long since brought to light" (Klaus Hamburger, "Illustrierter Religionsunterricht: Günther Sawatzki, 'Der Reformator', Dokumentarspiel über Martin Luther", in *Funk-Korrespondenz*, No. 45, Nov. 7, 1968, 18, reprinted in Horstmann, *Wandel*, 115).

104 Quoted in Horst G. Feldt, "Ein unromantisches und unheldisches Lutherbild", in *epd. Kirche und Film*, No. 41, Oct. 12, 1968, reprinted in Horstmann, *Wandel*, 112–114, here: 114: "Es gilt, fast gegen den gebräuchlichen Luther anzuspielen. Also kein heldischer Gottesstreiter, sondern ein Mensch in geradezu qualvollem Streben nach dem gnädigen Gott."

105 "Despite all intended alienation there was too much acting" ("Hier war offenbar, trotz angestrebter Verfremdung, noch immer zuviel Theater im Spiel") thus Dietmar Schmidt, 'Glaubenskriege' um Lutherfilme", in Trapmann, *Reformator*, 274.

106 John Osborne, *Luther*, London: Faber and Faber 1961, 7.

107 Michael Feingold, in *The Village Voice*, 2001, quoted according to the text printed in the leaflet issued with the DVD copy of the film.

108 Howard Taubman, "Theater: 'Luther' Stars Albert Finney", *New York Times*, Sept. 26, 1963, 41; Walter Kerr "'Luther' – Mighty Fortress Partly Breached by Britain's John Osborne", *Los Angeles Times*, Oct. 6, 1963, B20; "Few Smash Hits on N.Y. Stages", *Chicago Tribune*, Oct. 19, 1963, A5; Max Freedman, "Faults Invalidate 'Luther' Play", *Los Angeles Times*, Nov. 11, 1963, A5.

109 In 1965 the director was Alan Cooke and the producer Cedric Messina. It was broadcast on channel BBC1 on October 19, 1965. Cast: Martin Luther: Alec McCowen; Tetzel: Patrick Magee; Cajetan: Geoffrey Bayldon; Staupitz: Charles Carson; Knight: Ray Barrett; Hans: Jerold Wells; Lucas: Gerry Duggan; Weinand: Philip Stone; Miltitz: William Ingram; Katherine: Etain O'Dell; Eck: Fulton MacKay; Leo: Tom Criddle; Prior: James Cairncross. In 1968 the director was Stuart Burge, the producers were the BBC and InterTel Fernseh GmbH, Munich); Producer: Michael Style; television adaptation by Robert Furnival; Cast: Luther: Robert Shaw; The Pope: Robert Morley; Tetzel: Ronald Fraser; Cajetan: Max Adrian; Luther's father: Kenneth J. Warren; Wienand: Bernard Kay; Staupitz: Frank Middlemass; The Knight: William Marlowe; Hans: Reg Barrett; Katherine: Yootha Joyce; Eck: John Byron; Miltitz: Alexander Davion; The Prior: André Van Gyseghem. First broadcast on January 29, 1968, it ran for 90 minutes on ABC TV (British Film Institute, London, Film and TV database); it was broadcast a second time on December 21, 1968 on BBC 2, with a running time of 75 minutes.

110 "[…] a rather harshly cut version of Mr. John Osborne's *Luther*. This was "epic" not only in terms that the author would accept but in the Hollywood sense, too. Mr. Alan Cooke crowded the screen with people, linked scenes with obtrusive woodcuts, played photographic tricks and trained cameras down long perspectives which allowed his actors the freedom of a very big style; […] In concentrating on Luther as the archetypal rebel, who found his personal satisfaction in overthrowing authority because it exists, Mr. Osborne omits links from his intellectual chain, and these grow no less noticeable as time passes." ("Crowded Screen in Luther 'Epic'", *The Times*, October 20, 1965, 16).

111 Jack Gould deplored the cuts made to what had been such a successful production: "the pressures of the clock so common to TV including the unfortunate commercial interruptions, ultimately caused the study of the Reformation leader to lose momentum. […] the London interpretation caught the stature of Martin Luther in his challenge to the Roman Catholic Church and his stern belief that faith is not something not be formally structured but rather to be found in individual service to God" (Jack Gould, "TV: Robert Shaw Gives Intense Portrayal of Luther", *The New York Times*, Jan. 30, 1968, 83). Cecil Smith found the performance met all expectations of clichés: "John Osborne's Luther with Robert Shaw as the monk who 'lit a candle to God and started a bonfire with all Europe as the kindling,'

erupted with volcanic force on television's small stage [...] And although the British Intertel production [sic!] of the Osborn drama was considerably cut, particularly in the late scenes, to fit the ABC 90-minute time slot, the production still contained the sort of passionate, eloquent, provocative, dramatic involvement that is a rarity in the bland toothless world of TV. Osborne's play is essentially concerned with the man Martin Luther rather than the huge historical canvas of the Reformation. The play for all its probing into the dark heart of medieval Europe, for all the smoky excitement it contains in the stirring of revolt against the smug, corrupt Roman church, for all the thunderous power of its language, the repeated themes of blood, bone, flesh, is still the study of an angry young man, driven by private demons, who rips apart all Christendom because he is himself torn by his own need for something to believe." (Cecil Smith, "TV Review, John Osborne's 'Luther' Presented as ABC Special", *Los Angeles Times*, Jan. 31, 1968, C13). In Chicago it was the cuts that were chiefly regretted: "[....] the fraudulence of television's Luther was that what probably was a good production was cut with a meat axe. [...] On screen it [the play] had tantalizing glimpses of what might have been, primarily in the gaunt face of Robert Shaw as Luther" (Claudia Cassidy, "On the Aisle; Taut Drama Gets the Worst of It, Both on Camera and on Stage", *Chicago Tribune*, Feb. 5, 1968, B8).

112 Gary Arnold, "Cinema: Subscribing to the Idea That the Play's the Thing at AFT", *The Washington Post, Times Herald*, Sept. 9, 1973, L1.

113 Rex Reed, "You Can See It for Less Than It Costs to Take a Taxi to a Theater [...]", *The Washington Post, Times Herald*, July 22, 1973, F3.

114 "Landau is systematically ignoring all the conventional wisdom of the film industry." (Paul S. Clark, "Landau Pursues a Possible Dream", *Los Angeles Times*, Aug. 13, 1973, C13). On the number of locations and Stacy Keach's reputation at the time: Cecil Smith, "Keach: Tall in Napoleon's Saddle", *Los Angeles Times*, Aug. 15, 1973, E16.

115 Director Guy Green explained why he had chosen this setting: "My first inclination was to stage the play, as far as possible, in the actual locations where Martin Luther lived, but of course Erfurt, where Luther spent his early years as a monk, is now behind the Iron Curtain. Nevertheless, I found in Bavaria many places evocative of the times, especially a fourteenth-century monastery at Malbrun [sic! The author: Maulbronn is situated in Württemberg] which was wonderfully preserved and a pictorial dream. It was with great reluctance that I finally gave up this idea. There were two reasons. First, the logistics involved did not sit well with our less than lavish budget, and would also seriously restrict the choice of actors for the numerous taxing roles. Second, I had an uncomfortable feeling that I was staying too close to a conventional movie. During this time, I had seen several cathedrals and sensed the great dramatic possibilities they offered. Why not stage the *entire action* in a cathedral? It would be in keeping with the subject, but the play calls for great changes in place and time. By what logic could the monastery chapel at Erfurt become Juterbog [sic!] market place ten years later? The film must create its own logic. The transition just mentioned could be achieved by moving the camera from Luther [....] The idea was heartily endorsed by Ely Landau and his associates, and I now had to find the right cathedral. I searched in Germany, France and England. Although there were a number of good prospects, the problems of availability, light, and sound control seemed insurmountable, until our production manager said: 'How about building one? I can build you a cathedral, or at least a good-looking church.' So this was done magnificently, to the design of Peter Mullin, at Shepperton Studios in England [....]" (Guy Green, "On Staging the Film", in *Cinebill*; quoted from the text as reproduced on the DVD issued in 2003).

116 Act 1, scene 3, Osborne, *Luther*, 41.

117 Ibid., 1961, 91.

118 Jay Robert Nash and Stanley Ralph Ross, *The Motion Picture Guide*, L-M, 1927–1983, Chicago: Cinebooks 1986, 1779: "extremely well-acted [....] This is a classic example of

how some of the best written plays are inherently noncinematic"; Leslie Halliwell, *Halliwell's film & video guide*, edited by John Walker, 12th enlarged ed. London: HarperCollins 1996, 664: "Hard-to-watch filming [....] singularly theatrical play [....] Some good acting." C. P. Reilly, "Luther", in *Films in Review*, March 1974, 186: "Stacy Keach, [....], is so hopelessly miscast as Luther that the filming of John Osborne's play by the American Film Theater doesn't stand a chance [....] The production is claustrophobic, cutting off Luther from the world he was so deeply influencing"; by contrast: F. Meyr, "Luther", in *Variety*, Vol. 273, Feb. 6, 1974, 18: "Keach is brilliant as Luther, the sounding board for whom the others play off as strings on a finely tuned violin. He grows in the role from the fumbling, indecisive unsure university graduate who has entered a monastery to a key creator of the Reformation, though remaining unsure of himself throughout."

119 As early as 1946, Delannoy had made a name for himself by filming the André Gide novel *La Symphonie Pastorale* (German *Und es ward Licht*), which tells the story of a blind girl brought up by a Swiss pastor. Delannoy's film received two awards in Cannes. In 1950 he caused a stir with *Dieu a besoin des hommes* (1951 German version: *Gott braucht Menschen*) after the Henri Queffélec novel *Un recteur de l'Île de Sein* (published in 1944) since it depicts a Catholic congregation choosing an unconsecrated priest, that is, acting in accordance with the Protestant principle of freedom to choose clergy at congregation level (On this: Josef Hartmann, "Eine priesterlose Gemeinde auf der Suche nach Gott: ‚Gott braucht Menschen' von Jean Delannoy (1950)", in Josef Hartmann (ed.), *Spuren des Religiösen im Film*, 80–82).

120 "Interview mit Alexandre Astruc", in Trapmann, *Reformator*, 152f.: "In seinem Denken sind erste Keime der Aufklärung und der Französischen Revolution enthalten – kurz, Luther ist in meinen Augen einer der wichtigsten geistigen Protagonisten der Neuzeit. Aber in diesem Film wollte ich in erster Linie den Menschen Luther zeigen [....]. Im Gegensatz zu Calvin, diesem asketischen, gequälten Reformator, war Luther –, seitdem er zu der Erkenntnis gelangt war, dass es vor allem auf das Vertrauen ankommt, das man in Gott setzt –, ein sehr freier, sehr lebendiger und lebensvoller Mensch. [....] Ein Mensch von großer Kühnheit, der zu sagen pflegte: Pecca fortiter – sündige tapfer."

121 Schübel, *Luther*.

122 Olof Linton, "Ekklesia I (bedeutungsgeschichtlich)", in RAC 4, Stuttgart: Anton Hirsemann 1959, 915f.; Ernst Dassmann, "Kirche II (bildersprachlich)", in RAC 20, Stuttgart: Anton Hirsemann 2004, 967f. and 989–993.

123 Rainer Wolffhardt, "'Am farb'gen Abglanz haben wir das Leben'. Versuch über den Versuch der Versinnlichung des Stoffes", in Trapmann, *Reformator*, 60–69; here 68: "Herausforderung … den kirchlichen Spielort … einer immerwährenden Metamorphose zu unterwerfen: Von der Etablierung des mittelalterlichen Katholizismus bis zur In-Frage-Stellung all der darin enthaltenen Werte und der Etablierung des Protestantismus, der dann aber wiederum auch immer mehr in Frage gestellt wurde, im Zuge der Politisierung und Institutionalisierung."

124 *Religion im Film. Lexikon mit Kurzkritiken und Stichworten zu 2400 Kinofilmen*, 3rd enlarged ed. 1999, 343 (here the film is erroneously dated to 1996): "sinnbildhaftes Welttheater".

125 Thus Wolffhardt in the Geschichtsdidaktisches Kolloquium (Didactic History Colloquium) at Ludwig-Maximilians University in Munich, May 14, 2002.

126 "hätte [ich] allen Glauben, so dass ich Berge versetzte, und hätte der Liebe nicht, so wär ich nichts." (cf. 1 Cor 13,2)

127 Detlef Urban, "'Ein Genie sehr bedeutender Art'. Bemerkungen zu einem Lutherfilm im DDR-Fernsehen", in *Deutschland Archiv. Zeitschrift für das vereinigte Deutschland* 16 (1983), H. 12, 1253–1255; here 1253: "Zwar hat die SED offiziell das Jahr 1983 zum Karl-Marx-Jahr deklariert, aber für Martin Luther und dessen fünfhundertsten Geburtstag ist den Genossen nichts zu teuer."

128 Günter Vogler, "Luther oder Müntzer?: die Rolle frühneuzeitlicher Gestalten für die Identitätsfindung der DDR", in Hans-Joachim Gehrke (ed.), *Geschichtsbilder und Gründungsmythen*, Würzburg: Ergon-Verlag 2001 (Identitäten und Alteritäten, 7), 417–436.

129 Klaus Hilbig, "Warum muß Luther brüllen? Zu dem Fernsehfilm von Kurt Veth", *Sonntag* 43, 1983, 5 (press cutting in the Bundesarchiv-Filmarchiv in Berlin).

130 *Tagesspiegel*, Oct. 30, 1983: "Luther wird nicht weißgewaschen, er scheitert an seinen Grenzen. Aber er wird rehabilitiert. Der Volksverräter von damals ist heute ein frühbürgerlicher Revolutionär. Der Film unterließ es, ihm anstelle der theologischen politische Motive unterzuschieben. Das hatte er auch nicht mehr nötig. Mit diesem Film hat die DDR Luther für sich vereinnahmt – er soll Teil des nationalen Selbstbewusstseins sein."

131 "Solange ich lebe, will ich Gott darum bitten – Deutschland soll durch Krieg keine Not haben."

132 On that: Rotraut Simons, "Das DDR-Fernsehen und die Luther-Ehrung", in Horst Dähn/ Joachim Heise, *Luther und die DDR. Der Reformator und das DDR-Fernsehen 1983*, Berlin: Ed. Ost 1996, 99–185.

133 Cf. the report of this preview by Yvonne Matthes in a letter to Kurt Eifert, DEFA-Dokumentarfilmstudio, on May 6, 1982: "empfahl Prof. Laube, nach den Passagen über den gescheiterten Bauernkrieg einen wertenden Satz einzufügen, der die Tragik Luthers (siehe Rede Honecker) darlegt, d.h. [....] Luther klassenmäßig einordnet, der sich als Initiator einer großen Bewegung in seinen begrenzten Zielstellungen in der Rolle des Zauberlehrlings befand [...]. Ihm geht es um die klare Aussage, daß Luther nicht der Bauernschlächter war ...." (DRA, Standort Potsdam, HA Kultur Luther Wittenberg; cited according to the transcript at the website: http://www.staat-kirche-forschung.de/seiten/eBooks/RSimons/ Buerger%20Luther.pdf [26.1.2009])

134 Lew Hohmann directed the film for GDR television and it was produced at the "DEFA-Studio für Trickfilme" in Dresden (screenplay: Lew Hohmann; adviser: Professor Adolf Laube; camera: Hellmut May; length 460 m; format 35 mm, 1:1.33; picture/sound Orwo-color; first screening: 7 Oct. 1983).

135 Published on DVD, June 16, 2005 by Ottonia Media GmbH; length 45 min; format 4:3.

136 Susanne Hermanski, "Das Kreuz mit dem streitbaren Mönch", in *SZ-Extra*, Oct. 30, 2003; Matthias Drobinski, "Die Rückkehr des Reformators", in *Süddeutsche Zeitung*, Nov. 27, 2003, 3.

137 This has been maintained on many occasions (for instance Monika Goetsch, "Endlich reif fürs Kino: Der schöne Luther erobert die Herzen und bleibt ein Mann von Format [...]", in *Chrismon Plus*, July 2002, 51). In any case, anyone who knows the Osborne play would be unable to recognize any parallels.

138 "Ein Wildschwein trachtet danach, ihn [den Weinberg des Herrn] zu zerwühlen [...]." (Helmar Junghans [ed.], *Die Reformation in Augenzeugenberichten*, Düsseldorf: Rauch 1967, 87f.; cf. Holsing, *Luther – Gottesmann*, 426).

139 "Martin was ... all about [....] hope and compassion [....] I think we need a great deal of that today [....] a great wish [was] to [....] discover the human being failed, frail, insecure, aggressive ... obnoxious that time, very human [....] this was obscure and left out [....] We can't possibly satisfy theologians." (quoted from an interview with Eric Till in the bonus material supplied with the 2003 DVD version).

140 Monika Goetsch, "Endlich reif [....]", 50f.

141 See "Sir Peter Ustinov. Ein Interview zu seinem neuen Film 'Luther'", *Münchner Wochenblatt* 2003, 45, G5.

142 Quoted from the interview provided in the bonus material on the DVD of the 2003 version.

143 Hermanski, *Das Kreuz*.

144 Matthias Drobinski, "Die Kirche, die Krise und das Kino", *Süddeutsche Zeitung*, Oct. 31, 2003, 4: „um alles verschlankt ist, was keinen Spaß macht."

145 Susan Vahabzadeh, "Unbeichtbar. Mit seinen Sünden allein: 'Luther' – protestantisch betrachtet", *Süddeutsche Zeitung*, Oct. 29, 2003, 13; cf. Fritz Göttler, "Wilder Keiler. Auf Schauwerte bedacht: '"Luther' – katholisch gesehen": ibid.

146 Dirk Blothner, "Wirkungsanalyse: Veränderung mit Folgen", in Herbert Heinzelmann, *Luther, Eric Till: Deutschland 2003. Filmheft*, ed. by Bundeszentrale für politische Bildung, Bonn: bpb 2004, 16: "*Luther* fand im Herbst/Winter 2003 in den deutschen Kinos ein unerwartet großes Publikum. Ein Grund dafür mögen die in der Bundesrepublik anstehenden sozialen Reformen sein. Die Menschen ahnen, dass sich viele Dinge ändern müssen, aber sie haben noch keine konkrete Vorstellung davon. Der Film ermöglicht es, einen Prozess der Veränderung mit allen damit einhergehenden Versprechen, Risiken und Folgen nachzuvollziehen."

147 Steffens, *Luthergedenkstätten*, 59–91.

148 On that: Edgar Lersch / Reinhold Viehoff, *Geschichte im Fernsehen. Eine Untersuchung zur Entwicklung des Genres und der Gattungsästhetik geschichtlicher Darstellungen im Fernsehen 1995 bis 2003*, Düsseldorf: Landesanstalt für Medien Nordrhein-Westfalen, 2007 (Schriftenreihe Medienforschung der Landesanstalt für Medien Nordrhein-Westfalen, 54), 329f.

149 Cf. Ibid., 242.

150 Ibid., 113. Even in the Luther-year 2003 it was only 0.9%. In the German TV programs features about the history of the Third Reich hold the main part: It varied from about 7% to 11% in the years 1995–2003 (Ibid., 154 anc 155).

IV. Gender Roles in Luther Films

1   The expansion of Women's and Gender Studies to include research into maleness and masculinity is reflected in numerous studies, of which the majority on historical constructions of masculinity have appeared in the German-speaking countries in the past five to ten years. Overviews are provided by Wolfgang Schmale, *Geschichte der Männlichkeit in Europa (1450–2000)*, Vienna, etc.: Böhlau 2003; Ernst Hanisch, *Männlichkeiten. Eine andere Geschichte des 20. Jahrhunderts*, Wien etc.: Böhlau 2005; Jürgen Martschukat and Olaf Stieglitz, *"Es ist ein Junge!": Einführung in die Geschichte der Männlichkeiten in der Neuzeit*, 1st ed. Tübingen: Edition Diskord, 2005, 2nd ed. 2008. Unfortunately these studies have been overlooked by Anglo-American handbook-writers (for example: Kathy Davis, Mary Evans and Judith Lorber [ed.], *Handbook of gender and women's studies*, London etc.: Sage 2006).

2   For instance, Cohan/Hark, *Screening*: Claudia Liebrand, *Gender-Topographien: kulturwissenschaftliche Lektüren von Hollywoodfilmen der Jahrhundertwende*, Cologne: DuMont, 2003.

3   Spicer has drawn up a typology of all male roles in films between the 1940s and 1960s: Andrew Spicer, *Typical Men. The Representation of Masculinity in Popular British Cinema*, London and New York: I.B. Tauris Publishers 2001.

4   Raewyn (Robert William) Connell's concept, borrowing from Antonio Gramsci's use of the term hegemony, represents "a social ascendancy achieved in a play of social forces that extends beyond contests of brute power into the organization of private life and cultural processes [...] Ascendancy which is embedded in religious doctrine and practice, mass media content, wage structures, the design of housing, welfare/taxation policies" (R. W. Connell, *Gender and Power: Society, the Person and Sexual Politics*, Stanford, California: Stanford University Press 1987, 184; cf R. Connell, *Masculinities*, Berkeley: University of California Press 1995, chapter 3). Most historical Men's Studies have been based upon and further developed this concept, for instance in the volumes of studies edited by Martin

Dinges (ed.), *Männer – Macht – Körper. Hegemoniale Männlichkeiten vom Mittelalter bis heute*, Frankfurt am Main: Campus-Verlag 2005; as well as Ulrike Brunotte and Rainer Herrn (ed.), *Männlichkeiten und Moderne: Geschlecht in den Wissenskulturen um 1900*, Bielefeld: Transcript 2007 (Gender Codes 3).

5   Martschukat/Stieglitz, *Männlichkeiten in der Neuzeit*, 71.

6   Ibid., 82.

7   Ulrike Brunotte and Rainer Herrn, "Statt einer Einleitung. Männlichkeit und Moderne – Pathosformeln, Wissenskulturen, Diskurse", in Brunotte/Herrn, *Männlichkeiten und Moderne*, 9. Here the authors apply "abolition of celibacy" and, concomitantly, "desacrilisation of abstinence" as their criteria. Apart from the fact that celibacy was not obligatory for the Protestant clergy, the hegemonial concepts continued to be applied by the (Roman Catholic) laity (for instance, in the conquest of South America). Not until the 19th century did nobility as the classic leadership elite (based on this ideal of masculinity) begin to lose its primacy, and then only gradually–it also shaped gender roles in the (early) modern era: take, for example, the widespread influence of Castigliones *Il libro del cortegtiano* (Schmale, *Geschichte*, 27). The concept of the Protestant head of household as initiated by Luther can at best be viewed as a variant of the type of hegemonial masculinity. If, however, one follows Schmale in the premise that this concept can only be realized in a society of the masses with broad-based channels of communication (a thesis which has yet to be put to the proof), one has to admid, that this did not happen until the latter half of the 19th century (ibid., 151–154).

8   Thus the definition even in Connell, *Gender*, 184.

9   This is invariably true even in polyethnic cultures such as modern German society: Nina Baur and Jens Luedke [ed.], *Die soziale Konstruktion von Männlichkeit: Hegemoniale und marginalisierte Männlichkeiten in Deutschland*, Opladen, etc.: Budrich 2008, 16f.

10 See "Krise(n) der Männlichkeiten" in a themed issue of the European feminist history magazine *L'Homme* 19,2 (2008) and Brunotte/Herrn, *Männlichkeiten und Moderne*. On pacifism in this context: Hanisch, *Männlichkeiten*, 48–50.

11 On the eroticisation of male characters in cinema: Steve Neal, "Masculinity as Spectacle: Reflections on Men and Mainstream Cinema", in Cohan/Hark, *Screening*, 9–20, here: 13f.

12 On the various facets of this war experience, which are, so far as gender role concepts are concerned, also viewed as positive: Birthe Kundrus, "Geschlechterkriege: Der Erste Weltkrieg und die Deutung der Geschlechterverhältnisse in der Weimarer Republik", in Karen Hagemann and Stephanie Schüler-Springorum (ed.), *Heimat-Front. Militär und Geschlechterverhältnisse im Zeitalter der Weltkriege*, Frankfurt am Main: Campus-Verlag 2002, 171–187.

13 Spicer, *Typical Men*, ch. 3 (47–64); compare this pattern to other role models provided by British cinema (see Spicer's typology in Schmale, *Geschichte*, 244f.).

14 This part was played by Lyda Salmonowa (Strindberg, *Luther*, [94]), who became a famous actress in film; obviously she represented an oriental type of character, for example she played the part of Rabbi Löw's daughter Miriam in *Der Golem, wie er in die Welt kam* (1920).

15 That is not a specific phenomenon of documentaries on Luther: 'androcentrism' characterizes the whole genre as the study by Edgar Lersch and Reinhold Viehoff showed recently (Lersch/Viehoff, *Geschichte im Fernsehen*, S. 185).

16 Since this identification operates via the projection of universal desires, the gender of the figure upon whom they are projected is of secondary importance. Hence, women can also identify with male heroes if those heroes correspond to their ideals and are wish-fulfilling. On this complex process against the background of the issue of the masculine image in cinema: Neal, in Cohan/Hark, *Screening*, 10–15.

17 Most of the approximately 150 Luther plays, none of which can be classified as world-class literature, hand down the conventional image of Martin Luther's wife as a good housewife

and mother. There are, however, two notable exceptions: Friedrich Ludwig Zacharias Werner's *Martin Luther, oder Die Weihe der Kraft* and Thomas Mann's play *Luthers Hochzeit*, which was left unfinished when the author died in 1956. Werner's play for the stage might, as staged, have served at least partly as a model for the film *Doktor Martin Luther. Ein Lebensbild für das deutsche Volk*, particularly in the sentimental conception of Katharina. Otherwise, the two plays have had no verifiable effect on the history of viewer response to the character of Katharina von Bora. The exciting construct that she must decide between two concepts for her life in her choice of marriage partner (they are Luther and either the knight Franz von Wildeneck in Werner, or Hieronymous Baumgaertner in Thomas Mann) is never revisited (on this: Friedrich Weigend-Abendroth, "Luther – kein Held der Bühne. Ein Streifzug durch 500 Jahre Theaterliteratur", in Trapmann, *Reformator*, 247–257.

18 Lorrain Gamman and Margaret Marshment, *The Female Gaze: Women as Viewers of Popular Culture*, London: The Women's Press 1988, 1.

19 Christine Brückner, *Wenn Du geredet hättest, Desdemona. Ungehaltene Reden ungehaltener Frauen*, 1st ed. Hamburg: Ullstein 1983.

20 Birgit Stolt, "Luthers Sprache in seinen Briefen an Käthe", in Martin Treu (ed.), *Katharina von Bora. Die Lutherin, Aufsätze anläßlich ihre 500. Geburtstages*, Wittenberg: Stiftung Luthergedenkstätten in Sachsen-Anhalt 1999 (Katalog der Stiftung Luthergedenkstätten in Sachsen-Anhalt, 5), 23–32, here: 25f.

21 The text is preceded by a quote from the first Epistle of Paul to Timotheus, 3, 2: "A Bishop therefore must be […] the husband of one wife, […]" (*Martin Luther, oder die Weihe der Kraft*, Berlin: Johann David Sander 1807 [Mikrofiche-Ed.: Munich, etc, Saur, 1990–1994], title page. The play probably premiered as early as 1806 (Friedrich Weigend-Abendroth, in Trapmann, *Reformator*, 250f.).

22 "Schräg über seinem Stubenfenster wohnt eine Jungfrau minniglich. Kathrein von Bora war der Name. Der überfleissige Studio [sic!] ahnte nicht, dass röter ihre Wangen wurden, wenn er am Fenster sich tat zeigen."

23 "Es war der Jungfrau weh zu Mut. Der strenge Vater hatte es bestimmt, dass sie den Schleier nähme und in das Kloster Nimbschen müsse."

24 "Der alten Amme klagt sie wehmutsvoll ihr Leid. Seit sie Martinus Luther hat erblickt, ward es noch schwerer ihr der Weltlichkeit Ade zu sagen."

25 The cutaway technique had been used in American films since about 1903, but it would soon be replaced by complete changes in scene brought about through intercutting, which is the usual practice even today.

26 Werner, *Die Weihe der Kraft*, 140: "Ich muß ein Herz mir fassen – muß ich's doch / Dem Heiland selbst gestehn! – ich liebe Luther – Er ist das Urbild, das ich mir ersehnt." Werner also took up this motif elsewhere: when Luther meets Katharina in person before a Wittenberg city gate, she is only capable of gasping "Mein Urbild". This moment is illustrated by the copper engravings to the text (ibid., 71). Written in just a few months, the piece premiered in June 1806 at the preußisches Nationaltheater in Berlin, with Iffland in the leading role. After his conversion to Catholicism, Werner distanced himself from this text, notably in "Die Weihe der Unkraft" (1814), which was, however, primarily a statement of commitment to the cause of national independence – sparked off by the Battle of the Nations at Leipzig (Hans-Heinrich Reuter, "'Die Weihe der Kraft'. Ein Dialog zwischen Goethe und Zelter und seine Wiederaufnahme bei Fontane", in Regine Otto [ed.], *Dichters Lande im Reich der Geschichte: Aufsätze zur deutschen Literatur des 18. und 19. Jahrhunderts*, Berlin: Aufbau-Verlag etc. 1983, 145–160, 447–452; Uli Beuth, "Zacharias Werners Mädchen und Frauen", in Hubert Thoma, Ghemela Adler (ed.), *Romantik und Moderne. Neue Beiträge aus Forschung und Lehre. Festschrift für Helmut Motekat*, Frankfurt a. M. etc.: Lang 1986, 77–106).

27 "Kathrein von Bora brachte er gen Wittenberg ins Haus des späteren Bürgermeisters

Philipp Reichenbach, der sie als Lieben fast gern halten wollte. Bei Martinus begann sich stark zu regen das Wohlgefallen an der minniglichen Maid."

28 "Ihr schien es so, als sei's ein Traum. In Luther glaubt sie einen Heiligen zu sehn, als er gar milde sie zum Tor der Kirche führte."

29 "Um mit den alten Sitten ganz zu brechen, begann nun auch die Geistlichkeit den Zwang der Ehelosigkeit zu stürzen. Mit gutem Beispiel Luther ging voran, als er um Katharina von Bora freite."

30 "Wenn draussen Stürme toben, soll mein Heim von sorglich lieber Hand geordnet meine Zuflucht sein. Willst Du Kathrein dies Heim mir gründen helfen, so lass vor Gott und Mensch uns schließen eine ehrsam Eh!"

31 "Ein Ehmann soll geduldig sein, sein Weib nicht halten wie ein Schwein. Ein Hausfrau soll vernünftig sein. Des Mannes Weise lernen fein. Da wird Gott geben Gnad' dazu, dass ihm die Ehe sanfte tu."

32 *Evangelischer Filmbeobachter* March 4, 1954, 176, reprinted in Horstmann, *Wandel*, 89: "Luthers Käthe scheint nicht aus einem Kloster gekommen zu sein, sondern aus Hollywood, schade, auch Karl V. ist eine Fehlbesetzung."

33 "Es sei vermerkt, daß für unsere deutschen Vorstellungen die Rollen der Käthe Luther und Karls V. nicht glücklich besetzt [….] wurden." (quoted from reprint in Horstmann, *Wandel*, 93). It is unfortunate, particularly for this supranational study, that "German ideas" were not more precisely defined here.

34 This situation was also reflected in the first German postwar films (on these productions: Anja Horbrügger, *Aufbruch zur Kontinuität — Kontinuität im Aufbruch: Geschlechterkonstruktionen im west- und ostdeutschen Nachkriegsfilm von 1945 bis 1952*, Marburg: Schüren 2007).

35 Werner Hess, *Martin Luther: Eine Einführung in sein Leben: Mit Bildern aus dem Dokumentarfilm "Der Gehorsame Rebell" und dem Spielfilm "Martin Luther"*, Stuttgart: Evangelisches Verlags Werk 1954, 50: "Bruder Martin lernt es schwer, ein Ehemann zu werden. In einem Gemisch von Scheu und Herzlichkeit begegnet er seiner jungen Frau. Die aber entwickelt rasch sehr praktische Talente und beginnt einen Haushalt aus dem Nichts aufzubauen. Kein Geld, alles verkommen und verdorben, jeden Tag Freunde und Durchreisende, die an des Doktors Tisch mitessen sollen. Die einfachsten Geräte in der Küche fehlen, kahle Zimmer, leere Ställe, ein verwilderter Garten. Aber schon nach einem Jahr hat sich alles verändert. Nicht nur in Hof und Garten, sondern auch bei dem zaghaften Ehemann, der glücklich seinen kleinen Hans im Arm hält." Werner Hess was at that time Lutheran film commissioner (*Lexikon des internationalen Films*, Vol. G-H, 1931f).

36 Klaus Hamburger in *Funk-Korrespondenz*, No. 45, Nov. 17, 1968, 18, reprinted in Horstmann, *Wandel*, 115: "Im übrigen aber schritt diese präraffaelitische gezeichnete Kunstfigur durch entscheidende Lebensstationen unverändert, unberührt – ein romantisierter Reformator, dem gegen Ende des Spiels, wie mit schlechtem Gewissen, ein bisschen von dem beigegeben, nachgeliefert wurde, was eine bestimmte Popular-Presse in die Rubrik 'Menschlich gesehen' einordnet, also: das häusliche Idyll mit Katharina von Bora."

37 C. P. Reilly has tellingly summed this up: "Everyone else in the cast, [….], has only a moment or two to act as a sounding board for Luther's philosophy or some point in Luther's historical development." (C. P. Reilly, Luther, *Films in Review*, March 1974, XXV/3, 186); Although film critics' response to the work varied, the portrayal of Katharina was not discussed (Reilly ibid.; F. Meyr, Luther, *Variety* CCLXXIII, 13, Feb. 6, 1974, 18 and Halliwell, 456)

38 Osborne, *Luther*, 95 f.

39 Overview in Trapmann, *Reformator*, 301–304.

40 Angelika Schmidt-Biesalski, "Das Weib schweige in der Kirche", in Trapmann, *Reformator*, 192–203; here: 196: "Andererseits gibt er [Martin Luther], der die Briefe an seine

Frau mit 'Dein Herzliebchen' oder 'Dein Liebchen' zu unterzeichnen pflegt, ihr Aufträge, mit Druckern zu verhandeln, er teilt ihr – etwa aus Marburg – Ergebnisse theologischer Auseinandersetzungen mit, und er traut ihr auch zu, kluge Ratschläge zur Besetzung einer Pfarrstelle zu geben."

41 "But Katharina von Bora's household, her numerous activities from reading the Bible to responsibility for construction work, from taking care of her children to brewing beer: all that does not seem to have been so unusual. Girls were also given lessons even before Luther wrote to the town councillors, although the call for universal formal education for children of all classes was new." ("Aber etwa der Hausstand Katharina von Boras, ihre vielfältigen Aktivitäten von der Bibellektüre bis zur Verantwortung als Bauherrin, von der Kinderfürsorge bis zur Bierbrauerei, das scheint so außergewöhnlich nicht gewesen zu sein. Mädchen erhielten auch vor Luthers Schreiben an die Ratsherren schon Unterricht, wenn auch die Forderung nach allgemeiner Schulbildung für die Kinder aller Schichten neu war."); ibid., 202.

42 The minor importance attached to this role is visible in the fact that it is not included in the cast list in the *Lexikon der Fernsehspiele* (Achim Klünder [ed.], *Lexikon der Fernsehspiele* 1978–1987, Vol. 1, Munich: etc.: Saur 1991, 403).

43 Schübel, *Luther*, 111.

44 "Meine Käthe hat Ordnung in mein Leben gebracht."

45 Text: see ibid., 119–128.

46 A work produced by the Institut für Weltkunde with a running time of 19 minutes, it belongs to the initial phase of post-war cinema and was made by intercutting the 1953 American production with the German documentary film *Der gehorsame Rebell* (1952), which is laden with edifying and explanatory commentaries. As far as Luther's marriage is concerned, the film implies that it provided the Lutheran parsonage with role models.

47 The short documentary film made by Hans-Jürgen Weineck, which focuses on the political events of Luther's day, only cursorily touches on Luther's marriage to Katharina.

48 This film, which was made at the instigation of Haus der Kirche, the research centre of the Lutheran Church in Berlin, is filmed street theatre. In it, Luther is portrayed at five key stages or events in his life and the role is played by different actors in each of them (see "Luther ist tot", *Variety* CCCXVI/5, Aug. 29, 1984, 16; siehe also: Trapmann, *Reformator*, 301–304).

49 Christine Brückner, *Wenn Du geredet hättest, Desdemona. Ungehaltene Reden ungehaltener Frauen*, 1st ed. Hamburg 1983, 3rd enlarged ed. Berlin: Ullstein, 1996, 32–51.

50 "Wer war diese Katharina, die dafür sorgte, dass am Tisch des großen Reformators alle satt wurden?" (quotation from the film).

51 "zupackende Frau […], die selbstbewusst den Handwerkern sagte, was sie wollte und dem Gesinde Befehle gab […]" (quotation from the film).

52 "ihr Herrschaftsgebiet weit über das Haus hinausreichte und erst Pachtland und später sogar ein eigenes Gut umfasste" (quotation from the film).

53 For instance: Schmidt-Biesalski, in Trapmann, *Reformator*, 192–203.

54 Film critics also had something to say – and it was not even negative – on how Katharina was portrayed (for instance: Urban, Genie, 1253–1255).

55 Helga Schütz, *Martin Luther. Eine Erzählung für den Film*, Berlin and Leipzig: Aufbau-Verlag 1983, 95–117.

56 How embarrassing for an educational film that it shows Katharina von Bora fleeing from a covent in Torgau.

57 Thus the brief description in the EDV catalogue issued by the Lutheran media centres.

58 Martin Treu, *Katharina von Bora. Martin Luthers Frau*, 2nd unrevised ed., Wittenberg: Drei-Kastanien-Verl 1996. It should be noted in this connection that the monastery at Brehna

belonged to the Augustinian order, not to the Benedictine (see Alfred Schmidt, *Geschichte des Augustinerinnenklosters St. Clemens zu Brehna*, Brehna: R. Kiemle 1924, 4 f.).

59   Martin Treu, *Katharina von Bora. Bilder aus ihrem Leben*, Wittenberg: Stiftung Luthergedenkstätten 1998, 17: "Die immense Arbeitsbelastung Luthers erklärt, warum er seiner Frau die Gestaltung des häuslichen Lebens völlig überließ. Dahinter stand jedoch die Grundüberzeugung des Reformators von der biblisch gebotenen Gleichberechtigung zwischen Mann und Frau. Allerdings waren die Tätigkeitsfelder verschieden. Der Mann wirkte nach außen, der Herrschaftsbereich der Frau war das Haus. [....] Betrachtet man das Ausmaß dieser Hauswirtschaft, so ist von einer arbeitsteiligen Gleichberechtigung durchaus angemessen die Rede."

V. Church as Film Maker

1   Extensively on this period: Schmitt, *Kirche und Film*, 34, 105–150; cf. Julia Helmke, *Kirche, Film und Festivals. Geschichte sowie Bewertungskriterien evangelischer und ökumenischer Juryarbeit in den Jahren 1948 bis 1988*, Erlangen: Christliche-Publizistik-Verlag 2005, 72–77; on subsequent developments see also: Anne Kathrin Quaas, *Evangelische Filmpublizistik 1948–1968. Beispiel für das kulturpolitische Engagement der Evangelischen Kirche in der Nachkriegszeit*, Erlangen: Christliche-Publizistik-Verlag 2007.

2   E. g.: "Moving Pictures and Morals", *The Lutheran Companion* 42, May 5, 1934, 545; "Movies Alarmed by Church Fight", *The Lutheran Companion* 42, July 28, 1934, 931; according to Kahle/Lee, *Popcorn and Parable*, 127.

3   Robert Kahle and Robert E. A. Lee, *Popcorn and Parable: A New Look at the Movies*, Minneapolis: Augsburg Pub. House 1971, 82f.

4   Thus John R. May: "Contemporary Theories Regarding the Interpretation of Religious Film", in John R. May (ed.), *New Image of Religious Film*, Kansas City: Sheet & Ward 1997, 17–37; here: 24. There he cites: Kahle/Lee, *Popcorn and Parable* and a practical handbook: Robert G. Konzelman, *Marquee Ministry: The Movie Theater as Church and Community Forum*, New York: Harper and Row 1972.

5   Schmitt, *Kirche und Film*, 48.

6   Cf. Schmitt, *Luther*. 499–510; Walter Fleischmann-Bisten, *Der Evangelische Bund in der Weimarer Republik und im sogenannten Dritten Reich*, Frankfurt am Main etc.: Lang 1989 (EHS, 23: Theologie, 372), 194f.

7   Exemplary on the iconographic tradition: Armin Kohnle, "Luther vor Karl V. Die Wormser Szene in Text und Bild des 19. Jahrhunderts", in Stefan Laube and Karl-Heinz Fix (ed.), *Lutherinszenierung und Reformationserinnerung*, Leipzig: Evangelische Verlagsanstalt 2002 (Schriften der Stiftung Luthergedenkstätten in Sachsen-Anhalt, 2), 35–62. On the plays: Friedrich Weigend-Abendroth, "Luther – kein Held der Bühne. Ein Streifzug durch 500 Jahre Theaterliteratur", in Trapmann, *Reformator*, 247–257.

8   My query about copies was answered in the negative by the Filmarchiv in Frankfurt am Main, the Filmdokumentationszentrum in Vienna – there I was given a negative reply, moreover, for all archives under the Fédération Internationale des Archives du Film (FIAF) –, the Bundesfilmarchiv in Berlin and the F.-W.-Murnau-Stiftung in Wiesbaden. Nor is there a copy in the State Feature Film Archives in Moscow, where some films from the Reichsfilmarchiv have survived. Queries addressed to the Nederlands Filmmuseum in Amsterdam, the Cineteca Bologna and the British Film Institute in London have also yielded negative results.

9   *Der Kinematograph* No. 239, July 26, 1911.

10   *Lichtbild-Theater* 3, No. 35, Aug. 31, 1911.

11 Owned by the Litt family. Hermann Litt (b. in Zell near Bensheim in 1859, d. in Berlin in 1939) was a director and actor in 1908 at the Theater an der Spree in Berlin; subsequently in 1912 as actor and director at the Gustav-Behrens-Theater, also in Berlin; further, he was head director of the Deutsch-Südamerikanische Opern- und Operettengesellschaft between 1908 and 1910 (cf. *Neuer Theater-Almanach. Theatergeschichtliches Jahr- und Adressenbuch*, hg. v. der Genossenschaft Deutscher Bühnenangehöriger, Jg. 1908, 277 and Jg. 1912, 287). Litt also acted in the film *Die Macht des Goldes* with Asta Nielsen. As the Litt family tradition has it, Litt, who had been brought up in a Protestant family, converted to Catholicism in the Netherlands c 1880 and did not change his affiliation again (kindly imparted to me by Stefan Litt in May 2006).

12 Lamprecht, *Deutsche Stummfilme*, 180.

13 See findings of the censors of March 24, 1921 (Filmprüfstelle Berlin, Tgb. Nr. 1673) and April 20, 1921 (Film-Oberprüfstelle B.29.21, Jugendverbot) in the Deutsches Filminstitut Frankfurt am Main (Film-Oberprüfstelle B.29.21, finding of April 20, 1921, 3).

14 Thus the title of the copy of *Die Wittenberger Nachtigall* in the Bundesfilmarchiv in Berlin, which is shown as the first scene in this version. Since no other censorship records are known, the background and date of the title change are not clear. The film is, however, stored in the archives under its original title.

15 Georg Buchwald, *Doktor Martin Luther. Ein Lebensbild für das deutsche Haus. Mit zahlreichen Abbildungen im Text sowie dem Bildnis Luthers in Heliogravüre nach einem Gemälde von Lucas Cranach zu Nürnberg*, 1st ed. Leipzig etc.: Teubner 1902. What was of prime importance for the design of the film was probably the 3rd completely revised edition with numerous illustrations in the text and 16 plates after art works of the time published in 1916 ("3. völlig umgearbeitete Auflage mit zahlreichen Abbildungen im Text und auf 16 Tafeln nach Kunstwerken der Zeit").

16 Erwin Báron emphasized that he had "aimed at reproducing a cultural image from the turn of the 15th century and not representing a biography of Martin Luther" ("als Ziel die Wiedergabe eines Kulturbildes aus der Wende des 15. Jahrhunderts gesetzt [habe] und nicht die Darstellung einer Martin Luther-Biographie") and asked: "Who was to have the courage and the abilities to capture in pictures the spiritual greatness of a Martin Luther and the intellectual driving force behind this great Reformation? Where to find a public that would want to see the historical facts reproduced in the cinema in a manner faithful to nature?" ("Wer sollte den Mut und die Fähigkeiten haben, die geistige Größe eines Martin Luther und die intellektuelle Triebfeder dieser großen Reformation im Bilde fest-zuhalten? Wo fände sich ein Publikum, das sich im Kino die historischen Begebenheiten in naturgetreuer Wiedergabe ansehen wollte?"; *Erste Internationale Film-Zeitung*, No. 39, Sept. 1913, 117).

17 Ibid., 137.

18 Ibid., 136.

19 Erste *Internationale Film-Zeitung*, No. 39, Sept. 27, 1913, 136.

20 Filmprüfstelle Berlin, Kammer V, Tgb. Nr. 1673 (published online by the Deutsche Film-institut in Frankfurt am Main: www. deutsches-filminstitut.de [3.32009]).

21 Film-Oberprüfstelle B.29.21, 1 (published online by the Deutsche Filminstitut in Frank-furt am Main: www. deutsches-filminstitut.de): "Der Darsteller des Bildstreifens hat sich offenbar über die Geschichtsquellen, die jedem Gebildeten zur Verfügung stehen, nur in geringem Maße unterrichtet. So darf beispielsweise erwähnt sein, dass in dem vorliegenden Bildstreifen Martin Luther als der Sohn eines Tischlers oder Küfers geschildert wird."

22 "dass Katharina von Bora ihn bereits in jungen Jahren kennen lernt, bereits als junges Mädchen zu ihm eine Neigung fasst, dass gelegentlich seines Aufenthaltes auf der Wartburg das Ereignis der Bibelübersetzung überhaupt nicht erwähnt wird."

23 Film-Oberprüfstelle B.29.21, finding of April 20, 1921, 3–4: "Es war zu prüfen, ob diese

im übrigen von Anstößigkeiten freie Darstellung infolge ihrer historischen Ungenauigkeit und der damit verflachenden Charakteristik eines der größten deutschen Volkshelden geeignet war, im Sinne des § 1 des Lichtspielgesetzes beanstandet zu werden. [...] Nach diesem Gutachten [what is meant is the decision of March 24] sei der Film geeignet, das religiöse Empfinden protestantischer Kreise gröblich zu verletzen. Dieser Entscheidung konnte nicht beigetreten werden; die Gestalt Martin Luthers gehört der Geschichte an, sie ist aber nicht ein Bestandteil des evangelischen Glaubens, es kann sich also nicht um eine Verletzung des religiösen Empfindens, sondern etwa um eine Verletzung des (religiös [added later]) geschichtlichen Empfindens handeln und so war zu prüfen, ob eine solche Verletzung [...] geeignet sei, die öffentliche Ordnung zu gefährden. Diese Frage war zu verneinen."

24   Thus the 11th title of the version of 1913, quoted from the censorship cards (28814/19) in the Bundesarchiv-Filmarchiv, Berlin.

25   See the copies of the censorship cards (No. 28814/19) in the Bundesfilmarchiv in Berlin. The two exclamation marks are part of the original text.

26   Thus von der Heyden-Rynsch as head of the department for arts, sports and tourism of the city of Eisenach, in a letter of July 18, 1922 to the president of the *Deutsch-Evangelischer Kirchenausschuss*: "Court actor Wüstenhagen, who is enthusiastic about playing the role of Luther in the Leinhardt Festival put on here, has now suggested to me that I should make an important film which would depict the person of the great Reformer and spiritual hero Luther, his career and work by means of a text that is worthy of this great text and by using words of Luther's and melodies in vernacular imagery so that the idea of Luther might be borne to as wide circles as possible in Germany and abroad and thus initiate a reconciliation of peoples hitherto hostile or rather detached from it on the analogy of the Friedericus [sic!] Rex film. The undertaking should keep entirely away from the usual practices of making commercial films aimed only at making money. [...] What is needed to realize the thought underlying the idea is primarily trust and interest and the moral support of the Protestant church, especially, therefore, of the highest-ranking organisation of the German Lutheran Church Committee and the Evangelischer Bund and the Luther Society as well as, ultimately, also of the Luther (sites/cities [?])." ("Der für die Luthersache begeisterte Vertreter der Rolle des Luther in dem hier gegebenen Lienhardt'schen Festspiel der Hofschauspieler Wüstenhagen hat mir nun die Anregung nahe gebracht, um den Luthergedanken in möglichst weite Kreise des In- und Auslandes zu tragen und damit zugleich eine Versöhnung der sich bisher feindlich oder doch fern gegenüberstehenden Völker zunächst durch das Band der Glaubensgemeinschaft anzubahnen nach einer Analogie des Friedericus (sic!) Rex Films einen bedeutenden Film zu schaffen, der die Person des grossen Reformators und Geisteshelden Luther sein Werden und Wirken an der Hand eines der grossen Aufgabe würdigen Textes und unter Benutzung Lutherscher Worte und Melodien volkstümlich im Bilde vorführen soll. Das Unternehmen soll sich völlig fern halten von den landläufigen Praktiken der geschäftsmäßigen nur auf Erwerb gerichteten Filmfabrikation. [...] Um den der Idee zu Grunde liegenden Gedanken Verwirklichung zu bringen, bedarf es in erster Linie vertrauensvollen Interesses und der moralischen Unterstützung der protestantischen Kirche, insbesondere also ihrer obersten Spitzenorganisation des deutschen evangelischen Kirchenausschusses sowie des evangelischen Bundes und der Luthergesellschaft wie endlich auch der Lutherst[ätten/städte {?}])." (EZA, 1/2255 [Kirchenbundesamt. Acta betreffend Sonstige Luthergedächtnisfeiern]).

27   Thus also in the advertising released jointly by the Evangelischer Pressverband and the Evangelischer Bilderkammer (LAELKB, DW 2181 ★ Rep. No. 24 [formerly Bestand "Landesverein für Innere Mission", No. 401 T. I. Rep. No. 456]).

28   See the reply made by the OKR in November 1922 to Frhr. von der Heyden-Rynsch's query (see n. 26); both: EZA 1/2255.

29   Heinrich Assel, *Die Lutherrenaissance – Ursprünge, Aporien und Wege: Karl Holl, Emanuel Hirsch, Rudolf Hermann (1910–1935)*, Göttingen: Vandenhoeck & Ruprecht 1994. Jochen-Christoph Kaiser, "Der Protestantismus von 1918 bis 1989", in Thomas Bremer and Wolf Hubert (ed.), *Ökumenische Kirchengeschichte*, Vol. 3: Von der Französischen Revolution bis 1989, Darmstadt: Wissenschaftliche Buchgesellschaft 2007, S. 189f. For the impact of the "Lutherrenaissance" on visual culture see also: Steffens, *Luthergedenkstätten*.

30   Berndt Hamm, "Hanns Rückert als Schüler Karl Holls", in Thomas Kaufmann, Harry Oelke (ed.), *Evangelische Kirchenhistoriker im "Dritten Reich"*, Gütersloh: Kaiser, Gütersloher Verlagshaus 2002, 275f.

31   One report on the first public performance at the Wartburg has survived: EZA 1/2255.

32   *Kinematograph* No. 856, July 15, 1923, 9. The film had five acts and had an overall length of 1961 m (Lamprecht, *Stummfilme*, 133; cf. Schmitt, *Filmarbeit*, 333).
     Nor do any records survive of the Luther-Film G.m.b.H., founded by the director Karl Wüstenhagen in the Bayerisches Hauptstaatsarchiv in Munich. There seems to be no link with Lutherfilm-Gesellschaft m. b. H., which was established in Stuttgart in 1952 to distribute the American Luther film in Germany: see "Gesellschaftsvertrag and Geschäftsordnung" (contract of association and internal rules of procedure) of 1952 in the archives of the Diakonisches Werk der EKD in Berlin: ADW, HGSt 7777.

33   See LAELKB, DW 2181.

34   EZA 1/2255. Van der Heyden-Rynsch sent another copy to Wittenberg on March 3, 1923 (StadtAr Wittenberg 3746, fol. 55ff; cf. Stefan Laube, *Das Lutherhaus Wittenberg. Eine Museumsgeschichte*, Leipzig: EVA 2003, 315, note 221).

35   He was already an ardent pacifist in 1913, many of his sermons and publications show Nithack-Stahn's opposition to militarism and nationalism: *Der Christ und der Völkerfriede*, Stuttgart: Deutsche Friedensgesellschaft 1913; *Barbareien. Gedanken zur Gegenwart*, Berlin, Curtius 1913; *Kirche und Krieg*, Halle an der Saale, Fricke 1913; Matthias Wolfes, "Nithack-Stahn, Walter", in *BBKL* 20, Nordhausen: Verlag Traugott Bautz 2002, 1119–1125.

36   Walther Nithack-Stahn, *Luther. Festspiel in sechs Handlungen*, Breslau, Verlag der Evangelischen Zentralstelle 1921. A predecessor of this play was: *Luther in Oppenheim: geschichtliches Schauspiel in einem Aufzuge*, Halle: Fricke, 1920.

37   Scene: The Dance of Death: Death calls old men and child, Reich (Walther Nithack-Stahn, *Martin Luther. Ein Heldenleben in 7 Handlungen*, typescript n. d. [completed in 1923], 4; EZA 1/2255); 170. Scene: The Archangel Michael battles the Demon of Strife and fells him to the ground (Nithack-Stahn, ibid., 71); also see the scene cited in the following note.

38   For instance, the 79th scene: "A symbolic scene: Siegfried the Nibelung sets out to slay the dragon; puts his foot on its neck. [He] changes into the Archangel Michael, who bears Luther's facial features" ("Symbolisches Bild: Siegfried, der Nibelunge, zieht aus, den Drachen zu erschlagen; setzt ihm den Fuß auf den Nacken. Verwandelt sich in den Erzengel Michael, der Luthers Züge trägt."); Nithack-Stahn, ibid., 32; and the 143rd scene: "Vision of the Garden of Paradise; under flowering trees, angelic children are playing in white robes. Picking fruit, riding on hobby-horses, shooting little crossbows, dancing in circles, playing pipes and lutes. God the Father looks on. Luther himself comes with his four-year-old little Hans and asks for permission for him to play too. God the Father grants it, smiling. Little Hans joins the dancers in the circle. (after Luther's celebrated letter.)" ["Vision des Paradiesgartens, Unter blühenden Bäumen spielen Engelkinder in weißen Gewändern. Pflücken Früchte, reiten auf Steckenpferden, schießen mit kleinen Armbrüsten, machen Reigentänze, musizieren mit Pfeifen und Lauten. Gottvater schaut zu. Luther selbst kommt mit seinem vierjährigem Hänschen und bittet um die Erlaubnis, daß dieser mitspiele. Gottvater gewährt es lächelnd. Hänschen tanzt im Reigen mit. (nach Luthers berühmten Brief.)"]; Nithack-Stahn, ibid., 63.

39 The hand-out printed by the Evangelischer Pressverband für Deutschland contains an outline of the content of the individual acts (LAELKB, DW 2181).

40 "169th scene: Two men stand in combat in a bleak landscape. Title: 'Here the Pope – There Luther!' A woman designated as Germania, wearing mourning dress, wants to reconcile them as a mother would. They tear away from her and dash off, brandishing their swords, to each side. The woman breaks down, the crown falls from her head. [...] 171st scene: The apotheosis of the Reformation after the painting by W. Kaulbach *The Age of Reformation*. Enlarged by figures from more recent history, such as Frederick the Great, Bach, Handel, Wagner, Beethoven, Goethe, Schiller, Kant, etc. 172nd scene: Starry skies, the globe, from which flames are flickering. From the opening heavens, Christ steps to earth and stretches out his arms as the Peace Bringer." ("169. Bild: In öder Landschaft zwei im Kampfe stehenden Männer. Titel: 'Hie Papst – hie Luther!' Eine Frau als Germania gekennzeichnet, im Trauergewand, will sie wie eine Mutter versöhnen. Sie reißen sich von ihr los und stürmen, die Schwerter schwingend, nach beiden Seiten davon. Die Frau bricht zusammen, die Krone fällt ihr vom Haupte. [...] 171. Bild: Apotheose der Reformation nach W. Kaulbachs Gemälde Das Zeitalter der Reformation. Vermehrt durch Gestalten neuerer Geschichte, wie Friedrich der Große, Bach, Händel, Wagner, Beethoven, Goethe, Schiller, Kant usw. 172. Bild: Sternenhimmel. Erdkugel, aus der Flammen züngeln. Aus dem sich öffnenden Himmel tritt Christus auf die Erde und breitet als Friedebringer die Hände aus."; Nithack-Stahn, ibid., 71).

41 Janos Frecot, *Johann Friedrich Geist und Diethart Kerbs, Fidus: 1868–1948. Zur ästhetischen Praxis bürgerlicher Fluchtbewegungen*, Munich: Rogner & Bernhard 1972.

42 "Als ein ewig Lebender und lebendig Wirkender soll er [Luther] uns am Schlusse in der Seele verbleiben. – Einem Stoff von dieser Bedeutung mußte eine typische Form gegeben werden. Eine Art Prologbild kündet sie an. Luther bricht die erstarrende lateinische Welt – angedeutet durch einen r o m a n i s c h e n Bogen – und erweitert sie himmelwärts mit einer Gebärde des Glaubens zum Herzen hin. Er erschließt das Tor der Freiheit, für das nunmehr die g o t i s c h e Formenwelt die symbolische Linie gibt."

43 Cf. *Alte Pinakothek München. Erläuterungen zu den ausgestellten Gemälden, korrigierte und durch einen Anhang erw. Ausgabe*, 3rd ed., Munich: Edition Lipp 1999, 567f.

44 The author and the date of publication are unknown. All that is known is where it was printed: at the Vaterländische Verlags- und Kunstanstalt in Berlin, which is printed on the flyer itself (LAELKB, DW 2181): "Krankheiten, ergreifende Empfänglichkeit für die Leiden der Menschheit, kraftvolle Zuversicht und trotziger Wille, leiden zu wollen zum Heile der Welt, rollen als ergreifende, rührende, aufrüttelnde Bilder an uns vorüber."

45 This is implied in a letter of Nov. 13, 1926 written by Dean Johannes Kelber (Innere Mission) to the Ev.-luth. Dekanat [Deanery] in Augsburg, in which Kelber asks why the film was not permitted to be shown to the girls at the von Stettensches Institut even though it was cleared for youth (LAELKB, DW 2181). Dean Wilhelm Schiller answered that he had reservations, based on the quality of the film, about "forcing the girl pupils to attend the showing from school" ("die Schülerinnen zwangsweise von der Schule aus zur Aufführung hinzuführen"; Letter of Nov. 15, 1926, ibid.).

On the showing in Augsburg under the auspices of the Reformation celebration: *Augsburger Neueste Nachrichten* No. 255, November 3, 1926: "You must have thought it would be a bold undertaking to reproduce a personage of such overriding importance to world history as Martin Luther is, [...] in a moving picture. However, anyone who [...] has seen the Luther film, is sure to have noticed that these scruples [...] have become meaningless in several respects. [...] Thus we see at the end of the film how Luther opens up the gate to freedom to the people [...] It is not sensations that throb through the film; it is the fruit of serious work." ("Sie dachten wohl, es müßte ein gewagtes Unterfangen sein, eine Persönlichkeit von so überragender weltgeschichtlicher Bedeutung, wie Martin Luther ist, [...] im Laufbild nachzugestalten. Wer den Lutherfilm aber … gesehen hat, wird sicher festgestellt haben, daß diese Bedenken […] in mehrfacher Hinsicht gegenstandslos geworden sind. […] So sehen wir am Abschlusse des Filmwerkes das Volk, wie ihm Luther die Tore zur Freiheit öffnet […] Nicht Sensationen durchpulsen den Film, er ist die Frucht ernster Arbeit"; Press cutting in file LAELKB, DW 2181).

46 A letter of Oct. 5, 1927 written by Johannes Kelber to the Evangelische Bildkammer, Berlin-Steglitz: "Re: Luther film. If my memory serves me right, there was a scene in the 2nd act of the Luther film copies provided by Berlin last year in which the figure of Death enters a sickroom. We have now [corrected by hand to 'always'] adjudged that scene as impossible and have removed it for once and all from our Nuremberg copy. I should like to ask you to take this scene from the copies that have been ordered for us for the coming weeks and request that you confirm [this] so that I no longer need to look through this copy myself. With friendly greetings, signed J. Kelber" ["Betreff: Lutherfilm. Wenn ich mich recht entsinne, befand sich in dem im Vorjahre von Berlin gelieferten Lutherfilm-Kopien im 2. Akt eine Scene, in der die Gestalt des Todes ein Krankenzimmer betritt. Wir haben diese Scene jetzt [handschriftlich korrigiert in 'stets'] als unmöglich empfunden und in unserer Nürnberger Kopie ein für alle mal entfernt. Ich möchte bitten, diese Scene auch aus den für die kommenden Wochen für uns bestellten Kopien herauszunehmen und bitte um Bestätigung, sodaß ich diese Kopie nicht mehr selbst daraufhin durchzusehen brauche. Mit freundlicher Begrüßung gez. J Kelber", LAELKB, DW 2181).

47 See for instance the letter of Feb. 10, 1927 sent by Dean Kelber (Innere Mission) to Kirchenrat [member of the consistory] Dean Baum, Erlangen: "We showed it [the Luther film] about the Reformation era in 1926 in about 30 screenings, some in Nuremberg, some in Munich, Augsburg, etc. The response to it varied widely. The film was liked in Nuremberg, given grade 2–3 in Munich; in Augsburg Dean Wilhelm Schiller protested against it […]. The film undoubtedly has very fine parts, notably shots of beautiful scenery but the representation of Luther's psychomachy might have a peculiar effect on sensitive souls. The Nurembergers, however, do not seem to be among them. […]", "[…] wir haben ihn [den Lutherfilm] um die Reformationszeit 1926 in etwa 30 Aufführungen gezeigt, teils in Nürnberg, teils in München, Augsburg usw. Die Aufnahme war sehr verschieden. In Nürnberg hat der Film gefallen, in München mit Note 2-3, in Augsburg hat Herr Dekan Wilhelm Schiller dagegen protestiert […]. Zweifellos hat der Film sehr schöne Partien, vor allem schöne Landschaftsbilder; aber die Darstellung der seelischen Kämpfe Luthers kann auf feiner empfindende Gemüter vielleicht merkwürdig wirken. Die Nürnberger gehören aber scheinbar nicht zu diesen. […]" (LAELKB, DW 2181).

48 *Der Kinematograph* No. 856, July 15, 1923, 9: "Aus religiösen und nationalen Anregungen entsprungen, strebt es (das Erstlingswerk der Luther-Film GmbH) rein gleichen Zwecken wieder zu. […] Wenn der Vergleich nicht aus inneren Qualitätsgründen Blasphemie wäre, könnte man sagen, es sollte hier eine Art Film-Parsifal geschaffen werden. […] Die geniale Erfülltheit – voll des Unsagbaren – freilich fehlt. Man muß dafür die gute Absicht nehmen. Das Manuskript mag religiös und kirchlich einwandfrei sein, filmisch ist es nicht. Nicht weil es statt dramatischen Aufbaues nur eine beschauliche Bilderreihe gibt, sondern weil es dabei zu viel voraussetzt und darum auch an wichtigen Stellen Lücken läßt."
    The negative critique was justified as follows: "No one wanted to offend people of other persuasions and so the result was a rather un-Lutheran tepidity. Nevertheless, there were problems with censorship in Munich. This film is far less dramatic than Luther's life itself was. Accordingly, in representing it, [the authors] certainly went too far in the direction of immaculate angelic qualities, in intellectualisation to the extent of knavery." ("Man wollte keine Andersdenkenden verletzen und kam infolgedessen zu einer recht unlutherischen Lauheit. Trotzdem gab es in München Zensurschwierigkeiten. Dieser Film ist viel undramatischer als Luthers Leben selbst. In der Darstellung ging man entsprechend in

unberührter Engelhaftigkeit, einer Vergedanklichung bis zum Schelmenhaften sicher zu weit.")

49   Cf. especially the Jesus film genre, for instance: Lloyd Baugh, *Imaging the Divine. Jesus and Christ Figures in Film*, Kansas City, MO: Sheed & Ward 1997.

50   Letter of November 10, 1926 to the *Zentralstelle* for making a Luther film, "Lutherfilmdenkmal" (LAELKB, DW 2181): "Ich fand meine Anschauungen durchaus bestätigt, meine Befürchtungen sogar übertroffen. Den Aufführungen ging eine große Reklame vorher. Tagelang blickte der Kopf Luthers aus den Fenstern der Straßenbahnen. In den Zeitungen kamen Voranzeigen mit Berichten aus anderen Städten, z.B. Magdeburg, die etwas ganz Gewaltiges verhießen, auch über die Beteiligung hoher und höchster geistlicher Würdenträger zu berichten wußten. Der Zudrang zu den Vorstellungen war ein ganz gewaltiger. Was tatsächlich geboten wurde, war ein jämmerlicher Kitsch. Einige läppische Scenen aus der Kindheit, verunglückte Versuche[,] Luthers Seelenkämpfe darzustellen, die großen Scenen eindruckslos – [...] Ich gebe gerne zu, daß sich etwas weit Besseres schaffen läßt als dieser Film, der uns hier vorgesetzt wurde und nicht nur mich[,] sondern viele andere empört hat, während freilich die große Masse an diesem, wie an jedem Kitsch Gefallen fand. [...] Er (der Film) hat mir vielmehr bestätigt, daß es ein verkehrtes Unternehmen ist[,] eine Geschichte zu verfilmen, welche in ihrem Kern Geschichte eines inneren Lebens ist. Wer das unternimmt, hat entweder keine klare Vorstellung von den Ausdrucksmöglichkeiten des Films oder er hat kein Gefühl dafür, wie abstoßend es wirkt, wenn Pose, Geste und gewaltsame Mimik das heilige Ringen der Seele um Gott und mit Gott theatralisch wirksam machen. Dies ist der Hauptgrund, warum ich jedem Lutherfilm gegenüber eine radikal ablehnende Haltung einnehme. [...] Es liegt im Wesen des Films, daß er die Oberflächlichkeit fördert. Auf der flimmernden Leinwand eilen die Bilder rasch vorüber, ein Reiz für das Auge, aber kein Gegenstand der Betrachtung und des Nachdenkens. Sollen wir die Leute – ich denke vor allem auch an die Kinder – zu einer derartigen Betrachtung ernster, ja heiliger Dinge erziehen? – Eine der größten Illusionen derer, die Filme wie den Lutherfilm befürworten, ist die, daß man das Volk dadurch daran gewöhnen kann, anstelle schlechter[,] schädlicher Filme gute und wertvolle anzusehen. Ich fürchte vielmehr, daß die Kirche durch Pflege des Films Leuten den Geschmack am Kino beibringt, die sonst nicht hinein gehen würden. Sie werden nun verstehen, daß ich ein Gegner Ihres Unternehmens bin. Ich freue mich, daß meine Amtsbrüder meinen Standpunkt teilen."

51   LAELKB, DW 2181: "Ich bin vom Lutherfilm nicht restlos begeistert und hoffe sehr, daß das neue Lutherfilm-Denkmal des evang. Bundes noch besser wird. Denn tatsächlich fehlen viele wertvolle Scenen aus dem Leben Luthers. Wir haben daher den Lutherfilm bisher nicht allzusehr propagiert und warten auf das Kommende."

52   Letter of November 16, 1926 from Kelber to the Evangelische Bildkammer Berlin-Steglitz (LAELKB, DW 2181).

53   The association had been amassing funds since early 1926 by asking recipients to endorse share certificates (see printed advert in LAELKB, DW 2181). The Evangelischer Bund Bayern refused to have anything to do with Luther-Filmdenkmal since Luther-Filmdenkmal had not answered the Evangelischer Bund Bayern's query as to whether they might be allowed to influence the shape of the film if they [the Evangelischer Bund Bayern] declared themselves a promotional organisation (Letter of December 19, 1927 from Meinzolt for the Landesverein für Innere Mission to Pastor Hesselbach [ibid.]).

54   A letter written by Lutherfilmdenkmal e.V. to the Hilfswerk Ostern in 1928 reveals that about 65 0000 Reichs marks had been raised from Lutheran circles before the film was finished (ADW, CA/PD 299).

55   *Lexikon des Internationalen Films, völlig überarbeitete und erweiterte Neuausgabe*, Vol. 5, Reinbek bei Hamburg: Rowohlt 1995, 3529.

56   See the letter of July 6, 1926 written by Bundesdirektor Fahrenhorst to the *Deutsch-Evan-*

gelischer Kirchenausschuß, with the agreement enclosed (EZA 1/2256): "[…] 2. In making this film, the Evangelischer Bund secures to itself all possible conceptual support and after the film shall have been completed extensive aid in recommending and disseminating it. 3. The Evangelischer Bund declares its willingness to [provide] scholarly and artistic aid in the making of the film; in particular it will assume a paramount and crucial share in the writing of the script through its president, D. Döhring. The finished film is subject to final evaluation through a committee set up by the Evangelischer Bund." ("[…] 2. Bei der Herstellung dieses Films sichert der Evangelische Bund jede mögliche ideelle Unterstützung und nach Fertigstellung des Films weitgehende Hilfe bei seiner Empfehlung und Verbreitung zu. 3. Der Evangelische Bund erklärt sich zu wissenschaftlicher und künstlerischer Hilfeleistung bei der Herstellung des Films bereit; insbesondere wird er durch seinen Präsidenten D. Döhring sich an der Herstellung des Manuscripts maßgebend und entscheidend beteiligen. Der fertiggestellte Film unterliegt der abschließenden Beurteilung durch einen vom Evangelischen Bund einzusetzenden Ausschuß.")

57 "auf die Dauer von drei Jahren der Ausführung keines anderen Lutherfilms zuzustimmen"; this is once again expressly emphasized in the *Vorstandsblatt des Evangelischen Bundes* 1926, 204.

58 A letter written to the Landesverein für Innere Mission, stamp giving notice of receipt May 9, 1927, LAELKB, DW 2181; cf. on this the text of a folder (see n. 71): "Evangelische Vereine sind der Ausdruck evangelischen Gemeinschaftsgefühls. Ihre Aufgabe ist es, evangelisches Wesen zu pflegen und zu fördern […] 1. Unser Lutherfilm wird nicht ein gewöhnlicher Film wie irgend ein anderer sein, sondern eine die Herzen packende Versinnbildlichung der grossen Ideen der Reformation. Er wird in jedem Kino vorgeführt werden, die wohl das Kino, nicht aber die Kirche besuchenden Massen mit religiösen, evangelischen Vorstellungen erfüllen und dadurch in ganz hervorragendem Maße evangelisatorisch wirken. 2. Sie wissen, daß Rom die größten Anstrengungen macht, um Deutschland, das Land der Reformation, wieder zu erobern. So ist […] in der Zeit von 1913 bis 1925 die Zahl der männlichen Ordensleute von 6430 auf 11250, die der weiblichen von 63078 auf 77646 (einschl. 5926 Novizen) gestiegen. Wäre da nicht der Zusammenschluß aller Protestanten bei der Schaffung eines Lutherfilms ein würdiger und eindrucksvoller Protest? 3. Wir erbitten keine Geschenke, sondern ein rückzahlbares und trotzdem am Gewinn beteiligtes Darlehen. 4. Die Gestaltung des Films und die Geschäftsführung werden überwacht durch einen Ausschuss, an dem auch ein Kommissar der höchsten deutschen Kirchenbehörde, des Deutschen Evangelischen Kirchenausschusses, teilnimmt. Die Herstellung des Films erfolgt mit den denkbar vollkommensten und modernsten, künstlerischen und technischen Einrichtungen. Es ist also wirklich jede Gewähr für eine in religiöser, kirchlicher, wissenschaftlicher, künstlerischer und technischer Beziehung würdige Gestaltung des Films und für eine vornehme und einwandfreie Handhabung der Geschäfte gegeben. Es erscheint uns ganz selbstverständlich, dass bei einer evangelischen Sache von so überragender Bedeutung Ihr Verein [gemeint ist der Landesverein für Innere Mission] nicht abseits stehen darf. Wir rechnen zuversichtlich auf Sie! Mit evangelischem Gruß Luther-Filmdenkmal. Zentralstelle für die Schaffung eines Lutherfilms E.V. [gezeichnet mit den Unterschriftsstempeln der Vorstandsmitglieder, Freiherr Curt von Gillhausen (Vorsitzender), Werner Wilm (Direktor) und D. Repsold (Schatzmeister)].

59 "Und an die Stelle des Großkapitals sollst du treten, deutsches evangelisches Volk!"

60 Undated hectographed typescript (LAELKB, DW 2181): "[…] gern angebotene Unterstützung des zumeist nicht evangelischen Filmgroßkapitals unter allen Umständen entbehren zu können."; on the eminent role of the Jews in the early film industry especially in Berlin: Irene Stratenwerth, Hermann Simon (ed.), *Pioniere in Celluloid. Juden in der frühen Filmwelt*, Berlin: Henschel Verlag 2004.

61 Letter of November 19, 1930 from Dean Weigel, Landesverein für Innere Mission in der

Ev.-Luth. Landeskirche in Bayern, to the Evangelischer Oberkirchenrat (Evangelisches Zentralarchiv in Berlin, Akten des Kirchenbundesamtes EZA 1/2258).

62 Thus Werner Wilm, director of Luther-Filmdenkmal, in a letter of Dec. 31, 1930, 4, with the Evangelischer Bund letterhead to the Deutscher Evangelischer Kirchenausschuß (Evangelisches Zentralarchiv in Berlin, Akten des Kirchenbundesamtes EZA 1/2258).

63 See the report "Beim großen Lutherfilm" in *Der Wächter* Nos. 11/12, 1927, 15f. Picture postcards were also printed, with photographs showing visitors with Eugen Klöpfer (EZA). While the film was running, the printing press connected with the Evangelischer Bund also offered a set of twelve postcards with stills from scenes (an incomplete set is at the Konfessionskundliches Institut des Evangelischen Bundes in Bensheim [henceforward quoted as KI EB, Akte S 185.460.7]; advertising for it was placed, for instance, in *Die Wartburg. Deutsch-evangelische Monatsschrift* 27 (1928), 58 and 68.

64 Cf. Friedrich Wilhelm Bautz, "Bruno Döhring", in *BBKL* Vol. 1, Nordhausen: Verlag Traugott Bautz 1990, col. 1343. Döhring's autobiography was published in 1952 as *Mein Lebensweg. Zwischen den vielen und der Einsamkeit* (Gütersloh, Bertelsmann) a title that reveals a good deal of self-stylization.

65 On the issue of Protestant nationalism: Gangolf Hübinger, "Sakralisierung der Nation und Formen des Nationalismus im deutschen Protestantismus", in Gerd Krumeich and Hartmut Lehmann (ed.), *"Gott mit uns". Nation, Religion und Gewalt im 19. und frühen 20. Jahrhundert*, Göttingen: Vandenhoeck & Ruprecht 2000 (VMPIG, 162), 233–247. Manfred Gailus, Hartmut Lehmann (ed.), *Nationalprotestantische Mentalitäten in Deutschland (1870–1970). Konturen, Entwicklungslinien und Umbrüche eines Weltbildes*, Göttingen: Vandenhoeck & Ruprecht 2005 (VMPIG, 214).

66 Döhring, *Lebensweg*, 145.

67 Undated press release from the evangelischer Pressverband für Bayern (hectographed typescript in file LAELKB, DW 2181), which cannot have been written and issued before early January 1928 because it contains the viewer statistics for the first fourteen days of screening (20 000 viewers).

68 For instance: "Exhofpredigers Döhrings Lutherfilm", in *Aus der Welt der Kirche, Beiblatt zur Bayerischen Volkszeitung* of December 21, 1927. Reprinted in a compilation of articles with the subtitle "Exhofprediger Döhrings Lutherfilm. Eine Nürnberger Uraufführung. Klosterhetze, Romhaß, Ablaßrummel und Scheiterhaufen" in the *Allgemeine Rundschau* on January 11, 1928, which contains a statement addressed to the public by the Nuremberg clergy, in which they protested against the disturbance of interdenominational peace.

69 *Vorstandsblatt des Evangelischen Bundes* 1927, special ed. 1a, 53–56 and No. 2, 57–73.

70 Ibid., No. 2, p. 72f.: "Evangelischer Bund and Lutherfilm. The link between the Evangelischer Bund and the Luther film was established by D. Doehring, who according to the minutes of the board of governors session of May 19, 1926, told the board of governors that he was willing to collaborate on making a Luther film and invited the Evangelischer Bund to aid him in this undertaking. The actual work done by D. Doehring on this project would amount primarily to drawing up an outline for the screenplay, which, it had been agreed, was to be finished for summer 1926. We are delighted to inform [you] that D. Doehring, despite leaving the Evangelischer Bund, continues to collaborate on the screenplay and that this screenplay has, in essentials, been complete for some days now. Nor has the Evangelischer Bund any occasion to change its attitude to the Luther-film project [...]" ("Evangelischer Bund und Lutherfilm. Die Verbindung zwischen dem Evangelischen Bund und dem Lutherfilm ist durch D. Doehring zustande gekommen, der laut Protokoll der Präsidiumssitzung vom 19. Mai 1926 dem Präsidium mitteilte, daß er gewillt sei, sich an der Schaffung eines Lutherfilms zu beteiligen, und den Evangelischen Bund zur Mithilfe einlud. Die tätige Mithilfe D. Doehrings an diesem Werk sollte vor allem in der Herstellung eines Entwurfs zum Filmbuch bestehen, dessen Fertigstellung bereits für den Sommer 1926

zugesagt war. Wir freuen uns, mitteilen zu können, daß D. Doehring trotz seines Austritts aus dem Evangelischen Bund an der Herstellung des Filmbuchs weiter tätig bleibt, und daß dieses Filmbuch seit einigen Tagen im wesentlichen fertiggestellt ist. Auch der Evangelische Bund hat keinen Anlaß, seine Haltung gegenüber dem Lutherfilmunternehmen zu ändern […].")

71   "The spirit of Luther is missing in our times. Faith like Luther's has been lost in broad sectors of our people. The mission of our Luther film is to arouse and promote both: to revive Luther's spirit and to fill the hearts of the masses, who do go to the cinema but probably not to church, with Lutheran thoughts.

Moreover, its cultural mission is to be a witness for the culture of Germany and mankind grounded in the Reformation.

How will it fulfill these lofty tasks? We believe we have created all warranties that it will be able to do so: the author of our Luther film is D. Doehring, Preacher to the Court, shooting will be accomplished with the most perfect technical and artistic facilities imaginable [available to] the largest German film concern. The design of the film will be determined by a committee set up by the board of governors of the Evangelischer Bund, to which the Deutscher Evangelischer Kirchenausschuß has despatched a commissioner. All German clerical offices are well-disposed towards our work. […] Four fifths of the sum we must raise was realised by the end of March. But we need even more. Even though making the Luther film is now entirely assured so that it will be released in autumn of this year, because we can be assured of the outstanding sum from Big Film Capital. But we want to be fully independent of it and make the Luther film as a work of Lutheran communal awareness."

("Luthergeist fehlt unserer Zeit. Lutherglaube ist weiten Kreisen unseres Volkes verloren gegangen. Beides erwecken und fördern zu helfen, Luthers Geist wieder wach werden zu lassen, und die Herzen der wohl das Kino, nicht aber die Kirche besuchenden Massen mit religiösen, evangelischen Gedanken zu erfüllen, das ist die Missionsaufgabe unseres Lutherfilms.

Und seine kulturelle Aufgabe ist es, ein Zeugnis für die auf die Reformation sich gründende deutsche und Menschheitskultur zu sein.

Wie wird er diese hohen Aufgaben erfüllen? Wir glauben jede Gewähr dafür geschaffen zu haben: Verfasser unseres Lutherfilms ist Hofprediger D. Doehring, die Herstellung erfolgt mit den denkbar vollkommensten technischen und künstlerischen Einrichtungen des größten deutschen Filmkonzerns. Die Gestaltung des Films wird bestimmt durch einen vom Präsidium des Evangelischen Bundes bestellten Ausschuss, in den der Deutsche Evangelische Kirchenausschuß einen Kommissar entsandt hat. Alle deutschen Kirchenregierungen stehen unserem Werke sympathisch gegenüber. […] Vier Fünftel der von uns aufzubringenden Summe waren Ende März bereits gezeichnet. Aber wir brauchen noch mehr. Zwar ist die Herstellung des Lutherfilms schon jetzt völlig gesichert, sodaß er im Herbst d. Js. zur Vorführung kommen wird, weil wir den noch fehlenden Betrag vom Film-Großkapital erhalten können. Aber wir wollen von ihm völlig unabhängig sein und den Lutherfilm als das Werk evangelischen Gemeinschaftsbewußtseins schaffen."; printed folder enclosed with a letter from the chairman of the Luther-Filmdenkmal. Zentralstelle für die Schaffung eines Lutherfilms E.V. association in Berlin to the chairman of the Landesverein für Innere Mission in Nuremberg [receipt stamp of May 9, 1927], LAELKB, DW 2181).

72   Press cutting without sources (LAELKB, DW 2181).

73   "That angle was clear to me at once; the Luther film to be made can only accomplish its mission of bringing Luther's person and work again to the notice of a broad public only if it has justified prospects of actually reaching the broad masses of those who fill the cinemas day in day out. If that happens, it can be contended without exaggeration that a mission will have been accomplished. […]" ["Der Gesichtspunkt war mir sofort klar, der zu schaffende Lutherfilm kann seine Aufgabe, Person und Werk Luthers aufs neue in die

breite Öffentlichkeit zu tragen, nur erfüllen, wenn er begründete Aussicht hat, tatsächlich die breiten Massen derer, welche Tag für Tag die Kinos füllen, zu erfassen. Geschieht dies, so darf ohne Uebertreibung behauptet werden, daß damit eine Missionsaufgabe erfüllt wird. [...]"] (hand-out in form of a hectographed typescript n. d. [probably 1927], ADW, CA/PD 299).

74 ADW, CA/PD 299: "die wichtigsten Gesichtspunkte der Auswirkung der Reformation bis in die Gegenwart hinein zur Hebung kommen".

75 "Das Lied auf den Lippen starb Gustav Adolf zu Lützen den Heldentod"

76 See note 7 and ## for example.

77 Fleischmann-Bisten, *Der Evangelische Bund*, 63.

78 Schmitt, *Widerstreit* ND 1983, 60. However, the titling makes it occasionally unclear whether, in the lists of films shown, this really was the 1927 Luther film; the title *Dr. Martin Luther, der deutsche Reformator* appears in a report made by the Ev.-luth. Church in Hamburg to the Kirchenkanzlei of the Deutsche Evangelische Kirche in Berlin on August 30, 1939 (EZA 1/2253, Bericht [Report] 16).

79 For the year 1930, however, fifty-eight showings are recorded, for instance in the congregations of the regions under the aegis of the Hauptverein Hessen des Evangelischen Bundes: KI EB S 185.460.5 (1930): settlement of accounts on the profit margins from the screenings. In 1933 the film was shown at a "Luther-Celebration-Week" in Eisleben August 19–27 (Siegfried Bräuer, "Die Lutherfestwoche vom 19. bis 27. August 1933 in Eisleben", in Laube/Fix, *Lutherinszenierung und Reformationserinnerung*, 413f.). See also note 122 in this chapter.

80 Letter from the Evangelischer Bund of June 26, 1935 to the pastor of Bad Soden on the Taunus; KI EB S 185.460.5 (1930): "so gut wie gar nicht mehr verlangt".

81 According to the advertising handed out by the Hessischer Hauptverein der Gustav-Adolf Stiftung and the Hessischer Hauptverein des Evangelischen Bundes, which had acquired the joint rights to screening, from May 15, 1929 (KI EB S 185.460.5 [1930]).

82 "Ich habe gegen die Papisten geschrieben, weil sie mit Ablaßhandel das deutsche Volk aussaugen."

83 On the continuity of this motif in the 1930s see: Beate Rossié, "'Symbolhafte Sprache, die aus der Weltanschauung entspringt'. Kirchliche Kunst im Nationalsozialismus", in Stefanie Endlich, Monica Geyler-von Bernus, Beate Rossié (ed.), *Christenkreuz und Hakenkreuz. Kirchenbau und sakrale Kunst im Nationalsozialismus*, Berlin: Metropol 2008, 99f.; Review by Esther Wipfler in http://hsozkult.geschichte.hu-berlin.de/rezensionen/2009 (online since 14.5.2009).

84 Cf. Cantata BWV 20, Mvt. 1 Chorus: "O Ewigkeit, du Donnerwort, O Schwert, das durch die Seele bohrt, O Anfang sonder Ende! O Ewigkeit, Zeit ohne Zeit. Ich weiß vor großer Traurigkeit nicht, wo ich mich hinwende. Mein ganz erschrocken Herz erbebt, Dass mir die Zung am Gaumen klebt."

85 Strindberg, *Historische Miniaturen*, 181–199. Cf. Strindbergs play on Luther that premiered in Germany at the Künstlertheater in Berlin in Dec. 1914: August Strindberg, *Luther: (die Nachtigall von Wittenberg)*; [deutsche Historie in 10 Bildern]; Näktergalen i Wittenberg (1903) übersetzt von Emil Schering, München: Müller 1920.

86 "[...] in der Gefährdung der deutschen Volksseele nach ihren zeitlichen und ewigen Beziehungen"

87 "Daß rein protestantische Landesteile vornehmlich Preußens mit einem Netz von römischen Niederlassungen überzogen werden, auf daß sie dem Papst, der mit langen Zeiträumen rechnet, dienstbar würden, ist nicht mehr zu bestreiten." (Bruno Döhring, *Die Weltgefahr. Gedanken zum Reformationstage 1923 aufgrund von Epheser 6,10–17*, Berlin: Verlag des Evangelischen Bundes 1924, 4 and 8).

88 "inmitten des deutschen Volkes als ein Kämpfer mit dem Schwert des Geistes Gottes wider den Geist der Zeit" (Döhring, ibid., 5).

89 "Deutschland ist erst dann völlig besiegt, wenn der Luther in ihm erschlagen ist mit seinem Evangelium von der freien Gnade Gottes, die Charaktere schafft, an denen der Teufel sich mit seinen tausend abgefeimten Ränken umsonst versucht." (Bruno Döhring, *Weltenende – Und wir ?*, Berlin: Verlag des Evangelischen Bundes 1924, 7f.)

90 Döhring, ibid., 12.

91 Jochen-Christoph Kaiser, "Der Evangelische Bund und die Politik 1918–1933", in Gottfried Maron (ed.), *Evangelisch und Ökumenisch. Beiträge zum 100jährigen Bestehen des Evangelischen Bundes*, Göttingen: Vandenhoeck & Ruprecht 1986, 174–191; here: 181.

92 "daß durch das bayerische Konkordat außerdeutsches Recht innerhalb der Sphäre der deutschen Rechtshoheit sich eingenistet hat. [Rom ist nicht gewillt sich] mit der Selbständigkeit der reichs- und volkstümlichen Gegebenheiten einer Nation […] abzufinden. […] die römische Invasion [hat]… seit der Aufhebung des Jesuitengesetzes im Jahr 1917, in vielfach verstärktem Maße aber seit der Revolution eingesetzt." (Bruno Döhring, *Der deutsche Protestantismus in der Notwehr. Rede gelegentlich der 29. Generalversammlung des Evangelischen Bundes zur Wahrung der deutsch-protestantischen Interessen gehalten am 29. Juni 1925 zu Königsberg, Pr.*, Berlin: Verlag des Evangelischen Bundes n. d., 5-6).

93 Döhring, ibid., 11–12.

94 The use of light to configure the overall design is characteristic of Expressionist cinema (Rudolf Kurtz, *Expressionismus und Film*, Berlin 1926, Reprint Zurich: Rohr 1965, 59; cf. also the criss-crossing bunched rays in Lyonel Feininger: ibid., fig. 6 and in many works by Franz Marc). The light cross as used here, however, looks back on a long Christian iconographic tradition, one that had been energetically revived in Wilhelmine Prussia: Kaiser Wilhelm II had the Homburg Erlöserkirche equipped with a cross chandelier (Jürgen Krüger, *Rom und Jerusalem. Kirchenbauvorstellungen der Hohenzollern im 19. Jahrhundert*, Berlin: Akademie Verlag 1995, 227–254). It also appears in the illustration to Döhring's writings, where it illuminates the representation of the Prussian soldiers marching into battle above the text of his sermon on the occasion of the battle in Masuria on February 21, 1915 (to which he gave the title "Deutschlands Passion" and compared the sufferings of Christ with Germany's fate ["Jesu Passion – unseres Volkes Passion"]); Bruno Doehring (ed.), *Ein feste Burg. Denkmäler evangelischer und deutscher Art aus schwerer Zeit. Der "Predigten und Reden" 2., ausgew. und durch vaterländische Zeugnisse erw. Ausg.* [2nd ed. enlarged and supplemented by testimonials to the Fatherland], Berlin, Schmidt [1918], 184–193; here 184 and 186.

95 Willy Haas, "Film-Kritk. Luther, ein Film deutscher Reformation", *Film-Kurier* Nr. 42, Feb. 17, 1928.

96 Press cutting, n. d., without sources in file LAELKB, DW 2181: "Mächtig greift das Bild an die Seele, dieses Schlußbild aus Wittenberg, wo Luther, die blinkende Rüstung unter dem schwarzen Predigerkleid, auf der Kanzel der Kirche steht und die rasenden Bilderstürmer zur Vernunft ruft, zur Einkehr. Seine Worte, seine Art dämmen die Fluten des Hasses ein."

97 Regarding this response it is not comprehensible that Angelika Breitmoser-Bock did not define the scene as a "Key-Frame" ("Schlüsselbild") in her dissection of Fritz Lang's *Siegfried* (Angelika Breitmoser-Bock, *Bild, Filmbild, Schlüsselbild: Zu einer kunstwissenschaftlichen Methodik der Filmanalyse am Beispiel von Fritz Langs Siegfried (Deutschland 1924)*, München: Schaudig, Bauer, Ledig 1992 [Diskurs Film: Bibliothek, 5]).

98 "bedeutendste Menschendarsteller Deutschlands" (hectographed typescript n. d.; since in it it is mentioned that the film is close to being finished, the year 1927 is suggested; LAELKB, DW 2181). This verdict was expressed in a somewhat more moderate form by Johannes Kelber in his promotional efforts. In a newspaper article of December 15, 1927, he

wrote of the "outstanding German character actor" ("hervorragenden Menschendarsteller Deutschlands"; ibid.).

99   Copy of a letter of February 24, 1928 from Dean Weigel to the Bayerische Staatsministerium des Innern (Ministry of the Interior); ADW, CA/PD 299.

100 For instance the public statement made by the Catholic clergy in Berlin in the gazette *Germania* on February 17, 1928: the film offended "the most sacred religious feelings" ("heiligste[s] religiöse Empfinden") and disturbed the interdenominational peace.

101 See Schmitt, *Widerstreit* ND 1983. In the petition of February 24, 1928 submitted by the Erzbischöfliche[n] Kommissariat Nürnberg-Fürth to the Film-Oberprüfstelle in Berlin, to ban the film throughout Bavaria, it says *inter alia*: "the film [reveals] such an aggressive anti-Catholic bias that is at a far remove from purely historical representation […] that showing it would most severely offend Catholic feelings, disturb the religious peace and evoke incalculable prejudices." ("der Film [zeige] eine derart aggressive, von rein geschicht-licher Darstellung weit abweichende antikatholische Tendenz […], dass seine Aufführung das katholische Empfinden aufs schwerste verletzen, den religiösen Frieden stören und unabsehbare Unzuträglichkeiten heraufbeschwören würde.")

The records documenting film censorship in the 1920s have been published online by the Deutsches Filminstitut in Frankfurt am Main (www.deutsches-filminstitut.de): Zensurent-scheidung v. [censors' finding of] December 17, 1927: Filmprüfstelle Berlin B. 17622; length of film: 3308 m, approved; January 10, 1928: Filmprüfstelle Berlin B. 17863; length of film: 3220 m, approved; censorship record of February 24, 1928 (Bayerisches Haupt-staatsarchiv in Munich, henceforth cited as BayHStA); censorship document of March 22, 1928 (Oberprüfstelle O. 204; film length: 3117 m: passed but in part banned in the appeal; cuts: 93,35 m: censorship document and minutes: BayHStA).

102 Thus the Catholic reaction in the *Augsburger Postzeitung,* Jan. 10, 1928: In using the device of the apotheosis of Luther, the idea was to "breathe […] new elixirs of life into crumbling and disunited Protestantism" ("dem zerbröckelnden und in sich uneinigen Protestantismus wieder neue Lebenselixiere ein […]hauchen").

103 In the *Der Stürmer* column that was probably published in January 1928 "Diogenes. Streifzüge durch Nürnberg" (cutting, n. d., in file LAELKB, DW 2181), the author, who reveals that he is "Catholic", reports in a very positive tenor on the premiere of the film, which, he says, attained its zenith with the "intonation of the Luther hymn" ("Intonation des Lutherliedes"). However, the author's conclusion reveals that the film review only served as a vehicle for the Anti-Semitic defamation of a *Tagespost* journalist: "Yes, even the local Catholic parish officials have not hesitated to use the *Tagespost* Jew to scourge Christians." ("Ja sogar die hiesigen katholischen Pfarrämter haben sich nicht gescheut, sich des Tagespostjuden zu bedienen, um Christen zu peinigen.")

104 *Deutsch-Evangelische Korrespondenz. Mitteilungen des Evangelischen Bundes* 27 (1928), No. 6, Feb. 8, 1.

105 LAELKB, DW 2181.

106 "tatkräftige Wahrung der deutsch-protestantischen Interessen, wo und wie immer sich Gelegenheit dazu bietet." (Printed for instance in *Allgemeine Rundschau. Generalanzeiger für Nordbayern* 38 [1928], No. 53, March 2, 1).

107 "The bias offensive to the Roman world lies not in the film but in the Reformation, in Martin Luther and those of his intellectual cloth. What is offensive is not what the film shows and how it does it; what is fatal for the Roman soul is that these things, as tamely and sparingly as they are shown, are true." ("Die verletzende Tendenz für die römische Welt liegt nicht im Film, sondern in der Reformation, in Martin Luther und den Söhnen seines Geistes selber. Woran man sich stößt, ist nicht, was der Film darstellt, und wie er es tut, das Fatale für das römische Gemüt liegt darin, daß diese zahm und schonend gezeigten

Dinge wahr sind.”); *Deutsch-Evangelische Korrespondenz. Mitteilungen des Evangelischen Bundes*, 27 (1928), No. 9, 29. Feb., 2.

108 State made by leading Protestants in the Netherlands, Sweden and Hungary, which was submitted to the Generalsekretariat des Internationalen Evangelischen Bundes: *Protestantische Rundschau* 5 (1928), January, 155f.

109 The following scenes were among those that were shortened: “the first Roman monastic cell, in which various monks are seen feasting. [...] Brawl scene at Tetzel’s indulgence feast [...] the scene in which Tetzel is seen dancing with a female personage [....] the scene in which Tetzel personally taps the big beer cask [...]. Iconoclastic scenes and the destruction of the altarpieces [...] Burning-at-the-stake scenes” (“die erste römische Klosterzelle, in der man verschiedene Mönche beim Schmause sieht. [...] Schlägereiscene bei Tetzels Ablaßfest [...] die Scene, in der man Tetzel mit einer Frauenperson tanzen sieht [...] die Scene, in der Tetzel persönlich das grosse Bierfass ansticht [...] Scenen aus dem Bildersturm und der Vernichtung der Altäre [...] Scheiterhaufenscenen”; Protokoll der Verhandlung über den Antrag der Bayerischen Staatsregierung auf Widerruf der Zulassung des Bildstreifens *Luther* [Minutes of the negotiation on the petition submitted by the Government of the State of Bavaria to overturn the approval of the feature film *Luther*] of March 22, 1928, 8, BayHStA: published online at www.deutsches-filminstitut.de).

110 “Luther und unsere Zeit: Zur Aufführung des Lutherfilms”, in *Deutsche Tageszeitung*, March 6, 1928; Presseausschnittsammlung (Press cuttings collection) in the Bundesarchiv-Filmarchiv, Berlin; cf. on this the commentary in the *Bayerische Volkszeitung*, March 9, 1928.

111 *Fränkische Wacht. Über den Parteien. Für Christentum und Deutschtum im protestantischen Geist*, No. 2, Jan. 12, 1928, 9–11.

112 “Luther: Uraufführung im Ufa-Palast am Zoo”, press cutting, n. d. [probably from February 1928], without sources in the file LAELKB, DW 2181: “der Unhistorischste [...] auch der Unevangelischste [...] ein paar feststehende, unverrückbar volkstümlich klare Grundzüge vom Bilde Luthers und dem Wesen der Reformation”.

113 Newspaper article from 1928 conserved without indication of its source in the Bundesarchiv-Filmarchiv, Berlin: “Klöpfer, der den Luther spielt, hat seinen ganz großen Teil am Erfolge. Es ist so, als ob er mit der Rolle verwachsen sei, die keine Rolle mehr ist, sondern ein Stück seines Menschentums. Nicht eine theatralische Geste, immer der Unterton des Leidens eines im Grunde fröhlichen und festen Menschen, der die Dämonen der Seele kennt. Immer der Abschied und immer der Sieg”.

114 . Press cutting, n. d., without sources in file LAELKB, DW 2181: “Eugen Klöpfer als Luther fand die monumentale Linie. Er war Streiter, Dulder in Gewissensnot”.

115 “One realizes then also, what Luther’s feat meant to people then: freedom from the excesses of the Catholic Church of the time, from the traffic in indulgences, etc. but, above and beyond that, what was missing was elevating the figure of Luther to the atemporal and universal plane. Author-director Hans Kyser was not able to do that [...] from all known portraits of Luther, we imagine him as much stockier of build with the broad skull of the man absolutely driven by will-power; Klöpfer, however, gives [us] a mild Luther with melting Christ-like eyes, in a certain sense an idealized Luther” (“man begreift denn auch, was Luthers Tat den Damaligen bedeutete, die Befreiung von Auswüchsen der damaligen katholischen Kirche, von Ablasshandel usw., aber es fehlte darüber hinaus die Erhebung der Gestalt Luthers ins Zeitlose und allgemein Gültige. Das hat der Autor-Regisseur Hans Kyser nicht vermocht [...] nach allen bekannten Luther-Porträts stellen wir uns diesen viel vierschrötiger vor mit dem breiten Schädel eines absoluten Willensmenschen, Klöpfer dagegen gibt einen gütigen Luther mit sanften Christusaugen, gewissermaßen einen idealisierten Luther”; Fritz Olimsky, “Der Luther-Film: Ufa-Palast am Zoo”; Press cutting, dated by hand 17.2.1928 without sources in the Schriftgutarchiv, Filmmuseum Berlin, Stiftung Dt. Kinemathek).

116 "Kysers großer Luther-Film, Cob-Film der UFA: Ufa-Palast am Zoo", article signed "Maraun", press cutting, n. d. [probably February 1928], without sources in file LAELKB, DW 2181: "Luther ist nur das Symbol, lebendiger Ausdruck dieser Bewegung (Reformation), von einem an Schmerzen reichen Schicksal berufen, bewegende Kraft und zum Ziele leitender Führer zu sein. Diese Geburt aus Volk, Zeit und Raum, die Wesen und Notwendigkeit jedes großen Menschen in der Geschichte bestimmt, wird von dem Regisseur Hans Kyser vollendet zur Anschauung gebracht. Man bemerkt vielfach die Erfahrungen, die er als Mitarbeiter Murnaus beim Faust-Film gemacht hat [...]."

117 Press cutting without author and sources, dated by hand "6. 3. 1928" in the Bundesarchiv-Filmarchiv, Berlin: "Luther sicherte den Deutschen die nationale Individualität, er sicherte der gesamten Menschheit das Recht der freien geistigen Persönlichkeit und er gab zugleich dem einzelnen sein Eigentum zurück, indem er ihn von der Herde erlöste. [....] Sein Wort war eine Tat. Er sicherte uns die deutsche Freiheit. Halten wir dafür, dass wir sie nicht wieder verlieren. Und wenn die Welt voll Teufel wär!". The distributers compiled other positive critiques in the press in *Kinematograph* No. 1097, 1928, 6, including: "*Berliner Mittag*: [...] The film should be shown to our youth, who are in dire need of stimulation, now especially." ("Berliner Mittag: [....] Der Film soll unserer Jugend gezeigt werden, die gerade jetzt einen Ansporn bitter notwendig hat.")

118 On this Kaiser 1986, 190.

119 "Die Fehlleistungen der Nationalen Bewegung durch Adolf Hitler", in *Deutsch-Evangelische Korrespondenz* 29, 1930, quoted in Fleischmann-Bisten, *Der Deutsche Bund*, 62.

120 Stiftung Luthergedenkstätten in Sachsen-Anhalt, Lutherstadt Wittenberg, S 1018/7226: "Luther-Film. Der Freiheitskampf des deutschen Gewissens. Wir rufen heute alle nach dem großen Führer, der der deutschen Not ein Ende machen soll. Noch wissen wir nicht, ob er kommt, aber wir wissen, daß früher unserem Volke überragende Persönlichkeiten geschenkt waren, von deren Seelenstärke und Bekennermut wir heute noch leben. Ein solcher Führer war unser mitteldeutscher Landsmann D. Martin Luther. Sein Bild zu zeigen hat sich ein Film zur Aufgabe gemacht [...] Als ein Lebendiger steht er am Schlusse vor uns. Luther ist nicht tot, sein Geist wirkt in uns fort."

121 "So gibt es also doch etwas, das stärker ist als Rom und alle Päpste. Das deutsche Gewissen."

122 "A new Luther film? To be candid: we are still weary of the last one. We certainly were not to blame for it but we were encumbered by it. At that time there was no lack of Lutheran warnings about that production. Today it is as good as lost. In the silent film era, it would not have stood the test. [...] Now *Der Filmkurier* (No. 196) is talking about a new series of Luther films that may start at Frankenhausen. The author is allegedly Carl Leyst-Küchenmeister, the slant presumably the vernacular homeland play. The report is very vague and unclear. Judging from our previous experience, we should like to anticipate events by saying: Have a care, gentlemen!" ("Ein neuer Lutherfilm? Um es offen herauszusagen: wir haben noch von dem letzten genug. Wir waren bestimmt nicht an ihm schuld, aber man hat uns mit ihm belastet. Es hat damals nicht an evangelischen Stimmen gefehlt, die vor dieser Produktion gewarnt haben. Heute ist er so gut wie verschollen. In der Zeit des Tonfilms hätte er sich als stummer Film nicht halten können. [...] Nun weiß der *Filmkurier* (No. 196) von einer neuen Lutherfilm Serie zu berichten, die evtl. in Frankenhausen starten soll. Autor soll Carl Leyst-Küchenmeister sein, Anlehnung vermutlich an ein Heimatspiel. Die Notiz ist sehr vage und undurchsichtig. Nach unseren bisherigen Erfahrungen möchten wir von vornherein sagen: Vorsicht, meine Herren!"); Die Filmschere of Sept. 1, 1931, 8, cutting added to the records on December 3, 1931, EZA 1/2258.

123 Harry Julius Kreider, *The Beginnings of Lutheranism in New York*, New York: Author 1949.

124 For their history see for example: Thomas J. Müller, *Kirche zwischen zwei Welten: Die Obrigkeitsproblematik bei Heinrich Melchior Mühlenberg und die Kirchengründung der deut-*

schen Lutheraner in Pennsylvania, Stuttgart: Steiner 1994 (Transatlantische historische Studien, 2).

125 Michael Hochgeschwender, *Amerikanische Religion: Evangelikalismus, Pfingstlertum, Fundamentalismus*, Frankfurt am Main: Verlag der Weltreligionen im Inselverlag 2007.

126 Hartmut Lehmann, *Martin Luther in the American Imagination*, Munich: Fink 1988, 12.

127 Ibid.

128 Ibid. 25.

129 Ibid., 32.

130 Ibid.

131 Ibid., 33.

132 Ibid., 176.

133 Rev. Edward J. Jung: Ibid., 177.

134 Ibid., 178.

135 Ibid., 20.

136 For example in the part about Luther's roots: "Zu diesen Zeiten saß im Thüringischen, am Kreuzweg der deutschen Rassen von alters, zu Mora jenseits der Werra ein Bauernvolk, nährte sich schlecht und recht und blieb unwissend der bangen und herrischen Fragen [...] Sie wußten es nicht, ihr Erbgut an urtümlichen Deutschtum in ihrem vom Leben ihrer Ahnen kaum unterschiedenen Leben rein bewahrend, nüchtern gemacht durch ihr strenges und armes Dasein, doch wieder mystisch erschlossen dem großen heiligen Leben Gottes in der geheimnisvollen Natur, in der sie ihre Arbeit taten", Klara Hofer, *Bruder Martinus. Ein Buch vom deutschen Gewissen*, Stuttgart and Berlin: Cotta'sche Buchhandlung 1917, 11f.

137 Hugh McLeod, "*Religion in the United States and Europe – The 20th Century*", in Hartmut Lehmann (ed.), *Transatlantische Religionsgeschichte. 18. und 20. Jahrhundert*, Göttingen 2006, 132; Jay P. Dolan, *In Search of American Catholicism. A History of Culture in Tension*, New York: University Press 2002, 180f. Also in Europe, the feeling of a "Revival" was widespread (see for example the statement of Rev. F. P. Copland Simmons quoted in chapter V.3.4.2. and note 275 there).

138 Cf. Grant Wacker, *Religion in Twentieth-Century America*, in Jon Butler, Grant Wacker and Randall Balmer, *Religion in American Life: A Short Story*, Oxford and New York: Oxford University Press 2003, 364.

139 Ibid.; for the statistics see Will Herberg, *Protestant, Catholic, Jew: An Essay in American Religious Sociology*, Garden City, NY: Doubleday 1955, 174.

140 Jerald C. Brauer, *Protestantism in America: A Narrative History*, Philadelphia: Westminster Press 1953, 281.

141 Brauer, *Protestantism*, 278. The National Council was founded in 1930 as an alliance between the American Lutheran Church, which unified the three independent German Lutheran Synods, the Norwegian Lutheran Churches and the Augustana Swedish Lutheran Churches, the United Lutheran Church and the Missouri Synod Lutheran Church (ibid., 276).

142 Flückinger, *Protestantismus und Film*, 9.

143 Robert Fryer, *A Guide to the History and Art of the 'Martin Luther' Film*, Master thesis, 1964 (typescript in the Library of Columbia University, New York).

144 Fryer, *Guide*, 3.

145 "Mr. Maurischat [...] also had original Luther documents, imperial decrees, and church records duplicated or copied in English following the original format. Luther's pamphlet on the 'Freedom of the Christian Man' [...] appeared in English but looked exactly like the original German document" (ibid., 14).

146 Irving Pichel, "The Problem of Documentation", *The Quarterly of Film Radio and Television*, 8, 2, Winter 1953, 172–185: "The entertainment film aims, in general, to create the

illusion that is a record of actuality. [....] In the Luther film, there were both external and internal factors that imposed an obligation to adhere as closely as possible to the facts of the record. Inescapable was the purpose for which the film was made. It was commissioned by the Lutheran Church Productions, a coordinating body that produces films of religious education for all the Lutheran Synods of America. The film was planned to inform Lutherans particularly and Protestants generally of the issues over which Luther revolted against the Roman Catholic Church of his day, culminating in what has come to be known as The Reformation. It follows that the film, in selecting its material, should distinguish between events which were predominantly political or social or personal and those which have a residue of religious significance for an audience today; that it should necessarily emphasize the tenets of faith which remain a live issue for non-Catholics as against issues which were historically determined in the permanent record of the time and cannot affect any further the institutions involved. As historical facts, there is no need to do more than recount the indisputable occurrences: that is conceived by Luther and his followers that there were abuses in the Church [...]. The other issues noted [...] above were resolved in Luther's lifetime. The Reformation took place, an indisputable fact of history. However, the great issue ... had not been and may never be resolved. This made the telling of the story a parable of immediate applicability to a far wider audience than the sponsors may have at first had in mind. Again, it imposed upon us, the makers of the film, a responsibility to adhere completely to historic fact. [...] To make a noncontroversial film about a controversy may be impossible [...]. It makes bad drama as well as bad history, to set up a straw man for the hero to conquer. Therefore it was necessary to know and represent as truthfully and as fairly as possible the position of Luther's opposition, to view him also from the point of view of the Church."

147 Ibid., 185.
148 Fryer, *Guide*, 1.
149 Ibid., 2.
150 *Freedom: An Epic of Reformation* was distributed by "Reformation Films, inc." in New York (*American Lutheran* 12, June 1929, 27), it was celebrated as an "outstanding picture in every sense of the word" in the *National Board of Review Magazine* 3, No. 10, Oct. 1928; the front page of the magazine shows the scene "Luther Facing his Interrogators".
      The film *Martin Luther, His Life and Time*, released in the US by the "Lutheran Film Division" and first presented in the States in October 1924, was still available in the US in form of a VHS-copy made by Reel Images in Monroe, Connecticut, in 1980. A review of the 1920s praised the film as "being the genuine religious picture in the great library of film" and draws Luther's image like the icon of a saint: "The awakened Luther, near-martyr, man, and ever the leader, is then carried into enforced exile at the Wartburg, where he makes his other great contributions to religious freedom, the translation of the New Testament into the language of the people." On the other hand the author emphasized the authenticity of the film: "practically every incident was photographed on historic ground. Nine tenths of the scenes were made in Germany". The new intertitles were written by Dr. Scherer and a new score was composed by Edward Rechlin and Herman Spielter by using "classical Lutheran scores". Nevertheless, it had missionary character: "No Lutheran can see these pictures without being strengthened in his faith." ("The Life of Martin Luther in Motion Pictures", *American Lutheran* 8, March 1925, 7).
151 A copy is conserved in the ELCA Archives: LFA 0/8/2, Box 1. Nothing is known about the composition of the group.
152 Fryer, *Guide*, 17.
153 A report by Dr. Oswald Hoffmann and Henry Endress on October, 27–28, 1952, mentions that "'sperr marks' could not be used for the expenses of non-German citizens" (ELCA Archives: LFA 0/8/2, Box 1). For the intricate economic background see: Walter Lückefahr,

Sperrmark und Registermark, Dissertation Köln 1958, and Christoph Buchheim, "Rück-kehr in die Weltwirtschaft. Das Londoner Schuldenabkommen von 1953", in *Frankfurter Allgemeine Zeitung*, Sept. 23, 2003, Wirtschaft, Nr. 219, 13.

154 Fryer, *Guide*, 8.

155 Fryer, ibid. (the source Fryer indicated for this quotation, "Herbert G. Luft, 'Irving Pichel', *Films in Review* 1954, October" is not correct).

156 "Irving Pichel, Director and Actor, Dies at 63", *Los Angeles Times*, July 14, 1954, 5.

157 "Joseph C. Brun, ASC", *American Cinematographer* 80, Nr. 2, Feb. 1999, 127.

158 For the titles of the references used see Fryer, *Guide*, 7.

159 Cover letter and questionnaire signed by Henry Endress, executive secretary of the LCP (ELCA Archives: LFA 0/8/2).

160 "The Film Martin Luther", *The Listener*, Oct. 28, 1954, 707.

161 J.M., "Martin Luther, USA/Germany, 1953", *Monthly Film Bulletin* 21 (1954), 173.

162 H.H., *Films in Review* 4, No. 5, May 1953, 237; cf. "Martin Luther", *The Congregational Monthly*, Nov. 1954.

163 J.M., Martin Luther, 173.

164 Pichel, Documentation, 183f.

165 "Martin Luther", *New York Times* [New York City Edition] Aug. 23, 1953, SM26.

166 Henry McKean Taylor, *Rolle des Lebens*, 287.

167 Fryer, *Guide*, 14.

168 Ibid., 9.

169 Ibid.

170 Flückinger, *Protestantismus und Film*, 10.

171 See note 153.

172 Kate B. Griffiths, "Memories of Luther's Town", *The Baptist Times*, Sept. 1, 1955, 1.

173 Fryer, *Guide*, 11.

174 Pichel, Documentation, 183.

175 Report by Dr. Johannes Stuhlmacher, Luther Film GmbH, Stuttgart, on October 15, 1952, 1 (ELCA Archives: LFA 0/8/2, Box 1).

176 "Edinburgh Begins 7th Music Festival", *New York Times*, Aug. 24, 1953, 20.

177 "Religious News Notes", *Chicago Daily Tribune*, Sept. 5, 1953, 15.

178 "Of Local Origin", *New York Times*, Sept. 9, 1953, 38.

179 *American Lutheran* 9 (1926), May, 10.

180 *Los Angeles Times*, Sept. 6, 1953, C3.

181 *Los Angeles Times* , Sept. 10, 1953, A13.

182 Edwin Schallert, "Luther Life evokes Stir with Drama", *Los Angeles Times*, Sept. 11, 1953), A9.

183 *New York Times*, Oct. 9, 1953, 33.

184 *New York Times*, Oct. 23, 1953, 19; *New York Times*, Nov. 1, 1953, X7, *New York Times*, Nov. 20, 1953, 19; *New York Times*, Nov. 25, 1953, 33.

185 *New York Times*, Oct. 16, 1953, 33; *New York Times*, Nov. 27, 1953, 23; *Washington Post*, Nov. 1, 1953, L2; *Washington Post*, Dec. 9, 1953, 43.

186 This kind of religious Hollywood epic was very popular in the 1930s and the 1950s. It reflects the "great revival of moralism and community consciousness" that emerged from the Great Depression and "Cold War neurosis": Fraser, *Images of Passion*, 164.

187 See the letter sent on September 24, 1956 by Monte Kleban, Programmas de Televisión, Mexico, to Robert E. A. Lee, LCP about the problems in the Spanish translation: ELCA Archives LFA 0/8/6.

188 20th Century-Fox MAT–409; cf. MAT–120 and Mat–220 (ELCA Archives: LFA 0/8/5).

189 In a letter dated September 20, 1955, to Louis de Rochemont Associates, Bob Charvoz,

Gospel Film Incorporated in Dallas, Texas, asked for these commercials and transcripts of them (ELCA Archives: LFA 0/8/5).

190 ELCA Archives: LFA 0/8/7.
191 No date, probably shortly before October 31, 1953 (ELCA Archives: LFA 0/8/2).
192 ELCA Archives: LFA 0/8/5.
193 Ibid.
194 Ibid.
195 "The Film Martin Luther", *The Listener* 52, October 28, 1954, 707.
196 Bosley Crowther, "The Screen. Two Films Make Debut", *New York Times*, Sept. 10, 1953, 22.
197 Fryer, *Guide*, 57.
198 Ibid., 57f.
199 Quoted in Fryer, *Guide*, 27.
200 Ibid.
201 Albrecht, *Verkündigung*, 104f.
202 Gregory Lawrence Sobolewski, *Roman Catholic Reception of Luther in the Twentieth Century: Magisterial Positions and their Ecumenical Significance* (PhD Marquette University 1993), Ann Arbor, Mich., 1994, 190.
203 Sobolewski, *Roman Catholic reception*, 197.
204 Albert Hyma, *New Light on Martin Luther. With an Authentic Account of the Luther Film of 1953*, Grand Rapids, Michigan: Eerdmans, 1958 [©1957].
205 George Robert Garner III, "Music and the Arts", *Los Angeles Sentinel*, Nov. 5, 1953, A10.
206 Ibid.
207 "Theatres Refuse To Let Negroes See Religious Films", *Atlanta Daily World*, Nov. 25, 1953, 1.
208 Garner III, "Music and the Arts", *Los Angeles Sentinel*, Nov. 5, 1953, A10.
209 Richard L. Coe, "'Martin Luther' Shown on Merit", *The Washington Post*, Oct. 27, 1953, 14.
210 "Theatres Affirm Race Ban", *New York Amsterdam News*, Nov. 28, 1953, 1.
211 "Bias Nixes Sepia Patrons From Theatre Showing, 'Robe', Luther", *The Chicago Defender (National Edition)*, Dec. 5, 1953, 19.
212 "Louisville Theatres Nix Negroes' Admittance to See Religious Pix", *Pittsburgh Courier*, Dec. 5, 1953, 23.
213 Bosley Crowther, "Picking the Best Films of 1953", *New York Times* [New York City Edition], Dec. 27, 1953, X3.
214 E.g.: Richard L. Coe, "'Eternity' Tops '12-Best' Movie List", *Washington Post* (Jan. 3, 1954), B9: "'Martin Luther'. Distinguished by firmness of purpose, this drama makes much of the intellectual and theological clash of the sixteenth century, its fittingly professional production avoiding the religious passions which might so easily have been invoked by lesser handling."
215 "Quebec Movie Board Bars 'Martin Luther'", *New York Times*, Dec. 31, 1953, 10; "Quebec bans Film", *The Washinton Post*, Dec. 31, 1953, 3.
216 "Quebec bans Film", *The Washinton Post*, Dec. 31, 1953, 3.
217 "Lutheran Protest 'Martin Luther' Ban", *New York Times*, Jan. 1, 1954, 15.
218 "Toronto, Dec. 31", *New York Times*, Jan. 1, 1954, 15.
219 "Rap Quebec's Ban on Luther Film", *Chicago Daily Tribune*, Jan. 6, 1954, 4.
220 "'Luther' Ban Assailed", *New York Times*, Jan. 15, 1954, 14.
221 Ibid.
222 "Luther Biographer Admits He Was Red", *The Washington Post and Times Herald*, May 11, 1954, 11.
223 "Film, Video Writer Tell of Being Red", *New York Times*, May 11, 1954, 14.

224 "Luther Film Ban Explained By WGN-TV", *Chicago Daily Tribune*, Dec. 20, 1956, B9.

225 "Freedom to See", *Daily Defender*, Dec. 26, 1956, 9; also the chancellor of the Catholic archdiocese of Chicago confirmed: "Any protests were made by Catholics as individuals" ("Fight On for TV Showing Of Canceled 'Luther' Film", *Chicago Daily News*, Dec. 20, 1956).

226 "Since Luther was a real person, the story of his life can be read in innumerable books – although naturally of varying interpretation. That being so, we can think of no good reason why it should not be shown as a movie." ("Martin Luther", *Chicago Daily News*, Dec. 21, 1956).

227 See the letters to the editor page with statements divided between "against" and "for" the ban in the *Chicago Daily News* on December 28, 1956; cf.: Godfrey Sperling, "'Luther' TV Ban Stirs Public Opinion", *The Christian Science Monitor*, March 1, 1957, 3.

228 "Predicts Lifting of Luther TV Ban", *Chicago Daily News*, Dec. 28, 1956; in the film journal *Variety*, Martin Luther was called "television's most controversial personality in the upcoming 57th year of the 20th century" ("Chi Embroiled in Hot Religioso Hassle in TV Cancelling of 'Luther'", *Variety*, Dec. 26, 1956).

229 "Cancelling of Film on TV Protested", *New York Times*, Dec. 20, 1956, 34.

230 "Freedom to See", *Daily Defender*, Dec. 26, 1956, 9

231 So he wrote to the house committee: "any move to destroy freedom of speech in matters of religion is an un-American activity which you have a moral and legal obligation to investigate and expose." ("Ask U.S. Probe in Cancelling Luther Movie", *New York Times* Dec. 21, 1956, 19).

232 "'Luther' Action Urged: Chicago Group Asks F.C.C. to Revoke License of Station", *New York Times*, Feb. 21, 1957, 55; cf. *Robert Tate Allan's Washington Religious Report*, Feb. 15, 1957, No. 151, 2. The text of the petition has been preserved in ELCA Archives: LFA 0/8/7.

233 Unfortunately he does not even mention the moderate forms of Protestantism like Lutheranism, so his religious mapping of America is rather biased: Michael Hochgeschwender, *Amerikanische Religion*, 108–110, 121, 147, 155, 182. Even Shea mentioned Lutherans and Lutheranism only twice explicitly in his book about the relationships between Protestants and Catholics, although he defined the Lutheran Church as an evangelical Church (William M. Shea, *The Lion and the Lamb. Evangelicals and Catholics in America*, Oxford, Oxford University Press, 2004, 12).

234 "Jesuit Licenses For TV Opposed", *New York Times*, March 4, 1957, 46; "Granting TV Stations to Jesuit Schools Fought", *Los Angeles Times*, March 4, 1957, 13; "Protestant Protest Jesuit TV Licenses", *The Washington Post and Times Herald* , March 4, 1957, A13.

235 So Jack Gould, therefore, suggested that "the wiser example of broadcasting statesmanship would be to offer a companion program, on which exceptions to the film might be expressed." (Jack Gould, "TV: Battle Over 'Luther'", *New York Times*, Feb. 22, 1957, 43).

236 "Give Up Battle For Hearing On Luther Movie", *Chicago Daily Tribune*, March 15, 1957, 22. The opposing argument presented by the WGN before the Federal Communications Commission in Washington is recorded in ELCA Archives: LFA 0/8/7.

237 "Viewers to See 'Martin Luther' over Channel 7", *Daily Defender*, March 4, 1957, 7. Godfrey Sperling, "Chicago TV to Show 'Luther'", *The Christian Science Monitor*, March 4, 1957, 12; In the wake of the cancellation other TV stations had allegedly already signalled their intention to broadcast the film (George Dugan, "2 Lutheran Aides Going to Hungary", *New York Times*, Jan. 30, 1957, 15).

238 "Protestants, Catholic Paper Issue Comments on 'Luther'", *Chicago Sun-Times*, March 1, 1957 (ELCA Archives LFA 0/8/7).

239 "Martin Luther Film On Channel 7 Tuesday", *Daily Defender*, April 22, 1957, 7.

240 See for example "Cancelling of Film On TV Protested", *New York Times*, Dec. 20, 1956,

34; "Film 'Ban' Denounced", *New York Times*, Dec. 21, 1956, 18; "Ask U.S. Probe in Cancelling Luther Movie", *New York Times*, Dec. 21, 1956, 19; "Sponsor Sorry TV Film on Luther Was Canceled", *Chicago Daily Tribune*, Dec. 22, 1956, 4; "Freedom to See", *Daily Defender*, Dec. 26, 1956, 9; "Hit TV for Refusing To Show 'Martin Luther'", *Daily Defender*, Jan. 17, 1957, 19; Richard Philbrick, "Reveal Fringe Groups Lead In Church Gains", *Chicago Daily Tribune*, Jan. 30, 1957, B5; "Religion Group Asks FCC Study TV Ban On Film", *Chicago Daily Tribune*, Feb. 7, 1957, B4; "Churchmen go to F.C.C.: Chicago Group Retaliates In Barring Of 'Luther Film'", *New York Times*, Feb. 8, 1957, 19; "'Luther' Ban Piques A Catholic Weekly", *New York Times*, Feb. 8, 1957, 23; "'Martin Luther' Backers Hit TV 'Cancellation'", *Chicago Defender*, Feb. 16, 1957, 8; "300 Lutheran Churches Will Hold Missions", *Chicago Daily Tribune*, Feb. 17, 1957, N5; "'Luther' Action Urged: Chicago Group Asks F.C.C. to Revoke License of Station", *New York Times*, Feb. 21, 1957, 55; "Martin Luther Film To Be On Milwaukee TV", *Chicago Daily Tribune*, Feb. 27, 1957, A5; "'Luther' Film to Be Seen on TV", *New York Times*, Feb. 27, 1957, 22; "Movie on Luther to be presented on WBKB April 23", *Chicago Daily Tribune*, March 2, 1957, 10; Luther Film To Go On", *New York Times*, March 2, 1957, 41; "Jesuit Licenses For TV Opposed, *New York Times*, March 4, 1957, 46.

241 See undated cutting in ELCA Archives: LFA 0/8/7.

242 Bainton, *Bainton speaks* [1954]. Bainton replied in this text to Lon Francis' article in *Our Sunday Visitor Press* "The Martin Luther Movie, unhistorical, unbiblical, unfair" and the book of John A O'Brien, *Martin Luther: the priest who founded Protestantism*, New York, Paulist Press 1953. According to Bainton O'Brien errs in repeating the charge that Luther "built his religion around the state", on the contrary he was "regarded as menace" (*Bainton speaks*, 9).

243 Robert J. Welch, "The Martin Luther Film", *National Catholic Weekly Review*, XCVI, No 25, whole No 2497, March 23, 1957, 698.

244 Albert Hyma, *New Light on Martin Luther*, 1–7.

245 Robert J. Welch, "The Martin Luther Film", *National Catholic Weekly Review*, XCVI, No 25, whole No 2497, March 23, 1957, 698.

246 Ibid. 699.

247 WA TR 1, 177, 36f.

248 WA TR 1, 96, 6 (225) [Veit Dietrich; April 1532]; 177, 31–37 (409) [Veit Dietrich; Dec. 1532]; 441, 38–442,2 (884) [Veit Dietrich; first half of the 1530s]; nevertheless, Luther still saw himself as an Augustinian monk after 'the dismissal' by Staupitz; cf. Vera Christina Papst, *"....quia non habeo aptiora exempla.": Eine Analyse von Martin Luthers Auseinandersetzung mit dem Mönchtum in seinen Predigten des ersten Jahres nach seiner Rückkehr von der Wartburg 1522/1523*, Diss. Hamburg 2005, (online resource: http://deposit.ddb.de/cgi-bin/dokserv?idn=97588980x&dok_var=d1&dok_ext=pdf&filename=97588980x.pdf.), 53.

249 "Of Local Origin", *New York Times*, June 29, 1954, 21; cf. memorandum from Robert E.A. Lee of the Lutheran Church Productions to Paul C. Empie, dated July 17, 1954 (ELCA Archives: LFA 0/8/6).

250 According to Custen, *Bio-Pics*, 83.

251 There is virtually no material on these procedures in the ELCA records (LFA 0/8) apart from some newspaper articles. So in a reply published on June 23, 1953, Father J.A.V. Burke, honorary secretary of the Catholic Film Institute, vice president of the "Office Catholique International du Cinema" and member of the "Advisory Council of the Pontifical Film Commission" contends, that "it is quite untrue that any kind of ban has been placed upon this film, either in this country or in another." ("No ban on 'Luther'", *Kinematograph Weekly*, June 23, 1953). However, according to the British press in September, the film had been banned in Brazil (*The Star*, Sept. 5, 1955; *Birmingham Mail*, Sept. 8, 1955; *The Daily Mail*, Sept. 8, 1955; *News Chronicle*, Sept. 8, 1955) as well as in Egypt, Peru and

the Philippines (*Punch*, Sept. 7, 1955; *Northampton Independent*, Sept. 9, 1955; *Church of England Newspaper*, Sept. 16, 1955), but only a handout of unknown authorship and provenance is given as the source of this information!

252 Quoted in Haberer, *Bewegtes Lutherbild*, 59: "die breiteste Öffentlichkeit auf eine positive wirksame Weise als Kirche der Reformation."

253 Joachim Steinmayr, "'Martin Luther' kommt in die deutschen Kinos", *Süddeutsche Zeitung* Oct. 2, 1953.

254 Christoph von Imhoff, A. Betz, "Der amerikanische Lutherfilm. Eine evangelische und eine katholische Stellungnahme", in *Rheinische Post*, March 17, 1954.

255 Günter Dehn, "Glaubenskrieg um einen Spielfilm: Luther-Produktion erregte vor 30 Jahren die Gemüter", *Evangelische Wochenzeitung für Bayern/Sonntagsblatt* 1982, No. 43 quoted from the reprint in Horstmann, *Wandel*, 77f.: "Pfarrämter wurden zur Vorverkaufsstelle für weltliche Lichtspieltheater. Die Devise wurde ausgegeben: 'Dieser Film ist unsere Sache! Auch wer sonst keinen Film besucht, muss *Martin Luther* sehen!'"; "'Sollte sein Schritt Schule machen?'"

256 Dehn, *Glaubenskrieg*, 78.

257 Ibid., 77.

258 Dietmar Schmidt, "'Glaubenskriege' um Lutherfilme", in Trapmann, *Reformator*, 262 and 264.

259 F. M. Elsner, "Zum amerikanischen Lutherfilm", in *Film-Dienst* 7 (1954), issue 11 (March 12), reprinted in Horstmann, *Wandel*, 79.

260 "nicht wegen ihres theologischen Inhalts, sondern ebenfalls als Beispiele antipäpstlicher und antirömischer Polemik" (Albrecht, *Verkündigung*, 104f.).

261 Ibid., 74: "Manipulation der Geschichte".

262 One of the main points for criticism was, according to Albrecht, the displacement of Luther's Christology as "meaningful moderation" ("sinngebende Mitte") by the representation of his conflict with the Church of Rome. Moreover, Albrecht considered that the film presented late medieval theology erroneously, and the relationship between faith and the doctrine of justification in Luther was also inaccurately shown; see ibid., 73, 82 and 100.

263 Werner Hess, "'Martin Luther' – kein Filmheros: Ein Beispiel für die Möglichkeiten des religiösen Spielfilms", in *epd. Kirche und Film*, Feb. 1954, 2–4, reprinted in Horstmann, *Wandel*, 83–86; here: 83: "Gerade auf deutscher Seite wurde befürchtet, dass eine Verfilmung von 'Martin Luther' durch die amerikanischen lutherischen Kirchen die Gefahr einer falschen Heroisierung nicht vermieden werde. Um so überraschender war das Ergebnis. Der fertige Film war von einer derart starken, geistlichen Aussagekraft und zugleich von einer so durchgehenden inneren dramatischen Spannung, dass man ihn als eine großartige Leistung auf dem gesamten Feld des religiösen Spielfilms ansehen darf."

264 That institution was founded as a consequence of the Schalbach Resolution of 1950 to promote worthwhile films and impart quality standards to the public (Helmke, *Kirche, Film und Festivals*, 98f.).

265 *Handbuch für Evangelische Filmarbeit*, Gruppe I/b/2, Munich, Evangelischer Presseverband für Bayern, March 1954, 93: "für unsere deutschen Vorstellungen die Rollen der Käthe Luther und Karls V. nicht glücklich besetzt und die Konfirmandenszene nicht glücklich gespielt wurde." Unfortunately the statement does not reveal what would have met the criteria.

266 Kahle/Lee, *Popcorn and Parable*, 85.

267 Soul was born on August 28, 1943 in Chicago, Ill., as David Richard Solberg. His father, Dr. Richard Solberg, a Lutheran minister, was Religious Affairs Advisor to the U.S. High Commission in Berlin and Senior Representative for the Lutheran World Federation, a refugee relief agency actively involved in post-World War II reconstruction in Germany. Soul's brother is a Lutheran minister and social activist. Soul became very popular for

playing the part of Hutch in *Starsky and Hutch* (cf. http://www.davidsoul.com/biography. html [Sept. 6, 2008]).

268 See for example: "Luther Over Simplified", *Birmingham Post*, Oct. 18, 1954; "'Martin Luther' Film", *Irish Independent*, Oct. 18, 1954: "but it also possesses the very distinct disadvantages of being sponsored by Lutheran Church productions. The earlier scenes are well-balanced, but the hand of the propagandist becomes only too evident in the latter stages […] It is an idealised Luther that emerges on the screen. There is nothing here of the man who wrote the pamphlet urging the ruling classes to suppress the insurgents with all violence, and the unbending rectitude with which he is represented ill-accords with his sanction of the bigamy of Philip of Hesse"; "Luther in a thick coat of whitewash", *Universe: the Catholic newspaper*, Oct. 22[?], 1954: "In contrast to this whitewashing, nothing is shown of Catholicism but the current abuses, with most of the emphasis on the sale of indulgences."; "Talking At Random", *Tablet*, Oct. 23, 1954; "'Luther' Comes To Brighton At Last", *Brighton & Hove Herald*, Jan. 15, 1955: "The film portrays Luther as a gentle, saintly man. It stresses the favourable aspects of his life, his works and his personality, and ignores altogether his failings. Some of his opponents, on the other hand, it paints as rogues and schemers preying on the poor and the ignorant"; Peter Davies, "The Luther Film", *Merthyr Express*, April 23, 1955: "The accusation that Luther was anti-Semitic is unfortunately true, but hatred of Jews was universal in the Roman Church …"; "Niall MacGinnis A Gentle Luther. A Partisan Film, but Mild", *Manchester Guardian*, Sept. 3, 1955: "almost everyone (including Luther) is made nice and relatively quiet. And that frankly is a pity. It would surely have been more interesting if the film's sponsors had chanced their arms a bit more"; Grace Conway, "Luther comes to Town", *Catholic Herald*, Sept. 2, 1955.
The dates of the articles are usually cited as given on the newspaper cuttings in the ELCA Archives: LFA 0/8/5.

269 Ted Kavanagh wrote the lyrics that were to be sung to the tune of "Phil the Fluter's Ball": "Have you heard of Martin Luther from the town of Wittenberg? / They have made a film about him in a manner that's absurd. / They have covered him in whitewash till he looks a sorry knave, / So I'm sure hat poor old Martin is a-turning in his grave. / This film was made for and paid for by the Lutherans / And it's the dullest bit of bunk that ever has been seen, / For hour after hour you must listen to their flutherings / While miserable Martin fumes and fusses on the screen! Chorus: With no proof of the truth and a lot of tarradiddle-oh, / History in hiding and a lot of faddle-fillde-oh, / Teaching, preaching in bitterness and gall, / Oh, there isn't any gaiety in Martin Luther's Bawl! / There is a divil [sic!] of a hint in it of honest Christian charity. / The papshers are pilloried, the Pope is made a clown: / Melancthon [sic!] indulges in some most-pathetic parotry / And what a fine indulgence you could buy for half-a-crown ! / Off to Rome goes Martin in a tizzy now, / Do you blame the Pope for feeling he was just a bore? / With self-esteem poor Luther was all dizzy now, / And before he went to pieces nailed his thesis to the door. / Chorus / So Martin was startin' a hellish lot of trouble-oh. / Preaching here and teaching there a lot of roth and bubble-oh, / It's a sin and a shame that this film was made at all, / For there's not a word of honest truth in Martin Luther's Bawl!" (*Universe: the Catholic newspaper*, Sept. 9, 1955).

270 "'Martin Luther'", *Universe: the Catholic newspaper*, Sept. 2, 1955.

271 "'Martin Luther' in London", *The National Message*, Aug. 20, 1955.

272 "Martin Luther Film", *The Christian*, June 24, 1955.

273 "Freedom in Religion", Letter to the Editor, *Northampton Chronicle & Echo* (undated cutting, probably from 1955, in the ELCA Archives: LFA 0/8/5).

274 J. A. Friend, "'Martin Luther.' Film for Sydney Soon", *The Australian Church Record* Sept. 16, 1954, 8, column 3.

275 "Trade Show For 'Luther' October 15", *To-Day's Cinema*, Oct. 1954; cf. "'Martin Luther' Trade Showing", *Daily Film Renter*, Oct. 6, 1954 (ELCA Archives: LFA 0/8/5).

276 "'Coach-loads' expected for 'Martin Luther'", *Evening News* [Glasgow], Oct. 21, 1954, 15.

277 "439th Anniversary of Reformation to Be Feted", *Los Angeles Times*, Oct. 27, 1956, 10.

278 ELCA Archives: LFA 0/8/7.

279 For example: Larry Wolters, "Luther TV Film is set for Dec. 21", *Chicago Daily Tribune*, Dec. 12, 1956, B12.

280 Even as late as 1967 the script is cited in Lee, *Martin Luther.*

281 William Naphy, *The Protestant Revolution. From Martin Luther to Martin Luther King Jr.*, London, BBC Books 2007, blurb. Here is not the space to discuss all the theories about the consequences of the Reformation which have been developed during the last decades, especially in Germany. For the changing tendencies, see for example the journal *Archiv für Reformationsgeschichte* and the monographs *Schriften des Vereins für Reformationsgeschichte*. Nevertheless the knowledge about Luther of some Anglo-Saxon scholars seem to rely exclusively on secondary works in English, even though these authors are celebrated experts on the field of Reformation history: Dorothea Wendebourg, "Der ganze Westen kann nicht anders: Diarmaid MacCulloch will mit seiner ungeheuer reichen Geschichte der Reformation das entscheidende Kapitel Europas schreiben", *Süddeutsche Zeitung*, Oct. 13, 2008, 14 (Review of the German version of "Reformation: Europe's House Divided 1490–1700" by Diarmaid MacCulloch).

282 On that: Hartmut Lehmann, *Protestantisches Christentum im Prozeß der Säkularisierung*, Göttingen: Vandenhoeck & Ruprecht 2001; Hartmut Lehmann, *Transformationen der Religion in der Neuzeit. Beispiele aus der Geschichte des Protestantismus*, Göttingen: Vandenhoeck & Ruprecht 2007 (VMPIG, 230).

283 For a survey of all activities, see: Susan R Boettcher, "Luther Year 2003? Thoughts on an Off-Season Comeback", *Sixteenth Century Journal* 35, No 3, Fall 2004, 795–809.

284 Steven E. Bean, archives specialist at the ELCA, summarized the subsequent administrative history in the foreword to the records in the ELCA in 1991 as follows: "In 1955, representatives of LCP held several informal meetings to discuss possible future film projects. LCP was originally organized for the production of only one film and the amount of the corporate account was essentially fixed at the time of incorporation. Therefore in 1957, a second corporation was formed: Lutheran Film Associates (LFA) envisioned a corporate structure that would allow it to pursue a variety of projects over an indefinite period of time. The member organizations of LFA were the same as those of Lutheran Church Productions, with its purpose being: to produce, acquire, distribute, exhibit or otherwise utilize sound films in promoting church objectives of common interest to the participating church bodies and affiliated Lutheran agencies.

Having previously existed as an unincorporated association under the administrative wing of LCP, the LFA's task was to develop new subjects for filming. Incorporation was recommended when LFA came to the point of having script properties. After consultation with members and upon voice of counsel, the organization was structured so as to provide considerable flexibility in developing religious films, although its by-laws specifically prevented LFA from actually producing (i.e., financing and owning) a motion picture in its own name. However, LFA could supervise the production of a film for another group. The Board of Trustees of Lutheran Film Associates proposed in 1959 that their membership undertake the production and distribution of a motion picture whose screenplay explored the situation facing the Lutheran church in the midst of tensions between East and West Germany. The project was carried out through the creation of a stock corporation, LFA Productions Inc. (LFAP), organized for the specific purpose of producing and distributing the motion picture; LFA by-laws did allow for serving the needs of such a separate corporation. LCP, on the other hand, had an inherent charter limitation preventing it from film activity other than that 'related to the life and work of Martin Luther.'

LFA Productions Inc. borrowed funds in Germany for the production of 'Question 7' from Luther-Film G.m.b.H. in 1960. These funds had accumulated from the distribution of 'Martin Luther' in Germany. Their use in the production was consistent with the way in which LCP had financed its production of the motion picture 'Martin Luther' through the use of special German funds-sperrmark.

When the method of operation of the LCP-LFA-LFAP trio was discussed, a recommendation followed that Lutheran Film Associates serve as a service agency for LCP on one hand, and LFA Productions Inc. on the other. This had already been approved at the time of creation of LFAP and it was later decided that LFA should also service LCP, thus reversing the process that had earlier been in effect. The arrangement included the identification of joint accounts with local suppliers and utility firms (managed by LFA instead of LCP), and all joint administrative expenditures were paid by LFA check.

After the production of the film 'Question 7', the issue of LFAP's longevity was raised. The corporate status of Lutheran Church Productions was facing the same scrutiny. Because LFA was the 'housekeeping' agency for LCP and LFAP, it was a natural conclusion that LFA assume the functions and film management for the other two corporations. The necessary steps were initiated, and LFA was left as the single corporate entity. In 1965, the action was taken to transfer the assets of LCP and LFAP to LFA, and to dissolve the two former film organizations. When all of the foregoing had been executed, only Lutheran Film Associates remained. It owned all of the film assets and rights, including partnership in Lutheran Film G.m.b.H.

Lutheran Film Associates was faced with another change in 1967, when in the spirit of Lutheran unity the Lutheran Council in the USA was created. The establishment of LCUSA left the role of LFA in promoting inter-Lutheran activity in question. LFA eventually decided to merge into the LCUSA Department of Films operating within the framework and procedures of the Lutheran Council. Since the beginning of the LCUSA, the Board of Trustees of the LFA also served as the Standing Committee of the LCUSA Department of Films. Yet LFA was able to maintain its independent corporate status with the stipulation that it not engage in any activities beyond the review and approval of LCUSA. An administrative agreement was established in 1972, whereby LCUSA became the service agency for the Lutheran Film Associates by providing supervision, staff, facilities and communication.

LFA went through yet another period of transition in 1986, the eve of the dissolution of the Lutheran Council in the USA. Many discussions ensued regarding the corporation's future program, objectives and means for financing. LFA was at a point in its history where its film earnings were at a record low and when the future possibilities of its program and continued existence had to be considered. The executive secretary of LFA, Robert E. A. Lee urged the Board of Trustees to make one of three decisions: 1) pursue a future role for LFA aggressively with adequate funding that could provide for new staff; 2) dissolve the corporation; or 3) put it in dormancy. The Trustees voted to keep Lutheran Film Associates a separate incorporated agency beyond the life of LCUSA. LFA has been operating in a restricted mode since January 1, 1988 with an annual review of its status."

285 "Shortly after the turn of the 20th century, two grassroots groups - one made up of German Lutherans in Wisconsin and the other of Norwegian Lutherans in Minnesota - were concerned about the security and well-being of their fellow Lutherans. Each group was determined to start a fraternal benefit society that would provide Lutherans with life insurance. Aid Association for Lutherans was certified for business on Nov. 4, 1902, but only after several years of hard work by dedicated churchmen such as Albert Voecks, Gottlieb Ziegler, William Zuhlke and John Grupe. They canvassed Lutherans throughout much of eastern Wisconsin to sign up the 500 members required for the new organization to obtain its first charter.

The founding of Lutheran Brotherhood had its roots with the 1917 convention of the Norwegian Lutheran Church of America. Lifelong Lutherans Jacob Preus, a Minnesota insurance commissioner, and Herman Ekern, a former Wisconsin insurance commissioner, proposed launching a not-for-profit mutual aid society. After much debate, the proposal passed and the society began life as "Lutheran Union." Three years later, the organization was renamed "Lutheran Brotherhood." From the beginning, Aid Association for Lutherans and Lutheran Brotherhood offered similar life insurance products. [...] In September 29, 2001 [...] unanimous approval is granted to merge the two organizations. In January 1, 2002 the merged organization officially begins operation. The organization adopts the trade name of AAL/LB until a new name can be approved. In June 2002 – Members approve a new name - Thrivent Financial for Lutherans – following a mail ballot vote of adult contract benefit holders." (published on the homepage of the firm: http://www.thrivent.com/aboutus/history/index.html [18.5.2008]).

286 Janice Krahnt (Corporate Archivist/Historian Corporate Records Management, FSO Compliance, 4321 N. Ballard Road, Appleton WI 54919–0001), replied as follows on my query about their records of the film in an e-mail on March, 10, 2008: "The last film on Luther which was shown through out the United States has not reached the corporate archives as they are still dealing with questions and copyright questions. [...] I have very little documentation on 'Martin Luther'."

287 See "Corrections", *New York Times*, Sept. 14, 2003, AR4.

288 Sabine Horst, "'Luther würde heute nicht überleben': Der Regisseur Eric Till über Historienfilme, Religion und seine Arbeit an einer außergewöhnlichen Geschichte", *epd Film. Das Kino Magazin* 11 (2003), 22–25.

289 Ibid., 25.

290 Ibid., 23.

291 Dave Kehr, "At the Movies", *New York Times*, Sept. 25, 2003, E3.

292 Stephen Holden, "Martin Luther's Passion, Still Resonating Today", *New York Times*, Sept. 26, 2003, E11.

293 Ibid.

294 Boettcher, *Luther 2003*, 798.

295 Ibid.

296 Ibid, 800.

297 Jan Oppenheimer, "Luther Celebrates a Revolutionary Figure", *American Cinematographer* 84, 10, Oct. 2003, 12.

298 Robin Blaetz, *Visions of the Maid. Joan of Arc in American Film and Culture*, Charlottesville and London: University Press of Virginia 2001, xii.

299 Cf. ibid., xiv and p. 182.

300 Charles Musser, "Passions and the passion play: theatre, film and religion in America, 1880–1900", *Film History* 5 (1993), 419–456; German translation: "Leidenschaften und das Spiel vom Leiden. Theater, Film und Religion in Amerika, 1880–1900", in Reinhold Zwick and Otto Huber (ed.), *Von Oberammergau nach Hollywood. Wege der Darstellung Jesu im Film*, Köln: Katholisches Institut für Medieninformation GmbH 1999, 29–79.

301 Cf. McKean Taylor, *Rolle des Lebens*, 30.

302 Ibid., 48.

303 Ibid., 95.

Conclusions

1   On this for instance Kohnle, *Luther vor Karl V.*, 52–56 with extensive references.

2   Thus also the tenor in Diarmaid MacCulloch: "He [Luther] did not say the last word on the Protestant problem of liberty versus license, but he gave some profound answers for others to wrestle with, and he had released the word freedom (libertas) to ring through Europe and excite a bewildering variety of reactions in its hearers" (Diarmaid MacCulloch, *Reformation: Europe's House Divided* 1490–1700, London 2003, New York: Viking 2004, 127; cf. the German translation *Die Reformation 1490–1700*, Stuttgart: DVA 2008, 186); however, Luther was always solely concerned with religious freedom, which in his day even led to strife with the peasants.

   German experts have criticized MacCulloch's work and charged its author with being totally "uninformed" on Luther and ignoring most of German scholarship: thus also Dorothea Wendebourg, who summed it up as follows: "The statements on Luther and the Lutheran tradition are definitely among the weaknesses of the book" ("Die Ausführungen über Luther und die lutherische Tradition gehören zu den ausgesprochenen Schwächen des Buches"), Dorothea Wendebourg, "Der ganze Westen kann nicht anders", *Süddeutsche Zeitung*, Oct. 13, 2008, Literatur, 14.

3   On the discussion about the history and the interpretation of this process see for example: Heide Fehrenbach and Uta G. Poiger (ed.), *Transactions, Transgressions, Transformations: American Culture in Western Europe and Japan*, New York and Oxford: Berghahn 2000 and Lars Koch, "Zwischen Kontinuität und Innovation: Der westdeutsche Spielfilm 1945–1960", in Lars Koch (ed.), *Modernisierung als Amerikanisierung? Entwicklungslinien der westdeutschen Kultur*, Bielefeld, transcript Verlag 2007, 89–109.

4   H. Fehrenbach, "Persistent Myths of Americanization: German Reconstruction and the Renationalization of Postwar Cinema, 1945–1960", in *Transactions, Transgressions, Transformations*, 88.

5   This process is not mentioned by Michael G. Kammen, *Mystic Chords of Memory. The Transformation of Tradition in American Culture*, New York: Knopf 1991.

6   Werner Schneider-Quindeau, "Der Reformator als Leinwandheld: Lutherfilme zwischen Geschichte und Ideologie", in *Handbuch Theologie und populärer Film*, vol. 2, ed. Thomas Bohrmann, Werner Veith and Stephan Zöller, Paderborn, München, Wien and Zürich: Ferdindand Schöningh 2009, 195f.

7   Hermann Gerber, *Problematik des Religiösen Films*, Munich, Ev. Presseverband für Bayern 1962, 7: "daß ein gut Teil der Verkündigung von den Theologen auf die Laien übergangen ist."

8   Cf. Albert J. Bergesen and Andrew M. Greeley, *God in the Movies*, New Brunswick etc.: Transaction Publ. 2000, 177. (The 3rd edition, published in 2005, was not available to me.)

9   Report by the Protestant press agency "Evangelischer Pressedienst" (epd), Oct. 31, 2008 under the heading "Margot Käßmann und Ben Becker erinnern im Fernsehen an Luther" (epd 081031166).

10 Report by the epd, May 5, 2010 under the heading "Bavaria-Chef Esche hält neuen Spielfilm über Luther für möglich" (epd 100505057).

Bibliography

Abbreviations

ADW	Archiv des Diakonischen Werkes, Berlin
BBKL	Biographisches Bibliographies Lexikon
BSLK	Die Bekenntnisschriften der evangelisch-lutherischen Kirche herausgegeben vom Deutschen Evangelischen Kirchenausschuß im Gedenkjahr der Augsburgischen Konfession 1930.
EG	Evangelisches Gesangbuch: Stammausgabe der Evangelischen Kirche in Deutschland, Stuttgart: Biblia-Druck [1993].
EHS	Europäische Hochschulschriften
EKD	Evangelische Kirche in Deutschland
ELCA	Evangelical Lutheran Church in America
EZA	Evangelisches Zentralarchiv, Berlin
FsöTh	Forschungen zur systematischen und ökumenischen Theologie
GL	Gotteslob: Katholisches Gebet- u. Gesangbuch, Stammausg., 3. Aufl., Stuttgart: Katholische Bibelanstalt 1996.
HosEc	Hospitium ecclesiae. Forschungen zur Bremischen Kirchengeschichte
KI EB	Konfessionskundliches Institut des Evangelischen Bundes, Bad Bensheim
LAELKB	Landesarchiv der Ev.-Luth. Kirche Bayerns, Nürnberg
LCI	Lexikon der Christlichen Ikonographie
LMA	Lexikon des Mittelalters
LuJ	Lutherjahrbuch
RAC	Reallexikon für Antike und Christentum
RDK	Reallexikon zur Deutschen Kunstgeschichte
VerfLex	Die deutsche Literatur des Mittelalters. Verfasserlexikon, ed. by W. Stammler und K. Langosch, Vol. 1–5, 2nd. ed., Berlin und Leipzig
VMPIG	Veröffentlichungen des Max-Planck-Instituts für Geschichte,
WA	Luther, Martin, D. Martin Luthers Werke, Weimar: Hermann Böhlau 1883ff.: Schriften/Werke, Vol. 1–80 [WA], Tischreden [WA TR], Vol. 1–6, Deutsche Bibel [WA DB], Vol. 1–15, Briefwechsel [WA B], Vol. 1–18.

Archival Sources

Bad Bensheim, Konfessionskundliches Institut des Evangelischen Bundes [KI EB]
S 500.500.9d: Generalversammlungen des Evangelischen Bundes
S 185.460.5: Lutherfilme, -bühnenstücke

Contains stills from the 1927 Lutherfilm made by COB
S 185.460.7: Postcards made from the stills

Berlin, Evangelisches Zentralarchiv [EZA]

EZA 1/2248: Kirchenbundesamt. Akten betreffend Schauspiel, Film, Februar 1913–September
1927
(includes: Entwurf eines Gesetzes über die Prüfung von Bildstreifen vom 6.3.1920)
EZA 1/2249: Kirchenbundesamt. Acta betreffend Schauspiel, Film, Oktober 1927–Ende 1929
EZA 1/2250: Kirchenbundesamt. Acta betreffend Schauspiel, Film, Januar 1930–Februar 1931
Änderung des Lichtspielgesetzes, Entwürfe
EZA 1/2251: Kirchenbundesamt. Acta betreffend Schauspiel, Film; hierzu Drucksachen, März
1931–April 1934:
(includes: Änderung des Lichtspielgesetzes, Entwurf, Antrag Nr. 838 Reichstagssitzung am
6.3.1931, gedrucktes Protokoll, S. 1451b)
EZA 1/2255: Kirchenbundesamt. Acta betreffend: Sonstige Luthergedächtnisfeiern. 1920–1924
(includes Walther Nithack-Stahn, *Martin Luther. Ein Heldenleben in 7 Handlungen*, typescript
n. d. [completed in 1923].)
EZA 1/2256: Kirchenbundesamt. Acta betreffend Sonstige Luthergedächtnisfeiern, Okt. 1925–
Sept. 1927
EZA 1/2258: Kirchenbundesamt Acta betreffend Sonstige Luthergedächtnisfeiern
EZA 1/2259: Kirchenbundesamt. Acta betreffend Sonstige Luthergedächtnisfeiern
(includes press cuttings concerning the 1927 film)
EZA 7/P 254: Königl. Konsistorium der Provinz Brandenburg, Acta betr. Bruno, Georg Döhring
1904–1961
EZA 2/2800: Laufzeit 1954–1968 (includes material about Luther film 1953)

Berlin, Archiv des Diakonischen Werkes [ADW]

CA/PD 299: Lutherfilm der Lutherfilmdenkmal e.V., Schreiben von Ostern 1928 an ADW etc.
HGSt 7777: Lutherfilm-Gesellschaft mbH, Gesellschaftsvertrag und Geschäftsordnung von
1952
HGSt 7076: Pressespiegel zu Lutherfilm
HGSt 7077: Lutherfilm-Gesellschaft mbH: Schriftwechsel mit Lutheran Film Associates, N.Y.
1971

Berlin, Filmmuseum Berlin, Stiftung Dt. Kinemathek, Schriftgutarchiv.

Press cuttings

Elk Grove Village, IL, Archives of the Evangelical Lutheran Church in America [ELCA]

LFA 0/8/00 Lutheran Film Associates, Administrative History
LFA 0/8/1–10 Lutheran Film Associates, Luther film 1953
LFA 3/1–2 Lutheran Film Associates 1955 (- ongoing)

Lutherstadt Wittenberg, Stiftung Luthergedenkstätten in Sachsen-Anhalt

S 1018/7226: Pamphlet "Luther-Film. Der Freiheitskampf des deutschen Gewissens … ."

Nürnberg, Landesarchiv der Ev.-Luth. Kirche Bayerns [LAELKB]:

DW 2181 Rep.no 24 [formerly stock "Landesverein für Innere Mission", No. 401 T. I. Rep.
No. 456]).
DW 2155 Rep.no. 24 [formerly stock "Landesverein für Innere Mission", No. 420 T. I. Rep.
No. 475].

Secondary Works

Anonymous

1911, July 26: *Der Kinematograph*, No. 239.

1911, Aug. 31: *Lichtbild-Theater* 3, No. 35.

1913, Sept. 27: *Erste Internationale Film-Zeitung*, No. 39, 136.

1923, July 15: *Der Kinematograph*, No. 856, 9.

1925, March: "The Life of Martin Luther in Motion Pictures", *American Lutheran* 8, 32.

1926, May: *American Lutheran* 9, 10.

1927: *Vorstandsblatt des Evangelischen Bundes*, special ed. 1a, 53–56 and No. 2, 57–73.

1927: "Beim großen Lutherfilm" in *Der Wächter*, Nos. 11/12, 15f.

1928: *Evangelischer Bund zur Wahrung der Deutsch-Protestantischen Interessen e.V., Mitgliederblatt* 42.

1928: *Illustrierter Film-Kurier* 10, No. 810.

1928: *Kinematograph* No. 1096.

1928: *Kinematograph* No. 1097.

1928: *Deutsch-Evangelische Korrespondenz. Mitteilungen des Evangelischen Bundes* 27, No. 6, 1.

1928: *Deutsch-Evangelische Korrespondenz. Mitteilungen des Evangelischen Bundes* 27, No. 9, 29.

1928, Jan.: *Protestantische Rundschau* 5, 155f.

1928, Jan. 9–11: *Fränkische Wacht: Über den Parteien. Für Christentum und Deutschtum im protestantischen Geist*, No. 2, 12.

1928: March 1: *Allgemeinen Rundschau. Generalanzeiger für Nordbayern* 38, No. 53, 2

1928, May 4: *Nieuw Weekblad voor de Cinematografie* VI, 31

1929, June: *American Lutheran* 12, 27.

1928, Oct., 10: *National Board of Review Magazine* 3, No. 10.

1928, Nov., 9: *Nieuw Weekblad voor de Cinematografie* VII, 6

1930: "Die Fehlleistungen der Nationalen Bewegung durch Adolf Hitler", in *Deutsch-Evangelische Korrespondenz* 29.

1934, May 5: "Moving Pictures and Morals", *The Lutheran Companion* 42, 545.

1934, July 28: "Movies Alarmed by Church Fight", *The Lutheran Companion* 42, 931.

1927, Dec. 21: *Aus der Welt der Kirche, Beiblatt zur Bayerischen Volkszeitung* reprinted in a compilation of articles with the subtitle "Exhofprediger Döhrings Lutherfilm. Eine Nürnberger Uraufführung. Klosterhetze, Romhaß, Ablaßrummel und Scheiterhaufen" in *Allgemeine Rundschau* Jan. 11, 1928.

1928: *Die Wartburg. Deutsch-evangelische Monatsschrift* 27, 58 and 68.

1953, May: H.H., *Films in Review* 4, No. 5, 237.

1953, June 23: "No ban on 'Luther'", *Kinematograph Weekly*.

1953, Aug. 23: "Martin Luther", *New York Times* [New York City Edition], SM26.

1953, Aug. 24: "Edinburgh Begins 7th Music Festival", *New York Times*, 20.

1953, Sept. 5: "Religious News Notes", *Chicago Daily Tribune*, 15.

1953, Sept. 9: "Of Local Origin", *New York Times*, 38.

1953, Sept. 6: *Los Angeles Times*, C3.

1953, Sept. 10: *Los Angeles Times*, A13.

1953, Oct. 9: *New York Times*, 33.

1953, Oct. 16: *New York Times*, 33.

1953, Oct. 23: *New York Times*, 19.

1953, Nov. 1: *Washington Post*, L2.

1953, Nov. 1: *New York Times* [New York City Edition], X7.

1953, Nov 20: *New York Times*, 19.

1953, Nov. 25: *New York Times*, 33.

1953, Nov. 25: "Theatres Refuse To Let Negroes See Religious Films", *Atlanta Daily World*.

1953, Nov. 27: *New York Times*, 23.

1953, Nov. 28: "Theatres Affirm Race Ban", *New York Amsterdam News*, 1.

1953, Dec. 5: "Bias Nixes Sepia Patrons From Theatre Showing, 'Robe', 'Luther'", *The Chicago Defender (National Edition)*, 19.

1953, Dec. 5: "Louisville Theatres Nix Negroes' Admittance to See Religious Pix", *Pittsburgh Courier*, 23.

1953, Dec. 9: *Washington Post*, 43.

1953, Dec. 31: "Quebec Movie Board Bars 'Martin Luther'", *New York Times*, 10.

1953, Dec. 31: "Quebec bans Film", *The Washinton Post*, 3.

1954, Jan. 1: "Lutheran Protest 'Martin Luther' Ban", *New York Times*, 15.

1954, Jan. 1: "Toronto, Dec. 31", *New York Times*, 15.

1954, Jan. 6: "Rap Quebec's Ban on Luther Film", *Chicago Daily Tribune*, 4.

1954, Jan. 15: "'Luther' Ban Assailed", *New York Times*, 14.

1954, May 11: "Luther Biographer Admits He Was Red", *The Washington Post and Times Herald*, 11.

1954, May 11: "Film, Video Writer Tell of Being Red", *New York Times*, 14.

1954, June 29: "Of Local Origin", *New York Times*, 21.

1954, July 14: "Irving Pichel, Director and Actor, Dies at 63", *Los Angeles Times*, 5.

1954, Oct. 6: "Trade Show For 'Luther' October 15", *To-Day's Cinema*.

1954, Oct. 18: "Luther Over simplified", *Birmingham Post*.

1954, Oct. 18: "'Martin Luther' Film", *Irish Independent*.

1954, Oct. 21: "'Coach-loads' expected for 'Martin Luther'", *Evening News* [Glasgow], 15.

1954, Oct. 22[?]: "Luther in a thick coat of whitewash", *Universe: the Catholic newspaper*.

1954, Oct. 23: "Talking At Random", *Tablet*.

1954, Oct. 28: "The Film Martin Luther", *The Listener*, 707.

1954, Nov.: "Martin Luther", *The Congregational Monthly*.

1955, Jan. 15: "'Luther' Comes To Brighton At Last", *Brighton & Hove Herald*.

1955, June 24: "Martin Luther Film", *The Christian*.

1955, Aug. 20: "*Martin Luther* in London", *The National Message*

1955, Sept. 2: "'Martin Luther'", *Universe: the Catholic newspaper*.

1955, Sept. 3: "Niall MacGinnis A Gentle Luther: A Partisan Film, but Mild", *Manchester Guardian*.

1955, Sept. 5: *The Star*.

1955, Sept. 7: *Punch*.

1955, Sept. 8: *Birmingham Mail*.

1955, Sept. 8: *The Daily Mail*.

1955, Sept. 8: *News Chronicle*.

1955, Sept. 9: *Universe: the Catholic newspaper*.

1955, Sept. 9: *Northampton Independent*.

1955, Sept. 16: *Church of England Newspaper*.

1956, Oct. 27: "439th Anniversary of Reformation to Be Feted", *Los Angeles Times*, 10.

1956, Dec. 20: "Luther Film Ban Explained By WGN-TV", *Chicago Daily Tribune*, B9.

1956, Dec. 26: "Freedom to See", *Daily Defender*, 9.

1956, Dec. 20: "Fight On for TV Showing Of Canceled 'Luther' Film", *Chicago Daily News*.

1956, Dec. 20: "Cancelling of Film On TV Protested", *New York Times*, 34.

1956, Dec. 21: "Film 'Ban' Denounced", *New York Times*, 18.

1956, Dec. 21: "Ask U.S. Probe in Cancelling Luther Movie", *New York Times*, 19.

1956, Dec. 21: "Martin Luther", *Chicago Daily News*.

1956, Dec. 22: "Sponsor Sorry TV Film on Luther Was Canceled", *Chicago Daily Tribune*, 4.

1956, Dec. 26: "Chi Embroiled in Hot Religioso Hassle in TV Cancelling of 'Luther'", *Variey*.

1956 Dec. 26: "Freedom to See", *Daily Defender*, 9.

1956, Dec. 28: "Predicts Lifting Of Luther TV Ban", *Chicago Daily News*

1957, Jan. 17: "Hit TV for Refusing To Show 'Martin Luther'", *Daily Defender* , 19.

1957, Feb. 7: "Religion Group Asks FCC Study TV Ban On Film", *Chicago Daily Tribune*, B4.

1957, Feb. 8: "Churchmen go to F.C.C.: Chicago Group Retaliates In Barring Of 'Luther Film'", *New York Times*, 19.

1957, Feb. 8: "'Luther' Ban Piques A Catholic Weekly", *New York Times*, 23.

1957, Feb. 15: *Robert Tate Allan's Washington Religious Report*, No. 151, 2.

1957, Feb. 16: "'Martin Luther' Backers Hit TV 'Cancellation'", *Chicago Defender*, 8.

1957, Feb. 17: "300 Lutheran Churches Will Hold Missions", *Chicago Daily Tribune*, N5.

1957 Feb. 21: "'Luther' Action Urged: Chicago Group Asks F.C.C. to Revoke License of Station", *New York Times*, 55.

1957, Feb. 27: "Martin Luther Film To Be On Milwaukee TV", *Chicago Daily Tribune*, A5.

1957, Feb. 27: "'Luther' Film to Be Seen on TV", *New York Times*, 22.

1957, March 2: "Movie on Luther to be presented on WBKB April 23", *Chicago Daily Tribune*, 10.

1957, March 2: "Luther Film To Go On", *New York Times*, 41.

1957, March 4: "Jesuit Licenses For TV Opposed, *New York Times*, 46.

1957, March 4: "Viewers To See 'Martin Luther' Over Channel 7", *Daily Defender*, 7.

1957, March 4: "Granting TV Stations to Jesuit Schools Fought", *Los Angeles Times*, 13.

1957, March 4: "Protestant Protest Jesuit TV Licenses", *The Washington Post and Times Herald*, A13.

1957, March 15: "Give Up Battle For Hearing On Luther Movie", *Chicago Daily Tribune*, 22.

1957, April 22: "Martin Luther Film On Channel 7 Tuesday", *Daily Defender* , 7.

1957, March 1: "Protestants, Catholic Paper Issue Comments on 'Luther'", *Chicago Sun-Times*.

1963, Oct. 19: "Few Smash Hits on N. Y. Stages", *Chicago Tribune*, A5.

1965, Oct. 20: "Crowded Screen in Luther 'Epic'", *The Times*, 16.

1984, Aug. 29, "Luther ist tot", *Variety* CCCXVI/5, 16.

1999, Feb.: "Joseph C. Brun, ASC", *American Cinematographer* 80, Nr. 2, 127.

2003, September 14: "Corrections", *New York Times* (New York City Edition), AR4.

2003: "Sir Peter Ustinov. Ein Interview zu seinem neuen Film 'Luther'", *Münchner Wochenblatt* 45, G5.

2008, Oct. 31: "Margot Käßmann und Ben Becker erinnern im Fernsehen an Luther" (epd 081031166).

Albrecht, Gerd, *Film und Verkündigung: Probleme des religiösen Films*, Gütersloh: Bertelsmann 1962 (Neue Beiträge zur Film- u. Fernsehforschung, 2).

Alte Pinakothek München. Erläuterungen zu den ausgestellten Gemälden, korrigierte und durch einen Anhang erw. Ausgabe, ed. by Bayerische Staatsgemäldesammlungen, Munich: Edition Lipp 1999.

Arnold, Gary, Cinema: "Subscribing to the Idea that the Play's the Thing at AFT", *The Washington Post, Times Herald*, Sept. 9, 1973, L1.

Assel, Heinrich, *Die Lutherrenaissance – Ursprünge, Aporien und Wege: Karl Holl, Emanuel Hirsch, Rudolf Hermann (1910–1935)*, Göttingen: Vandenhoeck & Ruprecht 1994 (FsöTh, 72).

Babington, Bruce/Evans, Peter Williams, *Biblical Epics: Sacred narrative in the Hollywood cinema*, Manchester, etc: Manchester University Press 1993.

Bainton, Roland, *Roland Bainton speaks on the Martin Luther Motion Picture*, New York: Lutheran Church Production 1954.

Bainton, Roland, "Luther und seine Mutter", in *Luther* 44 (1973), 3, 123–130.

Bainton, Roland, "Luther und sein Vater: Psychiatrie und Biographie", in *Zeitwende* 44 (1973), 393–403.

Balász, Béla, *Der Geist des Films*, Halle an der Saale: Knapp 1930.

Balász, Béla, *Der sichtbare Mensch oder die Kultur des Films*, Vienna 1924, reprint Frankfurt am Main: Suhrkamp 2001.

Bamberger, Stefan/Everschor, Franz, *Religion im Film: Ein Beitrag zu Geschichte, Funktion und Gestaltung des religiösen Films*, Düsseldorf: Verlag Haus Altenberg 1963.

Barth, Hans-Martin, "Luther – der Mann und der Film: Zwölf Thesen", *Evangelische Orientierung. Zeitschrift des Evangelischen Bundes*, 2003, H. 4, 13.

Baugh, Lloyd, *Imaging the Divine. Jesus and Christ Figures in Film*, Kansas City, MO: Sheed & Ward 1997.

Baur, Nina/Luedke, Jens [ed.], Die soziale Konstruktion von Männlichkeit: Hegemoniale und marginalisierte Männlichkeiten in Deutschland, Opladen etc.: Budrich, 2008.

Bautz, Friedrich Wilhelm, "Bruno Döhring", in *BBKL*, Vol. 1, Nordhausen: Verlag Traugott Bautz 1990, col. 1343.

Beaucamp, Eduard, "Die Macht der Erinnerung: Geschichtsphantasie und Geschichtsreflexion im Werk Werner Tübkes", in Mosheh Tsukerman (ed.), *Geschichte und bildende Kunst*, Göttingen: Wallstein 2006 (Tel Aviver Jahrbuch für deutsche Geschichte, 34), 293–308.

Behrendt, Harald, *Werner Tübkes Panoramabild in Bad Frankenhausen: zwischen staatlichem Prestigeprojekt und künstlerischem Selbstauftrag*, Kiel: Ludwig 2006 (*Bau + Kunst*, 10).

Bergesen, Albert J./Greeley, Andrew M., *God in the Movies*, New Brunswick etc.: Transaction Publ. 2000.

Beuth, Uli, "Zacharias Werners Mädchen und Frauen", in Hubert Thoma and Ghemela Adler [ed.], *Romantik und Moderne. Neue Beiträge aus Forschung und Lehre. Festschrift für Helmut Motekat*, Frankfurt a. M. etc.: Lang 1986, 77–106.

Blaetz, Robin, *Visions of the Maid: Joan of Arc in American Film and Culture*, Charlottesville and London: University Press of Virginia 2001.

Boettcher, Susan R., "Luther Year 2003? Thoughts on an Off-Season Comeback", *Sixteenth Century Journal* 35, No 3 (Fall 2004), 795–809.

Bornkamm, Heinrich, *Luthers geistige Welt*, 1st ed. 1947, Gütersloh: Mohn ⁴1960.

Bornkamm, Heinrich, *Thesen und Thesenanschlag Luthers. Geschehen und Bedeutung*, Berlin: Töpelmann 1967.

Brandstetter, Gabriele, "Ausdruckstanz", in *Handbuch der deutschen Reformbewegungen: 1880–1933*, ed. Diethart Kerbs, Wuppertal: Hammer 1998, 451–463.

Brandt, Reinhard, *Lasst ab vom Ablass: Ein evangelisches Plädoyer*, Göttingen: Vandenhoeck & Ruprecht 2008.

Brauer, Jerald C., *Protestantism in America: A Narrative History*, Philadelphia: Westminster Press 1953.

Bräuer, Siegfried, Die Lutherfestwoche vom 19. bis 27. August 1933 in Eisleben, in Laube/Fix (ed.), *Lutherinszenierung und Reformationserinnerung*, 391–451.

Brecht, Martin, *Martin Luther. Die Erhaltung der Kirche 1532–1546*, Stuttgart: Calwer, 1987 (Martin Luther, 3).

Brecht, Martin, *Martin Luther: Sein Weg zur Reformation*, Stuttgart: Calwer, 1981 (Martin Luther, 1).

Breitmoser-Bock, Angelika, *Bild, Filmbild, Schlüsselbild: Zu einer kunstwissenschaftlichen Methodik der Filmanalyse am Beispiel von Fritz Langs Siegfried (Deutschland 1924)*, Munich: Schaudig, Bauer, Ledig 1992 (Diskurs Film: Bibliothek, 5).

Bremer, Thomas/Hubert, Wolf (ed.), *Ökumenische Kirchengeschichte*, 3: Von der Französischen Revolution bis 1989, Darmstadt: Wissenschaftliche Buchgesellschaft 2007.

Brückner, Christine, *Wenn Du geredet hättest, Desdemona. Ungehaltene Reden ungehaltener Frauen* (1st ed. Hamburg 1983), 3rd enlarged ed. Berlin: Ullstein 1996.

Brunotte, Ulrike/Herrn, Rainer (ed.), *Männlichkeiten und Moderne: Geschlecht in den Wissenskulturen um 1900*, Bielefeld: Transcript-Verlag für Kommunikation, Kultur und soziale Praxis 2007 (Gender Codes, 3).

Buchheim, Christoph, "Rückkehr in die Weltwirtschaft. Das Londoner Schuldenabkommen von 1953", in *Frankfurter Allgemeine Zeitung*, Sept. 23, 2003, Wirtschaft, Nr. 219, 13.

Buchwald, Georg, *Doktor Martin Luther. Ein Lebensbild für das deutsche Haus. Mit zahlreichen Abbildungen im Text sowie dem Bildnis Luthers in Heliogravüre nach einem Gemälde von Lucas Cranach zu Nürnberg* (1st ed. 1902), 3rd völlig umgearbeitete Auflage mit zahlreichen Abbildungen im Text und auf 16 Tafeln nach Kunstwerken der Zeit, Leipzig and Berlin: Teubner 1916.

Butler, Jon/Wacker, Grant/Balmer, Randall, *Religion in American Life: A short story*, Oxford and New York: Oxford University Press 2003.

Canossa 1077. Erschütterung der Welt: Geschichte, Kunst und Kultur am Aufgang der Romanik, Exhibition catalogue Paderborn 2007, Vol. 1: Essays, Munich: Hirmer 2006.

Carlyle, Thomas, *Thomas Carlyle's Works. The Standard Edition*, Vol. 4: *Sartor Resartus and On Heroes, Hero-Worship, and the Heroic in History*, London: Chapman and Hall, 1904; Vol. 6,2: *Critical and Miscellaneous Essays*, London: Chapman and Hall 1904.

Cassidy, Claudia, "On the Aisle; Taut Drama Gets the Worst of It, Both on Camera and on Stage", *Chicago* Tribune, Feb. 5, 1968, B8.

Clark, Paul S., "Landau Pursues a Possible Dream", *Los Angeles Times*, Aug. 13, 1973, C13.

Coe, Richard L., "'Eternity' Tops '12-Best' Movie List", *Washington Post*, Jan. 3, 1954, B9.

Coe, Richard L., "'Martin Luther' Shown on Merit", *Washington Post*, Oct. 27, 1953, 14.

Cohan, Steven (ed.), *Screening the Male Exploring Masculinities in Hollywood Cinema*, London u.a.: Routledge, 1993.

Connell, R., *Masculinities*, Berkeley: University of California Press, 1995.

Connell, R. W., *Gender and Power: Society, the Person and Sexual Politics*, Stanford, Cal.: Stanford University Press 1987.

Conradt, Walther, *Kirche und Kinematograph. Eine Frage*, Berlin: Verlagsbuchhandlung Hermann Walther 1910.

Conway, Grace, "Luther comes to Town", *Catholic Herald*, Sept. 2, 1955.

Crowther, Bosley, "Picking the Best Films of 1953", *New York Times*, Dec. 27, 1953, X3.

Crowther, Bosley, "The Screen. Two Films Make Debut", *New York Times*, Sept. 10, 1953, 22.

Custen, George F., *Bio-Pics. How Hollywood Constructed Public History*, New Brunswick: NJ Rutgers University Press 1992.

Dähn, Horst/Heise, Joachim (ed.), *Luther und die DDR: Der Reformator und die Medien anno 1983*, Berlin: Ed. Ost 1996.

Dassmann, Ernst, "Kirche II (bildersprachlich)", in *RAC* 20, Stuttgart: Anton Hirsemann 2004, 965–1022.

Davies, Peter, "The Luther Film", *Merthyr Express*, April 23, 1955.

Davis, Kathy/Evans, Mary/Lorber, Judith (ed.), *Handbook of Gender and Women's Studies*, London etc.: Sage 2006.

Dehn, Günter, "Glaubenskrieg um einen Spielfilm. Luther-Produktion erregte vor 30 Jahren die Gemüter", *Evangelische Wochenzeitung für Bayern. Sonntagsblatt* 43/1982, Ressort Kultur, 15, reprinted in Horstmann, *Wandel*, 77f.

Dieter, Theodor, *Der junge Luther und Aristoteles. Eine historisch-systematische Untersuchung zum Verhältnis von Theologie und Philosophie*, Berlin, etc. de Gruyter, 2001.

Dinges, Martin (ed.), *Männer – Macht – Körper. Hegemoniale Männlichkeiten vom Mittelalter bis heute*, Frankfurt am Main: Campus-Verlag 2005.

Doehring, Bruno (ed.), *Ein feste Burg. Denkmäler evangelischer und deutscher Art aus schwerer Zeit. Der "Predigten und Reden" 2., ausgew. und durch vaterländische Zeugnisse erw. Ausg.*, Berlin: Schmidt [1918].

Döhring, Bruno, *Der deutsche Protestantismus in der Notwehr. Rede gelegentlich der 29. Generalversammlung des Evangelischen Bundes zur Wahrung der deutsch-protestantischen Interessen gehalten am 29. Juni 1925 zu Königsberg, Pr.*, Verlag des Evangelischen Bundes, Berlin n. d. [1925/26?].

Döhring, Bruno, *Die Weltgefahr. Gedanken zum Reformationstage 1923 aufgrund von Epheser 6,10–17*, Berlin: Verlag des Evangelischen Bundes 1924.

Döhring, Bruno, *Weltenende – Und wir ?*, Berlin: Verlag des Evangelischen Bundes 1924, 7f.

Döhring, Bruno, *Mein Lebensweg. Zwischen den vielen und der Einsamkeit*, Gütersloh: Bertelsmann 1952.

Dolan, Jay P., *In Search of American Catholicism. A History of Culture in Tension*, New York: University Press 2002.

Drobinski, Matthias, "Die Rückkehr des Reformators", in *Süddeutsche Zeitung*, Nov. 27, 2003, 3.

Drobinski, Matthias, "Die Kirche, die Krise und das Kino", in *Süddeutsche Zeitung*, Oct. 31, 2003, 4.

Dugan, George, "2 Lutheran Aides Going to Hungary", *New York Times*, Jan. 30, 1957, 15.

Eckermann, Willigis, "Augustiner-Eremiten", in *LThK*, 3rd ed., Vol. 1, Freiburg i.B. etc.: Herder 1993, 1233–1237.

Eisener, Lotte H., *Die dämonische Leinwand* (1st ed. *l'écran démoniaque* 1952), 2nd rev. ed. Frankfurt a. Main: Fischer-Taschenbuch-Verlag 1980, 301.

Elm, Kaspar, "Augustiner-Eremiten", in *LMA*, Vol. 1, Munich and Zurich: Artemis Verlag 1980, 1220f.

Elsaesser, Thomas, *Filmgeschichte und frühes Kino. Archäologie eines Medienwandels*, Munich: Ed. Text + Kritik 2002.

Elsner, F. M., "Zum amerikanischen Lutherfilm", in *Film-Dienst* 7 (1954), issue 11 (March 12), reprinted in *Martin Luther. Zum Wandel des Luther-Bildes*, 79.

Erikson, Erik Homburger, *Der junge Mann Luther. Eine psychoanalytische und historische Studie* (*Young Man Luther. A Study in Psychoanalysis and History*, New York 1958, translated into German by Johanna Schiche), Munich: Szczesny, 1964.

Evangelisches Gesangbuch [EG]: *Stammausgabe der Evangelischen Kirche in Deutschland*, Stuttgart: Biblia-Druck [1993].

Faber, Richard, *Abendland: ein politischer Kampfbegriff*, 2nd ed. Berlin etc.: Philo-Verl.-Ges. 2002 (Kulturwissenschaftliche Studien, 10).

Fehrenbach, Heide/ Poiger, Uta G. (ed.), *Transactions, Transgressions, Transformations: American Culture in Western Europe and Japan*, New York and Oxford: Berghahn 2000.

Feldt, Horst G., "Ein unromantisches und unheldisches Lutherbild", in *epd. Kirche und Film*, No. 41, Oct. 12, 1968, reprinted in Horstmann, *Wandel*, 112–114.

Fleischmann-Bisten, Walter, *Der Evangelische Bund in der Weimarer Republik und im sogenannten Dritten Reich)*, Frankfurt am Main etc.: Lang 1989 (EHS, 23: Theologie, 372).

Flückinger, Alfred, *Protestantismus und Film*, Zurich: Wanderer-Verlag 1951.

Flügel, Wolfgang, *Konfession und Jubiläum. Zur Institutionalisierung der lutherischen Gedenkkultur in Sachsen 1617–1830*, Leipzig: Leipziger Univ.-Verl. 2005.

Forshey, Gerald E., *American religious and Biblical spectaculars*, Westport CT: Praeger Publishers 1997.

Fraser, Peter, *Images of Passion. The Sacramental Mode in Film*, Westport, CT: Praeger Publishers 1998.

Frecot, Janos, *Johann Friedrich Geist und Diethart Kerbs, Fidus: 1868–1948. Zur ästhetischen Praxis bürgerlicher Fluchtbewegungen*, Munich: Rogner & Bernhard, 1972.

Freedman, Max, "Faults Invalidate 'Luther' Play", *Los Angeles Times*, Nov. 11, 1963, A5.

Friedrich, Hans-Edwin/Jung, Uli (ed.), *Schrift und Bild im Film*, Bielefeld: Aisthesis-Verlag, 2002 (Schrift und Bild in Bewegung, 3).

Friend, J.A., "Martin Luther." Film for Sydney Soon, *The Australian Church Record* Sept. 16, 1954, 8, column 3.

Fryer, Robert, *A Guide to the History and Art of the "Martin Luther" Film*, Master thesis 1964 (typescript in the Library of Columbia University, New York).

Fuchs, Martina, "Martin Luther – Protagonist moderner deutscher Literatur", in *LuJ* 73, 2006, 171–194.

Fundsache Luther. Archäologen auf den Spuren des Reformators, Exhibition Catalogue Halle an der Saale 2008/2009, Stuttgart: Konrad Theiss 2008.

Gailus, Manfred/Lehmann, Hartmut (ed.), *Nationalprotestantische Mentalitäten in Deutschland (1870–1970). Konturen, Entwicklungslinien und Umbrüche eines Weltbildes*, Göttingen: Vandenhoeck & Ruprecht 2005 (Veröffentlichungen des Max-Planck-Instituts für Geschichte, 214).

Gamman, Lorrain/Marshment, Margaret, *The Female Gaze*, London: The Women's Press 1988.

Garner III, George Robert, Music and the Arts, *Los Angeles Sentinel*, Nov. 5, 1953, A10.

Georges, Karl Ernst, *Ausführliches lateinisch-deutsches Handwörterbuch*, Vol. 1, Hanover and Leipzig: Hahnsche Buchhandlung [8]1913.

Gerber, Hermann, *Problematik des Religiösen Films*, Munich: Ev. Presseverband für Bayern 1962.

Goetsch, Monika, "Endlich reif fürs Kino: Der schöne Luther erobert die Herzen und bleibt ein Mann von Format [...]", *Chrismon Plus*, July 2002, 51f.

Gotteslob [GL]: *Katholisches Gebet- u. Gesangbuch, Stammausg.*, 3. Aufl., Stuttgart: Katholische Bibelanstalt 1996.

Göttler, Fritz, "Wilder Keiler. Auf Schauwerte bedacht: 'Luther' – katholisch gesehen", *Süddeutsche Zeitung*, Oct. 29, 2003, 13.

Gould, Jack, "TV: Battle Over 'Luther'", *New York Times*, Feb. 22, 1957, 43.

Graf, Friedrich Wilhelm, "Die Lehrjahre des Epheben 'Luther'", *Frankfurter Allgemeine Zeitung*, Oct. 29, 2003, 35.

Griffiths, Kate B., "Memories of Luther's Town", *The Baptist Times*, Sept. 1, 1955, 1.

Gross, Friedrich, *Jesus, Luther und der Papst im Bilderkampf 1871 bis 1918. Zur Malereigeschichte der Kaiserzeit*, Marburg: Jonas Verl., 1989.

Gutzeit, Jutta, "Staatliches Schauspielhaus 1932–1945. Die Intendanz Karl Wüstenhagen", in *100 Jahre Deutsches Schauspielhaus in Hamburg*, Hamburg etc.: Dölling & Galitz 1999, 48–61.

Haas, Willy, "Film-Kritk. Luther, ein Film deutscher Reformation", *Film-Kurier* Nr. 42, Feb. 17, 1928.

Haberer, Johanna/Helmke, Julia, "Das bewegte Lutherbild im Wandel der Zeit – Durchsicht der Filme von 1927 bis zur Gegenwart", in Amt und Gemeinde: Theologisches Fachblatt 55, H 3–4, 2004, 55–63 (first printed in *Arbeitshilfe für den evangelischen Religionsunterricht an Gymnasien*, Folge II, 2003, 13–25).

Hahn, Johan G., "A Methodology for Finding the Filmmaker's Weltanschauung in Religious Films", in John R. May (ed.), *New Image of Religious Film*, Kansas City: Sheed & Ward 1997, 213–234.

Hanisch, Ernst, *Männlichkeiten. Eine andere Geschichte des 20. Jahrhunderts*, Wien etc.: Böhlau 2005.

Halliwell, Leslie, *Halliwell's film & video guide*, ed. by John Walker, London: HarperCollins [12]1996.

Hamburger, Klaus, "Illustrierter Religionsunterricht, Günther Sawatzki, 'Der Reformator', Dokumentarspiel über Martin Luther", in *Funk-Korrespondenz*, No. 45, Nov. 7, 1968, 18, reprinted in Horstmann, *Wandel*, 115.

Hamm, Berndt, "Hanns Rückert als Schüler Karl Holls", in Thomas Kaufmann/Harry Oelke (ed.), *Evangelische Kirchenhistoriker im "Dritten Reich"*, Gütersloh: Kaiser, Gütersloher Verl.-Haus 2002, 275f.

Handbuch für Evangelische Filmarbeit, Gruppe I/b/2, Munich: Evangelischer Presseverband für Bayern, March 1954.

Hartmann, Josef, "Eine priesterlose Gemeinde auf der Suche nach Gott. ,Gott braucht Menschen' von Jean Delannoy (1950)", in Hasenberg (ed.), *Spuren des Religiösen im Film*, 80–82.

Hasenberg, Peter (ed.), *Spuren des Religiösen im Film. Meilensteine aus 100 Jahren Kinogeschichte*, Mainz: Matthias-Grünewald-Verl., 1995

Heinzelmann, Herbert, *Luther, Eric Till. Deutschland 2003. Filmheft*, ed. By the Bundeszentrale für politische Bildung, Bonn: bpb 2004.

Helm, Melanie, "Jesusfilme in Geschichte und Gegenwart", in *Stimmen der Zeit. Zeitschrift für christliche Kultur*, March 2005, 161–170.

Helmke, Julia, *Kirche, Film und Festivals. Geschichte sowie Bewertungskriterien evangelischer und ökumenischer Juryarbeit in den Jahren 1948 bis 1988*, Erlangen: Christliche-Publizistik-Verlag, 2005.

Herberg, Will, *Protestant, Catholic, Jew: An Essay in American Religious Sociology*, Garden City, NY: Doubleday, 1955.

Hermanski, Susanne, "Das Kreuz mit dem streitbaren Mönch", in *SZ-Extra*, Oct. 30, 2003.

Hess, Werner, *Martin Luther. Eine Einführung in sein Leben. Mit Bildern aus dem Dokumentarfilm "Der Gehorsame Rebell" und dem Spielfilm Martin Luther*", Stuttgart: Evangelisches Verlags Werk 1954.

Hess, Werner, "Martin Luther – kein Filmheros. Ein Beispiel für die Möglichkeiten des religiösen Spielfilms", in *epd. Kirche und Film* No. 2, February 1954, 2–4, reprinted in Horstmann, *Wandel*, 83–86.

Hickethier, Knut, "Veit Harlans Film Jud Süß und der audiovisuell inszenierte Antisemitismus", in *Jud Süß*, Frankfurt am Main etc.: Campus-Verl., 2006, 221–244.

Hickethier, Knut, *Film- und Fernsehanalyse*, Stuttgart: Metzler ⁴2007.

Hilbig, Klaus, "Warum muß Luther brüllen? Zu dem Fernsehfilm von Kurt Veth", in *Sonntag* 43, 1983, 5.

Hoberg, Martin, *Mit und ohne H. Vogler. Das Bremer Gesangbuch 1917 und die Gesangbuchillustration des 20. Jahrhunderts*, Bremen: Hauschild 1982 (HosEc, 13).

Hochgeschwender, Michael, *Amerikanische Religion: Evangelikalismus, Pfingstlertum, Fundamentalismus*, Frankfurt am Main: Verlag der Weltreligionen im Inselverlag 2007.

Hodgson, Robert/Soukop, Paul A., *From one Medium to another: Basic Issues for Communicating the Scriptures in New Media*, Kansas City: Sheed & Ward 1997.

Hofer, Klara, *Bruder Martinus: Ein Buch vom deutschen Gewissen*, Stuttgart and Berlin: Cotta'sche Buchhandlung 1917.

Holden, Stephen, "Martin Luther's Passion, Still Resonating Today", *New York Times*, Sept. 26, 2003, E11.

Holsing, Henrike, *Luther – Gottesmann und Nationalheld. Sein Image in der deutschen Historienmalerei des 19. Jahrhunderts*, Cologne University doctoral dissertation 2004, online-resource: URL: http://kups.ub.uni-koeln.de/volltexte/2007/2132/)

Honselmann, Klemens, *Urfassung und Drucke der Ablaßthesen Martin Luthers und ihre Veröffentlichung*, Paderborn: Schöningh 1966.

Horbrügger, Anja, *Aufbruch zur Kontinuität – Kontinuität im Aufbruch: Geschlechterkonstruktionen im west- und ostdeutschen Nachkriegsfilm von 1945 bis 1952*, Marburg: Schüren, 2007.

Horst, Sabine, "'Luther würde heute nicht überleben'. Der Regisseur Eric Till über Historienfilme, Religion und seine Arbeit an einer außergewöhnlichen Geschichte", *epd Film. Das Kino Magazin* 11 (2003), 22–25.

Horstmann, Johannes (ed.), *Martin Luther. Zum Wandel des Luther-Bildes in der Geschichtsschreibung und im Film*, Schwerte: Kath. Akademie 1983 (Veröffentlichungen der Katholischen Akademie Schwerte, Dokumentationen, 8).

Horstmann, Johannes, "Kritik-Nr. 24 354", in *film-dienst* 36 (1983).

Hübinger, Gangolf, "Sakralisierung der Nation und Formen des Nationalismus im deutschen Protestantismus", in Gerd Krumeich and Hartmut Lehmann (ed.), *"Gott mit uns". Nation, Religion und Gewalt im 19. und frühen 20. Jahrhundert*, Göttingen: Vandenhoeck & Ruprecht 2000 (Veröffentlichungen des Max-Planck-Instituts für Geschichte, 162), 233–247.

Hürten, Heinz, "Der Topos vom christlichen Abendland in Literatur und Publizistik nach den beiden Weltkriegen", in Albrecht Langner (ed.), *Katholizismus, nationaler Gedanke und Europa seit 1800,* Paderborn u.a.: Schöningh 1985, 131–154.

Hyma, Albert, *New Light on Martin Luther. With an Authentic Account of the Luther Film of 1953,* Grand Rapids, Michigan: Eerdmans, 1958 [©1957].

Jacobsen, Wolfgang, *Geschichte des deutschen Films,* 1st updated ed. Stuttgart: Metzler 2004.

Johannes Calvin – Berufen zum Reformator, documentary (DVD: Hänssler Verlag, 2008, 60 min).

Junghans, Helmar (ed.), *Die Reformation in Augenzeugenberichten,* Düsseldorf: Rauch 1967.

Kahle, Robert/Lee, Robert E. A., *Popcorn and Parable: A New Look at the Movies,* Minneapolis: Augsburg Pub. House 1971.

Kaiser, Jochen-Christoph, "Der Evangelische Bund und die Politik 1918–1933", in Gottfried Maron (ed.), *Evangelisch und Ökumenisch. Beiträge zum 100jährigen Bestehen des Evangelischen Bundes,* Göttingen: Vandenhoeck & Ruprecht 1986 (Kirche und Konfession, 25), 174–191.

Kammen, Michael G., *Mystic Chords of Memory: The Transformation of Tradition in American Culture,* New York: Knopf, 1991.

Karalus, Paul, "Erstlich, dass man ihre Synagoge oder Schule mit Feuer anstecke ...", in Trapmann, *Reformator,* 223–240.

Kaufmann, Thomas, "Die Bilderfrage im frühneuzeitlichen Luthertum", in Peter Blickle at alii (ed.), *Macht und Ohnmach der Bilder. Reformatorischer Bildersturm im Kontext der europäischen Geschichte,* München: Oldenbourg 2002, 407–451.

Kehr, Dave, "At the Movies", *New York Times,* Sept. 25, 2003, E3.

Kerr, Walter, "'Luther' – Mighty Fortress Partly Breached By Britain's John Osborne", *Los Angeles Times,* Oct. 6, 1963, B20.

Klünder, Achim (ed.), *Lexikon der Fernsehspiele* 1978–1987, Bd. 1, München etc.: Saur 1991.

Koch, Lars, "Zwischen Kontinuität und Innovation: Der westdeutsche Spielfilm 1945–1960", in Lars Koch (ed.), *Modernisierung als Amerikanisierung? Entwicklungslinien der westdeutschen Kultur,* Bielefeld: transcript Verlag 2007, 89–109.

Köhler, Walther, *Dokumente zum Ablassstreit von 1517,* Tübingen: Mohr, 2nd revised ed. 1934.

Kohnle, Armin, "Luther vor Karl V. Die Wormser Szene in Text und Bild des 19. Jahrhunderts", in Laube/Fix (ed.), *Lutherinszenierung und Reformationserinnerung,* 35–62.

Konzelman, Robert G., *Marquee Ministry: The Movie Theater as Church and Community Forum,* New York: Harper and Row 1972.

Kracauer, Siegfried, *Das Ornament der Masse. Essays. Mit einem Nachwort von Karsten Witte,* Frankfurt am Main: suhrkamp 1977 (suhrkamp taschenbuch, 371).

Kraft, Friedrich, "Die bösen Bälge", in *Luther als Bühnenheld,* Hamburg: Lutherisches Verlagshaus 1971 (Zur Sache: Kirchliche Aspekte heute, 8), 75–86.

Kreider, Harry Julius, *The Beginnings of Lutheranism in New York,* New York: Author 1949.

Krüger, Jürgen, *Rom und Jerusalem. Kirchenbauvorstellungen der Hohenzollern im 19. Jahrhundert,* Berlin: Akademie Verlag 1995.

Krützen, Michaela, *Dramaturgie des Films: Wie Hollywood erzählt,* 2nd edition Frankfurt am Main: Fischer 2006.

Kundrus, Birthe, "Geschlechterkriege: Der Erste Weltkrieg und die Deutung der Geschlechterverhältnisse in der Weimarer Republik", in Karen Hagemann and Stephanie Schüler-Springorum (ed.), *Heimat-Front. Militär und Geschlechterverhältnisse im Zeitalter der Weltkriege,* Frankfurt am Main: Campus-Verl., 2002, 171–187.

Kurtz, Rudolf, *Expressionismus und Film,* Berlin 1926, Reprint Zürich: Rohr, 1965.

Lamprecht, Gerhard, *Deutsche Stummfilme 1913–1914,* Berlin: Druck V. Magdalinski 1969, 180.

Langenhorst, Georg, *Jesus ging nach Hollywood,* Düsseldorf, Patmos-Verlag 1998.

Langer, Bruno, *Evangelische Bilderwelt: Druckgraphik zwischen 1850 und 1950,* Bad Windsheim: Verlag Fränkisches Freilandmuseum 1992.

Laube, Stefan/Fix, Karl-Heinz (ed.), *Lutherinszenierung und Reformationserinnerung*, Leipzig: Evangelische Verlagsanstalt 2002 (Schriften der Stiftung Luthergedenkstätten in Sachsen-Anhalt, 2).

Laube, Stefan, *Das Lutherhaus Wittenberg: Eine Museumsgeschichte*, Leipzig: Evangelische Verlagsanstalt 2003.

Lee, Robert E. A., *Martin Luther: The Reformation Years. Based on the Film "Martin Luther"*, Minneapolis, Augsburg Pub. House [1967].

Lehmann, Hartmut (ed.), *Transatlantische Religionsgeschichte. 18. und 20. Jahrhundert*, Göttingen: Wallstein-Verlag 2006.

Lehmann, Hartmut, *Protestantisches Christentum im Prozeß der Säkularisierung* Göttingen: Vandenhoeck & Ruprecht 2001.

Lehmann, Hartmut, *Transformationen der Religion in der Neuzeit: Beispiele aus der Geschichte des Protestantismus* Göttingen: Vandenhoeck & Ruprecht 2007 (Veröffentlichungen des Max-Planck-Instituts für Geschichte, 230).

Lehmann, Hartmut, *Martin Luther in the American Imagination*, Munich: Fink, 1988.

Leppin, Volker, "Deus absconditus und Deus revelatus. Transformationen mittelalterlicher Theologie in der Gotteslehre von 'De servo arbitrio'", in *Berliner Theologische Zeitschrift* 22 (2005), H. 1, 55–69.

Leppin, Volker, "Geburtswehen und Geburt einer Legende", in *Luther* 78 (2007), 145–150.

Lerche, Otto, *Druck und Schmuck des deutschen evangelischen Gesangbuchs im 20. Jahrhundert*, Berlin: Eckart-Verlag 1936.

Lersch, Edgar/Viehoff, Reinhold, *Geschichte im Fernsehen. Eine Untersuchung zur Entwicklung des Genres und der Gattungsästhetik geschichtlicher Darstellungen im Fernsehen 1995 bis 2003*, Düsseldorf, Landesanstalt für Medien Nordrhein-Westfalen, 2007 (Schriftenreihe Medienforschung der Landesanstalt für Medien Nordrhein-Westfalen, 54).

Lexikon der theologischen Werke, ed. Michael Eckert etc., Stuttgart: Kröner, 2003.

Lexikon des Internationalen Films, völlig überarbeitete und erweiterte Neuausgabe, Reinbek bei Hamburg: Rowohlt 1995.

Liebrand, Claudia, *Gender-Topographien. Kulturwissenschaftliche Lektüren von Hollywoodfilmen der Jahrhundertwende*, Köln: DuMont 2003.

Linton, Olof, "Ekklesia I (bedeutungsgeschichtlich)", in RAC 4, Stuttgart: Anton Hirsemann 1959, 905–921.

Lipphardt, Walther, "Media vita in morte sumus (Deutsch)", in *VerfLex* 6, 1987, cols. 271–275.

Lückefahr, Walter, *Sperrmark und Registermark*, Quakenbrück: Trute, 1958.

Luther, Martin, *D. Martin Luthers Werke*, Weimar: Hermann Böhlau 1883ff.

Luther und die Folgen für die Kunst, Exhibition Catalogue Hamburg 1983/1984, Munich: Prestel 1983.

MacCulloch, Diarmaid, *Reformation: Europe's House Divided 1490–1700*, Ld. 2003, New York: Viking 2004.

M., J., "Martin Luther, USA/Germany, 1953", *Monthly Film Bulletin* 21 (1954), 173.

Malone, Peter, "Jesus on Our Screens", in John R. May (ed.), *New Image of Religious Film*, Kansas City: Sheed & Ward 1997, 57–71.

Martin Luther und die Reformation in Deutschland, Exhibition Catalogue Nuremberg 1983, Frankfurt a.M.: Insel-Verlag 1983.

Martschukat, Jürgen/Stieglitz, Olaf, "*Es ist ein Junge!*": Einführung in die Geschichte der Männlichkeiten in der Neuzeit* (1st ed. 2005), 2nd ed. Tübingen: Ed. Diskord 2008.

May, John R., "Contemporary Theories Regarding the Interpretation of Religious Film", in John R. May (ed.), *New Image of Religious Film*, Kansas City: Sheet & Ward 1997, 17–37:

McKean Taylor, Henry, *Rolle des Lebens: Die Filmbiographie als narratives System*, Marburg: Schüren 2002 (Zürcher Filmstudien, 8), 378.

Mecklenburg, Norbert, "Luther in Rom: Zur literarischen Fabrikation eines deutschen Mythos", in Conrad Wiedemann (ed.), *Rom – Paris – London: Erfahrung und Selbsterfahrung deutscher Schriftsteller und Künstler in den fremden Metropolen*, Stuttgart: Metzler 1988 (Germanistische-Symposien-Berichtsbände, 8), 321–334.

Meller, Harald (ed.), *Luther in Mansfeld. Forschungen am Elternhaus des Reformators*, Halle an der Saale: Landesmuseum für Vorgeschichte 2007.

Meyr, F., "Luther", in *Variety*, Vol. 273, Feb. 6, 1974, 18.

Möller, Bernd, "Thesenanschläge", in Joachim Ott, Martin Treu (ed.), *Faszination Thesenanschlag – Faktum oder Fiktion*, Leipzig: EVA 2008, 9–31.

Müller, Hedwig/Stöckemann, Patricia, *"... Jeder Mensch ist ein Tänzer". Ausdruckstanz in Deutschland zwischen 1900 und 1945*, Gießen: Anabas-Verlag 1993.

Müller, Thomas J., *Kirche zwischen zwei Welten: Die Obrigkeitsproblematik bei Heinrich Melchior Mühlenberg und die Kirchengründung der deutschen Lutheraner in Pennsylvania*, Stuttgart: Steiner 1994 (Transatlantische historische Studien, 2).

Münkler, Herfried, *Die Deutschen und ihre Mythen*, Berlin: Rowohlt 2009.

Musser, Charles, "Passions and the Passion Play: Theatre, Film and Religion in America, 1880–1900", in *Film History* 5 (1993), 419–456; German translation: "Leidenschaften und das Spiel vom Leiden. Theater, Film und Religion in Amerika, 1880–1900", in Reinhold Zwick/Otto Huber (ed.), *Von Oberammergau nach Hollywood. Wege der Darstellung Jesu im Film*, Köln: Katholisches Institut für Medieninformation GmbH 1999, 29–79.

Naphy, William, *The Protestant Revolution: from Martin Luther to Martin Luther King Jr.*, London: BBC Books 2007.

Nash, Jay Robert/Ross, Stanley Ralph, *The Motion Picture Guide*, L-M, 1927–1983, Chicago: Cinebooks 1986.

Netenjakob, Eugen, "Eine dramaturgische Leistung", in *Funk-Korrespondenz*, No. 5, of 28 Jan. 1965, 17f. reprinted in Horstmann, *Wandel*, 106f.

Neuer Theater-Almanach. Theatergeschichtliches Jahr- und Adressenbuch, ed. by the Genossenschaft Deutscher Bühnenangehöriger, Jg. 1908 and Jg. 1912.

Nickelsburg, J. E., "A Successful Publicity Tour", *American Lutheran* 9 (1926), Feb., 8f.

Nieberle, Sigrid, *Literarhistorische Filmbiographien: Autorschaft und Literaturgeschichte im Kino. Mit einer Filmographie 1909–2007*, Berlin: de Gruyter 2008 (Media and Cultural Memory / Medien und kulturelle Erinnerung, 7).

Nithack-Stahn, Walt[h]er, *Barbareien. Gedanken zur Gegenwart*, Berlin: Curtius 1913.

Nithack-Stahn, Walt[h]er, *Der Christ und der Völkerfriede*, Stuttgart: Deutsche Friedensgesellschaft [1913].

Nithack-Stahn, Walt[h]er, *Kirche und Krieg*, Halle an der Saale: Fricke 1913.

Nithack-Stahn, Walt[h]er, *Luther – Festspiel in sechs Handlungen*, Breslau: Verlag der Evangelischen Zentralstelle 1921.

Nithack-Stahn, Walt[h]er, *Luther in Oppenheim*: geschichtliches Schauspiel in einem Aufzuge von Walther Nithack-Stahn, Halle an der Saale: Fricke, 1920.

O'Brien, John A, *Martin Luther: The Priest who founded Protestantism*, New York: Paulist Press 1953.

Oelke, Harry, "Ein Bild von einem Reformator: Darstellung Martin Luthers als Identitätsfaktor des Protestantismus durch die Epochen", in *Einsichten. Berichte zur Forschung an der Ludwig-Maximilians-Universität* 2003, H. 2, 33–37.

Oppenheimer, Jan, "Luther Celebrates a Revolutionary Figure", *American Cinematographer* 84, Part 10, 12.

Osborne, John, *Martin Luther: A Play*, London: Faber and Faber 1961.

Paech, Joachim, "Vor-Schriften – In-Schriften – Nach-Schriften", in Ernst Gustav (ed.), *Sprache im Film*, Vienna: Wespennest 1994, 23–39.

Papst, Vera Christina, *"... quia non habeo aptiora exempla."*. *Eine Analyse von Martin Luthers Auseinandersetzung mit dem Mönchtum in seinen Predigten des ersten Jahres nach seiner Rückkehr von der Wartburg 1522/1523*, Diss. Hamburg 2005 (online resource: http://deposit.ddb.de/cgi-bin/dokserv?idn=97588980x&dok_var=d1&dok_ext=pdf&filename=97588980x.pdf. [2.3.2009])

Paulus, Nikolaus, *Geschichte des Ablasses im Mittelalter*, Vol. 1, 2nd ed. Darmstadt: Wiss. Buchgesellschaft 2000.

Philbrick, Richard, "Reveal Fringe Groups Lead In Church Gains", *Chicago Daily Tribune*, Jan. 30, 1957, B5.

Pichel, Irving, "The Problem of Documentation", *The Quarterly of Film Radio and Television* 8, Part 2 (1953), 172–185.

Quaas, Anne Kathrin, *Evangelische Filmpublizistik 1948–1968: Beispiel für das kulturpolitische Engagement der Evangelischen Kirche in der Nachkriegszeit*, Erlangen: Christliche-Publizistik-Verlag 2007.

Reed, Rex, "You Can See It for Less Than It Costs to Take a Taxi to a Theater [...]", *The Washington Post, Times Herald*, July 22, 1973, F3.

Reilly, C. P., "Luther", in *Films in Review*, March 1974, 186.

Reinitzer, Heimo, *Biblia deutsch. Luthers Bibelübersetzung und ihre Tradition*, Exhibition catalogue Herzog August Bibliothek Wolfenbüttel 1983.

Religion im Film. Lexikon mit Kurzkritiken und Stichworten zu 2400 Kinofilmen, 3rd enlarged ed. 1999.

Reuter, Hans-Heinrich, "'Die Weihe der Kraft'. Ein Dialog zwischen Goethe und Zelter und seine Wiederaufnahme bei Fontane", in *Dichters Lande im Reich der Geschichte: Aufsätze zur dt. Literatur des 18. und 19. Jahrhunderts*, hg. von Regine Otto, Berlin etc.: Aufbau-Verlag 1983, 145–160, 447–452.

Riess, Curt, *Das gab's nur einmal*, special ed. Gütersloh: Bertelsmann, 1957.

Robinson, Kenneth J., "Martin Luther", in *The Church of England Newspaper*, Sept. 16, 1955.

Rossié, Beate, "'Symbolhafte Sprache, die aus der Weltanschauung entspringt'. Kirchliche Kunst im Nationalsozialismus", in Stefanie Endlich, Monica Geyler-von Bernus, Beate Rossié (ed.), *Christenkreuz und Hakenkreuz. Kirchenbau und sakrale Kunst im Nationalsozialismus*, Berlin: Metropol 2008, 96–110.

Schallert, Edwin, "Luther Life evokes Stir with Drama", *Los Angeles Times*, Sept. 11, 1953, A9.

Scharfe, Martin, *Evangelische Andachtsbilder: Studien zu Intention und Funktion des Bildes in der Frömmigkeitsgeschichte vornehmlich des schwäbischen Raumes*, Stuttgart: Müller & Gräff, 1968 (Veröffentlichungen des Staatlichen Amtes für Denkmalpflege Stuttgart: Volkskunde, 5).

Schawe, Martin, Altdeutsche und altniederländische Malerei, Ostfildern: Hatje Cantz, 2006 (Alte Pinakothek, 2).

Schildt, Axel, *Zwischen Abendland und Amerika. Studien zur Westdeutschen Ideenlandschaft der 50er Jahre*, München: Oldenburg 1999.

Schilling, Johannes (ed.), *Martin Luther. Lateinisch-Deutsche Studienausgabe*, Vol. 2: Christusglaube und Rechtfertigung, Leipzig: EVA 2006.

Schmale, Wolfgang, *Geschichte der Männlichkeit in Europa (1450–2000)*, Wien etc.: Böhlau 2003.

Schmidt, Alfred, *Geschichte des Augustinerinnenklosters St. Clemens zu Brehna*, Brehna: R. Kiemle 1924.

Schmiedl, Joachim, "Luther – Der Film zur Reformation", in *Info: Informationen für Religionslehrerinnen und Religionslehrer, Bistum Limburg* 32 (2003), 248–249.

Schmitt, Heiner, *Kirche und Film: Kirchliche Filmarbeit in Deutschland von ihren Anfängen bis 1945*, Boppard am Rhein, Boldt 1979 (Schriften des Bundesarchivs, 26).

Schmitt, Heiner, "'Luther. Ein Film der deutschen Reformation' im Widerstreit der Konfessionen", in *Aus der Arbeit des Bundesarchivs: Beiträge zum Archivwesen, zur Quellenkunde und Zeitgeschichte*, Boppard 1977 (Schriften des Bundesarchivs, 25), 499–510, reprinted in Horstmann, *Wandel*, 51–61.

Schneider-Quindeau, Werner, "Der Reformator als Leinwandheld. Lutherfilme zwischen Geschichte und Ideologie", in *Handbuch Theologie und populärer Film*, vol. 2, ed. Thomas Bohrmann, Werner Veith and Stephan Zöller, Paderborn, München, Wien and Zürich: Ferdindand Schöningh 2009, 189–197.

Schubart, Christof, *Die Berichte über Luthers Tod und Begräbnis. Texte und Untersuchungen*, Weimar: Böhlau 1917.

Schübel, Theodor, *Martin Luther*, Munich: Droemer, Knaur, 1983.

Schulze, Manfred, "Thesenanschlag", in *Religion in Geschichte und Gegenwart*, Vol. 8, Tübingen: Mohr Siebeck [4]2005, 357f.

Schütz, Helga, *Martin Luther. Eine Erzählung für den Film*, Berlin und Leipzig: Aufbau-Verlag 1983.

Schwanitz, Dietrich, "John Osborne: The Entertainer – und John Osborne, the entertainer", in Heinrich F. Plett (ed.), *Englisches Drama von Beckett bis Bond*, Munich: Fink 1982, 100–117.

Segeberg, Harro, "Die großen Deutschen. Zur Renaissance des Propagandafilms um 1940", in Harro Segeberg (ed.), *Mediale Mobilmachung I*, Munich: Fink 2004, 267–291.

Shea, William M., *The Lion and the Lamb: Evangelicals and Catholics in America*, Oxford: Oxford University Press 2004.

Simons, Rotraut, "Das DDR-Fernsehen und die Luther-Ehrung", in Horst Dähn/Joachim Heise, *Luther und die DDR. Der Reformator und das DDR-Fernsehen 1983*, Berlin: Editon Ost 1996, 99–185.

Smith, Cecil, "TV Review, John Osborne's 'Luther' Presented as ABC Special", *Los Angeles Times*, Jan. 31, 1968, C13.

Smith, Cecil, "Keach: Tall in Napoleon's Saddle", *Los Angeles Times*, Aug. 15, 1973, E16.

Sobolewski, Gregory Lawrence, *Roman Catholic Reception of Luther in the Twentieth Century. Magisterial Positions and their Ecumenical Significance* (PhD Marquette University 1993), Ann Arbor, Mich., Microfiche ed. 1994.

Sperling, Godfrey, "'Luther' TV Ban Stirs Public Opinion", *The Christian Science Monitor*, March 1, 1957, 3.

Sperling, Godfrey, "Chicago TV to Show 'Luther'", *The Christian Science Monitor*, March 4, 1957, 12.

Spicer, Andrew, *Typical Men. The Representation of Masculinity in Popular British Cinema*, London and New York: I.B. Tauris Publishers 2001.

Steffens, Martin, *Luthergedenkstätten im 19. Jahrhundert. Memoria – Repräsentation – Denkmalpflege*, Regensburg: Schnell & Steiner 2008.

Steinmayr, Joachim, "*Martin Luther* kommt in die deutschen Kinos", *Süddeutsche Zeitung*, Oct. 2, 1953.

Stolt, Birgit, "Luthers Sprache in seinen Briefen an Käthe", in Martin Treu (ed.), *Katharina von Bora. Die Lutherin, Aufsätze anläßlich ihre 500. Geburtstages*, Wittenberg: Stiftung Luthergedenkstätten in Sachsen-Anhalt 1999 (Katalog der Stiftung Luthergedenkstätten in Sachsen-Anhalt, 5), 23–32.

Stratenwerth, Irene/Simon, Hermann (ed.), *Pioniere in Celluloid. Juden in der frühen Filmwelt*, Berlin: Henschel Verlag 2004.

Strindberg, August, *Historische Miniaturen*, Historska miniatyrer <deutsch> [nach der Übersetzung von 1908 rev. Edition von Roland W. Pinson], Essen: Magnus-Verlag n. d. (1985?).

Strindberg, August, *Luther: (die Nachtigall von Wittenberg)*; [deutsche Historie in 10 Bildern]; Näktergalen i Wittenberg (1903) übersetzt von Emil Schering, Munich: Müller 1915.

Swoboda, Gudrun, "Lavater sammelt Linien. Zu seinem Versuch einer universalen Klassifikation linearer Ausdruckscharaktere im Anschluss an Dürer und Hogarth", in Benno Schubiger (ed.), *Sammeln und Sammlungen im 18. Jahrhundert in der Schweiz. Akten des Kolloquiums Basel, 16–18 Oktober 2003*, Geneva: Slatkine 2007 (Travaux sur la Suisse des Lumières, 10), 315–339.

Taubman, Howard, "Theater: 'Luther' Stars Albert Finney", *New York Times*, Sept. 26, 1963, 41.

The New Testament of our Lord and Saviour Jesus Christ, Translated out of the Greek: Being the Version Set Forth A.D. 1611, Compared with the Most Ancient Authorities and Revised, A.D. 1881 and A.D. 1901, New York: T. Nelson 1901.

Thielicke, Helmut, *Kirche und Öffentlichkeit: Zur Grundlegung einer lutherischen Kulturethik*, Tübingen: Furche-Verlag 1947.

Thurnwald, Andrea K., *Weil ich Jesu Schäflein bin. Kinderleben und Kinderglauben im evangelischen Franken*, Bad Windsheim: Verlag Fränkisches Freilandmuseum 1995.

Tiemann, Manfred, *Bibel im Film. Ein Handbuch für Religionsunterricht, Gemeindearbeit und Erwachsenenbildung*, Stuttgart, Calwer Verlag 1995.

Tillmann, Frits et al [com.], *Religion im Film. Lexikon mit Kurzkritiken und Stichworten zu 1200 Kinofilmen*, 2nd ed., Cologne: Katholisches Institut für Medieninformation 1993.

Toeplitz, Jerzy, *Geschichte des Films*, vol. 1: 1895–1928, Repr. of the German edition Berlin: Henschel 1992.

Trapmann, Margret/Hufen, Fritz (ed.), *Martin Luther. Reformator – Ketzer – Nationalheld: Texte, Bilder, Dokumente in ARD und ZDF, Materialien zu Fernsehsendungen*, Munich: Goldmann 1983.

Treu, Martin, *Katharina von Bora. Martin Luthers Frau*, Wittenberg: Drei-Kastanien-Verl., 2. unveränderte Auflage 1996.

Treu, Martin, *Katharina von Bora. Bilder aus ihrem Leben*, Wittenberg: Stiftung Luthergedenkstätten 1998.

Treu, Martin, "Der Thesenanschlag fand wirklich statt. Ein neuer Beleg aus der Universitätsbibliothek Jena", *Luther* 78 (2007), 140–144.

Urban, Detlef, "'Ein Genie sehr besonderer Art'. Bemerkungen zu einem Lutherfilm im DDR-Fernsehen", *Deutschland-Archiv. Zeitschrift für Fragen der DDR und der Deutschlandpolitik* 16 (1983), H. 12, 1253–1255.

Vahabzadeh, Susan, "Unbeichtbar. Mit seinen Sünden allein. 'Luther' – protestantisch betrachtet", *Süddeutsche Zeitung*, Oct. 29, 2003, 13.

von Imhoff, Christoph/Betz, A., "Der amerikanische Lutherfilm. Eine evangelische und eine katholische Stellungnahme", *Rheinische Post* No. 64, March 17, 1954.

Voßkamp, Wilhelm, "Semiotik des Menschen. Bildphysiognomie und literarische Transkription bei Johann Caspar Lavater und Georg Christoph Lichtenberg", in Matthias Bickenbach (ed.), *Korrespondenzen: Visuelle Kulturen zwischen früher Neuzeit und Gegenwart*, Cologne: DuMont 2002 (Mediologie, 4), 150–163.

Warnke Martin, *Cranachs Luther: Entwürfe für ein Image*, Frankfurt a.M.: Fischer Taschenbuch Verl. 1984.

Weber am Bach, Sibylle, *Hans Baldung Grien (1484/85–1545). Marienbilder in der Reformation*, Regensburg: Schnell & Steiner 2006 (Studien zur christlichen Kunst, 6).

Welch, Robert J., "The Martin Luther Film", *National Catholic Weekly Review*, XCVI, No 25, whole No 2497, March 23, 1957, 698.

Wendebourg, Dorothea, "Der ganze Westen kann nicht anders", *Süddeutsche Zeitung*, Oct. 13, 2008, Literatur, 14.

Wendt, Simon, "Massenmedien und die Bedeutung von Helden und Stars in den USA (1890–1929)", in Daniela Münkel and Lu Seegers (ed.), *Medien und Imagepolitik im 20. Jahrhundert. Deutschland, Europa, USA*, Frankfurt/Main u.a.: Campus-Verl. 2008, 187–206.

Vogler, Günter, "Luther oder Müntzer?. Die Rolle frühneuzeitlicher Gestalten für die Identitäts-findung der DDR", in Hans-Joachim Gehrke (ed.), *Geschichtsbilder und Gründungsmythen*, Würzburg: Ergon-Verlag 2001 (Identitäten und Alteritäten, 7), 417–436.

Werner, Friedrich Ludwig Zacharias, *Martin Luther, oder die Weihe der Kraft*, Berlin: Johann David Sander 1807 [Mikrofiche-Ed.: München etc.: Saur 1990–1994].

Wipfler, Esther, "Das Luther-Bild im Spielfilm", in Volkmar Joestel and Jutta Strehle, *Luthers Bild und Lutherbilder. Ein Rundgang durch die Wirkungsgeschichte*, Wittenberg: Stiftung Luther-gedenkstätten in Sachsen Anhalt 2003, 85–89.

Wipfler, Esther, "Götzenbild oder Adiaphoron – Positionen protestantischen Bildverständnis-ses", in *Verbotene Bilder. Heiligenfiguren aus Rußland*, ed. Marianne Stößl, Munich: Hirmer 2006, 41–48.

Wipfler, Esther, "Katharina von Bora in den audiovisuellen Medien des 20. Jahrhunderts", in *Katharina von Bora, die Lutherin*, Exhibition catalogue Wittenberg 1999, Wittenberg: Stiftung Luthergedenkstätten in Sachsen Anhalt 1999, 318–334.

Wipfler, Esther, "Luther im Stummfilm: Zum Wandel protestantischer Mentalität im Spiegel der Filmgeschichte bis 1930", in *Archiv für Reformationsgeschichte* 98 (2007), 167–198.

Wipfler, Esther, "Luthers 95 Thesen im bewegten Bild: Ein Beispiel für Schriftlichkeit im Film", in Joachim Ott, Martin Treu (ed.), *Faszination Thesenanschlag – Faktum oder Fiktion*, Leipzig: EVA 2008, 173–197.

Wipfler, Esther, "Vom deutschnationalen Titan zum Herzensbrecher. Neunzig Jahre Luther-Film. Zur Geschichte des Luther-Bildes in Kinematographie und Fernsehen", in *Luther* 75 (2004), H. 1, 17–28.

Wipfler, Esther, "Review of 'Martin Steffens, *Luthergedenkstätten im 19. Jahrhundert. Memoria – Repräsentation – Denkmalpflege*, Regensburg: Schnell & Steiner, 2008'", in *Kunstchronik* 62 (2009), H. 5, 224–229.

Wolfes, Matthias, "Nithack-Stahn, Walter", in *BBKL*, Vol. 20, Nordhausen: Verlag Traugott Bautz 2002, 1119–1125.

Wolfgast, Eike, *Die Wittenberger Lutherausgabe. Zur Überlieferungsgeschichte der Werke Luthers im 16. Jahrhundert*, Nieuwkoop: B. de Graaf, 1971, Col. 122 and n. 656.

Wolters, Larry, "Luther TV Film is set for Dec. 21", *Chicago Daily Tribune*, Dec. 12, 1956, B12.

Zwick, Reinhold/Huber, Otto (ed.), *Von Oberammergau nach Hollywood. Wege der Darstellung Jesu im Film*, Cologne: Katholisches Institut für Medieninformation 1999.

Zwick, Reinhold/Lentes, Thomas (ed.), *Die Passion Christi. Der Film von Mel Gibson und seine theologischen und kunstgeschichtlichen Kontexte*, Münster: Aschendorff 2004.

Filmography

I. Movies

1. Doktor Martinus Luther (Germany 1911)
Production company: Bioscop (Berlin)
Cast
Hermann Litt (Martin Luther)

2. Die Wittenberger Nachtigall. Martin Luther (Germany 1913)
Additional Titles: Der Weg zur Sonne; Doktor Martin Luther. Ein Lebensbild für das deutsche Volk; Het leven en strijden van Maarten Luther, De macht van het lied.

Production company: Rubin Film (Berlin–Wien);
Copyrights since 1927: Marg.-Fried-Film GmbH (Berlin)
Director: Erwin Báron
Screenplay: Erwin Báron; skript revised by John Edward

Cast
Rudolf Essek (Martin Luther)
Margot v. Hardt (Katharina von Bora)
Ernst Wehlau
Fritz Alten
Jacques Morway
Max Zilzer

Rating "Jugendverbot" (ban for young people): Nr. B.29.21., 20-APR-21, "Verbot" (ban): Nr. Tgb.Nr.1673, 24-MAR-21
World premiere: 1. 9. 1913

Copy used: Berlin, Bundesarchiv – Filmarchiv; Amsterdam, EYE Film Instituut Nederland

3. Martin Luther (Germany 1923)

Additional Titles: Der Kampf seines Lebens; Martin Luther: His Life and Time, 1925, app. 2050 mtrs.

Production company: Lutherfilm GmbH
Director: Karl Wüstenhagen
Screenplay: P. Kurz
First draft: Walther Nithack-Stahn
Director of photography: Ewald Daub
Set design: Hans Wildermann

Cast
Karl Wüstenhagen (Martin Luther)
Charlotte Krüger
Elise Aulinger
Wilhelm Diegelmann
Viktor Gehring
Eugen Gura
Rudolf Hoch
Dary Holm
Raabe
Schwartze
Ulmer
Adolf Wohlbrück
Rating: Authorization on 28. 06. 1923

Copy used: Martin Luther, His Life and Time (Harmon Foundation, Inc., 1925) Washington, National Library (Harmon Foundation, Collection, Betacam; 1:23:00; call no. VBT 5352)

4. Luther – Ein Film der deutschen Reformation (Germany 1927)

Additional Title: Freedom: An Epic of Reformation
Director: Hans Kyser
Screenplay: Hans Kyser
First Draft: Rev. Dr. Bruno Döring
Director of photography: Otto Ewald; Sophus Wangøe
Music: Wolfgang Zeller

Cast
Eugen Klöpfer (Martin Luther)
Theodor Loos (Philipp Melanchthon)

Bruno Kastner (Ulrich von Hutten)
Karl Elzer (Frederick III, byname Frederick the Wise, Elector of Saxony)
Jakob Tiedtke (Johann Tetzel)
[Hermann (?)]Vallentin (Andreas Bodenstein von Karlstadt)
Arthur Kraußneck (Johann von Staupitz)
H. R. Müller (German Emperor Charles V.)
Max Maximilian (Hans Sachs)
Max Grünberg (Albrecht Dürer)
Rudolf Lettinger (Luther's father)
Livio C. Pavanelli (Luther's friend Alexius)
Elsa Wagner (Luther's mother)
Heinz Salfner (Captain Berlepsch)

Production company: Cob-Film GmbH (Berlin)
Producer: Josef Coböken

World premiere: nonofficial: 17. Dez. 1927 in Nuremberg;
Rating: Censored four times, the third version was authorized on March 22, 1928.

Copy used: Berlin, Bundesarchiv – Filmarchiv

5. Martin Luther (USA/FRG 1953)
Production company: Lutheran Church Productions Inc. (New York), Luther-Film GmbH (Stuttgart).
Producer: Louis de Rochemont; Lothar Wolff
Production manager: Kurt Hartmann
Unit manager: Hans-Joachim Sommer; Heinz Karchow; Anton Höhn
Production management: Hans Koch
Director: Irving Pichel
Assistant director: Fritz Stapenhorst
Screenplay: Allan Sloane; Lothar Wolff; Dr. Jaroslav Pelikan; Dr. Theodore G. Tappert
Director of photography: Joseph C. Brun; Kurt Grigoleit; Günther Senftleben
Still photography: Rolf Lantin
Set design: Fritz Maurischat; Paul Markwitz
Prop Master: Karl-Heinz Suhr; Helmut Deuckert
Costumes: Herbert Ploberger
Make-up: Carl Eduard Schulz; Ellen Schulz; Walter Andrä
Editing: Fritz Stapenhorst
Sound: Gustav Bellers
Music: Mark Lothar

Cast
Niall MacGinnis (Martin Luther)
John Ruddock (Johann von Staupitz)
Guy Verney (Philipp Melanchthon)
Pierre Lefevre (Georg Spalatin)
Alastair Hunter (Andreas Bodenstein von Karlstadt)
Philip Leaver (Pope Leo X.)
Hans Lefebre (German Emperor Charles V.)
Irving Pichel (Chancellor Brueck)
Annette Carell (Katharina von Bora)
David Horne (Frederick III, byname Frederick the Wise, Elector of Saxony)
Fred Johnson (Prior of the Augustinian Hermits in Erfurt)
Egon Strohm (Cardinal Aleander [Girolamo Aleandro])
Alexander Gauge (Johann Tetzel)
Leonard White (Gesandter)
Heinz Piper: (Johann Eck)
Jaspar von Oertzen (Knight)

Shoot : 04.08.1952: Taunus, Maulbronn, Eltville, Kloster Eberbach, Rothenburg ob der Tauber

Length: 2840 m, 104 min
Format: 35mm, 1:1,37

World premiere: 4. 5. 1953 in Minneapolis, USA
German premieres: 4. 3. 1954 in Hanover; 5. 5. 1954 in Nuremberg
Rating: FSK-Prüfung (DE): 27.02.1960, Nr. 07090 [2. FSK-Prüfung]; FSK-Prüfung (DE): 04.12.1953, Nr. 07090, ab 6 Jahre / feiertagsfrei

Distributor in the US: Louis de Rochemont, Twentieth Century Fox
Distributor in Germany: Luther-Film GmbH (Stuttgart)

Copy used: 2003 © Lutheran Film Associates, distributed by Vision Video, Worcester, PA

6. Der arme Mann Luther (FRG 1964)
Production company: Bavaria Atelier GmbH (München-Geiselgasteig) commissioned by Westdeutscher Rundfunk (WDR), Köln
Director: Franz Peter Wirth
Screenplay: Leopold Ahlsen
Set design: Gerd Richter; Helmut Gassner

Music: Wilhelm Killmayer
Director of photography: Karl Schröder; Gernot Roll

Cast
Hans Dieter Zeidler (Martin Luther)
Robert Meyen (Johann von Staupitz)
Lina Carstens (Luther's mother)
Heinz Baumann (Ulrich von Hutten)
Claus Clausen (Erasmus von Rotterdam)
Paul Hoffmann (Cardinal Cajetan)
Ernst Fritz Fürbringer (German Emperor Charles V.)
Margarete Carl (Katharina von Bora)

Length: 114 min
World premiere: 21. 1. 1965 ARD
Copy used: Cologne, Archive of the WDR

7. Luther (USA 1973)
Production company: Ely A. Landau, American Film Theatre
Producer: Ely Landau
Director: Guy Green
Screenplay: Edward Anhalt after John Osborne

Cast
Stacy Keach (Martin Luther)
Hugh Griffith (Johann Tetzel)
Alan Badel (Cardinal Cajetan)
Maurice Denham (Johann von Staupitz)
Judi Dench (Katharina von Bora)

Length: 111 min.
Copy used: DVD by Kino International Corperation, New York

8. Frère Martin (F 1981)
Additional Title: Bruder Martin
Production company: TF-1, Paris; SFP, Paris; Bayerischer Rundfunk; Taurus-Film, München
Director: Jean Delannoy
Screenplay: Alexandre Astruc and Roland Laudenbach
Director of photography: János Kende

Cast
Bernard Lincot (Martin Luther)
Philippe Clay (Johann Tetzel)
Georges Wilson (Johann von Staupitz)
Raymond Gerome (Frederick III, byname Frederick the Wise, Elector of Saxony)
Philippe Villiers (German Emperor Charles V.)

Copy used: Paris, Archive of TF-1

9. Martin Luther (FRG 1983)

Production company: Zweites Deutsches Fernsehen
Director: Rainer Wolffhardt
Screenplay: Theodor Schübel
Director of photography: Rolf Romberg

Cast
Lambert Hamel (Martin Luther)
Horst Sachtleben (Andreas Bodenstein von Karlstadt)
Michael Habeck (Johann Tetzel)
Heini Göbel (Johann von Staupitz)
Dieter Pfaff (Pope Leo X.)
Jörg Pleva (German Emperor Charles V.)
Karl Obermayr (Thomas Müntzer)
Britta Fischer (Katharina von Bora)

Length: 210 min

Copy used: DVD 2004 by Universum Film GmbH Munich

10. Martin Luther (GDR 1983)

Titles of the five parts: 1. Der Protest. - 2. Der Sohn der Bosheit. - 3. Die Geheimnisse des Antichrist. - 4. Hier stehe ich … - 5. Das Gewissen

Production company: DEFA-Studio für Spielfilme (Potsdam-Babelsberg) commissioned by Fernsehen der DDR (DDR-FS) (Berlin/Ost), supported by Filmstudio Barrandov, Prag, 1981-83
Screenplay: Kurt Veth; consultants: Dr. Gerhard Brendler; Prof. Dr. Herbert Trebs
Director: Kurth Veth
Scenario: Hans-Georg Kohlus
Director of photography: Erich Gusko

Set design: Harald Horn; Kurt Ihloff (Ausstattung); Werner Zieschang (Ausstattung); Richard Schmidt (Ausstattung)
Prop Master: Klaus Selignow; Frank Cochlovius
Costumes: Günther Schmidt; Werner Pleißner; Brigitte Pleißner
Make-up: Erich Runge; Frank Zucholowsky; Brigitte Welzel; Wolfgang Möwis
Editing: Renate Bade; Christine Schöne
Sound: Werner Krehbiel
Mixing: Gerhard Ribbeck
Music: Karl-Ernst Sasse

Cast
Ulrich Thein (Martin Luther)
Hans-Peter Minetti (Johann Tetzel)
Friedo Salter (Andreas Bodenstein von Karlstadt)
Otto Mellies (Lucas Cranach d. Ä.)
Herwart Grosse (Johann von Staupitz)
Frank Lienert (Thomas Müntzer)
Daniel Minetti (German Emperor Charles V.)
Barbara Schnitzler (Katharina von Bora)
Hartmut Puls (Georg Spalatin)
Renate Blume (Barbara Cranach)
Gesine Laatz (Kristina)
Thomas Rühmann (Valentin Böhm)
Ezard Haußmann (Pater Ludwig)
Jürgen Reuter (Kittlitz)
Bruno Carstens (Printer Grunenberg)
Hilmar Baumann (Schurff)
Klaus Piontek (Christoph Scheuerl)
Lutz Riemann (Amsdorf)
Rudolf Christoph (Mattstock)
Thomas Gumpert (Menz)
Jens-Uwe Bogadtke (Georg Agricola)
Arno Wyzniewski (Cardinal Cajetan)
Hannjo Hasse (Urbanus von Serralonga)
Peter Bause (Fugger)
Peter Sturm (Luther's father)
Ruth Kommerell (Luther's mother)
Rolf Hoppe (Schaumberg)

Length: 13514 m
Format: 35mm, 1:1.33
Picture/Sound: Orwocolor

First Screening: 09.10.1983, DDR-TV (Part 1); 09.10.1983, DDR-TV (Part 2); 16.10.1963, DDR-TV (Part 3); 20.10.1963, DDR-TV (Part 4); 23.10.1983, DDR-TV (Part 5).

Copy used: DVD (1–5) by Verlag Komplett-Media GmbH, Grünwald (Format: 4:3).

11. Luther (FRG/USA 2003)

Production company: NFP Teleart GmbH & Co. KG (Berlin) in association with Thrivant Financial for Lutherans; Eikon Film GmbH (München); Degeto Film GmbH (Frankfurt am Main), supported by Evangelische Kirche in Deutschland (EKD) and German Information Center (Washington D.C.)

Producer: Alexander Thies; Kurt Rittig; Dennis A. Clauss; Brigitte Rochow; Christian P. Stehr; AAL/LB (Aid Association for Lutherans/Lutheran Brotherhood).
Director: Eric Till
Screenplay: Camille Thomasson; Bart Gavigan
Director of photography: Robert Fraisse
Music: Richard Harvey

Cast
Joseph Fiennes (Martin Luther)
Jonathan Firth (Cardinal Aleander)
Alfred Molina (Johann Tetzel)
Claire Cox (Katharina von Bora)
Peter Ustinov (Frederick III, byname Frederick the Wise, Elector of Saxony)
Bruno Ganz (Johann von Staupitz)
Uwe Ochsenknecht (Papst Leo X.)
Mathieu Carrière (Kardinal Jakob Cajetan)
Benjamin Sadler (Georg Spalatin)
Jochen Horst (Andreas Bodenstein von Karlstadt)

Director: Eric Till
2nd Unit Director: Klemens Becker
Assistant director: Eva-Maria Schönecker
Screenplay: Camille Thomasson; Bart Gavigan
Director of photography: Robert Fraisse
Camera operator: Kevin Jewison; Klemens Becker
Optical effects: Thomas Zauner
Still photography: Rolf von der Heydt
Production design: Rolf Zehetbauer
Set design: Christian Schäfer; Ralf Schreck; Vaclav Vohlidal (Czech Republic);

Funding Filmboard Berlin-Brandenburg GmbH (Potsdam); Film-Fernseh-Fonds-Bayern GmbH (FFFB) (München); Mitteldeutsche Medienförderung GmbH (MDM) (Leipzig); Filmförderungsanstalt (FFA) (Berlin); Bayerischer Bankenfonds (BBF) (München)
Shoot: 16.04.2002-08.07.2002: Brandenburg, Bavaria, Italy, Czech Republic
Original distributor: United International Pictures GmbH (UIP) (Frankfurt am Main); Ottfilm Verleih GmbH (Berlin) in Cooperation with DVD distributor Universum Film GmbH & Co. KG (München)
Length: 3382 m, 123 min
Format: 35mm, 1:1,85
Picture/Sound: Farbe, Dolby Digital
Rating: FSK-Prüfung (DE): 27.06.2003, Nr. 94452, ab 12 Jahre / feiertagsfrei

First Screening in Germany: 28.10.2003, München, Neues Arri
Copy used: DVD 2004 by Universal Pictures GmbH and NFP teleart

II. German Documentaries with Re-enactments

1. Der Reformator (FRG 1968)
Production company: Zweites Deutsches Fernsehen
Director: Rudolf Jugert
Screenplay: Dr. Günther Sawatzki
Director of photography: Albert Benitz

Cast
Christian Rode (Martin Luther)
Ernst Fritz Fürbringer (Cardinal Cajetan)
Friedrich Schütter (Andreas Bodenstein von Karlstadt)
Dieter Wagner (Johann Tetzel)
Lukas Amman (Urbanus von Serralonga)
Jürgen Stöszinger (Georg Spalatin)
Dieter Borsche (Johannes Eck)
Henning Schlüter (Johann von Staupitz)
Wolfgang Hahn (Philipp Melanchthon)
Hermann Schomberg (Frederick III, byname Frederick the Wise, Elector of Saxony)
Andrea Dahmen (Katharina von Bora)

World premiere: October 31, 1968 ZDF
Copy used: ZDF archive

3. Martin Luther - Ein Leben zwischen Gott und Teufel (FRG 2003)

Production company: Mitteldeutscher Rundfunk
Director: Lew Hohmann
Consultant: Dr. Martin Treu (Stiftung Luthergedenkstätten in Sachsen-Anhalt)

Cast
Matthias Hummitzsch (Martin Luther)
Katharina (Henriette Ehrlich)

Speaker: Gunter Schoß

Length: 43.13 min.
Format: 4:3
World premiere: November 16, 2003 MDR

Copy used: DVD 2005 by Ottonia Media GmbH.

4. Martin Luther (FRG 2007)

Production company: Zweites Deutsches Fernsehen

Director: Günther Klein
Screenplay: Günther Klein
Camera: Ralf Gemmecke
Length: 45 min.

Cast
Ben Becker (Martin Luther)
Michael Hanemann (Berlepsch)
and others

Copy used: DVD 2008 Hänssler Verlag im SCM-Verlag GmbH & Co.Kg.

5. Luther und die Nation (FRG 2008)

Production company: Gruppe 5 Filmproduktion GmbH in behalf of ZDF
Producer: Uwe Kersken
Supervision: Peter Arens, Guido Knopp
Consultor: Prof. Heinz Schilling

Directors: Olaf Götz, Christian Twente, Stephan Koester, Erica von Moeller, Robert Wiezorek

Script: Friedrich Klütsch, Daniel Sich

Cast:
Georg Prang (Martin Luther)
and others

Format: 16:9 anamorph
Length: 43 min.

Copy used: DVD 2008 Complett Media, Grünwald

Credits

The author would like to thank the individuals and institutions who have kindly given permission to reproduce the illustrations on the pages listed below. In the other cases the owner of the copyright was not ascertainable.

Bundesarchiv – Filmarchiv (Berlin): 39, 69, 70; ELCA Archives (Elk Grove Village, Illinois, USA): 114; EYE Film Instituut Nederland (Amsterdam): 24, 25; EZA (Berlin): 95; KI EB (Bad Bensheim): 21 right, 27, 46, 99; LAELB (Nürnberg): 89, 90, 91, 94, 95; Litt Family: 21 left, 38; Lutheran Film Associates (St. Louis, Missouri, USA): 16; Neue Film Produktion, Media Rights GmbH & CO. KG (Halle an der Saale): 35.

Schlaglichter der Reformation

Gelehrt, mutig und glaubensfest

V&R

Sonja Domröse
Frauen der Reformationszeit
Gelehrt, mutig und glaubensfest

2. Auflage 2011. 158 Seiten mit 10 Abbildungen,
kartoniert
ISBN 978-3-525-55012-0

Sonja Domröse vermittelt in diesem Buch, in dem Frauen der Reformationszeit in ihrem Leben und Werk porträtiert werden, den weiblichen Einfluss auf die Reformation in Deutschland.

Nicht wenige Frauen fühlten sich berufen, durch eigene Publikationen aktiv in die Auseinandersetzungen der Reformationszeit einzugreifen und die inferiore Stellung der Frau zu bekämpfen. Das Buch soll durch die biographischen Stationen sowie die Würdigung des theologischen und schriftstellerischen Wirkens exemplarischer Frauen (Elisabeth von Calenberg-Göttingen, Argula von Grumbach, Ursula Weyda, Elisabeth Cruciger, Wibrandis Rosenblatt, Katharina Zell, Olympia Fulvia Morata, Ursula von Münsterberg) zu Beginn der Neuzeit deutlich machen, dass es bereits vor 500 Jahren Aufbrüche zu einer Gleichberechtigung von Frauen in Kirche und Gesellschaft gegeben hat. Nach der Darstellung der einzelnen Biographien setzt sich die Autorin mit dem Frauenbild Martin Luthers auseinander.

Vandenhoeck & Ruprecht